Myth and Memory in the Construction of Community

Historical Patterns in Europe and Beyond

P.I.E.-Peter Lang

Bruxelles · Bern · Berlin · Frankfurt/M · New York · Wien

A publication within the framework of the research project *The Cultural Construction of Community in Modernisation Processes in Comparison* in cooperation between the European University Institute, Florence and the Humboldt University, Berlin sponsored by the Bank of Sweden Tercentenary Foundation, Stockholm.

Bo STRÅTH (ed.)

Myth and Memory in the Construction of Community

Historical Patterns in Europe and Beyond

Series Multiple Europes
No.9

Die Deutsche Bibliothek – CIP-Einheitsaufnahme

Myth and memory in the construction of community :
historical patterns in Europe and beyond / Bo Stråth (ed.). – Bruxelles ;
Bern ; Berlin ; Frankfurt/M. ; New York ;
Wien : PIE Lang, 2000
(Series Multiple Europes ; No. 9)
ISBN 90-5201-910-X

*CIP available from the British Library, GB
and the Library of Congress, USA.*
ISBN 0-8204-4654-8

Cover photo: Maria Hedlund, «In the Lecture Room».
Nationalmuseum, Stockholm.

Cover: Safran, Brussels.

© P.I.E.-Peter Lang S.A.
PRESSES INTERUNIVERSITAIRES EUROPÉENNES
Brussels, 2000
E-mail : pie@skynet.be

ISBN 90-5201-910-X
D/2000/5678/01

Contents

MYTH AND MEMORY
IN THE CONSTRUCTION OF THE NATION

Preface

BO STRÅTH

As the editing of this book draws to a close, there are the first glimmers of hope that a settlement will be found for the war currently being waged in, or rather over, the Federal Republic of Yugoslavia. Once again, the media resound with the rhetoric of a just war. For much of Europe, the 'last' just war was World War II. The justness of this war was legitimised in the commemoration of the resistance and in the new myths and memories constructed after the conflict. New foundation myths which, in turn, were built upon older master narratives, promoted the idea of peace as an absolute European value, dearly-acquired through an act of violent resistance.

During the Cold War, this heroic past became entangled with ideas of economic growth as a basis for democracy. The pacifist peace in 1945 took on the proportion of an armed peace. Hitler, as the personification of the enemy, was gradually substituted by the figure of Stalin. However, the war remained 'cold', and the rhetoric of a just war was not directed at the battlefield, but at economic competition, and political and military influence in a world divided into spheres of interest.

This discursive framework changed with the end of the Cold War. The first response to the collapse of these established frameworks of interpretation was to call for a revision of the myths and memories of the resistance across Europe. The contours of a new history became discernible, a history that was less heroic and that placed more emphasis on various aspects of collaboration with the Nazis. Taken together with the erosion of the belief in the political provision of economic and social wellbeing, the basis for democracy, the implication was that the two corner-stones of (Western) European coexistence were undermined.

It is in this situation that new forms of meaning based on the ideas of a crusade for justice and of a justified war have come to be promoted once again. Hitler is recreated in the personas of Saddam Hussein and Slobodan Milosevic. The enormous difference in this construction of a new connection between present and past is that the war against Hitler was global and was imposed upon the world. Today's wars and today's Hitlers are local, not global, and they are delimited and targeted rather than globally imposed. The idea that democracy can be secured through bombs, this idea that emerged in the resistance myths of World War II, recurs today. But it recurs in a revised form, in the light of this difference between the war then and the wars today.

This is the backdrop against which this book on myth and memory in various parts of Europe and beyond (a few chapters address Israel and the USA) should be understood. The conceptual framework employed here is one in which history is continuously written and rewritten in order to cope with a recalcitrant present. The past is not the past as it was, but a translation of it to our times: it must be constantly re-designed in order to make the present understandable.

This book appears within the organisational framework of a research project on the cultural construction of community in processes of modernisation in a comparative view. This project started as a Swedish-German comparison, but has subsequently come to expand its comparative basis. It is sponsored by the Bank of Sweden Tercentenary Fund, and is a joint enterprise between the European University Institute (EUI) in Florence and the Humboldt University in Berlin.

The issues of myth, memory and history are all closely related to the problem of how community is culturally constructed. Taken together, they raise the question of how the past is mobilised in different but specific forms in order to come to terms with the present, and in order to deduce and legitimise historical origins.

With the aim of addressing this question, I organised a conference from 4th to 7th June, 1998, in Bivigliano, some 15 kilometres north of Florence. To some extent, this book can be seen as a spin-off from that conference, but it must be emphasised that these pages do not contain a conventional conference report. A number of the chapters represent a selection of the contributions presented at the conference, while other chapters have been written specifically for the book and were not presented at Bivigliano. Several of the chapters were also discussed at the EUI during the autumn of 1998, and these critical and productive discussions provoked considerable revision of the texts.

Mette Zølner provided excellent editing assistance during the autumn of 1998, and Michael Miller took over this job in January, 1999, when Mette moved from Florence to take up a position in Copenhagen. He has continued the work in a pre-eminent and no less excellent way. Benita Blessing participated in the task of editing with insightful comments and accomplished linguistic work.

Myth and Memory in the Construction of Community is the first in a new series on the plural Europe published by PIE-Peter Lang, and I am very glad to present this book within this framework.

Besides Mette, Michael and Benita, my special thanks go to all the participants in the conference at Bivigliano, and in particular to Hayden White, with whom I have had the privilege of discussing and working at various stages during the elaboration of the Introduction. I am also indebted to the participants in the seminar series at the EUI, who have contributed in various ways to the creation of this book. Additionally, I would like to thank Bernhard Giesen for his permission to include work he produced in the context of the study group on cultural trauma at Stanford University. This material is developed still further in his contribution to Neil J. Smelser and Jeffrey C. Alexander's forthcoming volume, *Cultural Trauma* (University of California Press, 2000) and in his own book, *Triumph and Trauma* (also University of California Press, 2000). Finally, I would like to thank the Bank of Sweden Tercentenary Fund and its Director, Dan Brändström, who, financially and in other respects, have supported the research project on the cultural construction of community in comparison.

Florence in June, 1999

Wolfgang Pavlik, Georg, Oil and Lacquer
on Canvas (165 x 130 cm) 1996. Courtesy of the Artist.

Prologue
Wolfgang Pavlik
The Image of the Other: *Ahnengalerie*

James KAYE

An exhibition of the work of Wolfgang Pavlik entitled 'The Image of the Other' was opened at Bivigliano on 5th June 1998, in the context of the conference 'Memory and Myth in the Construction of Community' (4th-7th June, 1998). It was this conference that laid the foundations for the present volume. The incorporation of this exhibition represented a ground-breaking attempt to broaden the significance of 'interdisciplinary' research within the framework of the project entitled 'The Cultural Construction of Community in the Process of Modernisation'.

The possibilities of representation and the thesis that our visual environment is manipulated through a metaphorical and figurative expression, replete with imagery and iconography, are not concerns exclusive to scientific research. These processes of construction and exploitation of myth and memory are central to a significant segment of 20th century artistic production and have been explored in numerous artistic exhibitions organised in recent years. Nevertheless, the artistic discourse is rarely juxtaposed with the scientific. 'The Image of the Other' was an attempt at just such a juxtaposition. By exploiting and distorting the ancestral portrait gallery *(Ahnengalerie)*, a mnemonic device long employed to create ties of kinship, lineage, memory and justification of power, the installation problematised the mechanism and put its established function in question.

Ancestor worship as a religion can be traced to antiquity; in Ancient Egyptian cults the ancestors of royalty were celebrated, in Babylon this was common among the ruling class, and in Rome it formed part of familial cult activities. Ancient Greek ancestor worship overlapped with the worship of heroes. The Greek Republics,

17

however, went as far as to prohibit portrait statues in order to suppress vanity. It should be noted that the portrait thrived in eras when human difference and individuality were of interest. It had little place in classical Greek societies where the ideal rather than human particularity was relevant. The same may be said of the Christian Middle Ages, when the human ideally lost his or her identity in the contemplation of God. Renaissance culture signalled a heightening interest in the status of the individual. In 15th century Italy, the sitter of authority was invented and power gradually began to replace piety in portraiture. As a result of these changes the first ancestral portrait galleries were realised, and these were subsequently to become integral parts of noble residences.

Wolfgang Pavlik's likenesses for the 'Image of the Other' differ in a fundamental aspect from the portraits which were normally housed in these galleries. Despite their designation as portraits, they deny identity. Although the arrangement of the portraits in the exhibition suggested the form of a family tree, they were almost devoid of identifiable content. Through the replacement, substitution or obfuscation of the visage by monochromatic fields, the portraits, which are of a photographic quality, became not only anonymous but also ambiguous. References to factors such as origin, social position and occupation of the subjects are absent. This void not only suggests the semantics of abstract art, but also the transformation which the perceptive sense has undergone due to the development of new medial technologies. The monochromatic field is suggestive of the eradi-cation of the subject, the development from the act of seeing to the non-personal apparatus of seeing. In the installation both seeing and the past lose their certainty and perpetually demand redefinition and criticism in their confrontation with identity, memory and iconography.

CHAPTER 1

Introduction
Myth, Memory and History
in the Construction of Community

BO STRÅTH

This book deals with the role of myth and memory when collective identities, and particularly national identities, are built. Myth and memory is history in ceaseless transformation and reconstruction, and the image of the past is continuously reconsidered in the light of an ever-changing present. History is an *image* of the past, rather than *the* past *wie es eigentlich gewesen*, as it really was.[1] From this perspective, history is memory and oblivion, it is a *translation* or *representation* of the past in the present.[2] In short, history and memory emerge as mutually constitutive.

The key question of this book is what role myth and memory play in the construction of communities, and what the distinction between

---

[1] The argument here is that the traditional configuration of history and memory as opposites can no longer be maintained. History and memory emerge as mutually constitutive. History as science, in a more conventional understanding of the term, means an opposition between history and myth. Myths can be the object of objective historical science only in a critical and destructive way – they must be revealed and unmasked. Scientific historiography and myth are, in this positivistic or objectivist view, insurmountable, antagonistic entities. In contrast, the point of departure of this book is that history, as a permanent process of reconsidering the past, means that demystification is remystification.

[2] For a discussion of the concept of representation, see Ankersmit, 1998.

collective myth and memory means. The assumption will be that myth and memory unify a community and shape its identity in a way that gives it essential proportions.[3] Collective memory occurs within the matrix or the plot that the myth provides. Such a matrix or plot emphasises certain values, such as Danish innocence with respect to the occupation during World War II (see Mette Zølner's contribution) or Swedish neutrality (my own chapter on Sweden). The plots constitute tropes in which legitimacy and historical meaning are sought and confirmed by emphasising specific values or characteristics, for instance Danish smallness or Swedish poverty. History takes on primordial proportions, yet a myth does not evolve from the 'nature' of a thing, and it is never eternal, rather, it has a specific historical foundation.[4]

Herder, the Grimm brothers, and other interpreters of the world among their contemporaries did not make a distinction between *Mythos* and *Märchen*, myth and fairy tale. However, with the Enlightenment discourse a separation gradually emerged between myth and science, a development that was also visible in theology and biblical exegesis for example. As this division widened, so there developed the positivistic programme based on essentialism. It is this separation which is now questioned by concepts like postmodernity.

One of the most frequent points of departure for myth construction has been the nation. Why have questions about memory and the nation become so topical at the present time? How should the identity boom be understood? A few decades ago there was no discourse on either national memory or national identity.

One answer to these questions can be found in the end of the Cold War and in the social and cultural fragmentation that ensued in East and West alike. World War II had produced cohesion through the resistance to Nazism, and many foundation myths that contributed to the construction of national identity were built on this idea. These myths continued to give meaning and cohesion during the Cold War. The language of a pacifistic peace in 1945 was, within a few years,

---

[3] According to Nora, the act of remembering is always related to 'the repository of images and ideals that constitute the social relations of which we partake', as Kritzman puts it in his foreword to the English translation of *Realms of Memory*. Nora, 1996, p. xi.

[4] Barthes, 1974, pp. 109-10.

transformed into the language of an armed peace in which the Soviet Union replaced Nazi Germany as the representation of evil. This was different to the development of interpretative frameworks and world views after World War I, when evil was seen much more as an historical category, and the Russian Revolution and the League of Nations, for a short while, seemed to offer the promise of a better world. There was, however, nothing to replace these loci of hope when the expectations faded away. In this context, there are similarities between the situation at the end of the 1920s and that of today, as the expectations invested in the market utopia after 1989 begin to fade away. It is indicative of this erosion of interpretative frameworks that the issue of resistance and collaboration during World War II has come under increasing scrutiny since the end of the Cold War, and many established truths have been questioned and challenged. This development, in turn, has brought the issue of collective memory to the fore. Questions about identity, about who we are and where we come from, are raised in situations where we do not know the answers. When we feel confident about who we are, we do not talk about it, and it is generally only in periods of identity crisis that we look for new identity and social community. It is in this framework that the issues of national identity and collective memory raised in this book should be seen.

A second reason why identity, memory and nation are currently at the forefront of our preoccupations is the emergence of a new epistemology indicated by concepts such as 'construction' and 'postmodernity'. This also involves the relativising of concepts like 'truth' and 'reality', which had previously been understood in absolute terms (for instance, reality may now be 'virtual'). The end of the Cold War and the new epistemological view have meant new challenges for professional historiography and have given a concept like history new perspectives, not least with the growing insight that there is no reality which can be conceptualised and analysed beyond the limits that language sets upon its meaning. The constraints of language when coping with reality mean, among other things, that the discourse creates its own interests. One might choose to see this 'linguisticism' as a burden, but it also justifies a certain optimism as a result of the interpretative freedom that it gives. Language is multivocal and constitutes a huge semantic field with vast ranges, and for this reason it offers greater freedom in the selection of perspective.

The historian does not stand above or beyond the processes that he or she is analysing, but is part of them through the language that, by means of the act of translation or representation, connects the present with the past. In the wake of Foucault, it is not only history, but also epistemological schemes in general that are ideological and political. This also means that the past is constantly changing with the present.

This approach emphasises that social cohesion and community are invented rather than discovered, that they are constructed rather than existing 'out there' and derivable, for example, from real economic structures. This does not mean, of course, that events as such are also invented. Rather the facts are constructed by reflection upon the documents that attest to the occurrence of the events. This distinction between fact and event is important, and Hayden White's chapter in particular develops this point. The construction of community means that images and myths emerge from the transformation of existing inventories of historical heritage and culture. Successful construction appeals to certain cultural chords and conceptual tropes, to narrative plots or discursive frames. Such tropes and plots are, of course, not primordial; they too are the products of human creation. In these processes of community construction, the *idea* of a collective memory and a specific history is a tool that bridges the gap between high political and intellectual levels and the levels of everyday life. What constitutes collective memory and what is consigned to collective oblivion, that is, taboos and what we do not talk about, is a highly disputed question, reflecting power relations in the definition of social problems.[5]

Identity emerged as a theoretical problem in the 1970s. While it is an old concept, with roots in ancient Greece, it remained a more or less technical term in philosophy for a long time. It came to the social sciences by way of psychoanalysis, a field in which it had become a key concept in the 1880s (see Lutz Niethammer's contribution on this point). Significantly, psychoanalysis also works with 'memory', which it problematises by distinguishing between 'memory traces', that are retrievable at will, and 'dynamically unconsciously repressed

---

[5] Nora holds that each nation has its canonical memories and myths that bind the community together and create social identities. Myth and memory give the community a narrative through which it can continue to forge its identity. The act of remembering is related to the repository of images and ideals that constitute the social ties of a community. Nora, 1996, pp. xv-xxiv.

memory traces'. From psychoanalysis, the concept of identity spread to debates and reflections on society. This happened, for instance, in the 1920s when, for a brief period after the First World War, there was talk about identity, and then again from the 1970s onwards.[6] In the interim, it was not a problem. During the Cold War, when political economies in the West were based upon economic growth, full employment and universal social rights guaranteed by the welfare states, we knew who We were, and we knew who the Other was, and there was no need to search for identity or evoke memory. Identity is not, for example, analysed in the German master-work on historical key concepts, *Geschichtliche Grundbegriffe*.[7]

Stuart Hall has formulated identification as a construction in a process never completed. It follows from this that identities are subject to a radical historicisation in a process characterised by constant flux and transformation. Hall's approach has a clear demarcation to naturalistic and essentialist conceptions of identity.[8] In a recent PhD thesis, Polymeris Voglis has problematised the connection between identity and construction and has demonstrated the contradictions in the constructivist approach.[9] This approach tried to restore the split between society and the individual through structuralist theories. In contrast to the humanist and liberal argument of the individual's free will, it emphasised the production of the subject in social processes and discourses. Such theories tried to find a middle way between determinism and free will, but in the long run they became determinist through the disappearance of the agent. This occurred because, by stressing the omnipresent social institutions and discourses, the role of the subject as an agent was minimised, and under the identity concept social subjects were seen as homogeneous. Here Voglis suggests a focus on the concept of subject as a solution. Subject has an ambivalent meaning, for it refers to the state of being subjugated to an authority, but also connotes an acting subject striving towards an object. The identity of a subject is linked to the politics involved in the construction of such an identity, and there is a contradiction between what an identity is, and the politics of the subject in the construction of its identity. Identity as a construction is

---

[6]   Lutz Niethammer in collaboration with Axel Dossmann, 1999.

[7]   Brunner, Conze and Koselleck, 1972-92.

[8]   Hall, 1996.

[9]   Voglis, 1999.

always an ongoing process, marked by flux, and it therefore does not correspond to the identities claimed by the subjects: unified, homogeneous, continuous, coherent and singular. In Voglis's convincing view, no constructivist approach to the identity concept can solve this contradiction.

The new conceptual and symbolic topography around concepts like identity and memory must therefore be understood in the light of experiences of intellectual disorientation and the erosion of earlier established frameworks of interpretation since the 1970s. These experiences have been the result of fundamental changes in epistemology, technology, and the organisation of economies, work and labour markets. These shifts have produced new views, both of the past and of the preconditions for history, the science of the past. History as 'science' is a translation from the German *Wissenschaft*. Since the 19th century, the writing of the past in Germany has been seen as analogous to the description of nature, the *Naturwissenschaften*. In English speaking cultures, history was never a science, but belonged to the faculty of arts. This distinction between the two linguistic cultures was ignored for a long time, but has recently begun to take on meaning. The insight that the writing of history is less a matter of the unproblematic discovery of a past 'out there' by means of refined techniques of source criticism, and more something dependent upon the context of the present in which questions about the past emerge, has come to be generally accepted.[10] The recognition of the role of narration poses new problems along the science-art axis.

Questions about the treatment of the past are also the underlying questions of this book. How culturally determined is the writing of the past? How are histories about the past constructed? How is the narration that aims to translate the past in order to give meaning to the present plotted? Why did the question of nation and the related issues of identity achieve such a predominant position in the debate from the late 1970s? To these questions, we might also add another; how does memory interrelate with oblivion? History and community are not

---

[10] For a groundbreaking development in this debate, see White, 1974. White has, however, built on a long tradition of philosophical thought. Spinoza developed a sceptical view on the opportunities of coming to terms with the past, as Thomas Hippler discusses in his chapter in this book. The Neapolitan philosopher of history and law, Giovanni Battista Vico (1668-1744), was an important source of information for White.

only built on memory, but also on forgetting. As Renan has observed, unity is created by assigning to oblivion that which divides a community:

> L'oubli, je dirais même l'erreur historique, sont un facteur essentiel de la création d'une nation, et c'est ainsi que le progrès des études historiques est souvent pour la nationalité un danger [...] l'essence d'une nation est que tous les individus aient bien des choses en commun, et aussi que tous aient oublié bien des choses...[11]

Chapter 20 offers an illustration of the importance of oblivion for the construction of community with the example of Ådalen in Sweden.

The linguistic or rhetoric turn, which argues that it is language that sets the limits when realities are constructed, brought the insight that there is a connection between myth and historiography through the form of narration, through the very way in which the story is told. Historiography is much more dependent upon its literary-textual organisation than has been recognised in more conventional views. Historiography cannot, as a matter of fact, be easily separated from myths and myth building. In the most radical versions of the linguistic/rhetoric methodological approach, historiography and mythography become more or less identical. Such views, however, are much older than the rhetoric turn. The idea that truth is contextual, rather than immutable and absolute, and that grounding myths are expressions of power, was clearly present in the works of Vico, Croce, Nietzsche, and Weber, long before White and Foucault.[12]

Myths assume the dimensions of reality in the sense, and to the extent, that people believe in them. From this perspective, they cannot be separated or distinguished from reality and truth, but rather they constitute this reality and truth through language. This means that reality and truth are contested and contextual entities. Grounding myths, the myths upon which societies ultimately rest, draw their power to legitimate from some specific connection to God, history or the truths of the social and economic sciences. It is within this context of legitimisation or *doxa* of everyday life that right and wrong are

---

[11] Ernest Renan, 1992 [1887], pp. 41-2.

[12] Vico, 1977 [1725]; Croce, 1963 [1941]; Nietzsche [1852-1889], 1988; Foucault, 1969; Peukert, 1989; Szakolszai, 1998.

25

defined and laws are promulgated which separate the proclaimed communities of destiny from the arbitrary and capricious.

Myth is not only the *object* of historiographic science, it is also its *product* in the form of constructed memory (which, at the same time, also means constructed oblivion). Processes of meaning production are processes of selection. The Holocaust and its preliminary stages took place before and during World War II, but it only became a theme in the 1960s, begging the question of why these events were more or less ignored in the late 1940s and throughout the 1950s. When, in the name of science, figures like Kennedy and Clinton, Hitler and Churchill, Catherine II and Voltaire, Atatürk and Atilla, or abstractions like Europe, nation, democracy and dictatorship are described and discussed, the point of departure is the myths created by history. This does not mean that these descriptions and discussions are all lies, but rather that the truths they convey are truths constructed from the *ex post* position. This idea of contextual truth was also present in the thinking of Spinoza, who considered that historical myths are not a false kind of historical knowledge, but rather that they reflect, in an imaginary manner, the relation of a society to itself (see Thomas Hippler's chapter). Constructed memories are continuously subject to critical scrutiny and revision in the framework of a history that is constantly written and rewritten from an ever-changing present. History is in flux; it is, like the present, in a permanent state of transformation. History does not exist 'out there', waiting to be discovered, but is permanently invented in order to give meaning to the present – and to the future – through the past.

Myth, in this sense of constructed memory and oblivion, is emancipated from its pejorative connotation and assumes the role of the provider of meaning, becoming a constituent element of politics and social cohesion. In this context, emancipation takes on a different meaning from that in the self-understanding of positivist historio-graphy, where activity in the name of science and source criticism is seen as an emancipation or liberation of the sources from the myths which enshroud them. This positivist approach was embodied by Leopold von Ranke and his followers, who believed that they stood outside and above the processes they studied. They believed that they were the judges or referees who were capable of disclosing the truth, *wie es eigentlich gewesen*, and failed to realise that they too were party to the production of the past.

26

In the European *Mythosforschung* of the 19th and 20th centuries, myth implied irrationality and was thus separated from rationality in the form of *logos* and reason. The key theoretical question which this dichotomy produced was whether mythical thought was prior to or parallel to scientific thought. It was through this debate that the myth of rational science emerged.

In the position we adopt in this book, the analysis of a myth cannot be restricted to examining its function. Analysing the function of a myth means *deconstructing* that myth, which, at the same time, provokes the question of what *new* forms of history are being *constructed*. To what extent can the new history, that is, our telling of history, be accepted as a definitive history based upon assumptions of discovery rather than invention? We can never recreate the past 'as it really was', at the moment before the future of that past was known, a future which has become, in turn, our past. We can only try to translate the past in order to produce meaning for ourselves, in our present. For this reason, we must make 'translation' a key methodo-logical concept. This translation can only be made from our point of view today, and never from the point of view of that past's present. In this sense, concepts like objectivity and Ranke's *wie es eigentlich gewesen* become ideology.[13] Both *wie es eigentlich gewesen* and the cumulative view of history as an inexorable process of mapping reality in a total and definitive sense through the addition of ever more and better data, become vain undertakings. The truths about the past are conditional and dependent upon the present in which they are formulated.

This was the point of view promoted by Lévi-Strauss when he described myths as something which order and give meaning to the universe, that is, they give us the illusion that we understand the universe. To create myth is to create 'order, an intellectual, cognitive order principally, an order that has as its focus the always problematic relations between man and nature'.[14] Barthes defines myth as a semiological system (form) and an ideology (content) consisting of three elements; form (signifier), concept (signified) and signification (sign). A myth hides nothing, but it distorts, that is, it functions in

---

[13] Cf. Iggers, 1999, pp. 281-301.

[14] Silverston, 1988, p. 28.

such a way as to give historical intention a natural justification.[15] In the view of Roger Silverston,

> Myth occupies a particular space in culture, mediating between the sacred and the profane, the world of every day common sense and the arcane, the individual and the social. Myth is a form of speech, distinct in its character, marked by definable narratives, familiar, acceptable, reassuring to their host culture. Myths are stories of which some are heroic but most are formulaic. They are the public dreams, the product of an oral culture musing about itself. Myths shade into folk tales, more secular, more literal, more narratively predictable or coherent, not asking to be believed in quite the same way, nor making so insistently the heartland of a society. Myths are associated with ritual, as beliefs to action, both together defining a transcendent and liminal space and time for a people in their otherwise mundane reality. Myths are logical, emotional and traditional and they are persisting though often in a diluted form, and, like some good wines, do not always travel well without at least changing some part of their character.[16]

It is obvious from these and many other similar views, that myths help build up social community and collective identities and that there is a connection between memory, myth and feelings of social community. What means are then available to enable us to study such connections?

Nora studies the metamorphoses of collective memory by investigating the history of the *lieux de mémoire*, by which he means any significant entity – a monument, for instance – which, by dint of human will or the work of time, has become a symbolic element in the memorial heritage of any community.[17] Le Goff suggests focussing on the connection between collective memory and power, because power lies with those who have mastered memory.[18] Lévi-Strauss holds that when studying a myth one should not ask whether a myth is true or not, but rather why do, or did, people believe in it.[19] According to Barthes, myth can be studied either diachronically or synchronically, by sketching contemporary myths. It is through the deconstruction of the myth that its distortion is revealed. This is a somewhat different

---

[15] Barthes, 1974, pp. 124-125.
[16] Silverston, 1988, p. 23.
[17] Nora, 1996, p. xvii.
[18] Le Goff, 1985, p. 109.
[19] Lévi-Strauss, 1978, p. 25.

view to that of Derrida, who considers the meaning of deconstruction to be the disconnection of truth from reason in order to discern the fundamental divide between the two. The combination of the sacred and the good with the rational and the reasonable is nothing other than Plato's project of logocentrism, which should be seen as yet one more cultural construction among others and therefore must also be deconstructed.[20] Lyotard expresses similar views when he argues that master formulations of myth must shatter under postmodern conditions, where no meta-narrative is possible. In particular, he considers that postmodern conditions are distinguished by their reliance on mass media of information and communication.[21] Yet, in the absence of alleged master narratives, discourses in these media are legitimised by micro-narratives that shape the message transmitted and give meaning to the flow of information.[22] This is what Hayden White illustrates in his chapter, where he analyses the Italian media coverage of the disaster in Sarno in May, 1998.

While the constructivist approach frees us from the quest for absolute truth, we should not accept the concept uncritically. In the framework outlined in this introduction, the concept of construction, which has become so central in the linguistic or cultural approach during last decades, *is* problematic. Its great merit is that it has mediated a view where history is no longer seen as an object lying out there waiting to be discovered. But what do we then mean when we say that history is invented?

The problem with concepts like construction is threefold. First, construction connotes a building industry, it connotes social engi-

---

[20] Derrida, 1972 and 1979. The writings of Derrida provide a language for the theorisation of difference. His point of departure is that Western systems of knowledge depend upon some original moment of truth or immanence from which our whole hierarchy of meaning springs. It is this guarantee of meaning transcending signification which is termed logocentrism. By invoking a claim to universal truth, a system of knowledge such as this hides cultural diversity and conceals the power structures that preserve the hierarchical relations of difference. Binary oppositions and distinctions are central to this logocentric form of thinking. 'Europe' and the 'Other' is one case in point. Another example is the construction of sexual difference through dichotomies like 'masculine-feminine', 'active-passive', 'rational-emotional', 'hard-soft' and so on. Cf. Rutherford, 1990 for a discussion of Derrida in this context.

[21] Lyotard, 1979.

[22] Combs and Nimmo, 1990.

neering, indeed it even connotes manipulation. Given this, it is not unreasonable to argue that the production of symbols, images and myths is an elite undertaking, that this construction/invention is simply the elite's manipulation of the masses. But cohesion and community may also be constructed from the grassroots level and may, as Michael Miller's chapter shows, challenge the meaning assigned to events and situations by elite groups. The second problem with the concept of construction is that, in modern Western-style societies at least, this process of production is something that occurs in a conflictual and oppositional context marked by social bargaining and negotiation with the aim of finding compromises. The ideas on the agenda are continuously transformed, so much so that it is often difficult to identify their origin. Symbols and myths, just like any politically fertile concepts, can be seen in many different ways and are therefore open to contestation. They do not mediate one indivisible view emanating from an originating elite. Their production is marked by conflict and compromise, but so is their mass reception. 'Construction' and 'invention' do not convey the idea that this is a two-way process, but this is how it must be studied if we are to understand the full implications of myth, memory and community construction.[23] Myths emerge from the matrixes of society (in this connection, see Michael Miller's chapter on the interaction between popular practice and the political act of urban planning in 'traditional' urban neighbourhoods, and Beate Binder's chapter, which uses a similar approach to investigate the construction of Berlin as the capital of a united Germany). The question is what role history and the social sciences play in making these myths into constitutive elements of collective identities. Construction as a concept can also be seen in contrast to a more positivist methodological/epistemological approach aimed at the discovery and mapping out of 'reality'. Construction in this sense means the building of interpretative frameworks, the construction of images of the past, images of the world, images of reality.

A third problem with construction is not so much the concept in itself, but how it has been employed. It has been used to express views on the actors in the society under scrutiny, but has been much less involved with those who perform the analyses, who tend to overlook

---

[23] Cf. Stråth, 1999 and Gerber, 1999, and the references therein to the phenomenology of Alfred Schütz.

that they too are engaged in construction. In other words, there is a problem of double construction. In their efforts to have history recognised as a science, professional historians have failed to recognise an important aspect of self-understanding, namely that history as a discipline is, like philosophy, a branch of ethics.

There are many different ways to consider the connections between memory, myth and history, and many different ways to approach the problems associated with construction. The contributions to this book offer an illustration of this variety. At first these perspectives might appear mutually exclusive, but, on closer inspection, it becomes apparent that they are not necessarily incompatible. The tension between the various views comes from the concepts of construction and invention. What do these concepts really mean with reference to myth, memory and history? At one extreme, the connection to some kind of elite activity, manipulation or otherwise, is emphasised. At the other extreme, weight is given to the structural preconditions of this activity. These structural preconditions might be like the prevailing epistemes in Foucault's sense, or like popular everyday practices and sentiments of a more anthropological kind. Hayden White, in his chapter, emphasises that construction presupposes a de-struction of something else, a fragmentation of a structure. The fragments can then be used to con-struct another one. In a verbatim sense, con-struction is re-con-struction by combining materials already at hand; 'Constructing a society implies remaking it out of elements already present.' However, this image of remaking is incompatible with the idea of modernity, which presumes a qualitative difference between present and past. When the fragments are re-composed, it is not the old building that emerges, but images of something new. A case in point is the best known Reconstruction of all, that which took place after World War II.

Is it then the aim to combine the two extremes, action and structure, into one conceptual framework, one cohesive *Denkfigur*? Would it not be a vain undertaking to try to dissolve and merge dichotomies and contradictions like action-structure, discontinuity-continuity, reflection/construction-practice and elite-everyday life? Would not a more complex understanding of the past mean that the past can be understood in various ways dependent on points of departure and viewpoints rather than looking for *the* past? Consider, in this connection, the distinction Hayden White makes in his chapter between 'disaster' in the literal sense of 'bad star', that is, a society's exposure to ill fate, and 'catastrophe', a term from Greek drama that indicates a turn for the worse that will eventually result in the revelation of meaning in the final scene. While 'disaster' suggests misfortune, 'catastrophe' is consciously constructed. In the Italian example of the mud slides at Sarno, we see how the shift from disaster to catastrophe was shaped in the reporting of *la Repubblica* – and in White's reading of this newspaper.

The chapters in this book represent various answers to the questions posed in the paragraph above, and taken together, they can be seen as analogous to Freudian theory. From the perspective of some of the contributions, myth and memory, like Freud's dreams, simply surface as expressions of the mental state of society. They are not governed or controlled. They provide a kind of cultural depository or heritage, and this depository is activated through specific codes. From the perspective of other contributions, this depository is used in discursive struggles over political, economic and social power. Myths and memories are interpreted and given form for power purposes (professional historiography might also be seen in this framework). From this point of view, there is a clear element of construction or invention, at least within certain limits. In this sense, memories and myths should be seen as multiple and subject to continuous contestation, even if, at certain historical moments, one view enjoys almost complete domination.

These perspectives on the concept of construction between (elite) action/reflection/construction and (everyday) structure/practice are not mutually exclusive, and are provided here simply as points of orientation. The intention of this collective volume is not to set up a dichotomy, but to draw together a range of approaches to myth and memory and place them in a context in which they can be constructively confronted and compared. No attempt was made to provide the contributors with a definition of myth and memory that, while encouraging a greater unity within the chapters, would ultimately have been unproductive and stiflingly restrictive. The essays collected in this volume demonstrate the richness and subtlety of the concepts of myth and memory.

It may be significant that few of the contributors speak explicitly about myth *and* memory – the majority choose to use either memory *or* myth. Already this suggests a blurring of the line between the two concepts. Furthermore, the majority of those who make use of the concept of memory seem to occupy similar academic ground, that is to say, there is a convergence of views founded upon the idea of collective memory and the distinction between socialised remembering and 'history'. Mette Zølner, for example, takes Halbwachs as the starting point for her chapter on Danish collective memories of the World War II. Here, collective memory is 'the result of a selective process of remembering and forgetting the past' and only exists where there is a group that remembers. From Zølner's perspective, collective memory is different from, but interacts with, deep-rooted myths of the national community. In a sense, these myths assign the limits to memory, defining what it is possible and what is impossible to remember.

The theme of self-awareness is also present in Bernhard Giesen's essay. Giesen suggests that 'memory supports or even creates the assumption of stability that demarcates identity in distinction to the incessant change of the phenomenal world'. The memories he refers to recall lost paradises and promised lands, founding heroes and the traumas of defeat, yet, Giesen argues, society does not necessarily experience these events as extraordinary in the moment they take place. Society comes to cope with this lack of awareness through the ritual re-enactment of these events in the form of commemoration. From this point of view, it is clear that myth and memory cannot be clearly demarcated.

From Péter Apor's perspective, memory is never innocent or neutral. His chapter shows how the events in a local pogrom trial in post-war Hungary were 'remembered' as fascist and anti-democratic, in a context where the Communist Party was striving to create the enemy it needed to justify its own particular notion of democracy. For Ewa Domańska, who offers the experiences of Poland, another former Communist country, the problem is not memory *per se*, but history as an academic discipline, which she sees as a powerful instrument of ideological manipulation.

The prominent exceptions to this view of collective memory are provided by Hayden White and Lutz Niethammer. Niethammer offers a critical and extremely insightful study of the contribution of Halbwachs to the intellectual discourses on memory and the 'feeling of identity' in the 20th century. White makes the important distinction between 'traditionalised memory' as information about, and accounts of the past latently stored in the corpus of traditional lore (fables, folk tales, gnomic commonplaces, customs, prejudices and conventions), and 'rationalised memory' as information about, and accounts of a community's past contained in its archives, and catalogued and processed in the form of written or visualised histories which can be accessed on demand. Traditionalised memory is at odds with rationalised memory – there is a tension between the two categories. Rationalised memory might comprehend traditionalised knowledge, but the reverse is not the case. However, this relationship means that there is not only tension between the two categories, but also a degree of overlap. White is as critical as Niethammer of collective memory, either in the Halbwachian sense, or in the Jungian sense of collective unconscious. He finds both these notions too dependent on the projection of the structures of an individual consciousness onto that of the collectivity. The distinction between myth and history as science is also emphasised by Ewa Domańska. She too discerns both tension and overlap when she considers myth and science, not as opposed. but as 'complementary modes of grasping a common reality'. She takes an extreme position in her argumentation for myth, where, as mentioned above, her own Polish experience allows her to adopt a critical view of scientific history with respect to this country.

If there seems to be a certain convergence with respect to the idea of memory, this is less the case for myth. However, a theme which continues to emerge, either implicitly or explicitly, is that myths find resonance when a society recognises itself in them. This is a key point in Thomas Hippler's introduction to Spinoza's work on historical myth. Spinoza, breaking down the dichotomy of history and myth, did not regard myths as false historical knowledge. Rather, myths reflect, in an imaginary manner, the relation of society to itself. For this reason myths must be regarded as containing a certain kind of truth, a vision, albeit confused, of society itself. This may offer a clue as to why some myths, even those promoted by powerful elites, fail to find resonance in society, while others constantly come to the surface without bidding.

Hayden White does not include myths in his category of traditionalised memory, but sees the relationship in the opposite sense, that is, myths constitute the organising principle of traditional lore. Tradition, in its original Latin meaning of 'handing over', is mythicised memory. For Wolfgang Kaschuba, history is the modelling clay of foundation myths, by which he means history in the numberless configurations of collective and national memories. The resonance of myths derives from their claim to universality which, in turn, provides their legitimacy. He defines myths as 'tightly woven fabrics of data and ideologies, of semantics and aesthetics, of values and practices. They represent extremely highly condensed cultural codifications which tell us "quote me, use me, believe me, but don't ask me"'. My own chapter on the Baltic Sea illustrates what happens when a myth, in this case, 'the Sea of Peace', quoted and used as a symbol of regional unity, is interrogated. At the end of the Cold War, a history of the region was constructed, drawing upon the myth of peace that recalled the Hanseatic web of pacific trade relations. However, if this myth is interrogated, a bellicose past emerges, a past characterised not by peace, but by division and war. In this sense, there are clear connections between the Baltic and European narratives.

In a similar approach, Marta Petrusewicz shows the emergence of a myth – the myth of Italy's *Mezzogiorno* – not as a conscious, instrumental construction, but as an outcome of the widespread disillusionment among the 'embittered heroes' of 1848. The myth of the *Mezzogiorno*, a traditional, agricultural, passionate and irrational land, emerged as a response to a trauma, as a means to fill the collective void left by failed aspirations. This Italian 'south' is set in a dualistic relation with the 'north', where the respective myths are, to return to Kaschuba, quoted and used, but never interrogated. Lars Berggren, on the other hand, presents myth as a choice, whereby actors can sift through the material of history in order to promote the myth that best suits their agenda. Moreover, from this perspective, myth is negotiable, and Berggren shows how, in late 19th century Italy, the government allowed different political and local groups to erect monuments according to their own version of the national myth, on the condition that this interpretation did not stray from the officially approved framework.

The instrumental use of myth as a stake in a struggle to obtain or maintain power is also well illustrated in the chapters by Steen Bo Frandsen and Arve Thorsen. Frandsen analyses Mussolini's manipulation of the idea of Ancient Rome to legitimate his fascist state, while Thorsen considers the way myth was used by elites to control the meaning of national day celebrations in France, Germany and Norway in the 19th century. Since the mobilisation of these myths had certain objectives, Thorsen is able to judge the degree of success or failure of each of these elite projects.

Other chapters show the difficulties involved in simply picking 'ready-made' myths off the shelf. This is clear in Andrei Zorin's perceptive and ironic analysis of the anniversary of the popular resistance to the neocommunist putsch in Russia in August 1991, and the public holiday to celebrate the 850th anniversary of Moscow in 1997. Zorin also makes the important observation that the attempt to create new national myths is as much about visions of the future as visions of the past. This 'future stake' is developed still further in Michael Miller's chapter, which shows how memory of the past is shaped and reshaped according to particular myths and, in turn, used to define a particular future. In Miller's contribution, the myth is the status of certain neighbourhoods as archetypal slums or communities, but even on this local scale, the myth must find resonance in order to mobilise collective memory. A similar position is adopted by Beate Binder in her study of the architectural developments in contemporary Berlin, as the city is shaped for its role as capital of a united Germany. Binder, however, chooses to use the term 'collective memory' rather than 'myth', and argues that buildings are places of memory, and therefore sites of contention over which particular collective memory is represented. Architecture is also the theme of one of Ron Robin's chapters in the volume. He considers the efforts of the United States to define the collective self through its embassy building project in the 1920s, and shows how history was mobilised to suggest continuity and evolution in American foreign policy. What Robin calls the 'mobilisation of history', others in this volume might call myth.

If society recognises itself in a myth, then the deconstruction of such a myth clearly becomes an arduous undertaking, and it is this that Ilan Pappe describes in his chapter on Israel's deep-rooted foundation myths. Ron Robin offers a provocative rejoinder to Pappe's paper, and provides a timely reminder to all of us working with the concept of construction that we can never step outside of myth and memory.

The chapters in this volume raise many questions, not least whether myth provides the limits to memory, or whether memory is the modelling clay of myth (both positions are represented among the contributions). Alternatively, one may conclude that the division is meaningless. One question which this book does not address, however, is whether myths are desirable or not. Myth cannot be seen in opposition to history, rather, history *is* myth and memory, in the sense that there is no sharp demarcation. Their relationship is like a Venn diagram of two overlapping discourses. The narrative or the story constitutes the overlapping field between the historical and the mythical discourses. Moreover, myth is not tested against historiography, as if its 'truth' or 'falsehood' could be demonstrated, on the contrary, it is historiography that defines itself against myth. The question this book poses then is how do myths emerge and what is the role of historians and other social scientists in this process? More specifically, how do different views of history emerge when community is constructed through the process of demarcation between Us and the Other, Now and Then? How are these views, these foundation myths, transformed, and what is the role of media, politicians, artists, architects, writers, film producers and so on? Like all these groups, professional historians also have a role to play, and they do it in their own particular way, through rules and methodology. And we certainly cannot consider historians to have a privileged position in this process, whereby others develop myths and the critical historians reveal these myths and tell the 'truth'. These questions are linked to the general issue of how community is constructed in the *Spannungsfeld* between images of the past and visions of the future, and how history has been interpreted and mediated in various settings. This in turn raises the question, made clear from the contributions in this book, of why symbols and myths so often emerge in the framework of the nation and become *Geschichtsmässig*.[24] 'Anti-fascism' can be seen as an example – although an extreme one – of how myths become *Geschichtsmässig*. Just as anti-fascism was 'moulded' to produce a very particular definition of 'democracy' in post-war Hungary, as shown in Péter Apor's chapter, so too in the German Democratic Republic, anti-fascism became the pivot of an ideology that defined 'democratic' in a remarkable way. Many German Communists had made sacrifices in their fight against the Nazi regime, and in this respect the emergence of anti-fascism as a *raison d'être* of the GDR is understandable. However, very soon after 1945, the idea of anti-fascism became fixed in distorted forms. For instance, it was anti-fascism which motivated and justified the erection of the Berlin Wall in 1961.[25] In the 1980s, Luther, Friedrich the Great and Bismarck were

---

[24] Cf. Schmale, 1997.

[25] In 1965, the East German Historian Ernst Engelberg stated: 'Both liberalism and Jacobin radicalism showed from the very beginning and show it time and again

all taken on board by the regime and merged with anti-fascism as elements in the historical justification of the GDR. However, a history where the Western *Bundesrepublik* comes out looking like a hero while the GDR is nothing more than a propaganda construction would be too simple. In the West, as Bernhard Giesen has shown, and also shows in his chapter in this book, the combination of memory and oblivion after the war played down the Nazi past. This was a memory strategy which was not only supported by the Allied powers after the war, but was actually initiated by them in order to prevent a repetition of the feelings of revenge provoked by the Treaty of Versailles. This strategy formed an important part of the framework of mental mobilisation during the Cold War that assigned guilt to the Nazi leaders for having seduced the German people who, in turn, were seen as being separate from the regime. Only with the Eichmann trial and the youth revolt in the 1960s did ideas of collective guilt emerge in which Nazi terror was not confined to a ruling core, but interpreted in the framework of a broader and, at the same time, more specific German history, the *Sonderweg*.[26] Whereas in Austria after 1945 a self-image as victim was constructed, in the GDR a modified victim thesis emerged which associated this evil with capitalism. It was on this basis that the image of being on the side of the victors in history was developed. The Federal Republic, on the other hand, presented itself as the anti-state to the Nazi regime, while simultaneously laying claim to the political, legal and moral legitimacy that was the heritage of the *Deutsche Reich*. There followed, however, unintended consequences which saw the FRG assume a certain responsibility for the Third Reich. Helmut Dubiel has demonstrated how this was given

---

that democracy and dictatorship are not contradictions. One always has to ask the question: Democracy for whom? Dictatorship against whom? [...] in reality, parliamentary bourgeois democracy is, on the one hand, a means to tune in the interests of the different parties of the urban and rural capitalists to each other; on the other hand, a means to press down the workers and the other labourers.'
Such an understanding of democracy, as Dutch historian Jan Herman Brinks has argued, bore strong similarities to the concept of democracy as it was articulated by the 'conservative revolutionary' Carl Schmitt, who was one of the trail-blazers of the Third Reich. As a matter of fact, 'anti-fascism' in the GDR represented the failure to purge the state and the SED adequately of Nazi adherents. West German authors as well as Simon Wiesenthal have observed that some former Nazis were allowed to find their way back into political life in the GDR. Historian Ernst Engelberg would, later on, write his great biography of Bismarck. Cf. Brinks, 1992.

[26]   Giesen, 1998.

expression in animated political and historical debates and conflicts over how to cope with the past, debates that have continued up to the present.[27]

The fact that today *Sieg Heil* salutes can once more be heard in the former GDR cannot, of course, be attributed to a single 'cause', but must be seen in the framework of a complex mythology. One element of this framework was the antagonistic and permanent dichotomy that emerged between Communism and Nazism. When Communism collapsed, radical adversaries of the state could tap into the process of interaction between memory and oblivion and turn it in new directions by means of old symbols. Victor Klemperer, whose recently translated diaries span the decades of the 1940s and 1950s in the GDR, was a contemporary who emphasised the continuity in language between Nazism and Communism. In July 1945, we find him asking whether there is any difference between Hitler's creation of language and truth and that of Stalin. 'Every day I observe the continuity from the Third Reich's *Lingua Tertii Imperii* to the *Lingua Quartii Imperii* in the Soviet sphere', he added in October of that year.[28] However, it was in Adenauer's Federal Republic that he saw the greatest evil. There he perceived the forces that had made Hitler's dictatorship possible still at work. From this perspective, the GDR was, despite all its faults, the more human alternative. This example shows that myths and collective identities, while they may appear to offer a clear demarcation between Us and Them, Now and Then, contain within them contradictions and overlaps.

Resistance during World War II also informs foundation myths in France.[29] In 1987, Henry Rousso published *Le syndrome de Vichy de 1944 à nos jours*, with the aim of crushing the national myth based on *la Résistance* and challenging the favourite metaphor of the older generation of historians whereby Vichy was presented as the shield and de Gaulle the sword.[30] In order to liberate France from the trauma that Vichy represented, Rousso recommended public debate. He had his request granted, and in 1996 he came back with a new book,

---

[27] Dubiel, 1999.

[28] Klemperer, 1999.

[29] For a general discussion of historians, foundation myths and World War II, see Bosworth, 1993.

[30] Rousso, 1987.

Vichy: un passé qui ne passe pas, written together with Eric Conan, in which, rather than public debate, they recommended a moratorium. The old myth was broken, but a new one about collaboration and guilt was about to take form. Rousso and Conan argued that the problem with this development was that historians had been pushed aside by journalists, who were better at producing hysteria than historical understanding.[31]

In Italy, historians after the war constructed a past in which the members of the resistance movement became the heroes, while the German occupation forces were the source of evil. The paradoxical consequence of this foundation myth, which was written from the perspective of the political left, was that the role of domestic Fascism was played down and the Italian war history became as heroic as that of the French, the Dutch, the Danish, the Norwegians and all other nations which had had a resistance movement. Playing down Fascism in Italy was, on the whole, an unintentional consequence of focussing on the resistance rather than the outcome of a conscious decision to ignore the Fascist past. The analysis of Fascism depicted a well-demarcated reactionary movement and, subsequently, a regime that, by means of violence, terror and surveillance, suppressed the democratic, progressive and popular Italian nation. In this respect, there was an obvious similarity between the mythology of the Federal Republic of Germany in the 1950s and the development of the myth in Italy by Liberals, Christian Democrats, Socialists, and Communists up to the 1970s. However, this foundation myth was seriously questioned in the 1960s by the conservative historian de Felice.[32] In the first volume of his biography of Mussolini, published in 1965, he gave serious consideration to the revolutionary socialist stance Mussolini' had adopted prior to 1915. He used this as a point of departure from which to problematise the antagonism between Fascism and Communism/Socialism, which is one of the key elements in the myth of the *resistenza*. He then continued step by step in his undertaking to demolish the myth. In the volumes on *Mussolini il Duce* (1974 & 1981), he argued that there had been a basic consensus between leader and people and that the *resistenza* had no popular backing until the fortunes of war turned. In his last triple volume (1990-7), he was very explicit in his questioning of the resistance movement, both as history

---

[31] Rousso and Conan, 1994.
[32] De Felice, 1965.

and foundation myth.[33] When he first launched his attack on the myth, De Felice was widely regarded as a maverick, but gradually his view came to be highly important in the field of fascism research. His campaign against the foundation myth should, however, be seen in a broader political framework, beyond the professional debate among historians. De Felice's work was an element of a wider campaign against the Communist Party that took place in the 1970s. At that time, the Italian Republic became problematised by the political Left as well as the Right, before being redefined by Craxi in the 1980s as a modern rather than an ahistorical democratic republic. In the most recent scholarly contribution to this field, the Italian debate on how to come to terms with the past is moving in the direction of synthesis, where emphasis is given to the plurality of memories. The Left, the Right and the Catholic world all have their views on the role of anti-fascism in developing the postwar republican *credo*. The revisionism initiated by de Felice in the struggle over memory has produced a critical response.[34]

The cases of Italy, Germany and France all illustrate that history in the form of foundation myths is not a given, set in stone for once and for all. On the contrary, this history is continuously reconsidered and renegotiated, and in this ongoing process some periods appear to be characterised by greater transformation than others.

Sweden was never occupied during World War II and could therefore not develop the same heroic story as Italy, France and the others. In order to repress the collective feelings of shame and guilt for not having shared the fate of the neighbouring Scandinavian countries, Swedish historians, political scientists and politicians built the myth of neutrality, in which the virtue of neutrality was argued to be the result of a choice made by Sweden in the early 19th century. Freud distinguished three levels of dream and, by analogy, three levels of myth; anxiety dreams, punishment dreams, and wish-fulfilment dreams. Employing this terminology, the Swedish myth was the development from anxiety to wish-fulfilment. Any historical evidence of deviation from the neutrality policy – before and during the Danish-

---

[33] De Felice's biographies of Mussolini: 1974, 1975, 1976a, 1976b, 1976c, 1981, 1990-7 and De Felice and Goglia, 1983. Cf. Pavone, 1991 and 1995. I am grateful to Nils Arne Sørensen for valuable comments on this point.

[34] See Paggi, 1999.

Prussian wars in 1848 and 1864, during the Crimean War, before World War I, during the short-lived euphoric belief in international security promised by the League of Nations and, finally, during World War II itself – was collectively forgotten. It is only in the 1990s that this view has come to be challenged by historians and alternative interpretations have been taken into consideration. In Denmark too, as Mette Zølner's chapter shows, the memory of the Second World War took on new dimensions in the 1990s.[35]

The Israeli foundation myth based on the David and Goliath metaphor is eloquently depicted and critically analysed by Ilan Pappe and Ron Robin in chapters 16a and 16b. Pappe's chapter is an excellent illustration of the main argument of this book, posing the question of why the Holocaust only emerged as a key theme for the legitimisation of the new state in the 1960s. Pappe and Robin also shows how the whole foundation symbolism is both defended and challenged by rival historical camps in an ongoing struggle over the 'correct' history.

The general pattern which emerges from these examples seems to be that foundation myths often emerge in the context of crisis situations, and particularly in response to a collective yearning to come to terms with these situations. They provide a framework for interpretation and understanding and seem to offer consolation, if not compensation, for present and past suffering and injury. Memory makes it possible to forget, in the same sense as Reinhart Koselleck has argued that, for public monuments, to reveal is to conceal: *zeigen ist verschweigen*.[36] This is a theme that is clearly present in Lars Berggren's chapter on 'The Making of Italy with Monuments'. But perhaps, rather than forgetting, it is a matter of not being reminded, and uncontested monuments signify a kind of agreement on the meaning of history as well as on the values of the present. We do not notice what we see around us every day, and it is in this context that myths take on the dimensions of common sense and truths that are never questioned. However, in new situations of crisis and loss of meaning, as during and after World War II, and in the 1990s when the

---

[35] Cf. also Sørensen, 1999.

[36] This concept was used by Reinhart Koselleck in his paper entitled 'Concentration Camp Monuments', presented at 'Art and Fact: The Possibilities of Representation', a workshop directed by Bo Stråth at the European University Institute, Florence, 19-20th April, 1999.

Cold War no longer provided meaning through the clear demarcation of Us and Them, myths become problematic and subject to renegotiation and revision.

The foundation myths in this book also address earlier periods than the post-1945 examples discussed above. There are chapters which deal with public monuments during the *Risorgimento* (Lars Berggren) and the emergence of the *Mezzogiorno* myth in Italy (Marta Petrusewicz), the national day celebrations in Germany, France and Norway around the turn of the century (Arve Thorsen), the representation of the USA through the form of its embassy buildings since the 1920s (Ron Robin), and the transformation of the Swedish foundation myth since the 17th century.

The nation does not provide the only example of the construction of territory. Three chapters in this book deal with the construction of place in a more localised sense; in Moscow (Andrei Zorin), Berlin (Beate Binder), and Glasgow and Roubaix (Michael Miller). Irrespective of whether we are considering the symbolic construction of a nation or a working-class district, the constructors promote an image of a bounded and unchanging territory which is distinguished by distinct and definitive characteristics. Successful constructions gradually permeate our way of seeing and thinking and until they finally reach essentialist proportions.

The question of how collective memory is constructed, maintained and transformed must also address the alternative histories that were never told. How is the collective memory assented to and officially canonised? Hayden White's contribution examines the role of media in this process, while other contributions emphasise the role of arts, architecture, and politics (Sten Bo Frandsen, Lars Berggren and Andrei Zorin, for example). However, it is also clear that it is difficult to exaggerate the importance of the role played by history and the social sciences in legitimating certain memories in the name of science. The practicians of these disciplines have appropriated this legitimating role through the pretension to stand above the processes they analyse. As discussed above, this position has, in recent decades, been challenged and severely weakened by the implication of the rhetoric or linguistic turn. The previously strict demarcation between history and myth is becoming blurred while, at the same time, concepts like objectivity take on new meaning and truth increasingly becomes a contextual category.[37]

Despite these developments, we are left to ponder an intriguing contemporary paradox: even as the claim to objectivity in history and social sciences is being seriously challenged, history is increasingly invoked as an objective science. From South Africa in the south to Sweden in the north, governments appoint 'truth commissions', whose brief it is to tell the final truth, *wie es eigentlich gewesen*, about the past. They are requested to reveal 'how it really was' during apartheid or how neutral Sweden 'really was' during the Cold War. But the question, 'was Sweden neutral or not?' only allows space for one answer, a clear 'yes' *or* 'no'. Truth commissions do not allow for ambiguity, tensions and contradictions – the answer cannot be 'yes' *and* 'no'. And everywhere historians unhesitatingly accept the request to tell the real truth. At the same time as this undertaking is being undermined from within the 'craft', through growing scepticism at the possibility of assuming an objective distance from the processes which are being studied, it is drawing new strength from outside, fed by the growing expectations of governments looking for legitimacy.[38] It is difficult to say how this paradox should be understood, but one might suspect that the money spent by governments on these truth-finding exercises, and the status and power derived from participation in the public debate, have a role to play. An interesting and illustrative example of the relationships between historical truth and political legitimacy is the fact that the Black Book on the crimes of Communism was published only several years after the implosion of

---

[37] See, for example, Combs and Nimmo, 1990.

[38] The use of history and historians for political legitimacy can also take the form of personal public relations campaigns. *Deutschlandpolitik in Helmut Kohls Kanzlerschaft* is a case in point. It is the first of four volumes, where a group of historians, at the request of the ministry of the interior, have been granted exclusive access to otherwise secret sources concerning the Chancellor's correspondence, meetings etc. with Mrs Thatcher, President Mitterand, President Bush, President Gorbachev among others, in order to tell the story of what really happened when Germany was reunified. For historians, journalists or others beyond this exclusive group, the sources will remain secret for at least another 20 years. On the other hand, to what extent is this kind of history taken seriously? Korte, 1998.

the Soviet Union, despite the fact that the historical data *per se* were, to a large extent, already well-known before 1989-91.[39]

The paradox intrinsic in the request that historians should tell the objective truth at the very time that truth is becoming inconstant and contextual and the concept of objectivity is becoming ideologically charged, leads, in turn, to another paradox. When the German and Czech governments appointed a joint commission of historians to come to terms with the past, history took on the role of being negotiable, while still claiming to be objective. The task was to find a version that could fit both sides. It is difficult to imagine a situation where the commission might have reported that it had failed and that there were, in fact, two stories. The report is testimony of the attempt to find a compromise without waiving the claim to objectivity.[40] The idea of negotiable history also seems to be the point of departure in the animated debate in Germany over whether and how to construct a Holocaust memorial in Berlin, a debate that has involved professional historians as well as the *Bundestag*.

From these examples, as well as from the contributions collected in this volume, it is clear that history is inherently political. Of course, medieval or 15th century Finnish history may not have immediate political implications, but when reading Ilian Pappe's contribution to this book, or indeed, any one of the contributions from Péter Apor, Lars Berggren, Beate Binder, Sten Bo Frandsen, Bernhard Giesen, Thomas Hippler, Wolfgang Kaschuba, Michael Miller, Lutz Niethammer, Marta Petrusewicz, Ron Robin, Arve Thorsen, Hayden White, Mette Zølner, Andrei Zorin or myself, the political dimension of history becomes much more obvious. History has a criticising, deconstructing function as well as one of legitimation and construction, and any denial that this is the case, by arguing that history is independent of politics, is itself a political gesture. The legitimating function, in turn, requires that history is conferred the status of a science. The solution to this problem is not to deny the political

---

[39] Courtois, Werth, Panné, Paczkowaki, Bartosek, Margolin, 1977. Cf. François Furet and Ernst Nolte, 1998.

[40] Professors Miroslav Hroch and Rudolf Vierhaus, both of whom were invited to sit on the Czech-German commission, developed this historical problematic in a joint seminar entitled 'East-West Dialogue: The German-Czech Case', organised by John Brewer and given at the Department of History and Civilisation, European University Institute, Florence on 11th May, 1998.

dimension, which would be a form of crypto-politics, but to recognise it and try to find its specific role in a general division of labour, a role which could preliminarily be called proto-politics. How exactly this proto-political role should be cast is a question which historians must address, but which goes beyond the scope of this book.

The essays in this volume share a common approach. This is an approach that does not aim to establish *wie es eigentlich gewesen* in a totalising, absolute and restricted positivist sense, but that strives instead to provide provisional interpretations and translations of the past which, while still source-based, are very different from Rankian history. Let me conclude by stressing that such an approach not only requires a diversity of views, but also a tolerance and a preparedness to consider these views. This is an approach in the best of Enlightenment traditions, far from the accusation of 'postmodern relativism'. This accusation is launched from positions that claim to possess a totalising and absolute truth, and it is claims such as these that, historically, have been one of the foremost points of departure in myth building. However, rejecting the concept of total and definitive truths does not necessarily mean denying the existence of truth as such. This distinction must be clear.

MYTH, MEMORY AND HISTORY

CHAPTER 2

Catastrophe, Communal Memory and Mythic Discourse: The Uses of Myth in the Reconstruction of Society

Hayden WHITE

In this volume, we are concerned with the relationships existing among a mode of discourse (myth), a human faculty (memory), and a specifically human activity (the 'construction' of societies). But myth is an idea whose conceptual content is difficult to specify. The term 'myth' has come to stand for any discourse deemed to be ahistorical, unscientific, illogical, and irrational; in a word, everything conceived to be 'uncivilised'. Indeed, in modernist discourses, myth cannot be dissociated from the 'primitive'. Therefore, even to suggest that myth might be of use in modern efforts at 'social construction' risks the accusation of atavism or of abandoning civilised thought and reason itself.

But if the concept of myth is indeterminable, the notion of 'construction' as applied to 'society' contains an ambiguity or equivocation. The word 'construction' derives from Latin 'construire', which indicates an activity of building by 'piling up' a number of pre-existing things, each being used as 'parts'. In other words, the concept of 'construction' presupposes a 'de-struction' of something else, a fragmentation of a structure, the remains of which can be used to 'construct' another one. In this way, it is not the elements of the constructed entity that will be new, but only their specific combination. Thus, while 'the construction of society' implies the notion of 'reconstruction', this is less as an innovation than a recycling of fragments of prior structures by recombination. It does not connote the activity of creating something new and original, but rather the activity of recombining fragments, shards, and orts taken from the rubble of formerly existing structures. Thus, when we speak of the activity of 'constructing' a 'society', we are suggesting a situation in which a whole is to be refashioned out of the parts remaining from a prior social structure. In a word, to construct, *sensu strictu*, is to reconstruct; it is to reconstruct by combining materials already at hand; and it is to combine by techniques more mechanical than organic in kind. In this way, the project of constructing a society implies remaking it out of elements already at hand and treated as usable parts of a mechanical totality. It does not imply the making of something new or original, or the invention or creation of that which did not exist before.

Now, this idea of building a form of life out of elements already present on the scene of construction is utterly alien to any ideology of modernism. Modernism presumes the possibility of qualitative differences between the 'now' of present time and all of the 'thens' of the past. For every modernism, the construction of anything whatsoever – from a self to a whole civilisation – presumes the presence of things on the scene of construction that are radically 'new'. And this is as true of the first religious 'modernist', St. Paul, as it is of the first philosophical 'postmodernist', Friedrich Nietzsche. Modernism, in short, always presupposes a change in the substance of things as well as in their form.

The same idea underlies the 'historical' conception of change. A historical conception of change presupposes a qualitative difference between any past and the present which follows it in time. In other words, history, like modernism, presupposes changes in the substance as well as in the form of things. No historian would take the resemblance between an ancient and a modern social institution as indicative of a substantive identity between them. For example, there are distinct ressemblances between certain institutions of modern European societies, such as the law and the state, and those of ancient Rome. These ressemblances may very well stem from the uses that these modern societies made of Roman institutions as models for 'constructing' their own legal and political institutions, but no historian would take this as sufficient reason to deny the substantive differences between modern legal and political systems and their Roman prototypes. Modern institutions presume different notions of persons, intentionality, responsibility, legality, citizenship, privacy, publicity and so on, from that of their Roman counterparts. Thus, while their formal attributes may resemble one another, they have a different substance of content. In modern historical thought, a change in the attributes of a thing is a sign, index, or symptom of a change in its substance. Thus, historical change is transubstantiative. In myth, on the other hand, all change is metamorphic.

In myth, all change is a result either of a 'dislocation' of a thing from its 'proper' place, or of it missing its 'proper' moment in time. When a thing or person is out of its proper place, or is early or late for its proper moment, nothing it does will be fulfilling. In myth, both time and space are conceived to be heterogeneous, distributed into 'lots' or 'portions', each with a substantiality 'proper' to itself. Whereas scientific time and space are conceived to be homogeneous and continuous, mythic time and space are mosaicked or fractated, and their units are incommensurable among themselves, both quantitatively and qualitatively. Thus, the life-world of myth is governed by the principle of 'propriety' and not 'causality'. Or rather, the only causality myth knows is that of 'propriety'. When the principle of propriety is observed, things go well; when it is violated, things go badly (cf. Genesis, 4:7, where the Lord says to Cain: 'If you do what is right, you will be accepted. But if you do not do what is right, sin is crouching at your door.')

Thus, myth emplots stories about specific actions and sets of events as manifesting the consequences of violations or observances of the rule of propriety. Space is localised, time is seasoned. Things are either in their places or moments or they are not. If they are properly located and seasoned, things go well; if they are not, things go badly. Ruination, destruction and disaster are consequences of dislocation or mistiming. Myth therefore explains or, rather, explicates the kinds of situations which we moderns might characterise as calling for a 'reconstruction of society', by charting, mapping, or identifying violations of the rule of propriety. This is why a mythic mode of conceptualising programmes of social reconstruction seems an apt alternative to historical and scientific techniques of analysing situations of social crisis or breakdown of a social system. For whatever else a 'society' may be, it is organised according to rules – customs, conventions, and laws – that define what is 'proper' and what is deviant behaviour, thought, and comportment in a given sector of human practice.

Myth explicates situations of social disaster by narrativising them. It not only represents them as displaying the form of the story told about them, but also attributes to them the meaning-content of the plot or generic story-type used to organise a congeries of events into a sequence segmented into the semantic categories of beginning, middle and end. Emplotment thus 'dramatises' complex processes of change by presenting them as conflicts between agents undertaking projects that are either 'proper' or 'improper' to the scenes (the places and moments) of their enactment. It is in this sense that 'narrativisation' can be said to 'moralise' what would otherwise have to be construed as a casual conjuncture of forces merely physical in kind. Thus, for example, a natural cataclysm, such as an earthquake or a flood, which had no effect on agents engaged in projects of a self-fulfilling kind, would be undramatisable ('drama', from the Greek '$\delta\rho\alpha\nu$': to do, act, or perform) and hence unnarratable. Having said this, in archaic cultures that might construe such cataclysmic events as effects of conflicts between the gods, they would be both dramatisable and narratable, and were in fact so presented in the canonical myths of Greece and Rome. But here again, the conflict envisaged is construed to be a result of violations of a principle of propriety which consigns the use of the powers possessed by individual gods to a specific domain ('$\mu o\iota\rho\alpha$' or portion) of the universe.

A mythic representation of a scene of disaster dramatises the scene by emplotting the events that occur thereon as effects, or rather as consequences, of a specifically moral conflict. It always focuses upon agents (natural or supernatural, human or divine) endowed with a sense of the necessity to act in ways that either conform to or violate the principles of propriety that inform the place and time of the action. I propose, therefore, that human beings, in their status as members of a specific society or social order, are inclined to have recourse to mythic modes of thought and expression whenever they have been subjected to processes, either natural or social, that both destroy the material infrastructure of their communities and exceed the powers of science to grasp or even to register their moral significance.

In situations of extreme social devastation, mythic discourse erupts and flows into the semantic space made vacant by the incapacity of science to recognise the moral significance of human suffering. This is because science cannot address the question of the *value* of human suffering. It may very well provide an explanation of *how* the disaster occurred and identify the factors, physical and social, that caused it, but *why* it occurred at the specific time and in the specific place that it did, and *why* its effects on the human population appear to the survivors to be a kind of 'cruel and unusual punishment', are questions that science, with its interest in fact rather than value, cannot even perceive, much less answer. From the standpoint of science, a disaster is always a matter of chance. It happened where, when, and as it did because different kinds of causal forces converged just there and not elsewhere. Myth factors moral forces into this equation and thereby transforms the face of 'disaster' (literally, 'bad star' or ill luck) into a visage of 'catastrophe' (we should note that the term catastrophe is a term taken from theatre, and denotes the point in a drama at which events take a sudden downward turn towards a condition of devastation, thereby setting up the revelation of the meaning in the drama's final scene.)

Myth and Communal Memory

I would now like to propose a hypothesis regarding the relationship between myth and communal memory. By 'communal memory' I mean two kinds of information about, and accounts of, a community's past. The first I call traditionalised memory. It consists of information about, and accounts of the past that are latently stored in its corpus of traditional lore (its fables, folk tales, gnomic commonplaces, customs, prejudices, and conventions, its jokes, spectacles, entertainments and language). The second kind of information I call rationalised memory, and it consists of information about, and accounts of a community's past, contained in its archives and catalogued and processed in the form of written or visualised 'histories', so that it can be 'accessed' on demand. I do not mean anything like the Jungian notion of a 'collective unconscious' or Halbwachian 'collective memory'. These notions seem to me to be much too dependent upon a projection of the structures of an individual consciousness onto that of the collectivity to offer utility for scientific examination. However, in traditional lore, on the one side, and archived and catalogued information on the other, we have enough approximation to what we can call a 'communal memory' to inquire into the relation between it and whatever we might mean by 'myth'. It should be noted that I have not included the category of 'myths' among the kinds of communal memory that I call 'traditional'. This is because I believe that the dominant myths of a society provide the organising principles of its traditional lore. Tradition, I wish to suggest, is mythicised memory. It is information about the past, organised in terms of its significance for comprehending the moral import of a community's relationship to its past. The word 'tradition' derives from Latin *tradere*, to hand over, and features the notions of 'transmission' and 'transfer' among its many connoted significances. By metonymy of the act of 'handing over' for the thing considered worthy of being so transmitted, the noun *traditio* came to indicate a body of lore inherently worthy of preservation and reverence by virtue of its origin in God's message to mankind regarding what He demanded of them as 'proper' conduct, thought, and feeling (as in God's commandments handed over to Moses, or the teachings of Jesus handed over to the Apostles).

Tradition thus mediates and regulates the exchange between a community's present and its past by providing norms of comportment, thought, action, and feeling specifically moral in kind. In traditional societies, or those parts of modern societies not yet modernised and thereby 'liberated' from the constraints of tradition, 'experience' is conceived to belong to the present, while 'meaning', or the moral significance of experience, is conceived as residing in the past – in mythicised memory. This part of the communal memory organised as tradition stands at odds with that part that has been rationalised, that is, organised, classified, co-ordinated, catalogued and stored in institutions created to serve as depositories of information. And this includes information about traditions, myths, and other kinds of non-rationalised knowledge. Thus, whereas rationalised knowledge comprehends traditionalised knowledge, the reverse is not the case. This is because traditionalised knowledge must confront rationalised knowledge as a threat and a danger, since the latter conceives rationality instrumentally and judges information in terms of its utility for problem-solving. This judgement of utility is brought to bear upon traditional knowledge itself in times of social disaster. 'Overcoming tradition', to use a phrase that served as a motto of Japanese modernists in the early 20th century, is a principal problem in situations of social disaster, because traditionalised knowledge is always more concerned with the moral import of an extreme event than it is with technical solutions to practical problems.

If we take this view of 'communal memory', we can begin to comprehend how a community's response to a situation that seems to call for social reconstruction can break down into three different kinds of discourse about 'what happened' and 'what is to be done'. First, the disaster can be assimilated to communal memory by its mythification. Secondly, it can be assimilated to communal memory by the conventions of classification, cataloguing, and storage techniques of the rationalising sciences. And thirdly, the disaster can be assimilated to communal memory in such a way as to force a revision and de-legitimation of traditionalised memory itself. Programmes for recovery from the disaster (or the reconstruction of the afflicted society) can thus be sublimated into public debates about the relative merits of different ways of construing the *causes* of the disaster. This is especially the case in societies in which discussions of public policy issues can be 'overloaded' with so much media-circulated information as to obscure both the 'facts' of a given matter and the resources necessary for the implementation of programmes of aid and succour. In these situations, governments can substitute actions with discourses and nothing need be *done* at all.

A Case in Point: The Disaster of Sarno

I now turn to a specific case in which the conflict between mythologising and rationalising approaches to the problem of reconstructing a social system devastated by a natural disaster ended in a decision to do 'nothing at all'. This was not because traditional knowledge triumphed over rationalising knowledge, but because the custodians of the latter produced mythic accounts of the nature of the disaster which afflicted a specific place within a national community that was engaged in the task of redefining its national 'identity'.

On 5th May, 1998, between 1500 and 1700hrs, after hours of heavy rain had saturated the volcanic soil of Mount Pizzo d'Alvano, to the east of Napoli, in the region of Campania, a massive avalanche of cold mud descended upon the town of Sarno (Salerno) to the west of the peak, and towards Quindici (Avellino) to the Northeast. The slide wiped out the town of Episcopio (Sarno), flowed through Sarno itself, and covered over parts of the towns of Siano, Bracigliano, Quindici, and San Felice a Cancello. Between 2345hrs of 5th May and 2100hrs of 7th May, the toll in human casualties in the area had mounted to 55 known dead, 200 'lost' and 'thousands of homeless'.

Once the extremity of the event had been registered, a virtual shower of discourses rained down on the opaque space created by the flow of mud, writing over it, encrusting it, and articulating it as only stories can do. Within a few hours, the disaster of Sarno was mythified.

The Italian national newspaper *la Repubblica* (Sede 00185, Roma, Piazza Independenza, 11/b) provided extensive coverage of the event from shortly after its beginning. This coverage constitutes an archive of the various kinds of stories that were told by and about survivors and rescue workers, as well as efforts of government agencies to deal with the disaster, journeys to the area, visits by politicians, humanitarians, volunteers and religious dignitaries, and expressions of sympathy and promises of aid by interested parties both foreign and domestic. It also conveyed an account of the impression that the disaster had made on observers, and, significantly, the impact that the response of government officials to the disaster might have on Italy's 'image' abroad, especially in Germany, where it was feared that German banks did not view Italy as a worthy associate in the emergent European Economic Union, and so on and so on. It also carried stories about the victims, how they had died, what had happened to their bodies, and how difficult it had been to recover them from the mud, identify them and provide for an appropriate burial.

By its manner of presenting the array of stories told about the event, stories by survivors, reporters, scientists, public functionaries, rescuers, politicians, and so on, *la Repubblica* constructed them as elements of a more comprehensive story. This story served as a 'master narrative', the function of which was to provide a plot-structure in terms of which 'facts' could be differentiated from 'fictions' and appropriately stored in the 'communal memory' of the *national* community. This process of archivisation established the 'relevance' of the facts about the 'disaster of Sarno' to the continuing task of constructing a national ('Italian') community capable of 'realistically' confronting certain concrete problems. These problems included 'modernisation' and, specifically, entrance into the European Economic and Monetary Union, to which Italy had just been admitted as a full, rather than second-class partner.

La Repubblica's treatment of this event can be taken as an example of how the 'collective memory' of the national community can be adjusted to accommodate an event which, at first glance, is apprehended as simply 'disastrous'. This adjustment was accomplished by mythification, by the progressive translation of the 'disaster' into a 'catastrophe', a scene of specifically 'moral' significance. This translation endowed the scene in which the event had occurred with a plot-structure by reference to which the moral importance of events could be identified, thereby permitting their classification in terms of good and evil, responsibility and negligence, nobility and baseness, guilt and innocence; in a word, in terms of their significance as a drama, specifically 'tragic' in kind.

This mythification of the scene of disaster, however, only paved the way for a further task of interpretation that was presented in the unfolding story as a de-mythification. Here, what had been inscribed as a tragedy was reinscribed as a scene of 'demonic farce' in which everyone – victims, survivors, and those governmental agencies responsible for the care of the community – was indicted as commonly complicit in the commission of a crime. The identification of the criminality that suffused the scene of the disaster permitted the assignment of the tasks of recovery to the State and its arm of law enforcement, the 'police'. But since the police themselves had already been 'archived' as fatally corrupt and incompetent in the nation's 'communal memory' by the very same techniques of mythification as those used to constitute 'Sarno' as a scene of 'demonic farce', the revelation of criminality in Sarno only had the effect of generating cynicism regarding what could be done to rebuild it as a 'place' worthy of membership of the larger national space.

In Italy, as they say, the situation, 'especially in the *Mezzogiorno*', is always disastrous, but never serious, because things always remain the same, which is to say, always a bit 'Third Worldish', a bit too 'Mediterranean', and a bit too 'African' to respond to modern and rational principles of social administration (see Marta Petrusewicz's chapter for a full discussion of the myth of the *Mezzogiorno*). It is this alibi that allows Italians to remain as sceptical about the national project of modernisation and entrance into 'the European Community' as a full, rather than second-order member. It is equally sceptical about the prospect of ever reforming the *Mezzogiorno* and making it worthy of partnership with the more progressive 'North', characterised by industry, business and commerce. (It should be noted that the debate over what was to be done with Sarno erupted at a moment in which some political representatives of the North were engaged in a movement to secede from the national community, leaving the South to wallow in its apparently irrecoverable condition of poverty, laziness, and corruption).

On Thursday, 7th May, *la Repubblica* carried on its front page the first news of the disaster in the headline: '*Una strage nel fango*' (*strage* means slaughter, massacre/ violent death of a large number of persons or animals/ destruction, ruin of things/ a collection of cadavers. *Fango* is mud). Thus began the paper's comprehensive coverage of the event. This coverage would extend over two weeks before the process of removing it from the category of 'news' and consigning it to 'history' began. Archivisation of an event such as this in the 'collective memory' required that it be provided with a definite plot-structure, a structure of meaning that permitted the collocation or configuration of events in terms of their 'relevance' to a social theme already familiar to readers as elements of its rationalised 'communal memory'.

An original moment of doubt or hesitation about the 'real' nature of an event in its social significance requires its translation from a 'problem' into an 'enigma'. The inauguration of this process in the case of Sarno was signalled by the large number of stories devoted to it, and also by the diversity of the kind of news printed alongside stories devoted to the event itself. Thus, on the same front page of the newspaper which first announced the cataclysm there were featured stories about Prime Minister Prodi's visit to the United States, in which it was reported that President Clinton had promised aid to the afflicted (Clinton is reported as saying: 'L'America vi aiuterà' – America will help you). On the same page, there was also a report on the capture of a sensational 'serial killer' who had struck terror in the populace of the Ligurian coastland for months before; the investigation of the murder of the recently appointed commandant of the Pope's Swiss Guard and his wife by a young corporal in the unit ('Sul delitto il Vaticano non ha detto la verità' – the Vatican has not told the truth about the crime); the flight of a convicted former head of P2, the outlawed Masonic Lodge ('Gelli è fuggito/il governo sott'accusa' – Gelli has escaped/the government is being blamed); the outcome of a soccer match ('L'Inter trionfa a Parigi' – Inter triumphs in Paris); two ads ('Domani con Repubblica il 1° di quattro straordinari CD di Frank Sinatra' – tomorrow with *Repubblica* the first of four extraordinary Frank Sinatra CDs, and 'CaseAbitare: Cambia il tuo modo di vivere' – change your way of living). Finally, and most prominently, there was an editorial signed by Giovanni Valentini, entitled 'Omissione di atti d'ufficio' – omissions in the official legislation – which began the process of relating the Sarno disaster to the malfunctioning of the Italian state apparatus.

The lead story was therefore surrounded by other stories and advertisements which, by their relationship of contiguity, effectively functioned as 'commentary' and 'glosses', having the effect of locating the Sarno event in a hierarchy of events, actions, and practices deemed to be of crucial interest to an Italian readership. Valentini's editorial treated the disaster and its effects as a synecdoche of the whole Italian social 'scene'. In fact, the editorial already prefigured the possibility of treating the event as something other than an 'unfortunate' (*i.e.* disastrous) occurrence.

In his editorial, Giovanni Valentini developed the theme of catastrophe:

> La fatalità, questa volta, non c'entra. L'alluvione [...] non é una 'calamità naturale' [...] É stato, piuttosto, il risultato [...] di una lunga catena di ritardi, errori e carenze, imputabili a precise responsabilità politiche e amministrative che chiamano in causa il governo nazionale, la Regione Campania e gli stessi Communi delle zone interessate, per un'omissione collettiva di 'atti d'ufficio'.[1]

In short, the event was already being at once politicised and moralised, endowed with human agency as one of its causes, if not its principal cause, and charged with sinister implications. This effect was augmented by the stories and ads that related by contiguity the events of Sarno with other ˙events, both serious and frivolous, occurring at the same time in Italy at large. Thus, the theme of political corruption was augmented by the story of the ease with which Gelli was able to escape police surveillance and flee from his impending trial for crimes as various as treason, murder, fraud and extortion.

---

[1] *La Repubblica*, Giovedi, 7 Maggio, 1998, p. 1. 'This time, fate has nothing to do with it. The flood [...] was not a "natural disaster" [...] It was, rather, the result [...] of a long chain of delays, errors and delinquencies, ascribable to precise political and administrative responsibilities that call into question the national government, the Region of Campania and the local councils of the afflicted zone for the collective omission of official legislation.'

These political and moral thematisations were concretised in the stories appearing on pages two and three of the paper, whose headlines intone:

'Fango e morte, scene da un disastro' (Mud and death, scenes of a disaster).
'Quella fuga nella notte dall'ospedale del terrore' (That flight into the night from the hospital of terror).
'Sotto la frana coi tre figli' (Under the landslide with three children).
'Anche Olga la "pasionaria" morta sotto l'ondata di fango.' (Olga the 'pasionaria' also dead under the wave of mud).

At this point, the cataclysm was still scripted as a natural disaster by the association of death with images of a sea of 'volcanic' and, therefore, black mud sweeping over and burying the innocent (children) and the virtuous alike (Olga was a well-known local opponent of the Mafia who had been endowed with the eponym of the famous female heroine of the Loyalist side in the Spanish Civil War).

The image of black 'mud' as the immediate cause of the 'massacre' locates its original cause in the most demonic aspects of a 'nature' indifferent to human suffering. The event is still 'naturalised', but its description is inflected in the register of the dark and malificent – in a word, Satanic.

But on page four, a turn towards a thematisation of the event as a 'catastrophe' is indicated by a coverage cast in three different discursive registers. First, there is the register of the facto-statistical. Here are displayed photos of the inhabitants of Sarno fleeing an avalanche of mud and of rescuers carrying survivors to safety. What is more 'factual' than a photograph? Then, we have a list (with pictures) of 'I grandi disastri in Italia (1923-1994).' – the great disasters in Italy. What is more 'factual" than a list? Finally, there is a table of statistics and characteristics of the great earthquake that struck Naples on 23rd November 1980. What is more 'factual' than a table?

This body of material can be said to balance and neutralise the horror evoked by the stories told of the suffering of the innocent victims of the disaster through their rationalisation. In these materials, the Sarno disaster is classified as to its scope, intensity, and impact on human beings, and it is shown to rank well below the Naples earthquake of 1980. Thereby, the Sarno event was 'domesticated' and 'provincialised' as it were. Indeed, it was domesticated by being provincialised. These tables, charts, and photos sent a message intended to be reassuring to the general public beyond the confines of Sarno. To the province of Salerno, the message was, 'Sarno is a disaster, but only one among many that have struck your region and, while bad, it is by no means the worst of its kind.' To Italy at large, the message was, 'Sarno is an event of the *Mezzogiorno*, and specifically of an area of the South commonly afflicted by such disasters.'

This discursive register is augmented by another, which I will call the *narrative-fabulistic*. The function of this register is to restore the event to its human significance and to empathicise it. Thus, there is a picture of a helicopter crew rescuing a family from an inundated dwelling, with the caption, 'In salvo con gli angeli del cielo appesi alla fune dell'elicottero' – in safety with the angels from the sky, hanging from a helicopter cable – while the military are quoted as saying, 'la missione più difficile? Rassicurare i piccoli.' – the toughest mission? To reassure the little ones. Another story on the same pages is entitled, 'Dopo 18 anni ricomincia il nostro nuovo terremoto.' – after 18 years our new earthquake has started again. Here some 'survivors of the disaster' speak about their ordeal. One family is quoted as saying, 'Avevamo un container, abbiamo perso anche quello sotto le macerie' – we had a container, and we lost even that under the debris. The intended effect of such 'human interest' journalism is to establish the general humanity that links the afflicted and their rescuers, the Sarnesi and other Italians, and Italians and other national groups, in a shared condition of 'sufferance'. We are all victims of the human condition which, as the Bible tells us, is a consequence of original sin and the 'fall' from the Garden of Eden.

Against these human-interest stories there is posed yet another discourse, which I propose to call the *desirative-consumerist*. This discourse is represented pre-eminently by the advertisements for consumer commodities spread over pages two to four, that announce the following:

'www.repubblica.it: oggi Daimler-Chrysler: tutti i siti del matrimonio dell'anno';
'New York in CD-Rom: Città in Cd Rom'; and
'Hallo Lloyd: Risparmio fino al 50 per cento sulla Polizza Auto'.

Thus, in the midst of news of disaster and deprivation, the readers of *la Repubblica* were offered access to (internet) *news* about the merger of the Daimler and Chrysler car firms; (computerised) *images* of New York City, the Paradise of a particularly modernist kind of commodity production and consumption; and an *invitation*, to save on the purchase of an insurance policy on the most desirable of modern consumer goods, the automobile. But pages six and seven continued with stories chronicling the government's failure to foresee the disaster and take steps to avoid it. There were stories of accusations leveled against Finance Minister Ciampi, who was accused of having blocked billions of lire marked for improving the ecostructure of Sarno ('Le accuse al Tesoro: "Ha bloccato miliardi."' – accusations against the treasury: 'it blocked billions'). To these accusations Ciampi replied, 'nessuna richiesta da quelle zone' – there was not one request for aid from those areas. So too, an insert on the same page carried news of the parliamentary opposition's demand for the resignation of the commissioner charged with handling such disasters: 'L'opposizione chiede che lasci l'incarico di commissario alle frane: "Rastrelli deve dimettersi".' – the opposition calls for the land-slide commissioner to leave office: 'Rastrelli must resign'.

An interview with the Minister of Public Works, Paolo Costa, headlined his opinion that, in areas at risk of natural disaster, it was incumbent upon inhabitants to carry insurance on their dwellings: 'nelle aree a rischio ci vuole l'assicurazione', while adding, 'Con i soldi che ci sono non potevo fare di più', – with the (public) funds available, I could not do more).

Another story, datelined Avellino, quoted the Undersecretary of Civil Protection, Franco Barberi, as saying that the funds available for relief were inadequate and could not be delivered in time to be of worth: 'fondi erogati in ritardo' and 'insufficienti le resorse per la protezione del suolo.'[2] In these stories, the disaster was being 'socialised', that is, removed from the category of natural events and assigned a function specifically political in nature. It was all a matter of insufficient money and the government's *inability* to deliver aid to a specific place at the right time.

Page seven contained more graphics. These included a photograph of an inhabitant of Sarno being saved by a helicopter, and two drawings, one representing the number and distribution of 'the victims of hydrological disasters' in Italy from Trentino to Sicily (3,488

---

[2]   *Ibid.,* p. 6.

victims in all, 631 in Campania alone in the last 50 years, and added the funds spent for damages during that period – 30 thousand million lire); and another representing 'The Principal Types of Landslides: Collapse *(crollo)* and Slide *(scivolamento)'*. These graphics are supplemented with a story on the Minister of the Interior, Giorgio Napolitano, who visited the scene of the disaster in a helicopter and is quoted as declaring it to be 'uno stato di calamità […] indegno di un paese civile' – a state of calamity […] unworthy of a civilised country.[3] The same story quotes Mayor Antonio Siniscalchi, of Quindici, the town to the north of Sarno which sustained extensive losses, as saying that he had requested aid from the government many times over the course of the last few years, but had received no assistance at all and virtually no response from government authorities to his pleas. Mayor Siniscalchi stated that the disaster was a result of criminal negligence and demanded that, 'chi ha versato sangue innocente deve pagare' – whoever has spilt innocent blood should pay.

Finally, however, there appeared a story reporting the opinion of Floriano Villa, President of the National Association of Geologists, that the area of Sarno contained too many illegally constructed dwellings – 'troppe case abusive' – thus making the likelihood of 'una sciagura', an extreme disaster, 'inevitable'.[4] This last story effectively *names* the event as an effect of human and, specifically, criminal agency. Who was responsible for building these *case abusive*, or allowing them to be built, or removing them and healing the damage done to the mountain? The story does not say. But in any case, the mountain itself can no longer be blamed for the disaster; it has to be seen as an innocent victim of human abuse. But now an authority, 'scientific' in nature, has identified the calamity, 'indegno di un paese civile', as an effect of criminal, if not sinful, intent.

Thematisation: Repetition, Substantialisation, Reduction, Naming

What is interesting about this process of interpreting the nature of the disaster of Sarno is the recognition on the part of *la Repubblica*'s reporters and editors that an appropriate 'archivisation' of the event

---

[3] *Ibid.,* p. 7.

[4] *Ibid.,* p. 7.

requires its classification as a catastrophe. I noted earlier that 'catastrophe' is a specifically theatrical term, indicating the moment in a plot in which things come apart (Greek: *sparagmos*), leading to the *dénouement* of the story and the 'recognition' (*anagnorisis*) of the event's 'deep' meaning, that is, what it tells us about human nature and the enigmas of a specifically 'social' existence. I also noted that 'catastrophe' is traditionally featured as a component of a course of events deemed to be emplottable as a 'tragedy'.

It is not surprising, then, that on 8th May, *la Repubblica* carried as its headline: 'La tragedia dei dispersi. Potrebbero essere oltre duecento. Allarme epidemia.' – the *tragedy* of the missing. There could be more than two hundred. Fear of disease. The contents of the next two pages were aimed at filling out what was now called a 'tragic' scenario in stories whose headlines are sufficient to indicate the meaning they wished to impute to the disaster:

'Il dramma dei dispersi. "Sono più di trecento." Barberi prima smentisce, poi corre a controllare.' – The *drama* of the missing. 'There are more than three hundred.' Barberi first denies this, then rushes to check.[5]

'La grande fuga dalla paura.' – the great flight from fear.[6]

'"Ci hanno lasciati soli" – Il grido di rabbia degli sfollati.' – 'they've left us on our own' – the evacuees' cry of rage.[7]

'Il pm Amato: "Sembra un nuovo terremoto. La gente ha diritto alla verità." Aperti due inchieste. Disastro colposo?' – State Prosecutor Amato: 'It seems like another earthquake. The people have a right to know the truth'. Two inquests opened.[8]

I have for the most part quoted only headlines and subheadlines. The stories themselves are elaborations of the topics announced, more or less informative, more or less opinionated depending upon the kind of authority to pronounce on calamitous events presumed by the individual writer or his or her 'sources'. But the headlines of the first couple of days following the avalanche announced the *themes* that would be used to establish the *multiple* meanings of the event in

---

[5]   *La Repubblica*, Venerdi, 8 Maggio, 1998, p. 2.

[6]   *Ibid.*, p. 2.

[7]   *Ibid.*, p. 3.

[8]   *Ibid.*, p. 3.

scientific, religious, legal, political and, above all, *moral* terms, over the days to come, as more 'information' regarding the scope, depth, and intensity of the destruction wreaked upon the towns most heavily affected by the avalanche came to light.

As I read the newspaper's coverage of the event over the two weeks following the avalanche, it seemed to me that the aim of everyone speaking about it was to get at 'the facts', and to substitute facts for opinions, speculations and, above all, 'polemics'. In this way, the work of rebuilding communities such as Sarno, Quindici, Siano, Episcopio and so forth would be moved to the top of the nation's priorities and undertaken with all possible speed. But one 'fact' that was being established beyond the shadow of a doubt was that everyone had a different conception of what the *community* consisted of and that, on the basis of the facts they pretended to possess, there existed real doubt – especially on the part of 'experts' – as to whether the community of Sarno in particular, but also the other towns of the region, were *worthy* of being rebuilt at all. In general, the journalistic coverage tended to focus on the question of the real 'identity' of the community that had been stricken and, above all, on its 'moral' identity. This raised the question of the worth or value of the community as it had formerly existed and whether, instead of *re*building it, it should not simply be moved to another site and *built* from scratch. Thus, it was suggested, it would be possible to set a new and purified community in the place of what was gradually being suggested to be the immoral and corrupt community which had been devastated. In a kind of act of divine justice, the mountain that the community had so abused, had finally struck back by unleashing upon this community what, in everything but the word itself, was described as a flood of 'cold' excrement.

On Sunday 10th May, a topic was introduced that would subsequently move to the centre of the coverage as the indicator of the sinister background of the event and would ultimately serve as its crucial explanation. This was the subject of organised crime, or the *camorra*. The subject of the *camorra* was first registered in *la Repubblica* on this date in a column entitled '*Il Caso*', the Case. This column reported a proposal by the doctors and nurses of Sarno for the construction of a new hospital to be built 'sui terreni della camorra' – on the lands of the *camorra*. The story explained that certain properties owned by the *(camorra)* 'boss Pasquale Galasso' had been recently confiscated. The citizenry, the anonymous writer of the article explained, were afraid that they would be deprived of their 'own hospital', and some of them had petitioned to take the property owned by the *camorra* boss on which to build a new one. 'Sarno deve rinascere,' – Sarno must be reborn – Doctor Ferdinando Volpe is quoted as saying, 'e quale migliore esempio di civiltà che costruire un ospedale proprio sul terreno che è stato sequestrato due anni fa alla camorra e che ora è entrata a fare parte del patrimonio dello Stato?'[9]

This story appeared on a page headed: 'Sarno, i temi, i disegni dei più piccoli. I volontari cercano famiglie disposte ad ospitarli. 'MA DIO NO, NON CI VUOLE BENE [...]''[10] This page also included news of Salerno's Series A soccer match with Venezia, which was to be dedicated to the memory of the victims, and a statement by Don Elvio Damoli, Director of *Caritas Italiana*, that this was a, 'Tragedia annunciata peggio del sisma dell' 80, etc.' – a foreseeable tragedy, worse than the quake of '80.[11]

The registration of the *camorra* as an actor in the drama provided a villain acceptable to the government as a cause, both remote and immediate, of everything that had made 'the tragedy of Sarno' possible. And this because the *mafia/camorra* had already been 'dramatised' as a player in a larger game featuring an inquiry into Italy's status as a near 'Third World' country in spite of the economic miracle (privatisation, mergers, cuts in social services and jobs, increases in taxes, etc.) that had made it worthy of being included in the European Economic Union.

Prior to this point, accusations of irresponsibility, inefficiency and lack of attention, care, and concern for Sarno on the part of officials and public agencies had flown back and forth among the towns, the regions and central government. On Monday, 11th May, however, the day on which *la Repubblica* ran front page stories on Juventus's 25th *scudetto* or league championship in football, and the victory of Israeli transsexual Dana International in the Eurovision Song Contest in

---

[9] 'And what better example of civility than to build a hospital right on the land that was sequestrated two years ago from the *camorra* and that has now come into the ownership of the state?'

[10] 'Sarno, the essays and drawings by the smallest little ones. The voluntary services seek families willing to put them up. "BUT NO, GOD DOES NOT LOVE US"'.

[11] *La Repubblica*, Domenica, 10 Maggio, 1998, p. 4.

London, it also reported the request to the Sarnesi for forgiveness by the President of the Italian Senate, Nicola Mancino: 'Lo Stato chiede scusa.' It was the season of such acts: the Pope had just apologised to the Jews for Christian 'anti-Judaism', and President Clinton had asked the forgiveness of Africans for slavery.

On 16th May, in a notice tucked at the bottom of page 12 of its Saturday edition, *la Repubblica* printed a story under the title '*La Denuncia*', the charge, and reported a statement by the Mayor of Sarno, Gerardo Basile, in which he named the cause of all of Sarno's troubles: 'Ma qui la camorra è sempre in agguato' – but here the *camorra* is always lying in wait. On Tuesday, 19th May, *la Repubblica* devoted only one page to the disaster (it had been moved to page 21). The page was headlined:

'Quattro paesi colpiti dall'alluvione inseriti nell' "area rossa" ad alto rischio. Barberi: "Scelta dolorosa ma necessaria"

SETTE MILA ABITANTI DA EVACUARE'[12]

There is one graphic, giving the statistics, 'I numeri dell'emergenza':

Communes at risk in the event of rain: 4

Persons to be evacuated in the event of precipitation: 7,000

Recorded landslides on 5th May: 132

Landslides which have overrun centres of habitation: 20

The duration of exceptional measures of security: 90 days.

This story bears the subheading: 'Quando il livello di acqua supererà i 60 millimetri, al suono delle sirene scatterà il piano di sgombero. E la popolazione verrà trasferita nei centri di accoglienza.'[13] Then, squeezed into the space remaining from five announcements of requests for firms to submit bids on various sales of equipment and on jobs of construction in Salerno, Siena, Cremona, and Buffalotta, there are two stories. One is entitled: 'Il piano antiframe della Protezione civile: scatterà in caso di pioggia' – the anti-landslide plan of the civil

---

[12] 'Four of the villages struck by the flood incorporated in the high-risk "red area". Barberi: "A painful but necessary choice". SEVEN THOUSAND INHABITANTS TO BE EVACUATED'.

[13] 'When the water level rises above 60 millimetres, the sirens will sound to initiate the evacuation plan. The population will be transferred to reception centres.'

protection services: it will be triggered in the event of rain. The other story, datelined Nocera Inferiore and labelled as 'L'Intervista', interview, bears two headlines: 'Lo sfogo del procuratore di Nocera Inferiore, Di Persia: É chiaro che la camorra sfrutterà anche questa occasione' and, 'È qui in provincia il vero regno dei clan'.[14]

The first story tells of a plan devised by the authorities and presented by the Undersecretary of Civil Protection, Franco Barberi, the basis of which is 'the map of the dangers' threatening the inhabitants of the afflicted area. This map indicates by a 'red circle' the areas which must be evacuated in case of alarm. But, according to the story, the Mayor of Quindici, Antonio Siniscalchi, was not impressed: 'We feel like the Jews deported by the Nazis. This is how you kill off a town already dying. We went to the doctor, but he gave us no medicine.' 'What will become of us?', the Mayor asked, 'we do not want to be driven away [...] you can't live out of a suitcase.' He mentioned a flyer announcing a meeting of the citizens, 'to defend our rights against the State.' 'Enough,' the Mayor concluded, 'we are fed up with being called *camorristi.*'

Mayor Siniscalchi was referring to the insinuations that had begun to be floated in the press that the cause of Sarno's problems was that it had always been a centre of *camorra* activity, more important and more virulent than either Napoli or Palermo. Indeed, it had been suggested more than once that the *camorra* owned Sarno and the surrounding area so completely that all of its problems – abusive construction that had destroyed the stability of the mountain, administrative inefficiency, insufficient social service resources to meet the challenge of the disaster, poverty, destitution, and drug-use – could be traced to the *camorra*'s hold over the area. It had been implied that the very citizens of Sarno, including its mayor, the victims and the survivors of the disaster, were in some way or another in league with the *camorra*. In this manner, and in good ideological fashion, the victims and survivors of the disaster would be transformed into the cause of their own suffering. This is what is meant by tragedy, and this would be the upshot of the stories about the catastrophe of Monte Pizzo d'Alzano reported in the newspaper over a period of about three weeks.

---

[14] 'The outburst of the attorney of Nocera Inferiore, Di Persia: It's clear that the *camorra* will also exploit this opportunity', and 'The real realm of the families is here in the provinces'.

The disaster of Sarno was being prepared for its consignment to the national 'communal memory' by techniques of discursivisation more like those of myth than those of science. But these techniques were being utilised, not by the common folk of Sarno, but by representatives of the political agencies responsible for providing aid for the afflicted community's efforts at 'reconstruction'. Under the guise of 'expert judgement' by technicians and administrators of public welfare, the authorities were preparing the groundwork (the alibi) for their abandonment of Sarno to its own 'traditional' devices for the survival of disasters. The Bishop of Episcopo emerged as the principal leader and spokesperson for the community as the authorised agencies of public relief dallied and offered excuses for their inability to accomplish anything substantive in the nature of 'reconstruction'. Here the *camorra*, in its phantasmatic role of hidden and elusive but, nonetheless, powerful *éminence grise*, provided a convenient scapegoat as both cause of the disaster and principal impediment to any effort to recover from it.

The preparation of 'Sarno' for consignment to the 'communal memory' as an 'unfortunate' event was accomplished by the use of discursive strategies typical of myth, but also featured in the rationalising discourse of 'historical' representation. By the use of these discursive strategies, 'the facts' were emplotted and re-emplotted as the elements of, first, a disaster, then a catastrophe, next a tragedy and, finally, a kind of demonic farce in which the effects of the disaster (devastation of the physical infrastructure, collapse of the social superstructure, depletion of the morale of survivors, reduction of the survivors to the status of victims, even death itself) could be put down to 'fate' and removed from the category of remediable human error.

This process of emplotment and re-emplotment had the effect of justifying the consignment of specific practical tasks for the reconstruction of the community, or at least of the space it had formerly occupied, to the police. Not surprisingly, the blank space 'Sarno', written over by a 'rationalising' or scientific form of mythic narrativisation, led to the conclusion that what was needed for the 'reconstruction of this society' was an expansion and augmentation of the surveillance and disciplinary powers of the political and legal apparatus. By the time the effects of the disaster had been thoroughly investigated and archived in the public memory, it appeared obvious – as a fact that went without saying – that Sarno's tragedy was a consequence of a disaster more 'criminal' than natural in kind, and that the criminals responsible for the crime were none other than the Sarnesi themselves.

It should not be thought, then, that this indictment of the Sarnesi as the causal agency of their own suffering was a result of the triumph of traditionalist modes of mythification over a 'scientific' analysis of the situation. On the contrary, the paradoxical conclusion that Sarno itself had been the cause of its own disaster was the conclusion of investigators claiming the objectivity, rationality, and methodological rigour of science (and objective journalism) itself. The myth of Sarno's responsibility for its own devastation, and therefore its guilt, was a product of a conflict between two orders of explanation, narratological, on the one side, and scientific, on the other. Both orders of explanation were based upon and addressed the same 'body of facts'. And both orders of explanation were directed to the task of naming the forces, agents, and agencies, actions, motives and purposes that conduced to transform Monte Pizzo d'Alvano from an ordinary place into the scene of a tragedy.

When the term 'tragedy' is used to characterise a real scene of social disaster, it is frequently misused to designate the facts that are calling for generic characterisation and the kind of illumination that the act of characterisation promises. This is because 'tragedy' properly names a situation in which human intention, motivation, responsibility, and guilt for the effects of a disaster cannot be identified and assigned. I do not say 'easily' identified; I say *cannot* be identified. For it is a presupposition of dramatic tragedy that the scene of social conflict is not disposable into categories of absolute good and evil. In a tragic vision of the world, everything and everyone inhabits a morally 'gray zone' in which good and bad are inextricably mixed. These two categories interanimate each other, and get sorted out, if at all, in images of that condition of ambivalence and ambiguity within which everyone but the criminally insane tries to 'construct' a meaningful life.

The identification of a real scene of social disaster as a 'tragic drama' in which absolute, or even 'relative' good and evil have met and done battle, destroying the good and leaving the survivors tainted with the evil which had victimised them is, therefore, a *mis*identification. Such a drama would be more properly identified as a 'demonic farce', a *Walpurgisnacht* or Witches' Sabbath, in which nothing but the forces of evil and malignity are present. A proper identification of the disaster of Monte Pizzo d'Alvano as a 'tragedy' (which I have no doubt it was) would authorise a response to the suffering of its survivors and victims that was somewhat more 'practically charitable' than that which indicts virtually everyone as criminally culpable. And yet this is what the stories published in *la Repubblica* manage to suggest. Thus, on Monday, 18th May, on pages six and seven, the coverage of the 'Disastro in Campania' carries four headlines.

The first quotes the Bishop of Episcopio as urging the local inhabitants to build a wall against the *camorra*: 'Il vescovo: faremo muro per fermare la camorra' ('You local inhabitants will be able to do it. No one can make you go away. You will stay in your neighborhoods. You were born here and you will stay here. You are like the grass and the trees.')[15] But at the same time, the government was warning the local inhabitants that, in case of another downpour of rain, it would be necessary to remove people from their dwellings, at least 'temporarily'. Thus, another headline intoned: 'Sgomberi temporanei quando pioverà tanto' – temporary evacuations in the event of heavy rains. 'It should be clear,' Cesare Landrini of the Department of Civil Protection states, 'that the people will not be "deported" but only evacuated while a danger remains. Keep calm, the situation is under control, day and night.'[16] (I cannot forbear noting that this story is put next to an advertisement for an analgesic nostrum for stomach gas: 'No-Gas Giuliani', 'Double action against gastric and intestinal swelling [...]' Was this inadvertent, planned, or simply 'casual'? You, dear Reader, must decide.)

In any case, by this time the survivors had become the principal objects of the authorities' concern – and control. This concern was manifested especially in a story, appearing on the same page, in which the local state prosecutor criticised the local mayor for cowardice and for suggesting that the *camorra* was not the problem: 'Se non ha coraggio vada via: Il pm contro il sindaco: dice che i clan non esistono' ('Io dico se il sindaco non ha il corragio di ammettere che la camorra esiste, [...] è meglio che se ne vada a casa [...] il suo ufficio

---

[15] *La Repubblica*, Lunedi, 18 Maggio, 1998, p. 6.

[16] *Ibid.*, p. 6.

avrebbe già aperto sul versante ricostruzione & camorra.')[17] The imputation was clear: either the mayor was afraid of the *camorra* or he was in league with them. But a lighter touch was provided by a story, on the same page, about a dog that had been saved from the rubble and was 'immediately baptised' *Frana* – landslide. The ultimate fate of this cur has not, to my knowledge, been reported. The activity of the *camorra* had become a topic of central interest. Indeed, on Sunday, 24th May 1998, it was reported that the *camorra* had fired shots at a truck being used (by a non-*camorra* sponsored company) to haul away the mud from Quindici.[18] But good news was in the offing for, on the same page, it is reported that the authorities had begun to use a computer in their efforts to control the activities of the *camorra* in the afflicted zone: 'Un computer contro i clan.'

The story was 'winding down', approaching its finale, preparing its audience for the withdrawal of attention from the disaster. Little by little, the story of Sarno was etiolated, moved to the interior pages of the newspaper and confined to occasional snippets of information about Sarno's condition. Soon it would be buried, if not forgotten, in the national 'communal memory'.

Conclusion

What does *la Repubblica*'s coverage of the story of Sarno tell us about the relationships obtaining among myth, memory, and the reconstruction of society? I must first note that this newspaper's coverage did not differ in any significant way from that of other Italian newspapers and magazines. They all treated the story in much the same way. It is not as if *la Repubblica* itself provided a metacommentary on the mythification of the event, except by its embedding of the various reports on it among a host of other stories and advertising that had the effect of removing 'the facts' of the matter from consideration as an event of genuinely national importance. The coverage of the event by *la Repubblica* simply made of it what, in the age of media treatment of news, it really was; an event being contested by different kinds of discourses, each of which had a different

---

[17] *La Repubblica*, Lunedi, 18 Maggio, 1998, p. 7. 'I say that if the mayor doesn't have the courage to admit that the *camorra* exists [...] it would be better if he went home [...] his office would have already begun to tackle the *reconstruction and the camorra*.'

[18] *La Repubblica*, Domenica, 24 Maggio, 1998, p. 20.

interest in emplotting this event in a different way. The various discourses in play produced the effect of an event that had no 'substance' at all. The event was, in a word, phenomenalised, which is to say, turned into a matter of no real importance for anyone other than the survivors. The overdetermination of the event – the result of being subjected to so many varying accounts of its real importance – sublimated it into a spectacle which could be forgotten once its drama had been played out.

Had the attention focussed on the disaster changed or importantly revised either the local or the national 'communal memory'? Had it resulted in a new appreciation of the problem of reconstructing 'society' in the wake of a disaster? Had it illuminated the relationship between mythic consciousness and scientific consciousness? It is impossible to give a simple answer to these questions for, as of the moment of my completion of this report on Italian society's 'communal memory' of this event (which is 5th May 1999, exactly one year after the disaster struck) precisely *nothing* has been done to assist the reconstruction of Sarno.

This morning I picked up my copy of *la Repubblica*. On page 25 of this issue, the section '*Cronaca*' featured two stories under the rubric: 'Un anno fa le valanghe di fango devastarono alcuni centri campani' – one year ago, the avalanches of mud devastated a number of settlements in Campania. In one of these stories, the headline reads: 'D'Alema [the current Prime Minister]: subito una legge per recostruire Sarno.' – a law to reconstruct Sarno immediately. This story reports the Prime Minister as saying that it would be necessary to pass a new law in order to give aid to Sarno, because the standing ordinances are 'insufficient'. At the same time, the Minister of the Environment, Edo Ronchi, is reported to have 'emitted signals' of a 'reassuring' kind: 'The Sarno basin has been secured,' he is quoted as saying, 'and there are no foreseeable dangers to the area.' But the parish priest of Episcopio, don Antonio Calabrese, reports that, 'Here the reconstruction has not begun.' Various canals have been built to divert the waters produced by heavy rainfalls, but, 'per il resto nulla', nothing else. 'We have even been denied the right to vote. They have removed the electoral sign from the schoolhouse. And it is now said that the same thing will happen on 13th June, when European and communal elections are scheduled to take place.' Government officials insist that billions have been spent to provide housing for the homeless, increase security and repair the mountain towering over Sarno.

The citizens of Episcopo remain unconvinced and unreassured. 'Today is a day of mourning in Sarno and the four other communes struck by the avalanche,' Ottavio Lucarelli reports. The Mayor of Siano, Gerardo Ricci, accuses the Undersecretary, Barberi, of having forgotten the disaster, '[...] these days he thinks only of Kosovo.' As for 'Robertino', a young survivor of the disaster, he thinks of nothing else. 'I was thinking about it,' he says, 'After three days and three nights among the rubble, my memory is empty. I don't know.'[19]

---

[19]   *La Repubblica*, Mercoledi, 5 Maggio, 1999, p. 25.

CHAPTER 3

Maurice Halbwachs:
Memory and the Feeling of Identity

Lutz NIETHAMMER

Although he was the leading French sociologist of the interwar period, there is no substantial body of literature on either the intellectual contextualisation of Maurice Halbwachs' work on collective memory or on the details of his life. His work was all but forgotten after his death in the concentration camp Buchenwald, and it was not until the end of the 1960s that he was rediscovered by a larger academic audience. His theory on memory, originally considered a minor area of interest, became a classic. Only recently have his unpublished manuscripts been made available to researchers. His working notes *(carnets)* therein have led to a revision of the fragments published in 1950 as The Collective Memory, re-edited and with an epilogue by Gérard Namer.[1] The result is that now the development of Halbwachs' thoughts about memory can be followed up until his death.

Halbwachs' posthumous influence initially seemed to be restricted to a technical and interdisciplinary audience in French sociology. Not until the 1970s, when increasing numbers of leftist social scientists began to turn to the 'subjective factor' in order to dismantle the illusions of '68, did Halbwachs – along with the American school of symbolic interactionism – become the insiders' tip for international theoretical inspiration. Since the 1980s he has become part of the

---

[1]   Namer (ed.), 1997. See especially the epilogue pp. 237-295.

canon for the rising wave of culturalism. His constructivism did not seem to be able to curb the postmodern instinct for whimsy: The same instrument with which Halbwachs attempted first to criticise the formation of a tradition of lies and power-abuse and then, later, desperately hoped could mobilise a counter-memory (although the work remained unpublished because of its inconsistencies) was now, in the hands of a successor generation, a manual for social construction of random and, of course, always well-intended future traditions. And, by calling on his (albeit exaggerated) sociological intervention, members of the academic field now saw the possibility of freeing themselves from the bothersome social fuss of the unsolvable question of reception.

Halbwachs' family originated from Alsace, where his father was a German teacher. After the Franco-German war and the annexation of Alsace to Germany 1871, the family moved to France. Halbwachs was born in 1877 in Reims and grew up in Paris in a liberal milieu of teachers, scholars and civil servants. He had two brothers, one of whom was a general, and the other a professor, and a sister, who received a PhD in philosophy. His schooling and studies at the lycée Henri IV and the École Normale Supérieure point to the elite education of a talented French family. As the child of a German teacher, Halbwachs spoke German, studied in Hanover and Göttingen (where he also taught), studied in Berlin on a research scholarship and, after his expulsion from Prussia (because he had written against Berlin police brutality in *Humanité*), went to Vienna. He wrote his first work on German philosophy and was a careful reader of German (and later American) sociology.[2]

Halbwachs published his sociology of memory in 1925.[3] The first chapter had already appeared in 1923 in a philosophical journal. It originated during the first years of Halbwachs' academic establish-

---

[2] Halbwachs' name and the fact that he died in Buchenwald have led many to believe that he was Jewish or of Jewish origins. In fact Halbwachs was married to the daughter of a Jewish intellectual, but he himself came from a Catholic family. As an adult he described himself as a rationalist and agnostic. See Charle, 1986, pp. 99-101. My appreciation to Patrick Fridenson for this reference.

[3] Halbwachs, 1991 [1925]. Cf. now the new edition from Gérard Namer, 1994, which includes a detailed discussion of Halbwachs' working notes (*carnets*). This and Namer's epilogue in Namer (ed.), 1997, because of their use of new materials, have largely superceded the only work to offer a detailed analysis of Halbwachs' own memory and consciousness (Namer, 1987).

ment and the interdisciplinary discussions in Strasbourg. Let us therefore read it as would a scientific community from top to bottom, first considering the index and footnotes and then the text, so that we might understand his working method, the context and the goal of his project. For the work of a brand-new socialist sociology professor, his citation index is noteworthy: 44 times it mentions Bergson, 17 times Jesus Christ, 14 times Durkheim (all other sociologists such as Max Weber and Thorstein Veblen receive far fewer citations), 11 times Freud, nine times the French history of Law by Esmein (which Halbwachs used to cross over the chasm of the history of society), eight times Rousseau and five times the livelong rebel pastor's son and Darwinist Samuel Butler (The Way of All Flesh). Butler was the *enfant terrible* of Victorian literature, who Semons (Freud's non-Jewish predecessor who elaborated a concept of an unconsciousness) had translated into English. Halbwachs in fact claimed that Butler had anticipated the basic elements in Bergson's thought 20 years earlier).[4]

The book is divided into an anthropological and a sociological section, each beginning with a citation from Durkheim. The first four chapters manifest the same pattern: at the beginning and end, the opponent arrives in the form of Bergson/Freud. In the middle of each chapter, a mountain of literature – psychological, physiological, linguistic and so on – is employed to scrutinise, respectively, dreams, language, the reconstruction of the past (here he contents himself with Butler) and the localisation of memory – thereby laying to rest the idea of an inner memory. Thus, the dual opponent in the form of Bergson/Freud, with his insinuations of internalness, or inner memory, is defeated and does not appear in the remaining three chapters about family, in the detailed one on religious groups, or in the discussion on classes and traditions. With the exception of the two chapters on memory in dreams and language, for which he still managed to trot out 13 titles against Bergson and Freud as well as Halbwachs' colleague in Strasbourg, Charles Blondel,[5] Halbwachs reserved his

---

[4]   Samuel Butler (1835-1902), translated Ewald Hering, (1870) and excerpts from Eduard von Hartmann: *Philosophie des Unbewußten*, Leipzig 1869 in: *Unconscious Memory* (London 1924 [1880]), pp. 69 ff. and 101 ff. In referring to the difference between consciousness of new developments and that of habit, Halbwachs used Samuel Butler in *Life and Habit: An Essay after a Completer View of Evolution* London 1878 (French 1922).

[5]   Cf. Blondel, 1924.

greatest literature attack for the higher forms of religious life, with 26 religious historical titles and sources, treating almost exclusively classical antiquity and Christianity. His primary sources were Matthew, Paul, St. Augustine and Luther.

We are therefore dealing with an author who knew the tone he wanted to set – which was not Jewish, post-Jewish or even one that considered Judaism other than from a Christian-secularised perspective. His standpoint on the origins of Christian-Jewish relations, which would have enraged even a 'godless Jew', as Freud had described himself, claimed 'that Christianity is foremost, especially in its articles of faith, dogma and rites, an expression of a moral revolution that became an historical event; of the triumph of a religion of spiritual content over a formalist cult and, at the same time, of a universalist religion that does not recognise races or religions over a strictly national religion.'[6]

The Religious Site of Memory as Social Artefact, or a Criticism of Civil Religion

This triumph was clearly so important to Halbwachs that he repeated this sentence verbatim a decade and a half later when he published The Legendary Topography of the Gospels in the Holy Land, his case study on cultural memory and religious sociology.[7] Namer, employing Halbwachs' private documents, discovered that this study was actually a subtle criticism – almost too subtle for today's readers, or for the contemporary censor – of the cultish productions of the contemporary allied totalitarian civil religions. Because this is the only thorough illustration of his concept of memory, we should take a small detour over this topography before returning to his sociology of memory. Halbwachs did not need the concept of identity for his case study, but it was developed here. This little book – published in the first year of German occupation and his last independent work to be published during his lifetime – was a

---

6   Halbwachs, 1994 [1925], p. 185.

7   Halbwachs, 1971 [1941], p. 140. Both times the sentence is in the middle of different texts is not emphasised and in its repetition is not cited with a reference to the original text. I did not find evidence of similar unreferenced self-citations. It would be conceivable that this sentence indicates such a basic conviction of the author that he did not even notice its repetition.

brilliant coup of enlightening erudition.[8] Like most of the case studies from the Durkheim school on distant cults, this too was primarily researched in Parisian libraries, but Halbwachs also undertook an impious pilgrimage in his car through the Holy Land in order to deconstruct his Christian cities of pilgrimage – in other words, he smashed the entire construction to pieces.[9]

In the footsteps of the 19th century Bible-critical scholarship on the life of Jesus, represented most prominently in France by Ernest Renan, Halbwachs proceeded to ruthlessly tear apart the New Testament, which he must have almost known by heart.[10] He then arranged its elements into two geographical groups. First, there were the witnessed teachings of Jesus and his life as preacher, which were associated with unspecified areas between the mountains of Galilee and the lake of Gennesaret. This was the 'moral revolution,' which spanned from the Sermon on the Mount to the parables, visions of miracles and other wandering preachers. It was a thoroughly human programme, well attended by the disciples who accompanied Jesus' travels. No place was named, either in the Scriptures or in cultish memory. There were no sites of pilgrimage, or else, like Nazareth, they developed only much later. 'But what good can come from Galilee?' Halbwachs stated that the message of the Sermon on the Mount would never have won the power of a religion had it not fused with essential elements of the Jewish religion and the history of the Jewish people.[11]

---

[8] The year of publication, 1941, is also the year of Bergson's death. In *Topographie* there are no explicit polemics against him (or Freud). However, in a tireless, academically dry mania for detail, the two main pillars of Bergson's panreligiosity – Judaism and Christianity – are presented as cultish-mythical inventions of successor generations, and point for point drawn up as opposing positions to his concept of consciousness: consciousness is not an internal show, but rather an external event; it is not about individuals, but of social groups; its dimension is not time, but space; and its images have nothing to do with the reality of the past, but change with the needs of the group in question.

[9] Even in the late British mandatory period, when Zionism and Arabian nationalism clearly were astir, Palestine was self-evidently for Halbwachs the Holy Land of Christians. The other two religions for which Jerusalem is holy appeared only in references to Christians or Muslims constructing on Jewish holy sites.

[10] Renan, 1863.

[11] Halbwachs, 1971 [1941], p. 140.

The second group of elements from the New Testament were the birth of Christ in the City of David (a lovely fairy tale, complete with ox and donkey, invented quite late, in order to fulfil the Scriptures), and his death and resurrection in the city of the Temple of Solomon. Between Bethlehem and Jerusalem there are, therefore, visible pilgrimage sites that anchor the supernatural in spatial dimensions, preferably by rechristening the cultural sites of Jews (at any rate, from 2nd century on, after the Romans destroyed the Temple and chased out the Jews, as testified to by pilgrims from the 4th century on).[12] In fact, everything that was supposed to have happened to the Son of Man along the cultish mile of the Jews between Bethlehem and Jerusalem was barely witnessed. There are no facts about his birth that would stand up to historical critical examination. In the most tragic hour of their Lord, the disciples fled, and the later joyous announcement was, at best, reported as hearsay or emerged from what they worked out on their own. A gap of memory stretches between the event and its cultural representation. The belief of the believers has nested in this hole, filling the space with their imagination. The furnishing of this room of memory was handled not by the poor first Christians (the Judeo-Christian Ebionites, the Roman catacomb painters, or the Gnostics who were told of a crucifixion or resurrection, for example), but by power. With the appropriation of Christianity by the Roman Emperor Constantine, the still timid sites of memory for the birth and death of the Son of God, as designated by the first pilgrims in post-Jewish Jerusalem, were (still during the 4th century) covered by an entire series of Christian sacred structures.[13] These in turn – after they had been partially razed during the Islamic occupation or forgotten – were renewed and enlarged by crusaders, whose sieges 'left no stone unturned'.[14] The crusaders then exported the symbols and mysteries of the medieval West to the East, where their origins could be visualised in culturally recognisable forms. And so on, and so forth.

---

[12] Halbwachs outdid himself with historical documentation, using pilgrims' testimonies from several centuries and in many languages to tear down brick by brick the reappropriation, dedication, new construction and growth of the holy sites.

[13] Halbwachs, 1971 [1941], pp. 150 ff.

[14] *Ibid.*, p. 156.

Halbwachs' concluded that Christianity became a religion because subsequent generations gave physical form to the foundations of a tradition rich in the representations of a cultural memory. These generations authenticated the supernatural by locating it spatially and amalgamating it with the already holy sites of the Jews. In contrast, the revolutionary programme of moral universalism as preached by the wandering Jew, far away from all places of worship in the hills of Galilee, did not need any *lieux de mémoire*. This was because it oriented itself towards reason and compassion, had plenty of witnesses, was formed early and lives on through its power of conviction from content and scriptures. But this power was even then not heavenly enough to make a religion out of it. The secret of the success of Christianity was not truth, but the amalgamation of both tradition and belief.[15]

Halbwachs even teased out insights into what he called collective memory from the religion's 'laws'.[16] The collective memory differs from history insofar as it consists of cultural representations of a group in space. This changes with the group's needs: thus, for example, the same event can be localised differently if there are groups who associate it with different places. Or alternatively, if various groups are integrated into a larger one and their local cult site has contradictory meanings, many events can be synthesised into one myth. This often results in what the German philosopher Ernst Cassirer once referred to as 'symbolic succinctness',[17] when images and narratives of an entire series of events or stories are fused into the memory of one single place or date.

---

[15] Namer, 1997, pp. 283 f. interpreted this text as a positive reconstruction of a religious consciousness, but I see no grounds for this in his work or, more specifically, in his language. I find especially problematic Namer's interpretation of the bitter-cool outlining of the early Christian cultural consciousness, if this was intended to be pro-religious, as an anti-totalitarian warning.

[16] Halbwachs, 1971 [1941], p. 145. Here he follows Locke's tradition (referring to the 'English school of idea association'), aspiring to study that in the consciousness of the Christian 'group' which Locke did for the consciousness of the individual; that is, 'how the representations are summoned, separated and united.' Locke referred to the feeling of unity which an individual has, in spite of the differences of social and cultural perceptions, as 'identity'.

[17] Cassirer, 1994 [1923-1929], pp. 222 ff. He referred though to the traces of Husserl and Leibnitz and the intentionality of the perceiving consciousness, or the now as *praegnans futuri*.

In general, the group memory retains only those events that are instructive. In this sense the Christian teachings were a story where, 'what can be seen are symbols of invisible truths.'[18] The collective memory reconstructs its memories in a manner that brings them into harmony with present ideas and preferences. The framework in which this occurs is 'a construction'. The entire life and teachings of Jesus collapsed into the illusory series of scenes of Holy Week. New representatives of the group – the Roman emperors, the crusaders – effected new representations in the space of memory, be it by taking on and reinterpreting old (Jewish) representations, or by creating new places. The meaning was always present for the group and was then given a space concretely and symbolically, because this is what the pilgrims 'wished to find again, to situate, to put into place. This attests to the fact that in each period the collective Christian memory adapts its recollections of the details of Christ's life and of the places where they occurred to the contemporary exigencies of Christianity, to its needs and aspirations.'[19]

Halbwachs was a demand-side theoretician of intellect: needs create the representations of the tradition and their accentuations in turn point to the needs and interests of the group in question.[20] His theory of memory travelled the hermetical circle of constructionism decades before it was given a philosophical programme. In contrast to Walter Benjamin's dictum, the origin is not the goal here, nor is it even the corrective.[21] It is an illusion – and the future of this illusion is religion. The traces of the past do not offer the present constructions true resistance, because they merely indicate the last level of interest-driven interpretations. Of course, it is possible to uncover each level and thus step down towards the march of time. 'Whatever epoch is examined, attention is not directed toward the first events, or perhaps the origin of these events, but rather toward the group of believers and

---

[18]   Halbwachs, 1971 [1941], p. 149.

[19]   *Ibid.*, p. 163. However the places and objects presented a certain material resistance to this attribution of cultural traditions, but the recourse to such resistances does not have the origin as goal, because they are products of consciousness construction of an earlier level.

[20]   What Eric Hobsbawm et al later referred to as 'the invention of traditions' breathes through and through this spirit of Halbwachs', but the authors do not refer to him explicitly. Hobsbawm and Ranger (eds), 1983.

[21]   Benjamin, 1990 [1940], pp. 619 f., here p. 701.

82

toward their commemorative work.'[22] The group creates its cultural origin in its own image.

In other words, Halbwachs threw the baby out with the bathwater. This process of historical-critical demythologisation tangled up his informative sociology in the whole cultish ballast of religious tradition in a relativist recourse *ad absurdum*, without resulting in an explanation of the faith or offering criteria to combat superstition. If one reads his topography of the holy gospels as a model of antitotalitarian education of contemporary civil religions, it can of course, ideologically, critically undermine such memory programmes as the 'Complete Artworks of Stalin' or Hitler's 'Word of Stone' (in the planning of dictator cities and cultish death monuments). This, of course, is no small accomplishment. A helpless anti-fascism (or anti-Stalinism) is at any rate better than a 'will to believe' in politics, as William James put this religious disposition. But we don't get any nearer to this will with Halbwachs' instruments. His realistic insight into the combined societal and ruling construction of all memory became an instrument of the emptying and randomness of every counter-memory because of the lack of criteria for his construction of memory. In the final count, all that remains – beyond relativism – along with 'progress' is nothing but another transcendence which refers not to the past but to the future. Nor does it show itself to be an internal truth, rather it is an external prejudice – in this case anti-Judaic flotsam and jetsam in post-Christian currents. The invented tradition of cultish sites of memory was only the (power-hungry and misguided) expression of a 'revolution of culture and mores', of a triumph of the intellectual/spiritual over a formalistic cult, and of the universal element (of Christianity) over the national (of Judaism).[23] The association of this *leitmotiv* caused me to digress from the memory theory of 1925 to the illustrative case study of 1941. Let us therefore take up the second part of his theory.

---

[22] Halbwachs, 1971 [1941], p. 163 (Coser, 1992, pp. 234-235).

[23] All the more surprising is his newer concept among followers of psychoanalysis, scholars of Jewish identity and even among those who point towards the promise of Jewish mysticism – the secret of salvation is remembering – as part of the responsible parties for Antisemitism.

Memory Gaps and the Feeling of Identity

We have gathered enough clues to recognise Halbwachs' offence against Bergson and Freud, and against the new concept of an inner, random memory and the fruitfulness of recursive memory work. Just as Bergson transformed his metaphysics of the mind into a metaphor of memory, Halbwachs employed this metaphor of the new paradigm in order to create the social mechanisms of tradition formation.[24] We need not trouble ourselves with the manner in which he took up Durkheim's lead – since we have seen the essential elements in the example of his holy sites.[25] But it is all the more important that we understand the final results of this process: 'the feeling of identity'.

At the beginning and end of Halbwachs' explanation, a certain something remains unstructured and unformed. This results from his introducing the concept of 'memory in its actual sense,' as he calls it, into the middle of his critical analysis. This concept is rationally more manageable, but was cut short in respect to the ideas about memory of his opponents. What he actually wanted to accomplish was to accept as 'memory' only a complete reproduction, accurate in details, of an earlier perceived reality (including its interpretation and verbalisation). Again and again, when his opponents tried to step forward with fragmented or inexact memory images as proof of the particular resources of an inner memory, he rapped their fingers, waving the yardstick of a *'mémoire proprement dit'* and growling, 'not identity!'[26]

---

[24] For a lengthy prehistory of metaphors for consciousness see Harald Weinrich's examination back to Plato's wax tablet and the 'storeroom' of rhetorical memoria teachings (Weinrich, 1964); and the much richer cultural historical development of Assmann, 1991. In the 20th century a significant change has occurred: although new metaphors continue to be invented for the not-yet understood consciousness (*e. g.* engram, paths, depository, network, etc.), 'consciousness' has become the metaphor for the now uncertain areas of perception, such as spirit, intellect, tradition and history.

[25] See the precise and concise explanation and criticism in German from Heinz, 1969.

[26] Cf. Halbwachs, 1994 [1925], p. 9, where he opposes psychoanalysis: 'We are not convinced that these reminiscences of childhood correspond to that which we call memories...' When, for example, childhood images only appear in dreams, 'what we find in them is reduced to too vague impressions and ill-defined images for these to have any real influence on actual memory.'

Thus, upon employing a logical-scientific measuring instrument that contradicts all culturally accepted concepts of memory, the memory of the individual can be emptied of all meaning, or at least turned into a positivistic means of access to an incomprehensible chaos. It is then ripe for the radical constructivistic collectivisation.[27]

The objectivisation and symbolisation of the culture of a group and the relationship network of their structure generally outlive the lives of the group's members, or at least their membership in the group. The members, who change over time, experience their membership and their past, regardless if experienced personally or supra-individually, in the re-encounter with these structures and their artefacts, which constitute a relative continuity for the space of memory.[28]

In a philosophical concluding remark, the question 'How could the container reproduce the contents?' led Halbwachs to the teachings of Plato and Spinoza on ideas, and he concluded that 'a collective perception' included everything that is necessary 'for the explanation of the production and reproduction of individual states of conscious-ness and especially of memories.'[29] After this seemingly accidental revelation, he had to quickly state, 'Let's remain on the solid ground of facts,' in order to mention another revelation: 'The observation of a fact, namely that one cannot while dreaming call forth the memory of events or complex images, has demonstrated the existence of the frames of the collective memory on which individual memory supports itself.'[30] The advantage of this idealistic construction over Plato's is that its societal materialisation of observation appears more accessible.

These changes, which a group takes on in the course of time in its objectified symbol apparatus, are normally visible through scholarly observation or reconstruction once the apparatus no longer satisfies the group's new interests and self perceptions. Thus, for example, when a group destroys a temple and builds a church there, or cons-tructs a department store on the planned site of a Nazi administrative

---

[27]   In the following I attempt to synthesise the three constructive chapters in Halbwachs, 1991 [1925], pp. 203 ff.

[28]   *Ibid.*, p. 237.

[29]   Halbwachs, 1994 [1925], pp. 279 and 281.

[30]   *Ibid.*, p. 281.

building, or when a party takes down the portraits of Stalin so that the number of its icons is reduced from four to three, the result is a 're-coding' of the space of memory.[31] Otherwise this space remains stable and recognisable in its structure and function. Through the transmission of the remainder of the social space, continuity remains in flux.[32] In contrast, the past itself, that is, the totality of the former objects, does not remain – it passes. Of these, only parts continue to be transmitted, and these, through exclusion and addition partially take on new meaning.

If we were to make Halbwachs' polemical deconstruction techni-que our own and then begin to grumble that this socio-cultural tradi-tion model (or 'cultural memory,' as it is termed today) does not allow for an objective memory either, we would find the author agreeing joyfully with us. In his transition from the criticism of psychological models of memory to the formation of a sociological one, he changed his unit of measure, his cognitive interests and his conceptualisations.

The unit of measure of the objective identity of that which is remembered through early perceptions turned out to be just a deconstruction tool for the internalness of his post-Jewish opponents. Even in his own social model of the formation of externalised tradition, in which concepts (normative structural-functional ideas) and images (transmission of persons and events) collapsed into one, there was no objective memory of that which had passed.[33] Instead there were perceptions, which appeared coincidentally or randomly in abbreviated form, or with additions, for a new totality of meaning. These perceptions are projected into the realm of experience of the present and thus differentiated from the past.[34] If one wanted to continue in this vein, there would be the option to keep the cognitive interest and change method. Or one sticks with his chain of thought and then something else comes out: a Philosphy of Tradition at once idealistic and sociologically based, in which concept and image, external and internal, present and past are forged into a series of

---

[31] These last two examples are of course not from Halbwachs. I have added them from our space of experience.

[32] Halbwachs, 1991 [1925], p. 162.

[33] *Ibid.*, pp. 371 f.

[34] From the practice of oral history, see the exemplary attempt at operationalisation by Lequin and Métral, 1980; also my critical remarks about the narrative form of memory molecule in the new and traumatic in Niethammer, 1995.

dynamic individual meanings that, regardless of their differences, present a collective identity.

Historicism – and in its wake psychoanalysis – has developed an historically critical method of recursive differentiation between 'leftovers' of the past and later repressions and covering-up in the formation of 'tradition'. It then, in an approach towards the origins – forever lost in their entirety – threw itself into the reading of fragmented traces, tentatively reconstructing them through circumstantial evidence, and into the search for other transmitted elements, etc. It therefore kept up the interest for the objectivity of that which was to be remembered, retreating to methods of convergence and interpretation. Halbwachs, on the other hand, maintained the positivistic method, wrote off the object of memory entirely and changed territory by concerning himself with the social and psychic function of remembering. It was therefore no longer about the identity of the remembered, but of the rememberer.[35] Thus the attained social identity, which he actually most often continued to call 'continuity' or 'tradition' in this text, was, for the time being, a disciplinary artefact.

The introduction of a precise measure of identity, by which all inner memory fails and all socially created reconstruction memories turn out to be deceitful fictions about the past, becomes the midwife of collective identity ideas. These only consist, however, of speculative knowledge of interactive relational conditions between individual memory and its social framework, as it were in societally supported, hermeneutical circles. They do not permit objectivity. These illusions about the past, rooted in society, achieve validity only by being appropriated by the subject. They are authorised by a subjective 'feeling'.

It is worth examining this decisive shift of a rational demand for precision into a metaphor of irrational individual continuity and societal tradition as it functions in Halbwachs' text. The 'feeling of identity' appears for the first time in his discussion of Freud's dream interpretations. The fact that we perceive the images in a dream as ours or related to us proves to Halbwachs that we 'maintain our conception of the ego while sleeping' as the 'feeling of continued,

---

[35] He thus admits the similarity of family memories, but explained that these are actually based on a common thought community whose members are able to recall memories of interest together. Halbwachs, 1991 [1925], p. 199.

both automatic and constructive influences' on these images. Society does not sleep. All of its 'frames', which constantly work together to construct thoughts and perceptions, do not leave the images out of the ego-control, not even for a night, not even when they appear to be unconscious or – as he states – automatic: '…[I]n a certain manner there is one thing behind them[36] which envelopes all of them and in which all of these images must take their places: the feeling of our identity.'[37] This looming background figure even keeps watch during our sleep so that our ego doesn't depart.

In the discussion on Bergson, this figure of a prerequisite feeling appeared a second time in order to dismiss mystical immediacy in the consideration of adults' childhood memories. 'From each stage of our lives, we retain some memories, which we reproduce over and over. In this manner the feeling of our identity perpetuates itself as in a continuous chain.' The metaphor gets difficult here, but is clearly necessary. Halbwachs posits continuity not only as a feeling, but even as a chain whose segments more resemble built-over buildings than the bones in a vertebrae. He continues, 'But precisely because these are repetitions, and because they are linked into very different conceptual systems of the different stages of life, they have lost their original form and aspect. These are not the intact vertebrae of fossilised animals, which might be used to reconstruct the being of which they were once part; they are more like the stones than can be found in certain built-over Roman buildings', whose 'faint traces of old characters certify their ancientness, but do not disclose either their form or their appearance.'[38]

We meet identity a third time – again in a discussion on Bergson – not as feeling and not as chain. This time we learn something about the nature of identity and are therefore brought, appropriately, into a metaphorical landscape of the edges of a storm, because the talk now turns to forgetting. 'One can in fact posit two hypotheses. Either [here he means Bergson] there is only a relationship of contact between the frame and the events that occur in it, but both would not be from the same substance, just as for the frame of a picture and the canvas in it. One might think of a riverbed, whose shores see the waters stream by,

---

[36] Here he means the 'more or less permanent frames' which allow us to cut up the visions of a night into a number of images.

[37] Halbwachs, 1994 [1925], p. 58.

[38] *Ibid.*, p. 89.

without projecting anything else on them but a superficial reflection. Or else between the frame and the events there is an identity by nature: the events are memories, but the frame is also made of memories. There is the difference between them that the latter are more stable and that in every moment they depend on us to notice them, for us to use them in order to refind and reconstruct the former. We will proceed with this second hypothesis.'[39]

This current of images rather resembles a cataract, but let's not even try to imagine a picture that hangs in a painted frame or a riverbed of muddy water. Let's leave that to the stream of forgetting, because this is what seems to me to signal Halbwachs' thoughts stretching to the edge of his conceptual abilities. In this moment of need, the concept of identity nails the frame onto the picture. Where we previously imagined the societal frame to be something solid that channelled the fluid memories, we now learn of two malleable materials that only differ in their degree of viscosity: the frame also consists of memories, but these are practically in a state of crystallisation. As for the societal frames, which are co-formed by all individual memories, there are not social structures or material transmissions of the cultural memory, but rather ideas about these things. These collective ideas, which contribute to the censoring, dimming and reconstruction of individual memories, are similar to these latter ones in their movement, although more sluggish, and fed by them. Who frames these frames and how they are moved remains a mystery.

When Halbwachs published his frame theory of memory in 1925, his closest Strasbourg colleagues, Marc Bloch and Charles Blondel, immediately distanced themselves from it quite clearly. It appeared to them to be an exaggerated construction of radical social constructivism. Blondel, who was interested both in Bergson and psychoanalysis, doubted most of all that Halbwachs had really proven that there were no true personal memories but only socially proffered reconstructions.[40] If this proof was unsuccessful, the entire polemic against Bergson and Freud, the largest part of his book, collapsed inwards. Bloch, the historian and mentor for the Annales who, after the German occupation, was persecuted and finally shot as a

---

[39] Halbwachs, 1994 [1925], p. 98.
[40] Blondel, 1926.

resistance fighter and Jew, wrote a lengthy article about 'Collective Memory, Traditions and Customs' in which he criticised *the 'raison-nements finalisantes'* of the Durkheim school, the abstract and teleological speculations of the sociologists about collective subjects and their legitimacies, purposes, desires, or even wills.[41] In other words, he argued against the determinable nature of societal futures. Instead he suggested that it was necessary to explain the mechanisms of tradition processes empirically, to identify their actors, and to examine observable and provable origins and effects.

The protests of his friends caused Halbwachs to start immediately a short book in 1925-7, probably intended for a broader audience, in defence of his theory of memory. He returned off and on to the manuscript for more than 19 years, (1932, 1935-8, 1943-4) until his internment, without being able to complete it. In the meantime, he did publish two more concrete texts: one about the memory of musicians, in which he described the frame of individual memory as a cultural code; and one on the topography of holy legends.[42] The latter we already know as the demythologisation of deceitful and power-forming cultural memory and I understand this as a response to Marc Bloch's challenge to research the mechanisms and actors of tradition formation. Besides this, it was also his attempt to bring together his theory in a compact form. However the project was probably so difficult to finish because he was unwilling to accept the criticisms of his friends – that there is inner memory, and that sociological fictions overlook history – in a positive manner, but wanted instead to dispel them.

These criticisms did not only have unacceptable implications for the Durkheim school, but also had common sense on their side. In questions of school, though, Halbwachs apparently would not retreat and thus allowed himself to think up further speculations, some of them certainly interesting (such as the social duplication of time and space categories), which would make his theory function after all. In reality, however, they made it increasingly complicated and more abstract and, when he wanted to correct this, vaguer.

---

[41]   Bloch, 1925.

[42]   Halbwachs, 'La mémoire collective chez des musiciens', first published in Spring 1939 in the *Revue philosophique* and now reprinted in *Namer*, 1997, pp. 19-50.

The indecision could not be overcome in the manuscripts for The Collective Memory. Halbwachs' instructional rationalism – especially in the 'black years' of the Second World War when the future not only of socialism but also of the French nation was called into question – got squeezed out in his desire to unite the values of the pre-war period of social classes with national ones and the conservation of the fictions of traditions. The outlined dimension for memory was no longer space but time. This was not, however, the time of external history, but the experiential space of experienced traditions:

> It was the defeat of democracy between 1938 and 1944 that characterised the transition: it was no longer about... defending history and progress, but about defending the past against the non-value of the present history [and] against the relapse represented by the totalitarian system. [...] It was about saving the past against the present; about reproducing it in its value and not reconstructing it in its reality.[43]

Now history became something increasingly discontinuous, external in its factuality, and valueless. It was presented with a new dimension of social time, in which the memory of non-institutionalised traditions transmits values. Stripped of history, its memories were still fictions, but they would guarantee collective identity for the future. The frame of the entire collective memory (the nation) could be joined together once more from the individual traditions: 'The identity of the rejoining would be illuminated by the new valuation of the experience of simultaneity: remembering means simultaneously finding oneself in the state of framing by the external (historical) time and to live the identity of the present time in the past.'[44]

In the context of a fragment of a remaining treatise on the differentiation between history and memory, Halbwachs pursued the question of the quality of memory of social frames of memory, in whose aporia we have discovered his theory of memory from 1925.[45] Now he attributed this, courageously and desperately (and appropriately enough given the exaggerated weight of its function of creating meaning in his theory) with its own subjectivity, and began to speak of 'collective memory', 'group memory', or even 'memory of the nation' instead of about tradition and continuity. Here he saw forms of

---

[43] *Ibid.,* p. 272.

[44] *Ibid.,* p. 260.

[45] Halbwachs, 1991 [1925], pp. 34 ff.

community knowledge with spatial and temporal dimensions that helped construct a unique memory of the group's past. The parameters of continuity and specificity of this knowledge – that is, its delimitation – were focused externally. Thus they were distinguished from history because their knowledge about the past broke away from group attachments, overstepped space-time validity (on the way to its actual goal, a universal historical synthesis) and emphasised change instead of continuity. The perception of real change countered this group memory: the group in question can only see itself internally and can only recognise itself in manifestations of transmissions as essentially unchanging. The external historical gaze on the other hand emphasised change, which had to remain unconscious for the collective memory. Anything really new can only be perceived to arrive from outside and would lead, as far as it changed the group, to a new memory.[46]

In this attempt at systemisation, Halbwach's concept of identity freed itself from its metaphorical function of helping in the fight against Bergson and Freud and took on social dimensions. It even employed almost the same language, but at the price of its inter-connection to pure traditional and in any profound sense unchanging collective subjects. Collective identity therefore became an ideological function of the definitional characteristics of a group and linked to its duration. Halbwachs could then state that a group looking back on its past perceived itself as having a continuously maintained identity.[47]

The enormous generality of this statement and its emptying of any meaningful content is the expression of a hope for an antifascist counter-memory of civilising values of the French Left and their fusion with the nation. In fact, the groups of the *résistance* were successful in activating such traditions, and then, after Liberation, in outfitting society with their hegemonic fictions. These included a communicated silence about the Collaboration and Vichy after the first wave of purges. A silence which only came to be broken after decades. The function of the identity postulate in the memory is the exclusion of the actual ruling difference.

The worth of such a validating 'we-feeling', based only on hope, is lost as soon as it is generalised. Halbwachs' sociology of memory, so

---

[46] Halbwachs, 1991 [1925], p. 75.

[47] *Ibid.*, p. 74

diverse and changing, can therefore not be synthesised verbatim; it must first be understood historically in order to see its important ideas about the societal participation in traditions. One must therefore consider very sceptically the dissolution of his undefined identity concept from its origin as an auxiliary in the defence against the post-Jewish discovery of a meaningful inner memory into a weak concept of a hopeful counter-memory. Such an open identity concept is ripe for any number of abuses and practically screams for ideological definition which would generally – if the national memory rules – be granted it. It must be emphasised that Halbwachs, an enlightener, wanted nothing less than this. Already with Topographie he had given an exemplary demonstration of how he wanted his concept of memory as reconstruction, with its stipulation of ruling symbol apparati and societal conditions, to be used. It was not to be used as a reinforcement of the totalitising rule over a randomly manipulable earth, but rather as a radically enlightening function of inciting the deconstruction of all forms of meaning staged by those in power and ostensibly traditional. There is no identity here.

CHAPTER 4

Spinoza on Historical Myths

Thomas HIPPLER

Introduction: Spinoza and History

Since his rediscovery in the early 19th century, Spinoza has been considered, especially in German philosophy, as the ahistorical thinker *par excellence*.[1] For Hegel, for instance, Spinoza's philosophy, being a pure deduction starting from the 'substance', was unable to think the 'particular' as such.[2] On the other hand, one should not forget the fact that Spinoza was not only the author of the *Ethics* but also of such a genuine historical work as the *Theologico-Political Treatise*. In this he sought to develop and employ an 'historical and critical method' for the interpretation of the Bible in order to reveal its political implications – the paradox of an ahistorical philosopher who is himself an historian.

In more recent research, most of which has come from France, questions of the political and historical impact of Spinoza's thinking have thus come to be given consideration.[3] Not without reasons, Spinoza has been seen as one of those classical thinkers who have something to say on the topic of historical and critical theory.[4] It may

---

[1]   Zac, 1989.

[2]   Hegel, 1971 [1833, 1844]; p. 170.

[3]   See Matheron, 1969 and 1971; Zac,1979; Tosel, 1994; Balibar, 1985; Laux, 1993; Moreau, 1994.

[4]   Norris, 1991.

therefore be fruitful to have a closer look at the implications of Spinoza's work for our understanding of contemporary theories of history.

Historically, the expression 'philosophy of history' is considered to be an invention of Voltaire.[5] Its originality lay in the way it linked together that which had previously been considered contradictory; philosophy as a science of truths of reason on the one hand, and history as a science that 'collects' empirical insights for practical purposes, and especially for political use, on the other.[6] In short, history deals with the social experience of contingency and variability in time, whereas philosophy is the sphere of eternal truth of reason.[7] The first sentence of the *Theologico-Political Treatise* reminds us that experience of contingency and instability in time is the basis for superstitious beliefs.[8] Challenging the belief of his contemporaries in prophecy and miracles, Spinoza's thinking may be understood as an attempt to reduce the effect of the arbitrary knowledge of contingency and instability in history. But there is another dimension of Spinoza's thinking, that which is found in the historical criticism of the Bible. His aim here was not so much to disqualify the 'mythical' knowledge of the Bible, but to reorganise this knowledge rationally, by 'scientific' methods. *In their order*, the stories in the Bible are perfect-

---

[5]   Voltaire, 1996 [1765]. See also the article 'Geschichtsphilosophie' Ritter, 1974.

[6]   See for example the opening of Bossuet's *Discours sur l'Histoire universelle*: 'Quand l'Histoire serait inutile aux autres hommes, il faudrait la faire lire aux princes [...] Les histoires ne sont composées que des actions qui les occupent, et tout semble y être fait pour leur usage.' See also the article 'Geschichte, Historie' in: Brunner, Conze and Koselleck, 1972-92; as well as Koselleck, 1989.

[7]   See Descartes *Discours de la méthode*: '[...] c'est quasi le même de converser avec ceux des autres siècles, que de voyager. Il est bon de savoir quelque chose des mœurs de divers peuples, afin de juger des nôtres plus sainement [...] Mais lorsqu'on emploie trop de temps à voyager, on devient enfin étranger en son pays; et lorsqu'on est trop curieux des choses qui se pratiquaient aux siècles passés, on demeure fort ignorant de celles qui se pratiquaient en celui-ci...'

[8]   'Men would never be superstitious, if they could govern all their circumstances by set rules, or if they were always favoured by fortune: but being frequently driven into straits where rules are useless, and being often kept fluctuating pitiably between hope and fear by the uncertainty of fortune's greedily coveted favours, they are consequently, for the most part, very prone to credulity.' Spinoza, 1883, Vol. 1, p. 3. The references to Spinoza are hence forth in this chapter referring to this publication of his chief works edited by R. H. N. Elwes.

ly true, even if the task of historical criticism is necessary to discover this specifically mythical order of truth.

In contrast to the tradition of the *Aufklärung*, for Spinoza there was no absolute opposition between the 'true' and the 'false', rather, one of the main characteristics of his thinking was the attempt to understand 'the truth of the false', which means considering the false not as a negativity, but as a coherent and necessarily existing being. Truth cannot emerge other than through a critical analysis of falsehood, or, to use Spinoza's term, of imagination. The imagination, as the mental function which gives rise to the social function of the myth, is one of the main themes of the second part of Spinoza's major work, the *Ethics*.

The Mythical Structure of Social Life

Surprisingly, this part of the *Ethics*, which deals with the human mind, begins with a definition of the body.[9] This reflects Spinoza's underlying philosophical conviction that the mind is nothing other than the expression of the body – the body that is felt and thought.[10] This does not mean, however, that the mind has an adequate idea of its body. On the contrary, mostly it has as inadequate idea of both its own body and that of others.[11] The mind, being the thought of the body, is an imagination because the body does not involve an adequate perception of reality. But Spinoza does not consider these inadequate perceptions as 'errors'. They are necessary results of the human constitution and as such, they involve even a certain type of truth. This is obviously not truth in the sense of an adequate representation of some objects in the world, but precisely the truth of the human body itself. Thus, 'imagination' does not necessarily mean 'error', for the mind has 'false' ideas only if it considers these bodily perceptions to be adequate ideas of reality.[12] Imagination, being nothing other than a set of ideas produced on the basis of bodily impressions, is not just a

---

[9]   'By *body* I mean a mode which expresses in a certain determinate manner the essence of God, in so far as he is considered as an extended thing.' *ibid.*, Vol. 2, p. 2.

[10]   Spinoza, *Ethics*, part 2, proposition 13, *ibid.*, p. 92.

[11]   Spinoza, *Ethics*, part 2, proposition 24, *ibid.*, p. 104, *Ethics*, part 2, propositions 27 to 31, *ibid.*, pp. 105-107.

[12]   Spinoza, *Ethics*, part 2, note to proposition 17, *ibid.*, p. 100.

reality on the individual level. On the contrary, one of the main functions of society is to work on the unification of its members' imaginations by elaborating an identical framework of bodily impressions.[13] Spinoza's case-study on this theme was the role of religious ceremonies in Ancient Israel.[14]

Human beings need to live in society, but since they do not always act reasonably, their passions tend to throw them into opposition.[15] For this reason, it is necessary to establish a political power that is able to defend the law and thus contain the antagonistic passions present in society. The means by which this pacification can be achieved are still passions, since humans, by definition, rarely act reasonably. More precisely, the passions used in pacification are hope and fear; hope for a better life in the future, and fear of punishment. But since 'human nature will not submit to absolute repression', it is better for a government to assure respect for the law through hope rather than fear.[16] It is imagination that provides the link between the social creation of hope and the stability of the state. According to Spinoza, this was the function of religion in Ancient Israel after the law had been received from Moses:

> This, then, was the object of the ceremonial law, that men should do nothing of their own free will, but should always act under external authority, and should continually confess by their actions and thoughts that they were not their own masters, but were entirely under the control of others.[17]

The ceremonial sanctification of everyday life, that is, the institutional supplement of 'meaning' to individual actions, thus creates a feeling of belonging to a wider community of sense by means of a social action on the body.[18] The very essence of religion is

---

[13] See Bertrand, 1983. There are striking parallels between Spinozas analysis of the social organisation of imagination and Foucault's description of discipline; see Foucault, 1975.

[14] Spinoza, *Theologico-Political Treatise,* chapter 5: 'Of the Ceremonial Law'.

[15] *Ibid.,* p. 73.

[16] *Ibid.,* p. 74.

[17] *Ibid.,* p. 76.

[18] This social action on the bodies is even more powerful if it leaves visible traces as, for example, in Jewish circumcision or in the Chinese's braid 'by which they keep themselves apart from everyone else, and have thus kept themselves during so

political. For each state it is necessary to institutionalise a social action which, in the bodily sphere, imaginarily represents the individuality of the state.[19] At the same time, these practices need some 'discursive' justification, and it is precisely the function of the myth to offer a kind of 'rationalisation'. With reference to Ancient Hebrew history, Spinoza considers this function in his description of prophecy and miracles in the Old Testament.[20]

For Spinoza, there was no doubt that prophecy was an inferior kind of knowledge that has its source in the vivid imagination of the prophet.[21] Nevertheless, even if prophecy is purely imaginary and 'highly dubious', this does not mean that it is simply false, since the question of epistemological truth and error in prophecy is accompanied by the socio-epistemological question of the kind of certitude it involves. According to Spinoza, prophecy is valid in socio-epistemological terms because the prophet is 'morally certain'[22] of his prophecy, and this moral certainty is founded on the fact that 'the mind of the prophet was given wholly to what was right and good'.[23] Given the fact that for Spinoza the categories of 'good' and 'right' do not exist outside of a political community, one can conclude that prophecy is valid because the prophet belongs to a community whose laws and rules he precisely embodies.[24] The social function of prophecy is to recall these norms in the memories of the members of society.[25] Prophecy, as a kind of knowledge, is entirely 'practical',

---

many thousand years that they far surpass all other nations in antiquity'. *Ibid.,* chap. 3, p. 56.

[19] 'Il faut remarquer qu'avec cette politique de l'adhésion, Spinoza excède la théorie classique de l'Etat. [...] Quand il commence à réfléchir aux conditions symboliques de l'adhésion des individus, le spinozisme déplace les questions de cette logique de l'obéissance. [...] il nous semble que la logique de l'adhésion et de l'identité devra attendre le XXe siècle, de Arendt à Habermas, pour retrouver un espace de lisibilité. Cet espace reste d'ailleurs à bien des égards en retrait sur la possibilité ouverte par les interrogations spinozistes.' Moreau, 1994, p. 495.

[20] Spinoza, *Theologico-Political Treatise* especially chapters 1 (Of Prophecy), 2 (Of Prophets) and 6 (Of Miracles).

[21] 'Therefore the power of prophecy implies not a perculiarly perfect mind, but a perculiarly vivid imagination.' *Ibid.,* chap. 1, p. 19.

[22] Spinoza, Theologico-Political Treatise chap. 2, p. 28.

[23] *Ibid.,* p. 29.

[24] Spinoza, A Political Treatise, chap. 2, sec. 23.

[25] See Spinoza, *Theologico-Political Treatise*, chap. 2, pp. 39 and 41.

which means that in society it has an exclusively moral function. Prophetic knowledge and the 'moral community' to which the prophet belongs, are strictly circular terms; a prophet is a prophet if, and only if, he or she belongs to a 'moral community', while prophecy essentially aims to strengthen the community's moral cohesion. To the extent that the existence of a community is determined by respect of these moral rules, it can be said that the prophet and his audience are, to a certain degree, the product of one another.

If this is true, then Spinoza's criticism of prophecy has to be reconsidered. If its main purpose is the de-sanctification of prophecy by means of a sociological functional analysis, then this involves a critical perspective on the way history is considered as a social function in social life. Through a critical analysis of the circle of mutual sanctification between the prophet's words and the political and religious rules of a given society, Spinoza in fact aims to destroy the sacred in history.

The same conclusion must be drawn from the analysis of the social function of miracles in Ancient Israel. Spinoza defines a miracle as 'an event of which the causes cannot be explained by the natural reason through a reference to ascertained workings of nature'.[26] Since nothing happens in nature without reason, a miraculous explanation of an event represents an imaginary interruption of the chain of rational causality. This form of reasoning is possible because one spontaneously imagines God as the author of miracles in the image of a king who can break the laws (of nature) just as he can decree them.[27] Myths of miracles tend to assure the Jewish people of the omnipresence of this form of divine intervention on their behalf and 'this idea was so pleasing to humanity that men go on to this day imagining miracles, so that they may believe themselves God's favourites, and the final cause for which God created and directs all things.[28] In this manner, myths of miracles tend towards the sanctification, not so much of nature, but of 'history', which comes to be perceived as the eternal presence of God in the life of a nation. 'History' is thus a form of social cement that has, like prophecy, a circular relation with a community's moral and intellectual values.

---

[26] *Ibid.*, chap. 6, p. 84.

[27] *Ibid.*, p. 81, see also the *Ethics* on this topic: part 2, note to proposition 3, p. 84.

[28] *Ibid.*, p. 82.

Myth is nothing more than a repetition of these values to a community that recognises itself in these stories – stories that are its 'history'. Since, however, the ground on which this circular definition works is an imaginary representation of nature, this form of social cohesion is itself imaginary. It is the goal of Spinoza's 'historical and critical' interpretation of the Bible to break this circle.[29]

Spinoza's Historical Criticism

It is in the 7th chapter of the *Theologico-Political Treatise* that Spinoza gives a theoretical account of the method for this historical interpretation of Scripture. The first stage of the analysis must be an 'archaeology of meaning', that is, an examination of the language of the Bible in order to determine all the possible senses of a word and so be able subsequently to reduce this diversity according to the context. After this, one must consider the 'external' – historical, social, cultural etc. – context of the situation in which the text has been written and transmitted. It is only in this way that the 'meaning' of Scripture can be understood, but this does not involve any knowledge about the 'truth' of what it says, 'meaning' and 'truth' being different things.[30]

The second stage of the analysis involves studying the 'mind of the prophets and the Holy Spirit'.[31] The method employed,

> does not widely differ from the method of interpreting nature – in fact, it is almost the same. For as the interpretation of nature consists in the examination of the history of nature, and therefrom deducing definitions of natural phenomena on certain fixed axioms, so Scriptural interpretation proceeds by the examination of Scripture and inferring the intention of its authors as a legitimate conclusion from its fundamental principles. By working in this manner everyone will always advance without danger of error.[32]

---

[29] Nevertheless, it should be noted that Spinoza's position differs from the mainstream Enlightenment tradition, inasmuch as he does not oppose a 'rational' model to a 'mythical' model of history. On the contrary, he insists in the social necessity of 'ideology' – otherwise there is the risk that 'science' itself may take the place of 'ideology'. There is a politico-ethical need for social 'differentiation'. I will return to this point later.

[30] *Ibid.*, chap. 7; p. 101.

[31] *Ibid.*, p. 104.

[32] *Ibid.*, p. 99.

The starting point must be an examination of that 'which is most universal and serves for the basis and foundation of all Scripture, a doctrine, in fact, that is commended by all the prophets as eternal and most profitable to all men'.[33] These general principles are, according to Spinoza, nothing but moral and political prescriptions. The beginning of the 7th chapter of the *Treatise* shows the importance of the political impact of the quarrels in scriptural interpretation. The theological debates of the 17th century have therefore to be understood as an ideological translation of political questions.[34] Unlike the 'theologians', who pretend to have the true interpretation independent of its practical effects, Spinoza affirms openly that the goal of his interpretation is 'theologico-political'.

It is also important to note that this practical approach to theological thinking is deduced from the very texts of the Bible, since the general principles of interpretation, what is called its 'universal doctrine', is just 'practical knowledge'. Beyond all difficulties of interpretation, 'we can easily follow the intention of Scripture in moral questions, from the history we possess of it, and we can be sure of its true meaning... it is most plain that we can follow with certainty the intention of Scripture in matters relating to salvation and necessary blessedness'.[35] According to Spinoza, there is little philosophical speculation in the Bible, and its goal is simply the political one of promoting social coherence.

> Scriptural doctrine contains no lofty speculations nor philosophic reasoning, but only very simple matters, such as could be understood by the slowest intelligence. [...] Scripture does not aim at imparting scientific knowledge, and, therefore, it demands from men nothing but obedience, and censures obstinacy, but not ignorance. Furthermore, as obedience to God consists solely in love to our neighbour [...] it follows that no knowledge is commended in the Bible save that which is necessary for enabling all men to obey God in the manner stated, and

---

[33] *Ibid.*, p. 10.

[34] 'When people declare, as all are ready to do, that the Bible is the Word of God teaching man true blessedness and the way of salvation, they evidently do not mean what they say. [...] we see most people endeavouring to hawk about their own commentaries as the Word of God, and giving their best efforts, under the guise of religion, to compelling others to think as they do: we generally see, I say, theologians anxious to learn how to wring their inventions and sayings out of the sacred text, and to fortify them with Divine authority.' *Ibid.*, p. 98.

[35] *Ibid.*, p. 113.

without which they would become rebellious, or without the discipline of obedience.[36]

Consequently, faith is the same as obedience and its contents differ according to people's mind *(ingenium)*.[37] If faith leads to blessedness, it does so only because it produces behaviour that is socially useful.[38]

From this position, Spinoza gives, in the 14th chapter of the *Treatise*, an account of what are the 'dogmas of universal faith of the whole of Scripture'. Beyond all contradictions that can be found in Scripture, there is a small set of theoretical convictions that can be found everywhere in the Bible and that must therefore be regarded as true – at least in a moral sense, which means 'politically true'. These dogmas are,

> That God or a Supreme Being exists, sovereignly just and merciful, the Exemplar of true life [...] That He is One [...] that He is omnipresent [...] That He has supreme right and domination over all things, and that He does nothing under compulsion but by His absolute fiat and grace [...] That the worship of God consists only in justice and charity, or love to one's neighbour [...] That all those, and those only, who obey God by their manner of life are saved; the rest of mankind, who live under the sway of their pleasures, are lost [...] that God forgives the sins of those who repent.[39]

Each of these dogmas is followed by a justification in a 'moral' sense. For instance, the 3rd dogma of omnipresence is necessary 'for if anything could be supposed to be concealed from Him, or to be unnoticed by Him, we might doubt or be ignorant of the equity of His judgement as directing all things.'[40] Spinoza's conception of the interpretation of Scripture as liberation from superstitious religious beliefs implies that interpretation has to be individually differentiated. After having established the 'dogmas of universal faith', Spinoza states that, 'every man is bound to adapt these dogmas to his own way of thinking, and to interpret them according as he feels that he can give them his fullest and most unhesitating assent, so that he may the

---

[36] *Ibid.*, chap. 13, pp. 175-176.

[37] *Ibid.*, pp. 180-181.

[38] *Ibid.*, chap. 14, p. 186.

[39] *Ibid.*, chap. 14, pp. 186-187.

[40] *Ibid.*, p. 187.

more easily obey God with his whole heart'.[41] The formulations of the dogmas leave enough space for personal comprehension, so that they can be interpreted in a 'superstitious' manner or in a 'spinozistic' way as the immanence of God in nature.

The claim of differentiated readings of Scripture is contrary to the view of a 'coercive' society in which everyone is subject to the same set of beliefs and the same set of bodily disciplines. For Spinoza, in fact, bodily submission to discipline and mental submission to mythical beliefs are complementary parts of social domination.[42] Such a differentiation in the interpretation of beliefs tends to the dissolution of the disciplinary form of the production of social cohesion and to the establishment of 'free' socialisation by means of adaptation, interpretation and the rational transformation of politico-religious beliefs. As a differentiated and 'powerful' imagination – for imagination corresponds to the degree of one's mental 'power' (*potentia*) – takes the place of a 'coercive' imagination, the 'society of discipline' becomes gradually emancipated from itself. But this kind of transformation is impossible if the texts of the historical myths that serve as ideological support are not accessible to historical criticism, for there is no other way in which to understand the social production of imagination. Like individuals, societies have to understand and recognise the mechanisms of their own submission in order to free themselves. The development of their 'power', activity and rationality has to be proceeded by an effort to transform their 'passions', myths and submissions.[43] Although commentators have made little of this point, one can say that in Spinoza's political philosophy, historical knowledge is in a ethically strategic position equivalent, on a collective level, to the individual's power of understanding. For

---

[41] Spinoza, *Theologico-Political Treatise*, chap. 14, p. 188.

[42] The 'parallel' structure of 'extension' and 'thinking' as two of God's attributes is one of the most fundamental ideas in Spinoza's philosophy; 'The order and connection of ideas is the same as the order and connection of things.' Spinoza, *Ethics*, part 2, proposition 7, p. 86.

[43] See the definitions of activity and passivity in the 2nd definition in the 3rd part of the *Ethics*; 'I say that we *act* when anything takes place, either within us or externally to us, where we are the adequate cause; that is [...] when throught our nature something takes place within us or externally to us, which can through our nature alone be clearly and distinctly understood. On the other hand, I say that we are passive as regards something when that something takes place within us, or follows from our nature externally we being only the partial cause.' p. 129.

individuals and for societies an adequate knowledge of the self is a necessary condition for transformation.

Spinoza's interpretation of the Bible differs from that offered by others in that it seeks to introduce the control of a rational procedure in its production of meaning in order to create an interaction between Scripture and reason in the theologico-political field of social beliefs. In doing so, the presence of reason in the practical matters of religion has an impact on social behaviour; 'it is an observed fact that men employ their reason to defend conclusions arrived at by reason, but conclusions arrived at by the passions are defended by the passions'.[44] If there is rationality in the interpretation of beliefs, there will also be rationality in their social consequences. On the other hand, 'passive' beliefs, that is beliefs that are created both by bodily submission to discipline and mental submission to myths, lead to a 'passionate' and irrational socialisation. In this way, the interpretation of the Bible, that is, the interpretation of beliefs with a social impact, is, at the same time, an interpretation of social reality that aims at the intelligibility of society as such. Treating inter-individual reality as a 'text' means destroying its opacity; individuals and words are spontaneously part of an imaginative structure, but both may be subject to interpretation, both may be 'organised' differently.[45]

In writing the *Theologico-Political Treatise*, Spinoza was taking a stand against those Protestants who, in 17th century Holland, sought to establish a state according to the religious norms of the Old Testament.[46] His 'party' was the liberal merchant bourgeoisie, which held power until the counter-revolution of 1672.[47] Nevertheless, it is important to note that Spinoza does not oppose one model of social organisation to another, considering one as rational and free and the other oppressive and irrational. On the contrary, as I have shown, according to Spinoza each society is 'imaginary' in some way, which means that each needs to establish a means of organising its beliefs or, in anachronistic terms, each society needs its ideology. Societies differ only in the degree that these beliefs are subject to interpretation, in the form of a methodical, controlled, rational transformation. A society is

---

[44] *Ibid.*, chap. 7, p. 99.

[45] See Laux, 1993, p. 117.

[46] See Balibar, 1985.

[47] See Feuer, 1958.

always and necessarily 'in imagination', because there is no society which does not have its myths. These myths do not have to be destroyed, but rather understood and interpreted. For any society, there is no *tabula rasa* outside of ideology and myth, and no new beginning 'in truth'.

History, Teleology and Democracy

When they are confronted with history, human beings tend naturally and spontaneously to imagine it as a teleologically organised process. In the appendix to the first part of the *Ethics* and in the preface to the *Theologico-Political Treatise*, Spinoza explains the mental laws that are necessary to understand why this is so.[48] Being conscious of their volitions and desires, but ignoring the causes which have disposed them so to wish and desire, human beings necessarily think in terms of means and purposes because they themselves do everything they do because they consider that it is useful for them. 'Thus it comes to pass that they only look for a knowledge of the final causes of events and when these are learned, they are content, as having no cause for further doubt.'[49] For Spinoza, finalism was the spontaneous but inadequate form of human thinking. Finding in nature many things that are useful to them, but which they have not produced, they deduce the existence of 'some ruler or rulers of the universe' (*rectores naturae*) who arranged everything for the benefit of human wellbeing.[50]

> They are bound to estimate the nature of such rulers (having no information on the subject) in accordance with their own nature, and therefore they assert that the gods ordained everything for the use of man, in order to bind man to themselves and obtain from him the highest honour.'[51]

On the other hand, Spinoza continued, they explain the hindrances in human life 'such as storms, earthquakes, diseases, etc.' by the god's anger about some faults committed by men.

---

[48] As Pierre-François Moreau has pointed out, the 'finalism in space' in the appendix has its complement in a 'finalism in time' in the preface. See Moreau, 1990, pp. 298-305.

[49] *Ethics, loc. cit.*, p. 75.

[50] *Ibid.*, p. 76.

[51] *Ibid.*

This 'prejudice towards finalism' causes human beings to interpret facts of human life as being in accord with 'God's will', which implies that some actions are classed as pious and others as impious. In this way they see God's judgement and justice as providing a certain 'rationality' in the distribution of good and bad fortune in the life of a person or a nation. Not even everyday experience, which demonstrates that fortune has no rational plan, has been able to change this 'providential' viewpoint:

> It was more easy for them to class such contradictions among other unknown things of whose cause they were ignorant and thus to retain their actual and innate condition of ignorance, than to destroy the whole fabric of their reasoning and start afresh. They therefore laid down as an axiom, that God's judgements far transcend human understanding.[52]

This idea is preciselyly the starting point of the *Theologico-Political Treatise*, which claims that this 'finalistic' structure of human reasoning is related to human 'passions', and so, 'being often kept fluctuating pitiably between hope and fear by the uncertainty of fortune's greedily coveted favours, they are consequently, for the most part, very prone to credulity'.[53] For Spinoza, fear is therefore the cause of superstition, meaning that everybody is potentially superstitious.[54] 'If anything happened during their fright which reminds them of some past good or ill, they think it portends a happy or unhappy issue and therefore... style it a lucky or unlucky omen.'[55]

At this point, their minds become inaccessible to reason and rational argument, and they believe in 'the phantoms of imagination, dreams, and other childish absurdities' such as 'the very oracles of Heaven'.[56] Thus, on a political level, fear, superstition and distrust in reason are the best means by which a tyrannical power can keep mankind in a state of intellectual and political dependence; 'The mob has no ruler more potent than superstition'.[57] Spinoza's attack on

---

[52]   *Ibid.*, pp. 76-77.

[53]   *Theologico-Political Treatise, loc. cit.* p. 3.

[54]   "Superstition, then is engendered, preserved, and fostered by fear. " *Ibid.*, p. 4.

[55]   *Ibid.*, p. 3.

[56]   *Ibid.*, p. 4.

[57]   'Hence anyone who seeks for the true causes of miracles, and strives to understand natural phenomena as an intelligent being, and not to gaze at them like a fool, is set down and denounced as an impious heretic by those, whom the masses adore as

finalistic prejudices has to be understood as an attack on the 'theologico-political bloc' that keeps the masses in its thrall.

> Such persons know that, with the removal of ignorance, the wonder which forms their only available means for proving and preserving their authority would vanish also.[58]
>
> But if, in despotic statecraft the supreme and essential mystery be to hoodwink the subjects, and to mask the fear which keeps them down, with the specious garb of religion, so that men may fight as bravely for slavery as for safety and count it not shame but highest honour to risk their blood and their lives for the vainglory of a tyrant; yet in a free state no more mischievous expedient could be planned or attempted.[59]

Teleological thinking in history has repercussions in politics and, moreover, there is a political interest in maintaining the theologico-political image of fluctuation between fear and hope for the masses (*multitudo*) in order to govern them more easily. Teleology informs a 'centric' view of society in two ways; on the one hand, it is a tool in the hands of a monarchist power, while on the other, it is the natural form of self-representation for a monarchist regime.

A teleological vision of history has thus to be understood as a translation 'in time' of a more fundamental finalism 'in space', that is, as a 'centric' vision of social totality. In this tradition, it is the king who is the axis for the construction and intelligibility of history, for he is the personification of the initial principles of social organisation.[60] Thus, monarchist historiography that considers society to be constructed around the king as centre and creator of social coherence, tends necessarily to imagine historical time as an eternal reproduction of those initial principles. Spinoza arrives by this route at the astonishing conclusion that the contemporary structure of a society determines its vision of history or, in other words, that the synchronic precedes the diachronic.

---

the interpreters of nature and the gods.' *Ethics, loc. cit.* p. 78. *Theologico-Political Treatise, loc. cit.*, p. 5.

[58] *Ethics, loc. cit.*, pp. 78-79.

[59] *Theologico-Political Treatise, loc. cit.*, p. 5.

[60] See, on French historiography, which is the ideal-type of monarchist historiography, Dubois, 1977, esp. pp. 18-39 ; and Tyvaert, no publ. year, esp. pp. 91-109.

On this basis, Spinoza's 'republican' standpoint necessitates another approach for the understanding of historical change.[61] Being a radical nominalist in his ontology as well as his politics, there is no place in Spinoza's philosophy for a king as a constitutive centre of society.

> Every natural thing has by nature as much right, as it has power to exist and operate [...] And so by natural right I understand the very laws or rules of nature, in accordance with which everything takes place, in other words, the power of nature itself. And so the natural right of universal nature, and consequently of every individual thing, extends as far as its power: and accordingly, whatever any man does after the laws of his nature, he does by the highest natural right, and he has as much right over nature as he has power.[62]

The perfect identification of right and power in nature means the denial of the idea of naturality of right in its common sense.[63] An unstable relation between individual powers that seek to maintain themselves in a complex interaction is prior to political power.[64] According to this, there is no naturality of relations of dependence and submission.[65]

The establishment of a political power [*potestas*] in society is thus possible only if the relations of individual powers [*potentia*] can be 'stabilised'. It is important to notice however, that human power is to be reckoned less by physical vigour than by mental strength, which means that political power has to use a 'passional' attachment.[66]

> He has another under his authority [*potestas*], he whom he holds bound, or from whom he has taken arms and means of defence or escape, or

---

[61] For Spinoza's republicanism see Walter, 1990.

[62] *A Political Treatise* in: *The Chief Works of Benedict de Spinoza... op. cit.* Vol. 1, chap. 2, sec. 3-4, p. 292.

[63] 'As, then, wrong-doing and obedience, in their strict sense, so also justice and injustice cannot be conceived of, except under domination.' *Ibid.*, sec. 23, p. 299 [*Ut itaque peccatum, & obsequium strictè sumptum, sic etiam justitia, & injustitia, non nisi in imperio possunt concipi. Tractatus Politicus.* in: *Spinoza Opera. Im Auftrag der Heidelberger Akademie der Wissenschaften herausgegeben von Carl Gebhardt.* Heidelberg (Winter) 1872, vol. 3, p. 284].

[64] See *ibid.*, sec. 8 and 14.

[65] *Ibid.*, sec. 9.

[66] *Ibid.*, sec. 11.

inspired with fear, or so attached to himself by past favour, that the man obliged would rather please his benefactor than himself, and live after his mind than after his own. He that has another under authority in the first or second of these ways, holds but his body, not his mind. But in the third or fourth way he has made dependent on himself both the mind and the body of the other; yet only as long as the fear or hope lasts, for upon the removal of the feeling the other is left independent.[67]

There are two types of power, of which one is physical and the other 'passional' or 'imaginary', even if its effects are not imaginary at all.[68] The former cannot constitute a stable relation of power, 'as there is no assurance of making it good'.[69] Thus, political power exists under the condition that it is the object of the hopes and fears of each member of society. In this way one can say that for Spinoza too, 'power comes from below', for the political power [*potestas*] is nothing but the 'confiscation' of the individual powers [*potentiae*] of the masses which it 'represents'.[70] Thus, according to his criticism of teleology in historical thinking, Spinoza analyses as imaginary the underlying vision of society as a 'centric' totality. Neither on the synchronic nor on the diachronic level is there transcendence of a king or a state, because both are nothing but instances of the imaginary representation of the power of the masses [*potentia multitudis*]. Nevertheless, imaginary representation does not mean that it is 'false'. On the contrary, the action of the imaginary is a basic determination of social reality.

Conclusion

Historical myths, in Spinoza's view, are not a false kind of historical knowledge, rather they reflect in a certain imaginary manner the relation of society to itself. The form and contents of myths are therefore not arbitrary at all; they are the imaginary expression of

---

[67]   *Ibid.*, sec. 10, p. 295.

[68]   Matheron, 1986.

[69]   Spinoza, *A Political Treatise,* sec. 15, p. 296.

[70]   Foucault, 1976, p. 124: 'Le pouvoir vient d'en bas'.
      'Le pouvoir véritable n'est donc rien d'autre que la confiscation, par le dominant, de la puissance du dominé. Confiscation imaginaire, car la puissance du dominé, physiquement parlant, reste la sienne. Mais confiscation qui a des effets réels dans la mesure où le dominé est réellement déterminé à l'accepter, et dans cette mesure seulement.' Matheron, 1986, p. 114.

society's own structure, just as the 'passions' and 'inadequate ideas' of an individual express his or her being in a certain way.[71] While being absolutely determinate, this relation of society to itself is nevertheless necessarily confused.[72]

The social imagination differs, however, from the individual one because the former is still 'in history'. A society's relation to its own past is one of the means of production of this social imagination that enables it to 'think' itself in its basic determinations. Such was the case, in Spinoza's study, for the history of Ancient Israel, its origins and its election by God. Any scientific investigation into this history must therefore proceed by means of criticism, which means that historical myths have to be analysed and understood for what they are.[73] In this way, there is a certain kind of 'truth' in the myth, but this truth demands methodical procedures in combination with scientific reason in order to be criticised.

The originality of Spinoza's position concerning historical myths lies in the fact that he does not simply claim to 'abolish' belief in myths by means of rational procedures, but argues that liberation is only possible as an interaction between beliefs and their rational 'deconstruction', which implies that their 'truth' must be recognised as such, and not only as an imaginary truth. More fundamentally, it is Spinoza's theory of 'errors' that enables him to consider them 'positively' and so look for the 'truth in what is false'.[74] In the field of

---

[71] 'The object of the idea constituting the human mind is the body, in other words a certain mode of extension which actually exists, and nothing else.' Spinoza, *Ethics,* part 2, proposition 13, p. 92. According to this one can say that the object of social representations is nothing other than the structure of a given society.

[72] 'Inadequate and confused ideas follow by the same necessity, and adequate or clear and distinct ideas.' *Ibid.* proposition 36, p. 109.
'[...] the human mind, when it perceived things after the common order of nature, has not an adequate but only a confused and fragmentary knowledge of itslef, of its own body, and of external bodies.' *Ibid.* corollary to the proposition 29, p. 106.

[73] Althusser was one of the first to see this implicit theory of historical knowledge in Spinoza: 'Que le premier qui ait jamais posé le problème du *lire*, et par voie de conséquence de l'*écrire*, Spinoza, ait été aussi le premier au monde à proposer à la fois une théorie de l'histoire et une philosophie de l'opacité de l'immédiat; et qu'en lui pour la première fois au monde un homme ait ainsi relié l'essence du lire et l'essence de l'histoire dans une théorie de la différence de l'imaginaire et du vrai [...]' Althusser, 1996 [1968], p. 8.

[74] See Moreau, 1975.

history, this means that there is no opposition between 'myths' and 'historical science', but rather a permanent interaction between the two.

In this way, Spinoza's criticism permits us to avoid being trapped by the dialectic of Enlightenment reason and the idea of a mythical function of rational scientific thinking. Thus, the 'supernatural' interpretation of those who think 'that the light of nature has no power to interpret Scripture' on the one hand, and, on the other, the 'philosophical' interpretation by Maimonides who claims that 'if the literal meaning clashes with reason, though the passage seems in itself perfectly clear, it must be interpreted in some metaphorical sense', share the position that reason (the 'light of nature') is completely exterior to mythical beliefs.[75] Spinoza therefore concludes that 'we should be unable to come to any conclusion about their truth'[76] 'In short, one party will run wild with the aid of reason, and the other will run wild without the aid of reason.'[77]

---

[75] Spinoza, *Theologico-Political Treatise,* chap. 7, p. 114.
   Ibid., p. 115. '*...aliter interpretandum censet...*' *Tractatus Theologico-Politicus*, p. 113.

[76] *Ibid.*, p. 116.

[77] *Ibid.*, chap. 15, p. 190.

MYTH, MEMORY AND REPRESENTATION

CHAPTER 5

Conflict in the Social Representation of Place: The Cases of Gorbals and Alma-Gare[1]

Michael James MILLER

The issues of foundation myths, architecture and public monuments have almost exclusively been dealt with as elements in the process of identity building for the region or the nation. The aim of this chapter is to consider these issues at a different scale, in an attempt to understand how *local* communities construct their own identity and, in turn, attempt to have this identity recognised and accepted by other actors. I shall draw upon two examples of neighbourhood construction. Both of these date from the period 1950 to 1980, which saw slum clearance and industrial construction techniques initially heralded as the panacea for the housing crisis in western European countries, and subsequently derided as key factors in the destruction of urban community life. One example considers the neighbourhood of Alma-Gare in Roubaix, a town in the north of France that, along with neighbouring Lille and Tourcoing, once formed the centre of the French textile industry. The other example is drawn from Scotland, and considers the Gorbals, a deprived area of Glasgow that, until its demolition in the course of the 1950s, 60s and 70s, housed some of the poorest sections of the city's population. In

---

[1] This chapter is based upon material from the author's PhD thesis. Archive references are ML for the Mitchell Library, Glasgow, AMR for the Archives du Mairie de Roubaix, ANE for the archives of *Nord Eclair*, Roubaix, and AIR, for the archives of the Association Inter-Quartiers de Roubaix. All translations by the author.

an article of 1959 in the *New Yorker Magazine*, the Gorbals was described as, 'the most notorious single slum area in the British Isles, and among the most notorious in the world.'[2]

The fundamental premise of this paper is drawn from recent geographical thinking on the idea of 'place', and in particular from the work of the British geographer Doreen Massey.[3] All places, at whatever scale, be it local or national, are constructions. These constructions, while being made to appear natural and neutral, in fact serve the interest of groups which enjoy hegemony in power relations. Massey uses the term 'essentialist' to describe this construction of place. An essentialist view is one which holds that any place, at whatever scale, is clearly delimited, and possesses distinct and definitive characteristics. Once an essentialist view is established, this squeezes ideas into a common shape, which marginalises any possible alternative interpretation of that place.

Taking this argument further, an essentialist view is legitimated by a particular reading of history, since it is impossible to think about a place without thinking about its past. Essentialist definitions presume a specific relationship between the assumed identity of a place and its history, pursuing a self-justifying linear logic from some supposed origin to the present day. Yet this origin is the work of a sleight-of-hand, for the past is distinguished and assigned meaning *in the present* by groups which sift through the past and identify elements which lend support to their social practices, while suppressing other elements which are not consistent with these practices (their construction is, in fact, re-construction, as Hayden White argues in chapter 2). This reading is then presented as a linear narrative which, rooted in some mythical origin, follows a seemingly inevitable path to the present, from which it is projected into the future in order to justify the continuation of the self-serving essentialist definition. The construction of myth, tradition, memory and, of course, oblivion, all feed into this process. Once an essentialist meaning is established, it becomes difficult to see it as a social construction and so, in considering a particular place, we are generally unaware that our thoughts are being shaped through it. Essentialist definitions of place are generally established by the group alliances which enjoy domination in social relations, but all the same, essentialist definitions do evolve, when

---

[2] Watts, 1959, p. 5.

[3] See, for example, Massey, 1995 and Massey and Jess, 1995.

agendas change, groups lose their power or when other groups succeed in imposing a counter-definition.

The essentialist definition of a place, at whatever scale, is, in fact, only one of many possible definitions attributable to that place, since history incorporates different rhythms, different scales, different observers, and different observation points.[4] To illustrate this point, let me borrow an example from Bernard Lepetit. Consider the case of a specific type of place; the city. The city exists in a social sense, and has a physical manifestation of social and cultural practices. Its activities, its institutions and its urban form are all historically rooted, but all these elements do not necessarily have the same rhythms, nor the same age. From Lepetit's perspective:

> The city [...] is never synchronous with itself; the behaviour of the citizens, the policies of urban, economic or social planning unfurl according to different chronologies. But, at the same time, the city is completely in the present. Or rather, it is completely located in the present by the social actors who shoulder all the temporal responsibility *(la charge temporelle).*[5]

The city thus consists of elements which are at one and the same time part of earlier ages, and part of the present time. The unifying principle for all these elements is provided by the social practices of the moment, and these social practices give different meanings to different parts of the city.[6]

The field of local politics and planning, particularly in the context of post-war urban renewal projects, offers a rich area in which to explore these themes. In brief, in order to construct a simplified and unified meaning when different meanings compete, a municipal council, often supported by development agencies, central government, real estate interest, the press and even local residents, would voice the 'common sense' view that certain areas of the city were slums or *taudis*.[7] This label was confirmed by pseudo-scientific

---

[4]   For example, this argument is explored in Lepetit and Pumain, 1993.

[5]   Lepetit, 1993, p. 293.

[6]   Lepetit, 1995, p. 293.

[7]   The terms 'slum' first came into use in the English language in the first half of the 19th century. Of slang or cant origin, it was initially used to designate a room, but by 1825 had been used to refer to a street or court inhabited by the very poor. While the contemporary meaning of *taudis* is ill-maintained or sub-standard

studies intended to quantify the extent to which housing was unfit or *insalubre*, and which often echoed 19th century hygienist ideas on ventilation, sunlight and sanitation.[8] The label of 'slum' could then justify the council's attempts to restructure the area, and indeed, demolition operations were normally underpinned by a discourse which tapped into issues of human dignity. Slum clearance was, as the mayor of Roubaix succinctly put it, 'in short, a social, human and fraternal undertaking'.[9]

In both Glasgow and Roubaix, the local political scene was traditionally dominated by socialist councillors, and the respective administrations presented a history of the Gorbals and Alma-Gare as one of private sector neglect and exploitation. For the Gorbals, the historical narrative took the form of a once respectable area of fine housing which had spiraled into decline thanks to the greed of landlords who had divided and sub-divided houses in order to exploit the poorest members of society. In Roubaix, the narrative started with the construction of poor-quality workers' housing by capitalist industrialists, incorporated the exploitation of the working-class, catalogued the physical disintegration of the urban fabric, to arrive at a present in which the residents of areas like Alma-Gare were compelled to inhabit 'degraded, unhealthy and dangerous housing stock'.[10] This history in turn justified a future where only the municipal council could 'efface the heavy heritage of the past' and, 'construct [...] a new neighbourhood in place of the slums constructed by the capitalists of the 19th century.'[11]

---

housing, its origin is middle French, *se tauder*, meaning 'to put under shelter'. *Taudis* was the shelter provided for workers engaged in preparing earthworks during a military siege.

[8] Both the UK and France have a list of objective measures to assess the condition of a house. In practice, however, the application of these criteria contains a strong subjective dimension. Technical documents generally did not use the terms 'slum' or '*taudis*', preferring terms such as 'unfit for human habitation' or '*logements vétustes*'. Others – politicians and journalists – did not pretend to be so objective. They used terms like 'slum' emotively, and tended to assign levels of moral and social meaning to areas of run-down housing.

[9] Victor Provo, Mayor of Roubaix, in AMR, 'Trois autres quartiers changent de visage', 1974, p. 3.

[10] *Ibid.*

[11] *Ibid.* ; ANE: *Nord Éclair*, 1977, p. 9.

In employing these narratives, the respective municipal councils sought to avoid any question of their own involvement in the perpetuation of the poor housing conditions in either Gorbals or Alma-Gare. Areas like these had been 'slums' for many decades, but only came to be targeted for improvement in the 1950s and 1960s. Before that time, they had served a purpose, housing reserves of cheap labour, be it for the textile industry in France or the various heavy industries in Glasgow. With the post-war decline of such activities, these areas came increasingly to represent a burden for the respective municipal councils. This burden was in part fiscal, but, in an era marked by a spirit of social reform, it was also part political. In this sense, the Gorbals was a particularly loaded place, not only achieving notoriety for its living conditions, but also for alcohol abuse and gang violence. Its folkloric status was such that it was identified as the first target for comprehensive redevelopment, not only in Glasgow, but in Scotland as a whole. The attention given to the Gorbals was in large part due to a novel of no great literary merit, published in 1935 and entitled *No Mean City*.[12] It told the story of Johnnie Stark, who grew up in the Gorbals to become the most feared street-fighter and 'Razor King' of his time. The book, which depicted the Gorbals as a desperate neighbourhood of violence, alcoholism and crime, provoked much debate in Glasgow; the library committee of Glasgow Corporation decided the city's libraries should not stock the novel, since the Labour administration objected to its depiction of working class life. Certain city bookshops decided to boycott the book and, as if this was not already enough to guarantee its success, the *Sunday Mail* then decided to serialise it in November 1935. This episode sealed the fate of the Gorbals which, to this day, bears the scars inflicted by the Razor King.

Of course, there were other factors at play which persuaded local councils to start clearing their slum areas. New planning theories were coming to the fore, based on the functional zoning of the city. In both Gorbals and Alma-Gare, one of the priorities identified by the planners was the rationalisation of land use and the improvement of the road systems of the respective towns. The physical re-arrangement which this involved offered the administrations a means to restructure the population profile of the city, shifting some of the poorest and therefore, in a period of industrial decline, some of the least

---

12   McArthur and Long, 1957 [1935].

productive inhabitants of the city, to peripheral locations. In Roubaix, the council made it clear that the restructuring of Alma-Gare was an attempt to distance the town from its traditional reliance on the textile industry and recreate itself as a centre for tertiary activity. The population of Alma-Gare, and the housing it occupied, was an unwelcome relic of an outmoded economic system.[13] Whether in Roubaix or Glasgow, however, all these motives were hidden behind the essentialist definition of certain areas as 'slums'. So long as this definition was considered to be natural, neutral and common sense, then nobody challenged the municipal agenda.

An important element in the essentialist definition of particular places as 'slums' was the urban morphology. In the Gorbals, housing was in traditional tenement form, built in blocks of four storeys around a central court in which were located communal facilities such as the wash house, drying greens and the 'middens', where refuse was collected. Inside each tenement a single stairwell served each floor, and there were normally at least three flats off each landing, as well as a communal WC. Interiors were generally cramped, and some of the apartments were 'single-ends', one room apartments which, all the same, often housed a large family. In Alma-Gare, the equivalent housing was the *courées*, poor-quality workers' accommodation built around tiny courtyards. This housing, which was brick-built, normally consisted of two rooms, built one above the other, and often lacked proper foundations. In the courtyard were the shared WCs and a communal water pump. Such was the emotive power of the term '*courée*' that Roubaix's municipality could use it as a direct substitute for the term *taudis*. The *courées* were presented as symbols of shame, accessed by 'these doors that led to despair' (see fig. 1).[14]

---

[13] Paradoxically, the shift to the tertiary sector was supported by the more traditional, family-run textile firms in Roubaix which, recognising the decline of the French textile industry, were keen to move into other sectors, particularly mail order services.

[14] AMR: 'Trois autres quartiers changent de visage', 1974, p. 16.

Fig. 1 – Views of passageways leading to the *courées*, with the original heading supplied by Roubaix's municipal council. From 'Trois autres quartiers changent de visage', *Périodique d'information municipale*, August 1974, p 16, (AMR).

There is no doubt that living standards in both Gorbals and Alma-Gare were extremely poor, and it is therefore not surprising that the populations of these areas were initially keen to tap into the dream of the new future place. Indeed, some of the earliest protests organised by residents of these areas were sporadic actions intended to encourage the local councils to speed up the demolition, rebuilding and rehousing process. From this common starting point, however, the two stories take somewhat different directions.

Gorbals, Glasgow

In Gorbals, despite a series of false starts and delays, the modernist vision was carried through. The press, politicians, and also local people spoke of the 'miracle of the Gorbals' as, starting in an area called Hutchesontown, 'old Gorbals' was progressively cleared and replaced by 'new Gorbals'. The community newspaper, which in later years was to become highly critical of the new Gorbals, hailed the transformation:

> The miracle of the Gorbals! After years of wordy and empty promises from politicians, and highly coloured sensationalism in press and on television, it all began to happen [...] And not only buildings were new created in Hutchesontown. A people were created – with a common voice to be heard, in Ward Committee and Tenants Association.[15]

Moreover, this same article assigned a positive, if somewhat apocalyptic role to the bulldozer, which was sweeping away the tenements, 'And now – 1968 – we are at the beginning of the end. Now the bulldozers, mindless avengers of years of neglect, are grinding out at last the final solution for Gorbals.'[16] Some two-thirds of the Gorbal's inhabitants found themselves shipped out to peripheral housing estates, while the remainder moved into the new flats. Important architects, Basil Spence and Robert Matthew, were employed to carry out the main phases of the development and, in June 1961, the queen was invited to lay the foundation stone of the Spence development of towers and 'hanging gardens'.[17]

The transformation from old to new Gorbals involved many delays, and sections of the population were left in terrible living conditions while waiting to be rehoused. These delays provoked protest, both from local priests and ministers, who saw the conditions as 'an affront to human dignity', and from the newly formed tenants associations.[18] For example, the Gorbals and Hutchesontown Tenants Association sent a petition to the Secretary of State for Scotland complaining of rat-infested houses:

---

[15]   ML: *The Gorbals View*, p. 1, no. 10, Jan 1968.

[16]   *Ibid.*

[17]   *Glasgow Herald*, 10 June 1961, 1f, 'Royal Visit, June'.

[18]   *Glasgow Herald*, 24 June 1964, 5h, 'Priest wants Gorbals Property Demolished'.

A mother of four children said that rats were being killed but the bodies were not being removed with the result that they were floating in pools of green scum in the common back courts. 'Our children are running about the backs throwing dead rats at each other' the woman said.[19]

Given the living conditions in old Gorbals, those families who did move into the new flats were delighted to find their own bathroom and toilet, and a bedroom for each family member. For these people, the miracle of the Gorbals, as championed by the city council, was a tangible phenomenon. There was a feeling that there was a chance to make a new start. This is clear, for example, from the distress provoked by the siting of a public house in the new development in 1967. At a meeting held by the Hutchesontown Tenants Association, fears were expressed that the plan for the pub would take the area 'back to the old Gorbals'. The local MP tapped into a collective shame over the past of the area, 'If we're going to have a New Gorbals let us make it without a pub at every corner. I think the site of the public house is disgraceful and I'll fight it to the bitter end', while another speaker made the link with the essentialist definition of the area's slum past even more explicit, 'The women especially have lifted their families above the dreary image of Gorbals depicted in "No Mean City" and our councillors should be urged to raise at all levels the question of the siting of the pub.'[20]

Despite the early optimism, the dream of the new Gorbals went sour remarkably quickly. The physical fabric of the new homes deteriorated, lifts frequently broke down, and households found themselves socially isolated in high flats. Indicatively, Spence's A block came to be nicknamed Alcatraz, the B block became Barlinnie, Glasgow's own prison, while the C block was christened Sing-Sing. Interestingly, in the context of concerns about the lack of community facilities that began to emerge in the course of the 1970s, the old public houses, once despised as moral and economic drains upon the community, became the focus of a new wave of nostalgia, and it was reported that many of the former residents of Gorbals now living in peripheral estates still returned at weekends to drink in the few pubs which had survived the transformation.[21] But while the lack of

---

[19] *Glasgow Herald*, 12 June 1964, 18g, 'Rat Infested Houses: Petition to Mr Noble'.

[20] *Glasgow Herald*, 13 June 1967, 20c.

[21] See *Glasgow Herald*, 23 Jan 1975, 7a, 'Reviving Old Spirit in New Gorbals'.

community facilities was lamented, it was to prove to be defects in the physical structure of the new Gorbals project which presented the real challenge to the city council's vision. In particular, the industrially-built deck-access units proved to be problematic. These had originally been introduced with the aim of overcoming some of the problems of isolation associated with tower blocks, and as such had been welcomed by Gorbals residents. James Rae, chief city planner, painted a positive picture of the possibility of uniting innovation with tradition, 'These "streets in the air" will form definite places and thoroughfares and will contain familiar street objects such as telephone kiosks, post boxes, seating benches, planting etc., and also shops.'[22] But the 'familiar street objects' never materialised, and the deck-access units, in particular a development named Hutchesontown 'E' block (opened in 1972, again with a royal ceremony), proved to be particularly prone to problems of water penetration and dampness, so much so that 'Hutchie E' entered the city's consciousness as 'the Dampies'.

For the tenants of these new flats, water penetration meant infestations of beetles, black mould growing on walls, unpleasant odours, damp beds and ruined carpets and furniture. And beyond the threat this posed to physical good health, there were also risks to the tenants' mental health due to the stress induced by these living conditions. The city council spent years strenuously denying that the problem lay with the physical structure of the new Gorbals, and blamed the lifestyle of the tenants for creating excessive condensation. Residents were advised to turn up their heating and open their windows, hardly practical advice for low-income households, particularly during the Scottish winter. At one point the council even accused their tenants of 'breathing too heavily'.

In these circumstances, the essentialist view promoted by the city council, like the physical fabric of the new Gorbals, began to fall apart. The distinction between old Gorbals, the slum, and new Gorbals, the modernist housing dream, became increasingly blurred. A local councillor, having visited Hutchesontown 'E' described some of the flats as 'cave dwellings', while a labour MP was reported as saying that the flats, 'Were not the type of accommodation people should have to be using in the 1970s.'[23] The population of the new

---

[22] ML: *The Gorbals View*, p 13, No5, August 1967.

[23] *Glasgow Herald*, 21 December, 1976, 4a, 'Ministers Back Tenants in Damp Row'.

Gorbals began to construct a counter-place. They remembered the old Gorbals as an area of close social bonds and mutual aid, they generated a nostalgia for the times which were hard but good, and they turned their resentment on the council, which, they believed, had robbed the community of its strength. Here is a personal version of this history from the secretary of the Gorbals-Laurieston Rehousing Association. It not only suggests that the Gorbals community has been lost, but also overturns the myth of the old Gorbals by suggesting that new Gorbals is even more dangerous;

> I was born in Cavendish Street, only a few hundred yards from here. Then the area was a community, as this area was when I moved into the house 16 years ago. Then there were many butchers' and grocery shops and the things which go to make a community. Now people go to Shawlands to shop because new developments here have left no room for shops except general stores. I will not let my three younger children out on the street because of the rising rate of muggings and assaults. There is no place for them to play.[24]

Residents of damp-ridden flats began to claim that their life had been better in their old tenement houses:

> When I moved in I was quite happy. We spent every penny we had on it [the new house] and I expected to stay there for the rest of my life. Now to say I am disappointed would be an understatement. I was far better off in the old tenement property.[25]

Ironically, dampness made certain rooms unusable, and some families found themselves crowding into one room, unwillingly re-creating the classic conditions of overcrowding that had been so prevalent in old Gorbals. In all this, life in the old tenements came to be celebrated. Indeed, the physical arrangement of the tenements was credited with engendering the Gorbals' sense of community: 'The tenements [...] provided homes for generations of Gorbals families. They created a community which worked and lived well together, sharing good times as well as bad and sad times.'[26]

---

[24] *Glasgow Herald*, 3 August 1977, 4e 'Angry Gorbals Families Call for Better Homes'.

[25] Treasurer of the Laurieston and Hutchesontown Tenants Association, cited in *Glasgow Herald*, 16 September 1977, 5b, 'Mildewed Settee Goes to Court as Angry Tenants Seek Rates Cut'.

[26] The Gorbals History Reasearch Group, n. d. [1990], p. 42.

The local tenants associations drew much inspiration from the community myth. Their original purpose had been to ensure the smooth running of tenant life in the new 'miracle' homes, but they soon adopted a more conflictual position with respect to the city council. These associations united to form the Anti-Dampness Campaign in October 1975. The campaign's earliest activities involved sending hundreds of letters to the council and other authorities, and organising petitions and deputations. The campaign activists also mounted a picket of a mobile exhibition unit which had been launched by the city council to instruct tenants how to combat dampness in their homes. Gradually their activities became more ambitious, including a court action in 1977 against the council. This was attended by some 200 tenants, who brought with them as evidence a mildewed settee, bottles containing beetles taken from their homes, and examples of damp wallpaper. On 1st May 1977, the Anti-Dampness Campaign held its most successful meeting, succeeding in filling the entire Citizens' Theatre in the Gorbals. The meeting was marked by a festive atmosphere and included a theatrical skit featuring Mrs. Ivy Mould, a council house tenant, and the 'housing manager' of Glasgow District Council. Apart from invited speakers, the meeting also featured Mr. Fungus, Mr. Anti-Dampness, and a five-man 'monster', the Dampness Monster. The action of the protesters was directed at all properties affected by damp in new Gorbals, but the symbolic centre of the campaign were the flats in the Hutchesontown 'E' development, where, it was claimed, more than 70% of the units suffered from dampness.

In time, the Anti-Dampness Campaign succeeded in obtaining a rates reduction, some £500,000 of compensation from Glasgow City Council and, by 1982, the rehousing of all the residents of 'The Dampies'. At this point, the community newspaper could joke, "'E" for Empty'[27]. Even once all the residents had been rehoused, the campaign continued until, in 1987, the council undertook the demolition of the flats. The demolition of Hutchesontown 'E' marked a form of urban exorcism, as well as representing a painful and costly parody of the council's slum clearance techniques. These flats, which had started as an architectural symbol of a better future provided by the city council, had become a symbol of the destruction of a community, and this historical interpretation began to be incorporated

---

[27]   ML: *The Gorbals View*, August 1982, p. 1.

in a range of autobiographical and historical works. For example, the Gorbals History Research Group (note how Gorbals history has become something to be researched rather than escaped) wrote:

> Lots of people who used to stay in the Gorbals, as well as many who reside there, have fond memories of the old place. It was a place throbbing with vitality where neighbours chatted from their windows and gossiped at street corners [...] Many of those who have a warm nostalgia for the area do not like to be reminded of the fact that the Gorbals was allowed to fall into a disgraceful state [...] By the inter-war years it had deteriorated into slum conditions with some of the worst housing in the city.[28]

From this perspective, post-war planning operations were not an attempt to rectify these conditions, they were simply a continuation of this process of decline:

> When the area had so deteriorated the final stroke which well-nigh killed-off its social fabric as well as its crumbling built environment was the intensive blanket treatment of Comprehensive Redevelopment in the 1960s and 1970s [...] but the planners' schemes went awry. Utopia was stillborn – much of the Gorbals of the dreams has now been laid waste once more.[29]

The memory of old Gorbals was rehabilitated, and the myth of the slum was replaced by the myth of the community.

Alma-Gare, Roubaix

Let us now consider the example from France. The operation for the redevelopment of Alma-Gare, which lies just to the north-west of Roubaix's town centre, was originally scheduled for 1966, but was consistently delayed until it was finally started, in a limited area, in 1973. In Alma-Gare, and in contrast to the Gorbals, the pressure of local activists galvanised the population *prior* to demolition of their 'slum' housing.[30] The ensuing protests finally resulted in the

---

[28] The Gorbals History Reasearch Group, n.d. [1990], p. 15.

[29] *Ibid.,* p. 16.

[30] These activists belonged to the APF, the *Association Populaire Familiale*, an organisation, with Catholic roots, that worked for the improvement of the domestic environment and attempted to politicise home life.

municipal council abandoning their project for the *résorption* of the area.

In Alma-Gare, as in Gorbals, the plans for redevelopment were initially welcomed and, indeed, encouraged by residents keen to escape the *courées* and tap into the municipal council's new future. However, delays in the planning process created uncertainty and allowed the population to witness the fate of other areas of the town that were subject to the process of *résorption*. In short, the residents of Alma-Gare witnessed the original populations of these areas being decanted, after which the neighbourhoods underwent complete demolition, such that even the old street patterns were erased. Only a small proportion of the original inhabitants had either the legal right or the financial means to take up residence in one of the new flats that were constructed to replace the *courées*. Spurred on by the activists, a campaign was launched which claimed that the population should be allowed to participate actively in the planning of the new area, and that all residents who wished should be allowed to remain in Alma-Gare after the planning operation. In any case, protesters were determined that the new neighbourhood would not consist of the modernist industrial architecture or, as they put it, the 'rabbit hutches', which they saw springing up in neighbouring areas of the town.

The activists constructed a counter-place to the municipal definition of Alma-Gare as '*courées*', confronting it with a definition of Alma-Gare as '*quartier*', a term which incorporated both a social and a spatial dimension. They used the concept of *quartier* to give not only dynamism, but also coherence, to an area that, in fact, consisted of a myriad of interest groups founded upon age, ethnicity, gender, housing tenure and so on. The evident diversity of the population, which included Spanish, Polish, Portuguese and North African groups, meant that the opponents of the activists, and principally the municipal council, could have too easily discredited a definition of Alma-Gare as '*communauté*'. In February 1972, local activists held a public meeting at which they decided to set up a place where the population could meet and discuss with officials and technicians involved in the planning process, and so give concrete form to their own ideas for the area. The *Atelier populaire de l'urbanisme* (APU) thus came into being, taking as its slogan 'It's possible. We act. We reflect. We build'.[31] The organisation was open to all, and the only

---

[31] 'C'est possible. On agit. On réflechit. On construit'.

requirement for membership was part spatial and part social: 'to live in the *quartier* and to want to fight to stay there.'[32]

In the affirmation 'we're staying' *('on reste')*, the activists were assigning positive value to the *quartier*, presenting it as a place where people wished to stay and make a life. In this way, they directly confronted the municipal council and the associated clearance and rehousing organisations, which presented Alma-Gare as uninhabitable and, therefore, undesirable. While the activists associated with the APU made use of the more conventional protest tactics, such as those discussed in the Gorbals example, they also employed certain other more innovative tactics, aimed both at creating a common purpose among the inhabitants of Alma-Gare and at challenging the essentialist view of the area. They occupied strategic places, notably construction sites and the headquarters of ORSUCOMN, an organisation established specifically to clear the *courées*.[33] They also enacted examples of what they considered should be the tasks of the authorities, for example, organising a maintenance service for houses that were still inhabited, and bricking-up derelict properties in order to prevent pillaging, vandalism and illegal dumping. These kinds of activities made life more bearable for the people remaining in Alma-Gare, and helped slow the exodus from the area. Moreover, the APU began to create a memory for the *quartier* through the creation of symbolic moments. These moments were most often *fêtes* or celebrations, to which all residents of Alma-Gare were invited. On 1st May, 1975, for example, a parade of clowns moved through the *quartier* and the activists and local volunteers cleared an area of wasteland in order to create a play space for the local children. The collective memory was also reinforced by a theatrical rendition of the population's history and struggles. In November 1975, the APU organised a day during which 'outsiders' were invited to visit Alma-Gare. There were presentations on the *quartier*, and visitors were invited into homes to eat a meal and chat with residents about the events in Alma-Gare. The evening was concluded with music and dancing. This action served both to reinforce the collective identity of the *quartier*, and to encourage the visitors to see beyond the definition of *courée* slum and understand Alma-Gare as 'home' to a section of Roubaix's population.

---

[32] APU-CSCV, 1982, p. 26.

[33] Organisation pour la Suppression des Courées de la Métropole du Nord

The protesters constructed a history which tapped into the myth of the resistance and cohesion of the textile workers in the past. Ironically, while the activists even borrowed the language of workplace militancy – 'Workers organised in the factory, we also want to organise our domestic habitat *(cadre de vie)*' – few of the population of Alma-Gare belonged to what might be termed the 'traditional French working class'.[34] In particular, the North African immigrant population was viewed with hostility by the unions, who saw them as a threat to jobs and wage levels. Nonetheless, the APU promoted the myth of a cohesive community which, as in Gorbals, flourished in the spatial arrangement of the housing which had originally been constructed for the textile workers:

> One could say that the thing which gives strength to the movement in the *courées* in Roubaix – its durability, its imaginative power in its objectives and in the forms of its actions, its partial successes – is its strong and vibrant popular roots.[35]

The militants claimed that, notwithstanding their capitalist origins and deplorable living conditions, the *courées* of Alma-Gare had contributed to a collective cohesion which was the greatest strength of the community. They argued that any future development of Alma-Gare should seek to reproduce this organisation of space. Furthermore, they launched a direct attack on the municipal agenda of complete demolition by claiming that as much as 40% of the housing stock in the area could and should be preserved. In this way, they challenged the fundamental conclusion of the council's essentialist definition, namely that the only possible future for Alma-Gare was complete demolition. In all this, the bulldozer, which the municipal council had depicted as a harbinger of good, was depicted by the APU as the machine that would sweep away, indiscriminately, the life of the community.[36] Thus, for example, a widely distributed text from 1977 read, 'It's evident; if we don't put up a struggle, the bulldozer,

---

[34] From AIR: *Bulletin d'adhésion*. A sketch of two men, one in work clothes, outstretched arms interlinked, joins the image of the factory to the image of the home environment. Below, a pair of female hands hold a series of four images; *école, santé, logement* and *consommation*.

[35] APU, 1976, p. 13.

[36] The municipal publication 'Trois autres quartiers changent de visage' of 1974 which triumphantly announced the plans for the renovation of Alma-Gare and two other areas, featured a large photograph of a bulldozer sweeping away the rubble of a *courée* on the back cover.

which is now in *rue Archimède*, will continue on its course and will destroy the life of the *quartier*.'[37] It should be noted, however, that for the activists the idea of the *quartier* went deeper than social solidarity – the definition that they sought to promote was also self-serving since the *quartier* was the object which legitimised their very existence and which, since they had no official mandate, gave credibility to their claim to represent the population of Alma-Gare.

While the actions of the APU were many and varied, let us consider a particular example that provides an informative insight into the construction of local community. The 1st of May, 1974, marked what the activists chose to remember as 'a key moment in the history of the *quartier*'.[38] The APU undertook the unofficial, and indeed, illegal, rehousing of an elderly woman who lived in a *courée* in Alma-Gare. This woman, 74 years old, had lived in the *quartier* for 20 years, and had been forced to remain in her *courée* home without electricity for eight days. At the same time, other houses, in much better condition than her own, had been designated *insalubre* and were therefore legally uninhabitable. The contradictions of this situation were the result of a technical definition of *insalubrité* combined with the slow pace of the clearance process which meant that many inhabitants were left waiting for months in deplorable conditions to be rehoused, while other streets and houses, sometimes less run-down, received immediate attention. The symbolic aspect of the rehousing was emphasised to the full by the activists. A public and mock-official presentation of the keys was made to the old woman, who was known by many as '*memère*' or 'granny'. In a sense, in choosing to rehouse this woman, they were symbolically rehousing the *quartier*, its memories and experiences. The conferral of the keys, and the opening of the 'new' house in a street which was located in the geographic core of the *quartier*, was witnessed by many of the inhabitants of Alma-Gare. As an event, it was conceived in such a way as to carry the fullest impact at the level of the *quartier*, and the issues it addressed – the contradictions of the planning process, the delays in rehousing, the daily struggle against the degradation of the physical environment, and the right to 'stay where we are' – were all issues common to the population of Alma-Gare. The action was repeated on 1st May of the following year, when the activists rehoused the family

---

[37] AIR: CSCV, APU, letter re. la réunion du Groupe de Travail, 8. 6. 77.

[38] APU-CSCV, 1982, p. 26.

of an unemployed man who had recently been evicted from their home.

The APU had no intention to rehouse *all* those living in the poorest houses in Alma-Gare. In an attempt to initiate a dynamic, they appropriated the role of the re-housing authorities, but only temporarily, and moreover, the solution they presented was in itself only temporary. Their aim was to persuade the municipal council to take on this responsibility by confronting the technical definition of *insalubrité* with the social one, the definition as lived by the residents of Alma-Gare. For the activists, it was essential that the elderly members of the population should be seen to wish to remain in the area. Without them, any claim to historical continuity, any assertion that the *quartier* was an entity that existed across time, and not just in geographical space, would begin to sound hollow. They needed to create a place of continuity in the face of a reality where many of the residents of Alma-Gare were new arrivals in the *quartier*, some having fled clearance operations in other parts of the town. Thus the newsletter produced by the activists featured a cartoon strip in which an old woman explained why it was important to fight for the right to stay in the Alma-Gare and to have a say in how the future *quartier* should be planned:

> Jules – 'You seem to be in good form!'
> Old woman – 'That's because we're fighting'
> Jules – 'They want to give you a hard time too?'
> Old woman – 'They'd like to dump us who knows where in homes [...] full of old folks! But we all want to live, not die in there. I hate playing cards and I haven't worked 50 years to be treated like a kid. Now I'm staying put! Youngster!!'[39]

Critically, the concept of *quartier* directly opposed the image of Alma-Gare promoted by the municipal council, and challenged Roubaix's councillors to look beyond the idea of the *courées* as mere slums. At the same time, it encouraged the population to share in a wider concept of the idea of 'home', and provided them with a collective identity which helped to overcome the fractures and conflicts of interest that otherwise characterised the inhabitants. In part due to the efficacy of this campaign, and in part due to changing methods in the field of planning in the course of the 1970s that gave

---

[39] APU, 1976, p. 15.

more importance to public participation, the activists succeeded in achieving the majority of their goals. Indeed, in studying the events at Alma-Gare, it becomes clear that once the municipal council began to give ground on small points, for example, agreeing to wall-up vacant properties, this effectively represented a recognition of the alternative definition of Alma-Gare and offered a small foothold from which the activists could launch their next initiative.

This appraisal of the events in Gorbals and Alma-Gare has been necessarily brief. The aim here has not been to undertake a comparison of the two cases, but rather to use them to identify common themes in the construction of community at the local level. All the same, it is clear even from these short summaries that there were certain fundamental differences between the two cases. In Gorbals, the general issues concerning the redevelopment of an area of the city became crystallised around a very specific theme – that of water penetration in the new flats. The ensuing protest activity was more remarkable for its determination rather than its innovatory qualities. On the whole the Anti-Dampness Campaign employed what might be termed 'conventional' protest tactics, and opportunely rode a wave of nostalgia for the old community rather than actively created this phenomenon. In contrast, the actions in Alma-Gare were much more consciously politicised, and the final aim was especially ambitious, namely to take charge of the shaping of the urban environment, not only in physical, but also in social and economic terms. In keeping with the originality of this demand, many of the protest tactics employed were particularly innovative. These tactics suggest that the Alma-Gare activist made a conscious effort to substitute *quartier* for *courées*.

Despite these differences, it is possible to draw certain general conclusions from the two examples. First, in both the cases, the projects to demolish and reconstruct the areas were justified by an essentialist version of 'place' that, employing a specific reading of history, presented these areas as slums of one sort or another. In this dominant discourse, emphasis was placed upon the physical structure of these areas. This view was challenged by a counter definition which emphasised the idea of community and cohesion. This counter-place was founded upon a social definition of the neighbourhoods, and even appropriated their supposedly flawed physical morphology as a factor contributing to this exceptional solidarity. As the meaning of the physical structure of these areas changed, so too the meaning changed of the mechanism which brought about these changes – the 'bulldozer', as a generic term, was transformed from the herald of a new future to the destroyer of the community. It should also be noted that, in both cases, none of the actors created identities *ex nihilo*, but rather each appropriated, resurrected or promoted material which already existed in the collective memory, be it the struggles of textile workers or the exploits of razor gangs.

The second point for consideration refers to the memory invested in the bricks and mortar of these areas. The tenements and *courées* were clearly not constructed as monuments, but this is effectively what they became. They assumed the role of 'empty monuments' which were filled with meaning as the situation required, and the collective memory of the community was adjusted accordingly. Thus, the *courées* went from symbols of exploitation to symbols of resistance (although they continued, simultaneously, to have negative connotations). In Glasgow, the physical removal of the tenements meant that they existed as symbols of community cohesion *only* in the collective memory, and in this sense, they were less problematic than the *courées*. Their original, negative significance was transferred to the system-built blocks provided by the city council, which in turn became the new slums.

Lastly, it may be useful to reflect upon the meaning of these events with respect to national identities. It should be pointed out that both these examples concern traditionally marginalised members of society – to a large extent these populations represented an urban underclass and not, despite the rhetoric of the Alma-Gare activists, a cohesive working-class community. For this reason, there was little scope for either movement to tap into national class discourse. Perhaps it is telling that the housing model which the APU in Alma-Gare finally selected as being most appropriate for the *quartier* was derived from a middle-class residential suburb of Brussels. The two populations were not only socially marginalised, they were also geographically marginalised. Roubaix and Glasgow are both provincial with respect to the respective national cores of economic and political power, and those who most often attempted to locate their position with respect to a national reference were the city councils rather than the activists. In Roubaix, the socialist council repeatedly put the blame on Gaullist central government for the early delays in the Alma-Gare operation, while Glasgow City Council blamed central government for having encouraged the use of industrial construction techniques. Moreover, as a result of Glasgow's council dragging its feet over the implementation of Margaret Thatcher's Conservative government's programme in the 1980s to sell off council housing, central government imposed spending restrictions upon the council. These prevented it undertaking the massive repairs required by the city's public housing stock.

On the other hand, the tenants groups in both Alma-Gare and Gorbals rarely referred to national government. When, in 1980, the Gorbals community newspaper ran the headline, 'Free Sponge With Every Council House! 1 out of every 5 council houses suffer from dampness = is this why Maggie Thatcher calls council tenants spongers?', this was a rare example of tenant discontent finding expression with respect to Westminster.[40] Moreover, it can justifiably be pointed out that these few examples have much more to do with political partisanship than with resentment in the periphery being directed at the national centre. Perhaps we should not be surprised by these findings. By necessity, both movements fed upon their local history and experience, finding their dynamism from the 'interior', for how else could they justify their claim to community strength

---

[40] ML: *The Gorbals View*, April 1980, p. 1.

CHAPTER 6

Political Stage-Setting. The Symbolic Transformation of Berlin[1]

Beate BINDER

After the fall of the Berlin Wall in 1989, German reunification in 1990 and the decision of parliament in 1991 to move the government from Bonn, the city of Berlin has become a massive building site – sometimes considered to be the largest in Europe. 'Free' areas in the middle of the city, particularly along the line of the former wall, have been given new uses and new owners, and the building density in inner city areas has increased. The reshaping of the city has not only been driven by commercial projects; the planned move of the government from Bonn to Berlin has been followed by substantial rebuilding and reconstruction work, as well as by projects for new buildings. A visit to the Info-Box at Leipziger Platz, where two of the major players in this process, the public transport company and the marketing corporation Partner für Berlin (Partners for Berlin), present the projects that are under way around Potsdamer Platz and Leipziger Platz; a walk through the exhibition at the former Staatsratsgebäude (the building of the State Council at the Schloßplatz) in which the

---

[1] The following paper is part of a research project entitled 'The Staging of Power: Making the Berlin government quarter a representational space', which started in January 1998 at the Institute of European Ethnology in Berlin. In very general terms, this project aims to follow up and describe, in ethnographical terms, the process of rebuilding the city of Berlin for its role as the capital of Germany and preparing it for its governmental functions. Many thanks to Christian Kumpe and Tatjana Eggeling for the translation of this text.

German government explains the planning of the governmental buildings; or a look at the government's homepages, all show that the rebuilding project does not concern only the material shape of Berlin.[2] Before the projects materialise in stone, glass and concrete, the readings of the 'New Berlin' will be designed and elaborated, and it is this which will provide the motivation and the legitimation for the changes to come, and facilitate their integration. In short, in the transition from the divided city to the new capital, the focus will mainly be on the symbolic transformation of Berlin. Only this double rebuilding – the physical one and the cognitive-symbolic one – will produce a Berlin that will be the symbol of, and the setting for the new *Berliner Republik*. Even this term, which has been used more frequently since 1996, indicates that, with the move of the government, something new will begin. An historical place of political power will once again be made the setting for national politics – a unique process in 20th century Europe. Consequently, there are complex problems of interpretation connected with this move. At the same time, the city has to be prepared for its new duties of representation.

In this complex process, history becomes a key source of contestation. Drawing upon elements of *Berliner*, German and, to some extent, also European and international history, the past is remembered in such a way as to give these changes the highest possible degree of plausibility and legitimacy. Images of history are being reconstructed, collective memory and national identity re-shaped, traditions founded and places of memory and symbols of representation 'morphed' into urban landscape, all with the intention of making Berlin a representative capital.

In the course of the rebuilding process and the search for, or construction of, meaningful references, there is a confrontation of different concepts and interpretations. There are concepts of the 'correct' representation of Germany, and the impact of the 'old, new capital' in domestic, European and international terms, and there are the interpretations of the continuities and discontinuities as they are perceived in both Berlin's and Germany's histories. The actors in these quarrels are mainly politicians, experts and local, national and, to some extent, international elites, as well as spokespersons for local and supra-regional interest groups. With this recourse to history, a

---

[2] <http://www. berlin. de/deutsch/politik/hauptstadt/standorte_parlament /B1S3D/index. html. >

new discursive space has been opened for the debate over the future shape of the city. The strategy of historical legitimation offers at least two perspectives. On the one hand, that Berlin's physical rebuilding and reconstruction, as well as its symbolic transformation into a representative capital, can be justified and made meaningful. On the other, that it is possible to historically justify counter-concepts that put the official plans into question. Between these extreme positions lie a whole range of intermediate strategies. In each case, the politics of historical argumentation aim at establishing a certain reading of Berlin, both for the city as a whole and for particular areas. In this way, both big and small stories and narratives of the city's history are woven into the urban texture and the urban space becomes an interpreted landscape.

In this chapter, I will take a closer look at the connections between the politics of history and the perceptions of the city, and I will examine the social conflicts that emerge in the course of this reinterpretation. From the perspective of the built environment, it is also interesting to examine the role which architecture and urban design play in the process of reconstructing collective identities.

Yi-Fu Tuan emphasises that the perception of a city as a historically-grown product may be misleading: 'A landscape littered with old buildings does not compel anyone to give it a historical interpretation; one needs a "discerning eye" for such a viewpoint.'[3] Of course, the diverse architectural styles that exist side by side in European cities make it easy to consider the passage of time and history, but this is only because the 'discerning eye' is connected to a system of meanings and interpretations and is thus embedded in individual and collective identities. Different meanings are added to both new and historical objects, depending on the social context. Therefore the perception and interpretation of a historically grown city is always connected with collective memory and shared images of history.

Two different approaches might bring us closer to understanding the nature of this connection. In the context of his reflections on the functioning of collective memory, Maurice Halbwachs has already drawn attention to the fact that what is seen on a walk through a city is

---

[3] Tuan, 1997, p. 192.

always determined by the view of other persons.[4] Pierre Nora has emphasised the meaning of *lieux de memoire* for the construction of national identities, but has given less attention to the juxtaposition of conflicting interpretations and the process of producing shared imagined spaces of history.[5] Whereas Nora's approach emphasises the meaning of historically impregnated geographical spaces as a constituent part of structures of collective identity,[6] geographical and ethnological investigations first consider the social appropriation of urban space. Thus Sharon Zukin focuses on the point that the attempt to establish a certain perception of landscape is one of the central strategies in current social quarrels about the appropriation of space.[7] These 'politics' have the aim of giving space a singular and essentialist identity and, at the same time, of establishing a certain use of that space.[8]

From this double perspective, the history of a particular place becomes an important point of contention and source of social conflict. This point of departure of my chapter is the same as the viewpoint of Michael Miller in the previous chapter. A certain space can be turned into a place for the identification of a given social group through the assignation of historical narratives to that place, thus making the history of the group visible. Personal experience associated with a certain place plays only a minor role in the construction of collective identity. Rather, historical images are connected with the constructed environment in such a way that it appears to be an objective manifestation of history. As elements in the construction of identity, both history and urban space are fragile and, within certain bounds of plausibility, they undergo constant reinterpretation. They are therefore products as well as objects of social processes and debates. In the course of globalisation, and the changed meaning it has given to the local, the shape of a city acquires a central function: by

---

4   Halbwachs, 1994 [1925]. Cf. Lutz Niethammer's chapter for a discussion of Halbwachs.

5   Cf. Nora, 1984-1986. Although Nora does not limit *Lieux de mémoire* to places that exist in a geographical sense, his considerations are certainly valid for them.

6   Cf. Assman, 1988, here p. 11.

7   Zukin, 1992 and 1995.

8   Cf. Massey, 1994; Massey and Jess, 1995.

becoming the source of images and memories, it accordingly decides on who 'belongs' to the city and who does not.[9]

For the remainder of this chapter, I will develop my argument by means of a specific example. The debates about the future location of the German Foreign Office in Berlin clearly show how different historical interpretations of the site in question structure the actual perception of the place and its surroundings and serve as justification for either the acceptance or refusal of the plans. I will start with a brief description of the different perspectives and the conflicts associated with them. I will then focus on the strategies by which the official reading of the site selected for the Foreign Office has been established, and I will question the strategies that have been used to represent the corpus of historical images with the aim of fixing the identity of a place.

Two groups of experts, planners and historians, play a major role because they supply central figures in the debate. Architects and city planners emphasise aesthetic values and spatial structures. Their presentation technique, which usually involves plans and elevations as well as computer simulations, visualises their interpretation.[10] In this context, the *Berliner Republik* is mainly established by the shape of façades and sequences of urban spaces. Historians, on the other hand, evaluate the past and develop criteria for what is worthwhile preserving in our urban surroundings and what is not. By connecting historically complex processes with buildings, squares or streets, a profound dimension is added to the visible surface representing Germany.

The Space: The Schloßplatz

The Foreign Office is one of ten ministries that have to transfer their headquarters from Bonn to Berlin. About 2,000 employees will move to Berlin, while some 300 will remain in Bonn. After the capital resolution in June 1991, when the federal government together with the Berlin senate developed the initial concept for the distribution of government functions in Berlin, it was planned to construct a new building for the Foreign Office on the Schloßplatz, still known then as

---

[9]   Zukin, 1995.

[10]   Cf. Fischler, 1995, pp. 13-58, esp. pp. 23 ff.

Marx-Engels-Platz.[11] Situated in the former East Berlin, the square is still dominated by government and official buildings of the GDR which frame an empty space. After the demolition of the heavily damaged city castle (Stadtschloß) in 1950, the first building to be built on the southern edge of the square was the Staatsratsgebäude, headquarter of the *Staatsrat*, the Council of State of the GDR. Included on the front of this building, which was constructed in the 1960s, there is a small piece of the old city castle – a portal with the balcony from which Karl Liebknecht proclaimed the German Republic in 1918.[12] The building has been classified as an historical monument. The eastern edge of the square consists entirely of the Palast der Republik, built in the tradition of the culture houses of the workers' movement, and including the assembly hall of the former *Volkskammer* (the parliament of the GDR), conference rooms, restaurants, cafes, a theatre, a bowling club and a youth club. The Palast der Republik was built in the 1970s and opened in 1976. Due to asbestos contamination the building was closed in 1990 and has been vacant ever since. The western side of the square was demarcated by the GDR's Ministry of Foreign Affairs. The building was torn down in 1995 and replaced by an area of grass. The northern side is formed by the Unter den Linden Strasse, with the Lustgarten, a museum and the dome on the opposite side.

In 1992 a competition for the urban development of the whole area was announced, with the briefing that it should 'prepare the reordering of the urban development of Berlin'.[13] The explanatory notes given to the competitors permitted them to demolish all three buildings. These notes also invited the participants to find locations for the Foreign Office, the Ministry of the Interior and a conference centre, and to develop – with regard to historical structures – a new urban concept for the whole area. Although the budget committee of the German

---

[11] Senatsverwaltung für Bau- und Wohnungswesen Berlin, 1993.

[12] Cf. Michel, 1993.

[13] *Internationaler Städtebaulicher Ideenwettbewerb Spreeinsel.* 2. Phase. Ausgelobt von der Bundesrepublik Deutschland und dem Land Berlin, vertreten durch das Bundesministerium für Raumordnung, Bauwesen und Städtebau, die Bundesbaudirektion, die Senatsverwaltung für Stadtentwicklung und Umweltschutz. Durchführung: Arbeitsgemeinschaft Wettbewerb Spreeinsel. Berlin, Bonn, Januar 1994 (The Spreeinsel International Competition for Urban Design Ideas). The competition area covered the whole Spreeinsel, so it was much bigger than the Schloßplatz.

government demanded that use be made of the old state-owned buildings, the plans for a new Foreign Office were maintained. Klaus Kinkel, Foreign Minister from 1992 until 1998, justified his demand for a new building by stressing the special importance of his department and claiming that, together with the President and the Chancellor, his ministry was supposed to embody the appropriate representation of Germany.[14] But while this was going on, the Marx-Engels-Platz and its surrounding buildings had become 'contested space', and the plans for its future were brought into question. There are three distinct readings of the square which confront each other, and the influence of each of these readings depends upon the power of the actors who support them. This chapter will examine each of the three in turn.

1) The Platz as Developing Area

The organisers of the competition made a point of expressing the hope 'that with a convincing design, the historic spatial centre of Berlin can be reclaimed.'[15] This formulation provides two interpretations of the area. First, it considers that the area is in need of development, that something has been lost that must now be found. Secondly, this formulation implies that this task is of the highest priority because this inner city district is equated with the 'historic centre' of Berlin. This is a reference to Berlin's early history, when, more than 750 years ago, the city consisted of the two villages of Berlin and Cölln, both located in this very area. Nevertheless, the designation of this area as the historic centre is by no means self-evident. Town planner and urban sociologist Harald Bodenschaft convincingly shows that Berlin had no distinct 'central point' until 1945, not only because of its polycentric structure that resulted from the incorporation of many smaller urban centres, but also because the governmental and business centre was not fixed and tended to 'shift' from one part of the city to another.[16] When the area of the first settlement is identified as the centre of town, all this complex history will be ignored, and the city will be described as being centred around a single, fixed core. It will take some time to become accustomed to this restructuring, especially from the perspective of the former West

---

[14] *Die Tageszeitung* 7.12.1992, p. 25; *Tagesspiegel* 17.5.1994, p. 7.

[15] Internationaler Städtebaulicher Ideenwettbewerb Spreeinsel, pp. 125 f.

[16] Bodenschatz, 1995, pp. 11-15.

Berlin since, for a long time, this area has been barely accessible.[17] Moreover, the contemporary form of the square can only be regarded critically when compared to its 'historic' meaning. Nor does it seem to live up to the role of 'pulse generating', as the metaphor of the heart implies. The square has been described as empty and deserted and, consequently, as unworthy of the central function assigned to it. At the same time, the government of the GDR, with its concept of 'socialist city planning' has been condemned as being responsible for 'an almost complete loss of historical identity' because the 'inflationary width' of the square shows no feeling for scale and proportion, thus making it impossible to comprehend the structure of the historical city.[18] By means of this argument, the existing 'socialist city planning' is transformed into a symbol of undemocratic government. The square was planned as a huge field for parades and mass events and was framed by buildings which exemplify the failure of urban development under the sign of modernity. Since the present situation is seen as a failure, the new shaping of the square does not aim to invent, but rather to reconstruct a lost identity. The future form of the area is supposed to orientate itself as far as possible upon the historical structures that lie under the surface of the square. These structures are considered to be the real link to history and so offer the possibility for the area to achieve a positive identification for itself.

At the same time, according to this reading, identity should also be created by the construction of urbanity. Recent discussions have avoided a precise definition of the term 'urbanity', but it generally refers to a mixture of urban specific functions coupled with as high a development density as possible in order to compel people to encounter the 'strange'. Thus the term 'urbanity' means the search for 'lively street life'. The historical ideal is the image of a 'European City' which also incorporates pre-war Berlin. When the tradition of the European city is adopted in this idealised way, it remains unsullied by overcrowding, dirt, social problems and unemployment. Without all these negative aspects, the image of a lively urban culture develops into a landscape of stimuli in the urban space.[19] Although the former Schloßplatz, as the centre of the imperial *Kaiserreich*, never fitted this image of diversity and liveliness, the concept of urbanity is

---

[17]   Cf. *Stadtforum* No 3, 1991, p. 8.
[18]   Cf. *Stadtforum* No 7, 1992, p. 1.
[19]   Cf. Häussermann, 1995, pp. 12-14.

144

nevertheless claimed for this place and, moreover, taken as the basis for future plans. The competition papers mention that the reordering is supposed to pick up 'former qualities' and, in doing so, 'create a centre for Berlin that unites social life and social activities'.[20]

2) The Platz as Space of Experience

In opposition to these perceptions, the majority of interest groups in East Berlin claim that the existing buildings are part of their history and represent a resource for an 'Eastern' identity. From this perspective, the history of the GDR, through which the square took its contemporary form, is pushed into the forefront while the proposals contained in the new plans are seen as part of the widespread colonisation of the east. In contrast to the dominant reading that characterises the buildings as ugly and, with respect to the old city, destructive, the square is perceived as a link to a special experience in German history. In particular, the Palast der Republik is described as a place of lived experience, as a place where corporate celebrations, wedding parties and other family events took place, or simply as a place where some happy hours could be spent. When, in March 1993, the so-called *Hauptstadtbeschluß* (the decision that Berlin should be the new capital) included the proposal to demolish the Palast der Republik, around 1,000 people marched around the building carrying signs that read, 'This house is property of the people' or 'Peace to the Palace because it's the people's hut'.[21] At the same time, the cultural experience associated with 'Erich's Lampshop' – the nickname given to the Palast der Republik – is pushed into the centre of the debate, and it is claimed that the building represents an experience of being a Berliner that goes beyond all strict political ideologies. Embedded in the discourse concerning German reunification, this interpretation has become so powerful that, to this day, all planned projects for the area of the Palast der Republik have been prevented.

This position directly puts into question the aesthetic categorisation of urban space as promoted by the planners and architects. This reading of the square seeks to make it clear that identity cannot be designed by means of buildings and blueprints alone, but that the

---

[20] Internationaler Städtebaulicher Wettbewerb Spreeinsel, p. 116.

[21] Die *Tageszeitung* 29.3.1993. In this context the following booklets are also interesting: Ellereit and Wellner (Hg), 1996; Hertl, no year.

people living in the city create identity by using the buildings. A communicative memory close to everyday experience is given priority over a collective memory frozen in a monument and urban ground plans.[22]

3) The Platz as an Expression of a Lost Identity

The situation has become more complicated since a third element has entered the scene, making demands for the reconstruction of the Stadtschloß, the old City Castle. One of the strongest promoters of this idea is the Förderverein Berliner Stadtschloß e.V., which unites the most important pro-reconstruction interests. This group describes the demolition of the castle in 1950 as an act of barbarism and claims that only a reconstruction of the old castle, as close as possible to the original or, at very least, the reconstruction of its façade, can resurrect the historical centre and so re-establish Berlin's identity. A further argument says that if the castle is not rebuilt, everyone will believe that it was destroyed in World War II and, therefore, that Germany as a whole was to blame for its destruction. In fact, the GDR government alone was responsible for this act, because they had the power to preserve or destroy the building.[23] This interpretation focuses on the Schloß, and declares it as the centre of *Gesamtkunstwerk* Berlin: 'Berlin was not home to the castle, Berlin was the castle' is one of the group's key slogans. Only the castle, as a symbol of *Berliner*, Prussian and German history before 1933, is able to reconstruct the identity of the city. In 1993-4, in order to recreate the visual impression of the old Schloßplatz, a metal framework was erected and clad with canvas, on which the old façade had been painted. Through this construction, the imaginary shape of the castle assumed physical dimensions, and the calls for its reconstruction were given a visual reference. Meanwhile, the remains of the castle cellar have been excavated, and the association has installed an exhibition that shows the former dimensions of the castle on the basis of the existing remains.

All three positions discussed above attempt to connect architecture or cityscape to distinct readings of history. The value they assign to the present form of the square is founded upon the past in order to

---

[22] Cf. for this distinction Assmann 1988.

[23] For example, I have heard this argument in a discussion organised by the *Verein Historisches Berlin* on 23.9.1998. Fc. as well: Berliner Extrablatt. Hg. vom Förderverein Berliner Stadtschloß e. V., Januar und Juli 1998.

derive legitimacy and justification for future construction initiatives. From the theoretical position of Sharon Zukin, all three try to establish a specific reading of the area in order to obtain (political) power in the process of its design and so have their own identity constructions added to the use and representation of the cityscape.

Although all three employ the past in order to legitimise both the present appearance and the future plans, these linkages are constructed in different ways and different symbolic spaces of collective memory are built. The present of the place is interpreted through particular elements of the past, which are partly imagined, like an archaeological stratum buried under the visible surface. The excavation is supported by films, pictures, *memoires* and stories of 'old Berlin' which are referred to as representations of the 'real' past, and are particularly adept at evoking the square's pre-war status. Exhibitions, guided tours of the city and public discussions fix these pictures of the past. In particular, it is the advocates of the Palast der Republik and of the Stadtschloß who use their particular constructions of the past to mobilise group-specific emotions and to lend themselves cohesion. The buildings, and to a certain degree also the square itself, are described as safe places for memory, protecting it against contemporary confusion while giving support to civic identity.

Yet, until now, none of the views that have been outlined here has been able to win completely. The listing of the Staatsratsgebäude as an historical monument is no longer questioned.[24] On the other hand, it is still disputed whether the Stadtschloß should be reconstructed and whether the Palast der Republik should be demolished or integrated into this reconstruction or, alternatively, whether completely new plans should be drawn up. There is no end to these discussions. Many call for a decision soon, because the emptiness of the square is perceived as a wound in the city, while interim solutions, for example, the use of the square as a circus or fairground, are felt to be too painful. But in contrast to other parts of Berlin, like the Potsdamer Platz with its new buildings nearing completion, the Schloßplatz

---

[24] At the moment the building is used by the Ministry for Spatial Planning, Building and Urban Development. On the ground floor there is an exhibition entitled '*Bundeshauptstadt Berlin und Bundesstadt Bonn*', while on the first floor Förderverein Berliner Stadtschloß e. V. shows a mock-up of the Schloßplatz before World War II. Until the completion of the new Chancellor's residence near the Reichstag, the Chancellor will have his office here.

remains almost unchanged. All the same, Marx-Engels-Platz was rechristened with its former name, Schloßplatz, as early as autumn 1994. In this sense, the interests that wanted to revise post-war developments and link present-day Berlin to the situation prior to 1933 have had the upper hand. But this change did not come about without severe arguments on the political level between the district administration, legally responsible for changes in street names, and the Senate of Berlin, which had the final say on city matters (*Fachaufsicht*). While the district supported the East Berlin view which interpreted the renaming as an expropriation of a special experience, the Senate based its decision on the necessity to reconstruct the historical centre of Berlin. It therefore followed the recommendations of a commission, which included several historians, that had been appointed by the Senate itself. In their final report the commission wrote that, with the old name, the 'wish of the public to appreciate this urban, historically significant area in the appropriate manner' would be complied with. Historically significant and known beyond the bounds of Berlin, the old name would allow 'the recollection of the place of the former castle, which had been a centre of the city, and upon which the centre of Berlin had been focused'.[25] Furthermore, the Senate of Berlin and the commission declared that street names are part of the process of tradition founding. In this sense, the honourable remembrance of persons, especially in 'the prestigious parts of the city like the governmental districts or historical centres', is regarded as 'a declared confession of the capital as well as of the whole nation'. Therefore, Marx and Engels should no longer be commemorated, at least in this part of the city. In the act of renaming, it became clear that the establishment of the structures of collective identity in the cityscape is linked to political power. In the end, the images promoted by the political decision-makers will be the visible ones, but the memory of the 'dissidents' will have no material basis and so become nearly invisible.

The Building: The Foreign Office

Despite the seemingly endless struggles over the future design of the Marx-Engels-Platz and the Schloßplatz, the project for the governmental move was urgent. Because of the designation of the Staatsratsgebäude as an historical monument, this relatively small

---

[25] Senatsverwaltung für Verkehr und Betriebe, 1994.

building could not be altered to meet the requirements of the huge Foreign Office. Finally, the nearby Reichsbank was chosen as the new residence of the Foreign Office, and there is an extension currently under construction.

As the Berlin newspaper *Der Tagesspiegel* pointed out, the Reichsbank is 'a building that impressively unites German past and present.'[26] It's construction was originally intended to be on the basis of an architectural competition in the early 1930s (in fact, the last such competition in which the *Neues Bauen* architects took part prior to the advent of National Socialist architecture), but the results of the competition were ignored and the Nazis took the opportunity to erect their first prestige building project in Berlin. The Reichsbank was built between 1934 and 1938 on the plans of Heinrich Wolff. After World War II, the virtually undamaged building became first the centre of the Berlin *Stadtkontor*, and then, from 1950 on, it was home to the Ministry of Finance of the GDR. From 1959 until 1989, it was the seat of the Central Committee of the SED. In 1990, following the closure of the Palast der Republik due to asbestos, it served as the 'House of the Parlamentarians' until reunification in October 1991. During this period it housed the 'one and only freely elected' parliament *(Volkskammer)* of the GDR. With reunification, the building became property of the Federal Government.[27]

For Minister Kinkel, the decision to move the Foreign Office to the Reichsbank involved the task of giving the building a new image. This image had to connect the future function of the building with its history. Although he had fought long for the construction of a new building, Kinkel now had to give his public support to the opinion that the Reichsbank building was the best location to provide a home for the Foreign Office in Berlin. As a result of public comments and criticisms that, with the redesignation of Berlin as its capital, Germany was on the way back to centralism or, even worse, Fascism, Kinkel employed a strategy of historical legitimation, while hardly mentioning the practical and functional requirements of an administrative building at all. He used the symbolic meaning of the

---

[26]   *Der Tagesspiegel*, 25.8.1996, p. 12.

[27]   Vgl. *Foreign affairs,* 1997, p. 44. In 1991 the building was given the official title of *Haus der Parlamentarier* in the papers of the design competition, and it remained such until it was renamed according to its original function.

new headquarters in a twofold way: on the one hand he referred to the building itself, which, in keeping with the societal discourse, he presented as a 'witness' of the past; on the other hand, he reverted to the location of the Reichsbank in Berlin. In this way, the aesthetics of the reconstruction work and the new location of the Foreign Office are interpreted as symbols of change, while history guarantees that the nature of these changes is 'correct'. For this purpose, continuities and discontinuities in German history are pointed out, and the various uses of the building are related to phases of German foreign policy, all the time maintaining a strict separation between Us and the Other. In this construction, the aims of future German foreign policy can be positively positioned, and, in recent years, these interpretations have become more and more established as a canon of values and images that appear as a set of standard phrases in all statements.

On the occasion of the foundation-stone ceremony for the extension building, Kinkel declared in an interview given to a Berlin newspaper that, 'The spirit of a building is made by its residents. The Foreign Office will change "Honecker's Fortress" into an international and open house – for the people of Berlin, for 20,000 visitors a year and for all our partners all over the world.'[28] Kinkel then went on to connect the various historical layers of the building and the phases of German foreign policy with the 'correct' emotions. So he promised to preserve the 'good traditions', especially the role the foreign service played in the resistance against Nazism (while not forgetting 'their faults and their share of guilt before 1945'). At the same time, he pointed out the symbolic character of the building 'for the people in the eastern parts of our country who, after 1945, had their freedom refused by the central committee of the SED from this house.' Finally, he emphasised that he is proud to work in the building where the first freely elected *Volkskammer* of the GDR had decided upon the accession of the five new states to the FRG. Kinkel made use of one of the central strategies of contemporary German historical discourse whereby the past, and especially Nazism, is not ignored, but there are means to separate this past from the present without denying the continuities (cf. Bernhard Giesen's chapter in this book on the construction of German identity after Nazism). All references to German history are used in accordance with the rules provided by the societal discourse. In this way, 'good traditions' can be separated from

---

[28] *Der Tagesspiegel*, 7.4.1998, p. 11.

bad ones and become part of one's own construction of tradition beyond complex historical analysis.

In his interview, Kinkel also connected different political eras with different urban spaces. The old Foreign Office had been situated on the Wilhelmstraße, the street in which the main government functions of National Socialist Germany had been concentrated. Now the Foreign Office would start its work at the Werderscher Markt, in the heart of old Berlin – in the so-called 'historical centre'. This new location was presented as a guarantee of the changed image of Germany and of the quality of the future *'Berliner Republik'*, which would not return to the old centralistic governmental forms of the years before 1945.

In the building itself, all historical elements will be preserved. The architect Hans Kollhoff, whose firm is responsible for the reconstruction, has worked out a concept that accepts the substance of the building and will keep alive the different historical layers contained within it. Echoing Kinkel's remarks, Kollhoff's office points out that the construction and design will add a third layer to that which already exists, thus giving sense to the new function and meaning of the house, while all historical layers will remain legible. On this principle, the former cash hall will be restored to its condition in 1940, while the interior of the adjoining chamber will be kept as it was in the era of the GDR. In this way, the building will become a place of memory for very different parts of German history that, together, form a mosaic of historical particles. To prevent any association with the striking monumentality of the National Socialist buildings, a new colour scheme will add yet another layer to the building, starting with the entrance hall, which will acquire an air of spaciousness and representativeness.[29] Although no one today can gauge the impact the building will have upon its future visitors, the presentation and the interpretation of the new concept already form a horizon of expectations that will tune the 'discerning eye' according to the optical impression.[30]

---

[29] Cf. Häussermann, 1995, pp. 28-30, or the exhibition panels in the *Staatsratsgebäude*.

[30] Of course the groups that do not agree with the governmental move reject this interpretation. The exhibition *'Baustop. Randstadt'* (NGBK 28.8.-11.10.1998) makes this position explicit by reading the governmental move as part of the

While the old building of the Reichsbank receives its new image through reinterpretation, the extension to its front has already been planned and designed as a symbol of a democratic government, demonstrating transparency and openness. Its two architects, Thomas Müller and Ivan Reimann, provide an interpretation of their proposals that fits the general aims of the government move to an astonishing degree: 'The building does not want to be an isolated block, but a part of the city. In its open courtyards it manifests the public character of the building itself.'[31] The two architects proposed glass façades and wide halls, and used architectonic techniques that evoked the desired goals of transparency and, above all, of democracy.[32] The published images of the extension building show the view from inside the hall, looking out. The observer looks at the old city framed by the new windows. The Friedrichswerdersche Kirche and the Schinkelsche Bauakademie, yet to be rebuilt, will become points of reference for the 'new', freezing the past in a picture and creating a place for German foreign policy.

Performing the Future

The integration of the new Foreign Office into the city as a representation of the new capital that now stands for co-operation and openness is not only supported by words and images, but also by symbolic performances. These events put the newly constructed images of both the Reichsbank building and the Foreign Office to the test. The design of such events, their programme and their speeches try to put the image and the historical-political interpretation of both the building and the government office on stage. On such occasions, the design of Berlin as Germany's capital is tested and established. The Foreign Office has already carried out a number of such events, with the aim of addressing different target groups. In 1996, for example, an open house event took place in the Reichsbank building.

---

ongoing politics of expelling people who do not fit into Berlin's new image as capital.

[31] *Foreign Affairs*, p. 69. The two architects, Müller and Reimann, won the second prize in the architectural competition. Max Dudler's blueprint, which took 1st prize, 'does not live up to the task of a Foreign Ministry, which wants to open itself up to the centre of the city at the very least architecturally, if not otherwise.' Thus, Minister Kinkel and Töpfer, the Minister for Construction, quickly gave their support to the 2nd prize.

[32] Cf. Haberlik, 1997, p. 15.

Then in 1997, Kinkel invited the diplomatic corps on a boat trip through the historic centre of the new capital. Of course, the tour passed the new home of the Foreign Office. In the same year, an exhibition of German foreign politics from 1870 until the present was opened at the State Library. Finally, the foundation-stone ceremony was held in April 1998. All these event-like productions allowed different interest groups to experience the rebuilding of the city which, until that time, had remained largely rhetorical and imaginary. The celebratory and festive atmosphere of such events helps to develop positive feelings for the promised future. For a moment, the outlined future becomes reality, while the tasks that lie ahead for Berlin and the Foreign Office are connected to the space where this future will take place. The politics of ritual performance complete the strategy of historical legitimation in the process of symbolic transformation by integrating people into the designed image of the future.

Paul Connerton has demonstrated that taking part in social commemorative performances conveys and sustains collective memory and the order of the past.[33] He shows very convincingly how societies construct or maintain their historical and social memories through a repertoire of public rituals, political ceremonies and symbolic acts. Banquets, exhibitions and festivals are, furthermore, suitable for controlling the collective memory and thus legitimising political ideologies and goals. In his argument, Connerton refers mainly to the meaning of collective memory for contemporary social life. The acts in and around the Foreign Office can also be interpreted in this context because they are intended to establish the new interpretation of the building and to structure its history. But they also highlight another aspect of the relationship between the intentions behind this construction of memory and its efficacy. Precisely because the celebrations and events point to the future, the building or the area in which they take place plays a special role in the mediation between past and future. It is at the very moment of stepping into the area and walking through the building that individual and group memories become co-ordinated and, at the same time, are committed to the new structure of memory. Participation produces the meaning of the area, and the symbolic connotations of the acts correspond to its historical structure.

---

[33] Connerton, 1989.

A closer look at the open house event illustrates this argument. The slogan of the day was 'The Foreign Office is looking forward to Berlin.' Considering the great resistance of many civil servants in Bonn to the transfer of the government, this slogan is very positive and shows clearly the enthusiasm of the Foreign Office for its new home. At the same time, it demonstrates the efforts to reconcile Berlin with its new duty as capital. On the one hand, the open house event offered an opportunity to present the work of the Foreign Office and inform visitors about its working methods. On the other, it introduced the building as a place of memory. As visitors walked through the building and visited Erich Honecker's former study or the conference room of the last *Volkskammer*, they conquered one of the most secret and closed spaces of the old GDR, a space that was an icon of this centralist and anti-democratic socialist government. In this way, they simultaneously illustrated and made real the image that had been designed for the Foreign Office, that of an open house. As Kinkel pointed out in his speech, they turned Honecker's Fortress into an open house long before the actual move. Representatives of more than 20 nations completed this image of openness by offering culinary specialities in the courtyard.

Conclusion

The cases discussed in this chapter have demonstrated some of the dimensions of the symbolic transformation of Berlin. Because of the massive actual and historical problems of interpretation connected with the move of the government, this move is accompanied by the reconstruction of images of history and the restructuring of places of memory, or memoryscapes. The strategies of historical legitimation and ritual performance serve both to give the sought-after changes a high degree of plausibility and to represent the corpus of images, to shape the way they are experienced and so strengthen the coherence of the desired development. Both strategies are connected to architecture and cityscapes and aim at establishing a definite interpretation of the urban space. The examples also show the importance of the constructed physical environment for the construction of collective social identities. In buildings and cityscapes, unstable social constructions can be connected with something apparently 'fixed', which seems to have an existence of its own. But a closer look at the interpretations of the constructed environment shows that this too is the result of efforts to definitively fix the way it is perceived and therefore is also a product of socio-cultural processes and discussions. On the one hand, the symbolic transformation of Berlin into the capital of Germany is part of the comprehensive discourse of societal self-understanding. On the other, the competition between different designs and different interpretations of the role of Berlin shows that this discourse is socially structured. It is impossible to introduce and represent all designs in an equally powerful way. The creation of a new symbolic cityscape will finally decide who is represented in the new city, and in which way.

CHAPTER 7

Italian Fascism and Roman Heritage:
The Third Rome of Mussolini

Steen Bo FRANDSEN

Roma è il nostro punto di partenza e di riferimento;
è il nostro simbolo, o se si vuole, il nostro Mito.[1]

Benito Mussolini in *Popolo d'Italia*, 21 April 1922.

Mussolini discovered Rome relatively late in his career, even if he
said – on the occasion of receiving Roman citizenship in 1924 – that
the city had always been on his mind since his youth.[2] Mussolini was
a *romagnolo* from the town of Predappio in the hills south of Forlì,
and he spent a substantial period of his life in Milan, Italy's self-
proclaimed *capitale morale*. It was there he received his political
education and went on to become a leading figure among the socialists
who advocated Italy's entry into the First World War. He was
expelled from the Socialist Party for these interventionist views and
became increasingly attracted to nationalist circles. In Milan he
founded his journal *Il Popolo d'Italia* in November 1914 and then
later, in November 1921, his own political movement, the *Fasci di*

---

[1]   'Rome is our starting point and our point of reference; it is our symbol, or if you
      like, it is our myth.'

[2]   In 'Lotta di Classe' Mussolini in 1910 called Roma an enormous 'città-vampiro
      che succhia il miglior sangue della nazione'. Cf. Cederna, 1980, p. 30. Cederna's
      introduction to the theme of Mussolini and the Third Rome remains important in
      the literature about this subject.

Combattimento. Fascism would remain largely a phenomenon of Northern Italy until the march on Rome of 28th October, 1922.

The official chronology of the Fascist movement began with Italy's entry into the First World War in 1915. The heroic experience of the war and the hard-earned victory became central points of reference for the movement, as did the conviction of having been cheated of the spoils during the peace negotiations. During the critical months following Vittorio Veneto on 4th November 1918, Mussolini denounced 'the mutilated victory', demanded a position among the victorious powers, and spoke of the necessity of an expansionist and imperialist foreign policy. It was during this process that the future *Duce* discovered Roman continuity as an element for his political propaganda.

During the *Risorgimento*, a number of cities had been considered for the role of Italy's capital, but in the end no other city could compete with the enormous weight of the mythological idea of *Roma Capitale*. But even if the decision was inevitable, it still had its critics.[3] Liberal democrats argued that its long tradition of universalism, despotism and oppression disqualified Rome as capital of a liberal democracy, while Catholics found the decision an intolerable insult to the Pope.[4]

With the conquest of Rome in September 1870, the eternal city became capital of the Italian nation-state. This marked the beginning of a new, a Third Rome (following the First Rome of the ancient Romans and the Second of the Pope), but in spite of the consecutive numbering, the Third Rome represented a break rather than continuity with its predecessors. Liberal Italy never succeeded in reconciling the paradox of having a national capital with an outspoken universalist tradition. No solution was found to the problem of *coabitazione* with the Pope, with whom the liberals remained on bad terms, and the new democracy also felt somewhat uncomfortably with antiquity.

Rome had never before been the capital of Italy, and despite all the fascination with the idea of Rome as the centre of the nation-state, it remained a difficult choice and the city never succeeded in becoming an Italian Paris. It was the political centre, but other cities were able to

---

[3] Galasso, 1970, pp. 5-24.

[4] See for example Chabod, 1951, where the last part of the second chapter – dedicated to the idea of Rome – deals with the opponents of *Roma Capitale*.

set the agenda in economy, culture and, very often, politics too. National ideology had never regarded antiquity as a suitable point of reference, even if the Roman past was always echoed in the idea of uniting the peninsula. The mainstream of Italian nationalism was orientated towards the Middle Ages as the glorious moment of the past: it was the medieval city-states of North and Central Italy that were idealised rather than the Roman Empire. In this respect, the choice of Florence as Italian capital after Turin, which had widely been considered to be too French, seemed to mark a step in the direction of a more genuine Italian development.

These problems of tradition and historic ideals also had an influence upon the architectural debate in the new Italian nation-state. Classicism was rejected on the basis that it was an unsuitable style for an Italian democracy. Napoleon Bonaparte had favoured classicism during his rule in Italy, and the Habsburg Emperor had also preferred this style for representative architecture. Associated with the enemies of the Italian nation-state, the classic style was therefore compromised in the eyes of nationalists. During the period of *Firenze Capitale* (1865-1870) in particular, architects searched for a new Italian style. Giuseppe Poggi, who was responsible for the plan that was to turn Florence into a 'real' capital, chose a *neo-cinquecentesco* style as the new national style. This was the first of a number of eclectic styles, based on different glorious pasts, that would, for decades, dominate the architecture of the Italian nation-state.

Although Rome symbolised something completely different to Florence, representing universalism and classicism instead of the city-republic and the Renaissance, the architects and decision makers of the new capital never adopted classicism as the exclusive style. It was unavoidable, however, that antiquity and classicism gained a much more prominent position in a city with many ancient monuments and a strong symbolic meaning. Immediately after the conquest of the city in 1870, excavations began in the area of the Forum and later a so-called *passegiata archaeologica*, an archaelogical itinerary, was constructed in order to facilitate visits to some of the most famous Roman monuments. Throughout the history of liberal Italy however, antiquity always remained part of a highly elitist culture. Sometimes symbolic parallels were too obvious, and, for example, liberal politicians would not hesitate to draw upon the Roman tradition to defend their imperialist projects in Africa. All the same, antiquity did not figure as a prominent part of state ideology: it did not provide the justification for the new Italian state, and the liberals were not always concerned with presenting themselves as the Romans of the 19th century.

Fascism took a different approach to these questions. Arguably, Mussolini was the last political leader to take historical continuity seriously in his propaganda, and it is impossible to read his Third Rome without a historic perspective. Fascism claimed to take up old Italian traditions, and, although Mussolini denounced liberal democracy, *plutocrazia*, as a foreign and 'un-Italian' import, he was often portrayed as a tribune of the people or a *condottiere* to underline the tradition of populistic leaders and men of action, before he finally became the *il Duce* (DVX).[5]

Mussolini's interest in Rome grew stronger during 1920 and 1921, as his nationalistic fervour turned into an imperialistic project. He declared that 'Our imperialism is Roman, Latin and Mediterranean. The Italian people must be, of necessity, expansionist'.[6] He demanded colonies and claimed the Mediterranean as *mare nostrum*, as it had been to the Romans.[7] In this particular context, the Roman ideology

---

[5] 'Siamo monarchici? Io parto anzituto da questo aforisma: un popolo deve sempre avere quelle istituzioni che sono adatte alla sua indole. Vi sono state delle repubbliche aristocratiche e oligarchiche; e vi sono delle monarchie popolari, come quella inglese, in cui il re non è che un simbolo di rappresentanza. Se domani la monarchia fosse per il progresso italiano un ostacolo, noi, che non siamo legati da pregiudiziali circa la forma di governo, l'abbandoneremmo. E oggi, 1920, non crediamo utile di accettare una pregiudiziale repubblicane'. Discorso di Cremona, September 5th 1920, cf. *Opera Omnia di Benito Mussolini*, 1954, p. 185.

[6] At the second *adunata fascista*, 29. maggio 1920. Here cit. after del Boca, 1996, pp. 415-437. Here p. 417.

[7] One of the earliest examples can be found in the important speech delivered in Trieste on the 50th anniversary of the conquest of Rome, 20th September, 1920. 'Roma è il nome che riempie tutta la storia per venti secoli. Roma dà il segnale della civiltà universale; Roma che traccia strade, segna confini e che dà al mondo le leggi eterne dell' immutabile suo diritto. Ma se questo è stato il compito universale di Roma nell' antichità, ecco che dobbiamo assolvere ancora un altro compito universale. Questo destino non può diventare universale se non si trapianta nel terreno di Roma. Attraverso il cristianesimo, Roma trova la sua forma e trova il modo di reggersi nel mondo. Ecco Roma che ritorna ancora una volta centro dell'impero universale che parla sua lingua. Pensate che il compito di Roma non è finito, no, perchè la storia italiana del medioevo, la storia più brillante di Venezia, che regna per dieci secoli, che porta le sue galee in tutti i mari, che ha ambasciate e governi, governi di cui oggi si è perdute le semente, non si è chiusa.

was a brilliant move. It not only postulated a historical right by referring to Roman times, but it also promised a solution to the problems of the Italian capital. If the nation-state was to be surpassed by an empire, the problems of continuity not only vanished, but this very continuity, this tradition, was the justification for Mussolini's programme. Rome would become the centre of a re-created empire, of a new, a third, a Fascist civilisation. The Third Rome – very soon the Fascists monopolised this terminology to a degree that it has almost been forgotten that the liberals also used it – re-established continuity and took up the tradition of classical Rome. The period from 1870 to 1922 was virtually ignored and, as Fascist power became indisputable, Mussolini was in a position to conclude the *conciliazione* with the Pope. The Italian capital was no longer in conflict with the universal tradition. The Third Rome became inseparable from the idea of the empire and of *Romanità*, the cult of antiquity, and this was clearly reflected in Roman urban planning, the scenography of power. The creation of a worthy capital, characterised by a hitherto unknown monumentalisation of the city, occupied Mussolini in his first 15 years in power. In this perspective, the use and abuse of antiquity became a means to promote and diffuse the idea of the continuity and historical tradition of an empire.

During the *anni del consenso*, when the Fascists enjoyed total control of the political scene and the media, they made considerable efforts to convince the Italians that an empire was necessary if Italy was to survive the relentless rivalry among the international powers. The Fascist regime, building upon mass-mobilisation and authoritarian rule, saw propaganda and coercion as a means of achieving integration. The spreading of ideas such as the importance of an empire and the necessity of having many children and the promotion of the concept of the Italians as the true descendants of the Romans and the necessity of acquiring Roman virtues, became central elements in the politics of mobilisation. It is interesting how Fascism in this respect represents an endeavour to educate the masses using certain traditional ideas of a classic, historical and, ultimately, elitist

---

La storia dei Comuni italiani è una storia piena di prodigi, piena di grandezza, di nobiltà. Andate a Venezia, a Pisa, a Amalfi, a Genova, a Firenze, e voi troverete là sui palazzi, nelle strade, il segno, l'impronta di questa nostra meravigliosa e non ancora marcita civiltà.' Cf. Discorso di Trieste, September 20th 1920, cf. *Opera Omnia di Benito Mussolini*, 1954, pp. 217 f.

tradition. In a society that still had a high level of illiteracy and a modest circulation of newspapers, the radio and the visual media were assigned a new and decisive role. Fascist propaganda can sometimes appear rather crude and repetitive, but it was trying to sell a message to the masses and not to an educated elite.

In his speech delivered on Rome's 2677th anniversary on 21st April 1924, Mussolini dealt with the future city, stressing two main themes – *necessità* and *grandezza*. The question of necessity was primarily concerned with infrastructure and housing in a city that was expected to reach a population of four to five million inhabitants, whereas the question of greatness was directly connected to the ideological construction of the capital of an empire. On this occasion Mussolini declared, 'We must liberate classical Rome from all those mediocre buildings that disfigure it, but side by side with the Rome of Antiquity and of Christianity, we shall also construct the monumental Rome of the 20th century'.[8] Mussolini had already chosen the anniversary of the founding of Rome as the day of the Fascist party, and under Fascism it was an annual occasion for the delivery of decisive proclamations.[9] One year later, in 1925, he delivered one of his most important speeches regarding the Third Rome. He promised that in 15 years Rome would present itself to the world in such an impressive condition that it would recall the Empire of Augustus. New open spaces would be created around the Capitol, the Theatre of Marcellus and the Pantheon as everything that evoked the centuries of decadence would be swept away: 'The millenary monuments of our history must stand like giants in their necessary solitude.'[10]

Few could have envisaged what would happen in the following years. The monumentalisation of Rome and the creation of vast open spaces was concentrated around the area of the Capitol and the fora of

---

[8] Cf. Cederna, 1980, p. 51.

[9] On 1st December, 1921, Mussolini stressed the importance of this day and of the Roman tradition in the ranks of his party in a speech in Parliament: 'Noi fascisti, unici fra tutti i partiti italiani, abbiamo scelto giornata di festa il 21 aprile [...] noi, per tutta la nostra forma mentis, per tutto il nostro stile, siamo degli esaltatori di tutto ciò che è romano [...] ed io in particolar modo insorgo e protesto contro certe manìe provinciali, perchè la storia è stata sempre fatta dalle grandi città. Può qualche volta la storia finire in un piccolo villaggio, ma è concesso soltanto alle grandi agglomerazioni umane, alle grandi città, di determinare gli eventi capitali della storia.'

[10] Cf. Cederna, 1980, p. 51.

the Roman emperors, but the *Mausoleo Augusto* was also 'liberated' in order to mark the grandiose celebration of the 2000th anniversary of the birth of Augustus, the greatest of all Romans.[11] Archaeologists were important protagonists in this project, which was more concerned with *sventramenti* (demolitions) than with the construction of new buildings. Among the key figures was Corrado Ricci, who had already, 20 years previously, drawn up plans for huge excavations of the fora. Given this, it is hardly surprising that he and his colleagues did not hesitate when Mussolini demonstrated a willingness to realise these ideas.[12]

Mussolini did not represent the coming to power of an antiquarian or neo-classical tradition, although a great number of Italian and foreign archaeologists, classical philologists and historians of antiquity honestly believed this to be the case. The *Duce* never celebrated antiquity and Roman tradition for its own sake, but he used it extensively for his own purposes, as ambitious rulers had done before him, and he was the first to bring classical tradition into mass politics.

Shortly after the march on Rome in October 1922, Mussolini proclaimed that it would soon be possible to see from Piazza Venezia to the Colosseum. This seemed a rather fantastic idea, but in October 1931 work began on this project. Corrado Ricci was in charge, but Mussolini took an active part in the demolition. In a famous representation he is shown swinging his pickaxe on the roof of one of the doomed buildings. Houses, churches, streets and *piazzas* were demolished, the Velia hill was dug away and the inhabitants of this traditional Roman neighbourhood were removed to *borgate* on the periphery of the city. In September 1932, Via dell'Impero was ready to be inaugurated by Mussolini during the celebrations for the first decade of Fascist rule on 28th October of the same year. The inauguration, an illustration of the re-established continuity, was linked with the opening of the *Mostra della Rivoluzione Fascista*, an exhibition that was forward looking in its orientation.[13]

---

[11] A thorough book on this aspect is Scriba, 1995.

[12] Ricci, Colini, Mariani, 1933.

[13] This famous exhibition was held in Palazzo delle Esposizioni in Via Nazionale, very close to Via dell'Impero, where the eclectic 19th century-palace had been transformed into a large red cube (symbolizing the Fascist martyrs) with four

Via dell'Impero represented the most evident combination of Fascism and *Romanità* in the Third Rome. It created a perfect scenography that showed the might and modernity of Fascism alongside the monumental evidence of the ancient magnificence that had been revived by Mussolini. In so doing, it offered both the historical and the contemporary legitimation for the Fascist regime. It is no wonder that Mussolini preferred to use this entrance to the new capital when he received Hitler in 1938. The railway station at Ostiense was also built for this occasion in order to avoid the *Führer* arriving through the decadent 19th century streets that led from the old Termini station to Piazza Venezia.[14] Following the triumphal entrance to Rome, the visitor would encounter the impressive Baths of Caracalla, the Obelisk of Axum (which Mussolini's victorious army had brought back from Ethiopia where the new empire had been founded) located in front of the modern Fascist Ministry for the African Colonies (today the headquarters of the FAO). Moving on, he would then pass the Circus Maximus, the Palatine Hill and the Arches of Constantine and Titus before arriving at the Colosseum. Here, in front of the most impressive of all the ruins, the visitor would turn almost 90 degrees into the straight Via dell'Impero leading to Piazza Venezia, to arrive in front of the famous balcony of the Palazzo Venezia, from which Mussolini had delivered some of his most important speeches. Via dell'Impero ran parallel to Via Sacra on the Forum, and was conceived to function as a road for triumphal processions. Foreign statesmen bore witness to this Fascist *grandezza*, and on at least one occasion British prisoners of war were led along this road. It made use of some of the most famous Roman ruins like the backdrop of a theatre; the temple of Venus and Rome, the Basilica of Maxentius, the *Forum Romanum*, the fora of Augustus, Caesar, Nerva and Trajan, and it took the visitor directly through the greatest era of the past to the actual centre of power, without any reference to the decadent centuries in between. The useful Roman monuments were 'liberated' from the buildings within which they had been incorporated (according to a long architectural tradition in Rome). Now they towered in their solitude in wide open spaces. Alongside the road some statues of Roman emperors were erected and on the wall of the Basilica four plaques showed the extension of the Roman Empire

---

fasces, the emblems of authority, on the front. The exhibition was planned and designed by some of the most important modern architects, among them Libera.

[14] Bottazzi, XLIV, 5, May, pp. 607-614.

from the nucleus of Rome to the culmination during the reign of Trajan. After the proclamation of the empire in 1936, a fifth plaque was added showing the modern Fascist empire.

Corrado Ricci and his colleagues had their massive excavation, but they were encouraged not to waste time. Mussolini boasted that he had had dozens of truckloads of old stones driven away. Some antique monuments were destroyed because they did not fit into the plan or because they were considered uninteresting.[15] All the same, the archaeologists obtained their archaeological zone alongside the road and they successfully managed to prevent the construction of any new buildings in that area. In 1934, a major competition was held for the design of the Fascist party's headquarters, to be build opposite the basilica of Maxentius. Several important Italian architects participated in the competition, with daring projects that reflected the ideals of Italian *razionalismo*. Party members and archaeologists opposed this provocative modern architecture and managed to block the plans. At that time, Mussolini himself had already lost interest in this area and wanted to construct a centre in a new location.

Via dell'Impero was the biggest and most ambitious project of Fascist Roman ideology realised in central Rome, but the liberation of the mausoleum of Augustus and the opening up of a new space around it also represented an important example of the link made between the two golden ages.[16] Next to this huge ruin a 'pavillon' was built to contain the reconstructed Ara Pacis. On the wall facing the mausoleum was written the text of Augustus' political will.[17] Celebrations for the 2000th anniversary of the birth of Augustus included the large and famous *Mostra Augustea*, an exhibition that once more stressed the inseparable connection between Fascism and Roman civilisation, and that demanded that the Italians should ensure that the glories of the past were surpassed by those of the future.

---

[15]   Most famously, the destruction of the base of the colossal statue of Nero and the Meta Sudante, both of which were partly reconstructed in later years.

[16]   From Piazza Venezia a new road was built, 'liberating' the facade of the Theatre of Marcellus. This was the beginning of the Via del Mare – the road to the sea and to the new port of Ostia. There was also an idea to construct a new centre outside the city in this direction, and the project of the World Exhibition of 1942 – E42 or later to be called EUR – was a part of this idea.

[17]   The way in which the church was also incorporated in this space was an indication of the *conciliazione* that Mussolini had meantime reached with the Pope.

Cheap train tickets brought thousands of Italians from all parts of the country to see this exhibition, which lasted for 14 months. Augustus was given a central position, and Mussolini was presented as a sort of reincarnation of this greatest of all Roman rulers. The way in which the *Duce* had brought an end to chaotic democracy and opened up a new era of prosperity and progress, as well, of course, as recreating the empire, seemed to demonstrate obvious parallels with the biography of Augustus.

Parallels between the past and the Fascist era were repeated again and again. For example, Mussolini was often portrayed as a Roman emperor. One of his admirers published a book with biographies of a number of selected Roman emperors in which their deeds and personalities were all compared to Mussolini. Indeed, in reality almost every chapter of the book was more concerned with the *Duce* than with his Roman predecessors.[18] Mussolini proclaimed the empire from the balcony of Palazzo Venezia, and the Luce newsreel of the speech shows the *Duce* and, behind him, the king and the profile of Augustus. The celebration of Augustus produced a number of books about *Romanità* and the titles, like that of Ettore Pais' *Roma. Dall'antico al nuovo Impero* often made reference to this continuity.[19]

Roman inspiration was a widespread phenomenon, and could be seen in the insignia of the party, the standards of the army and the Roman greeting, but there were also more surprising examples of its reuse. The black and white mosaics from the Roman ruins inspired a decorative style which was used repeatedly in official monuments. If the figurative language was Roman, the message was often contemporary. A good example of this can still be seen at the *Foro Italico*, formerly the *Foro Mussolini*, where classical motifs and figures are re-used alongside Fascist slogans and representations of contemporary sports, aeroplanes, tanks, Fascist *squadristi* and the conquest of Ethiopia.

The Roman past was also used as inspiration or legitimation for modern politics, like the project of bringing Rome back to the sea by building a harbour at Ostia, and even more so in the large scale

---

[18] Viganoni, 1937.

[19] Ettore Pais, 1939.

draining of the *Agro Pontinia*.[20] Here the Fascists worked on sacred ground and boasted that they had achieved what not even the Romans had succeeded in doing. The project in the *Pontinia* was, in many respects, a sort of trial run for what would happen in the colonies, with the fertilisation of wasteland, the founding of new towns and the organisation of a society of colonists. The civilising aspects of *romanità* were everywhere.

Fascism undoubtedly left its mark on Rome during the *Ventennio*. Although often discussed, no radical policy to destroy the monuments of Fascism was ever adopted. Only a few buildings were demolished, for example, the tower of the Fascist party headquarters in Littorio, the capital of the *Agro Pontino*.[21] There were plans to blow up the buildings of the World Exhibition which had been planned for 1942, but after some years of discussion the area was actually opened. This satellite quarter soon developed into an important centre of economic activity, and the architecture of the 1930s inspired postwar architecture in Italy and beyond. After the fall of Fascism there were several, mostly half-hearted cases of reviving the old Roman practice of *damnatio memoria*, and while inscriptions were often damaged, they were seldom totally erased. As the reaction to Fascist monuments is a phenomenon which has scarcely been studied, there is an element of speculation in dealing with it, but it is probably necessary to adopt a perspective of continuity in this question too. It cannot be explained by political or bureaucratic inertia, nor by veneration for sources and monuments of the Fascist period. It is not even the outcome of a general satisfaction with these monuments. From another point of view, a view often to be found in Italy, Fascism might simply represent another past history. Many Fascist monuments are no longer perceived as 'Fascist', and their more subtle propaganda effects are no longer understood. Perhaps a growing amnesia when it comes to history might explain a part of it, but it should be remembered that this is happening in a country, and in this case in a city, where successive epochs have left their marks, and where there have been many despots and many ambitious founders of ephemeral greatness.

---

[20] The project at Ostia, involving the reclamation of land, the excavation of the harbour and the construction of a highway was not originally a Fascist idea, but Mussolini took over the work which had already been started and turned it into a Fascist project.

[21] This Fascist model-town also had its embarrassing name changed to Latina.

In this sense, the Fascist monuments, like the monuments that preceded them, have simply been absorbed in present-day Rome, a huge city of a very long collective memory. Seen in this perspective, even Fascist monuments with their claims of founding and representing a new civilisation become ironic comments on Fascist propaganda. At *Foro Mussolini* – today *Foro Italico* – the setting created for the Olympic Games of 1940 and for the education of the *Balillas* survive intact.[22] Behind the obelisk – a *carrarese* monolith with the well-preserved inscription *Mvssolini Dvx* – lies a large rectangular piazza with mosaics. This was restored before the finals of the football World Cup in 1990, and even some of the most propagandist mosaics underwent restoration. Two rows of marble stones flank the *piazza*, and each stone bears an inscription that recalls an important date in Fascist history. Together, they establish a chronology containing the glorious moments of the *Ventennio* which the regime wished to commemorate. The visitor can stroll along history, starting with the entry into the First World War and moving on to the creation of the Fascist state, the founding of the new cities in the Pontinia, the war in Ethiopia and, on the seventeenth stone, the proclamation of the empire. On the eighteenth stone there is the inscription: *Fine del Regime Fascista*. The following two stones record the abolition of the monarchy and the introduction of the republican constitution in 1948. After Fascism the monument was not destroyed, but rather these three additions succeeded in turning the story upside down.

---

[22] Del Debbio, the leading Fascist architect, became the superintendent of the *Foro* after the war, and this probably explains why it was hardly changed at all.

CHAPTER 8

Monuments in the Making of Italy

Lars BERGGREN

Since the fall of the 'Iron Curtain', public monuments have increasingly attracted the attention of the general public. Questions about destruction or preservation of monuments erected by the fallen regimes, their value as objects of art, their function as instruments of propaganda, and their utility as sources for history in general are at present debated with an intensity that recalls the situation in Europe a century ago. Scholars from a variety of disciplines have joined the battle and have thus provided a powerful impetus to research in what was formerly a largely neglected field of study. On the whole this is a good thing, but my concern is the superficiality of many recent works, a superficiality that stems from an academically conditioned inability to fully appreciate the complexity of the artefacts in question.

Pioneers like Thomas Nipperdey and George Mosse, who wrote their seminal studies on monuments and nationalism in the 60s and early 70s, have recently acquired a large following among historians.[1] Consequently, discussion still tends to focus on how monuments were used by authorities as instruments for shaping and manipulating the collective memory of societies. There is, of course, nothing wrong with that. The problem is that historians, and scholars from other disciplines as well, still insist on treating monuments more as simple manifestations of the political situations in which they were erected, and less as the outcome of long and complicated processes that they

---

[1] Nipperdey, 1968, Mosse, 1975.

actually were. As a result, the role of authorities in these processes is often overstated, the 'messages' of monuments are simplified and the levels at, and ways in which, monuments were expected to operate misunderstood. The main reason for these shortcomings is, as usual, lack of relevant knowledge.

Public monuments are extremely complex artefacts, which, if they are at all to be used as sources for history, require several levels of investigation and explanation. The political ideas, financial status and artistic preferences of commissioners, the workings of cultural and political control mechanisms, the current iconographic conventions and the very definition of a monument, all had their impact on the finished product. No matter the context, the handling of monuments requires special knowledge in a number of different fields that traditionally, and unfortunately, belong to different academic disciplines. Thus, most historians lack not only the basics of iconography but also the necessary tools for a more refined visual analysis, while art historians – presumably in possession of this part of the equipment – are not generally capable of providing the relevant historical contextualisation. None of them seem to be fully aware of the composite character of public monuments.

In this paper, I will focus on two fundamental but – for the reasons given above – largely ignored issues in the study of monuments in the process of nationalisation; the political significance of monuments in Europe during the 'long 19th century', and the ways the Italian Government tried to control the materialisation of the national myth in monuments during the period following the *Risorgimento* period.

My research work on the public monuments erected in Rome during the last quarter of the 19th century has made me acutely aware of the multitude of different, more or less incompatible, ways in which scholars use the word 'monument'.[2] It turns out that this terminological confusion is in fact one of the serious obstacles to the development of an interdisciplinary dialogue. I will therefore start by

---

[2] The results are to be found in the volume *L'ombra dei grandi. Monumenti e politica monumentale a Roma 1870-1895,* in which the histories of some 43 monument projects, launched in Rome during its first 25 years as capital of the united Italy, are studied with special attention to their origin, interaction, and other factors that affected their fate, design, siting and political significance.

giving a representative 19th century definition of the objects with which we are dealing:[3]

> A monument is a work of art, sculpture and/or architecture, erected in a public place to keep alive the memory of remarkable persons and events, and to arouse in the mind of the beholder feelings towards these persons and events, strong enough to implant in him civic virtues and patriotic feelings. It should be made of durable material – ideally bronze and marble – and be provided with an inscription clarifying its meaning and intent. The works of art suited for this purpose are triumphal arches, columns, pillars, obelisks, pyramids, trophies, statues and combinations of these elements.[4]

This definition is of course very general, indeed I think it would have passed without much opposition throughout European history, from ancient Greece to the beginning of our century. To get a more precise idea of what the term 'monument' normally stood for, a couple of observations on practice must be added. Since a certain size and degree of complexity was required, ordinary inscription-tablets or portrait-busts were not regarded as 'true' monuments. Nor were buildings or other constructions that served a mainly practical purpose; a ministerial palace, a church or a bridge, for instance, could be both commemorative and monumental, but they were not monuments in the full sense of the term. Funerary monuments were normally not included among monuments proper, since the places where they belonged – cemeteries and churches – were public only in the restricted sense that visiting them was an option for almost everybody. The inclination to make and to sharpen these distinctions increased more or less continuously, as did the tendency to single out as paradigmatic the monument consisting of a bronze statue on a stone pedestal placed in a central square. Figure 2, '*Die Höchsten Monumente*', gives a good idea of what, by the end of the century, was normally accepted as a true monument.

---

[3]   The sloppy use of the term tends to blur the fact that during the 19th century it had a rather distinct meaning. This is vital to the understanding of both the central position of monuments in the construction of national identities, and the 'monumentomaniac' explosion of the last decades of the century.

[4]   The definition is derived from a number of publications, though mainly from Sulzer 1798. For a fuller discussion of the subject, see Berggren, 1991, pp. 19 f.

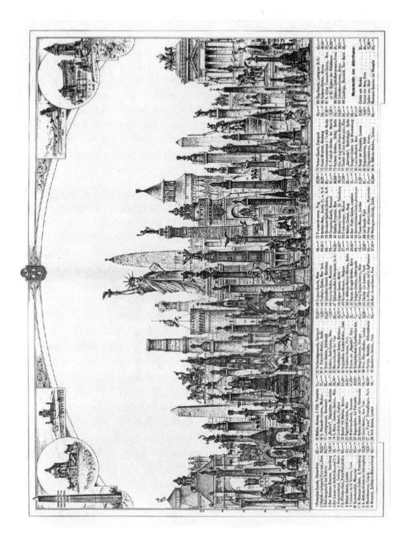

Fig. 2 – 'Die Höchsten Monumente' (ca 1895), published in the series
Monumente und Standbilder Europas (Wasmuth),
Berlin 1894-1904.

True monuments were destined for eternity and must therefore speak an eternal language. Naturally, the design was affected by changes in taste, and varied with locality and time, but on the whole it remained within the framework established in ancient Greece and Rome. In fact, the traditional types of monuments were perceived as parts of a supra-historical language of forms that constantly referred back to the historical roots of western civilisation. Straying too far from the original models meant running the risk of being forgotten by posterity, of being misread, of not getting one's message through at all, of being accused of a lack of classical erudition, or, generally, of being derided for not knowing the rules of the game. It is therefore not surprising that 19th century monuments look more or less the same all over Europe, and, indeed everywhere that European culture was dominant, and that the same forms in different contexts could be used to carry widely different messages.

19th century monuments differ from those of earlier centuries not so much in terms of basic symbolic function or typology as in what the cultural and political elite believed could be obtained by using them. From rather simple status symbols, designed to emulate the Roman emperors and to induce fear of and loyalty to feudal lords, monuments were turned into instruments for the active manipulation of the minds of men. Roughly speaking, the change took place during the last quarter of the 18th century, when men like Sulzer, Voltaire, Rousseau, Diderot and d'Alembert developed a new model for the ideal function of art in society.[5] Basing themselves on egalitarian ideals, the authority of classical authors and the *tabula rasa* theory of visual perception, they claimed that the broad masses of the population could and should be transformed into good and useful citizens by being constantly exposed to powerful images of the right kind. All the arts, and especially public monuments, should work in concert to bring about progress, liberal reform and a uniform national identity. Public gardens and squares should be converted into 'schools of virtue and patriotic feeling' by means of the erection of monuments dedicated to worthy and outstanding men. The concept was spread in a number of highly influential publications, such as Diderot's *Grande*

---

[5]   Bloch, 1990, pp. 194 ff. ; Leith, 1965.

Encyclopédie and Sulzer's *Allgemeine Theorie der Schönen Künste,* and was extensively adopted in the French Revolution.[6]

By the close of the Napoleonic era, the idea of monuments as supremely efficient instruments for communicating moral and political messages to the broad mass of the population was firmly established. Linked from the beginning to the project of 'nationalising the masses', this concept became recognised and institutionalised as an integral element in the building of national states, or rather, the visualisation of their ideals and myths. From that point on, monuments were regarded as symbols of a special status conferred by the nation – and not by God – on men, events or even concepts which were judged to be worthy of this supreme honour.[7] Provided that the monument was designed according to the standards prescribed by tradition, it served as material proof of an officially acknowledged greatness. Conversely, the capability to produce Great Men was demonstrated by the presence of monuments; their number, size and quality serving as an index to the cultural, economical and technical level reached by a nation.

Social unrest and political change further stimulated the general interest in monuments. For the ruling classes, the growing industrial proletariat was becoming an ever more dangerous element that had to be dealt with, preferably without the use of violence. The gradual extension of suffrage made it increasingly important for both govern-ments and opposition parties to reach larger groups with their propaganda. The nationalist revolutions and wars of liberation that characterised the century provided an ample supply of heroes and

---

[6]   Agulhon, 1981, pp. 18 ff.

[7]   The redefinition of the monument's social aims and effects automatically widened the social range of 'monumentable' individuals. This status was – at least in theory – based on personal merit and thus something that could be earned by all citizens alike. Distinctions were made, however, between different kinds of merits and different levels of importance for society, and although frequently hotly debated in individual cases, a number of rules were generally agreed upon. Equestrian statues were reserved for rulers, while statesmen, military commanders, and other such heroes should be eternalised in standing statues. For cultural heroes, such as artists, philosophers and other thinkers, portrait-busts or minor statues were considered proper, though they belonged in parks and gardens, and not in squares in the centre of the city. In most countries, ordinary politicians, rank and file soldiers, and women were not considered worthy of the bronze and marble of eternity until the end of the century. Berggren, 1991, pp. 24 f.

martyrs suitable for 'monumentalisation', not to mention the host of mythical figures and historical personalities from a more distant past whom various political movements hailed as precursors and idols. Convinced of the propagandistic potential of monuments, and urged on by famous writers and practical example, people in all countries and all political camps began to show the symptoms of what was later to be labelled 'monumentomania'.

The nationalist elites of Italy were no exception to this rule, but since the idea of an instrumental use of public monuments was, from the beginning, closely linked both to the liberal left and to nationalism, their opportunities to erect real monuments were initially limited. The question of how to make Italians with monuments became a practical issue after the constitution of the Kingdom of Italy in 1861, and only became really acute with the ascendance to power of the left in 1876. I will give a short outline of the situation with respect to monuments on the Italian peninsula during the 19th century. To simplify matters, I have divided the century into three periods; from the start of the century until the official proclamation of the Kingdom of Italy in 1861, from 1861 until the shift of parliamentary power from right to left in 1876, and from 1876 onwards.

1800 to 1861

During the first half of the century precious few monuments were realised in marble and bronze. The political situation in the aftermath of the Napoleonic wars was unstable in terms of both internal and international relations, and the conservative governments all over the peninsula avoided project for monuments, since they were highly charged and always potentially provocative. Not only did they start no projects of their own, they also stamped out all initiatives that hinted at political opposition. However, this does not mean that 'monumental' activities were not going on. On the contrary, this was the great period for the revival of Italian historiography, and everywhere writers of widely different political views were busy constructing a national unity out of the peninsula's chaotic past. In this process monuments played an important role.

Devoid of territorial, political, or even ethnic unity, the Italy-to-be was constructed as a cultural unity, vaguely defined by reference to a common classical heritage that included language, architecture and liberal arts, and to the presence of a national spirit, or rather *Volksgeist*. Monuments offered tangible manifestations of this elusive entity, as did the list of Great Italians which, neatly arranged in genealogical series from antiquity to present, served to illustrate the concept. Real historic monuments and imaginary ones, dedicated to the heroes of the day, were mingled in books, pamphlets and broadsheets. In the words of the contemporary philosopher Bertrando Spaventa, these collections served to 'heighten the Italians' conceptual consciousness of the national question and to give them a unitarian historical tradition, with the object of furthering Italy's cultural resurrection and the legitimation of its political unification.'[8]

In the long term, even the failure of the insurrections of 1848-1849, strengthened the unitarian movement (the *Risorgimento*) by providing it with clear-cut heroes and enemies. Designs for monuments dedicated to the leaders of republican resistance (such as Mazzini and Garibaldi), and especially to the martyrs of the Italian cause, flooded the underground market. The external enemies, clearly indicated as such, were of course the French and Austrian troops that crushed the republics. But the new internal enemy, the Papacy and, to a lesser extent, the whole Catholic Church, was even more in evidence, being regarded as infinitely worse because it had betrayed the national cause and called in foreigners to fight against it. However, very few projects were started; real monuments were too dangerous to be considered even by nationalistically minded regimes.

1861 to 1876

This situation changed radically a decade after the convulsions of 1848. The idea of an Italy united under the House of Savoy gradually materialised through the incorporation of Lombardy, Emilia, Tuscany and finally the Two Sicilies, and the official proclamation of the Kingdom of Italy followed in 1861. Incorporation into Italy unleashed a wave of 'monumental' activities in the new provinces. The event itself, its leading protagonists and the local martyrs of the 'patriotic battles' were commemorated in bronze and marble in cities, towns and villages. The new government not only permitted monuments with an explicitly nationalistic content, sometimes even with a republican or democratic bias, but also allowed manifestations directed against the

---

[8]   Garin, 1983, p. 53.

only remaining serious obstacle to the *Risorgimento* – the Catholic Church. Three projects for monuments to famous heretics were started in their native towns immediately after the Italian take-over; to Arnaldo in Brescia, to Girolamo Savonarola in Ferrara and to Giordano Bruno in Nola.[9] All three were officially resurrected and elevated to 'monumentable' status as precursors of Italian nationalism and exponents of various liberal virtues, although the most important themes present in these projects were anti-clerical and anti-temporal. The monuments were designed to demonstrate that the power of the church was broken, and to divert the strong anti-clerical currents into mainstream national thinking.

The invasion of the Papal States in 1870 and their formal annexation to the Kingdom of Italy triggered the same kind of reaction – projects for monuments started everywhere. Only in Rome, the new capital, did the Government discourage and even actively oppose all such initiatives. There were several reasons for this, but the strongest one, at least initially, was probably the urgent necessity of avoiding all actions that might provoke the Catholic powers (France, Spain, and Austria) into a military intervention on behalf of the Pope.

On the whole, the new-born Italian State, or rather its Parliament under a succession of right-wing governments, maintained a low profile in questions of monuments during this period, and very few projects for national monuments were started. The reasons for this were both political and financial. Especially from 1870 on, the extremely strained financial situation of the state demanded strict economy, and moreover there was the necessity to avoid offending foreign powers, including the Vatican with which some kind of agreement would eventually have to be sought. However, this does not mean that the state regarded questions of monuments as unimportant, but rather than taking its own initiatives, it chose to

---

[9]   Arnaldo da Brescia was executed and burnt in Rome 1155. An international subscription was started in 1860-1, and the monument was inaugurated in 1882. Girolamo Savonarola was strangled and burnt in the Piazza della Signoria in Florence 1498. The project was initiated in 1859 and the monument was unveiled in 1875. Giordano Bruno was burnt at the stake in Campo dei Fiori in Rome in 1600. Monument projects were started in the early 1860s in both his native Nola and nearby Naples; the former was erected in 1867 and the latter in 1864. Berggren, 1991, pp. 43 f; 52 f.

concentrate on controlling the activities of other agents in the field, such as municipalities, veteran organisations and political clubs.

1876 Onwards

The beginning of the third and last period was inaugurated by the shift in political power from right to left that occurred in Parliament in 1876. As in most European countries, the political left was considerably more inclined to believe in the efficiency and necessity of monuments than the right. The shift in parliamentary power therefore immediately resulted in a less strict surveillance of monument projects in general, and the lifting of the interdict on new monuments in Rome. It also saw Parliament reserving for itself both the right to and the responsibility for the erection of 'national monuments'. As a result, monumental activities of all kinds proliferated, not only in Rome but all over the country, and the period from 1876 to the turn of the century is the one that most properly fits the description of 'monumentomaniac'. Nobody knows how many monuments were erected, but counting only those dedicated to the two greatest heroes of the *Risorgimento*, King Vittorio Emanuele II and Giuseppe Garibaldi, we arrive at a figure of at least 500. To get an idea of the magnitude of the whole phenomenon, I suppose we must imagine a much higher figure.

Who erected all these monuments? Who paid for them? What intentions lay behind them? The answers to these questions are varied and extremely complex, indeed, the only thing all monuments had in common was their official justification through their reference to the nation, and the necessity to pass through the control mechanisms of the government. Of the three principal categories of agents in the field – governmental organisations, municipalities and a wide range of private and semi-private organisations – the first was largely concerned with the surveillance of the other two. Authorities invariably regarded questions of monuments as top priority, watched all projects closely, and, if necessary, intervened without hesitation.

Governmental Policy on Monuments

The remaining part of this paper is dedicated to governmental monument policy, and especially to the functioning of its control mechanisms. The state itself erected comparatively few monuments –

all in all only about a dozen, of which five were located in the new capital. Many more were suggested, but most of them could not muster the parliamentary support needed to attain the formal status of 'national monument'. Such monuments were thought of as manifestations of the whole nation, politically as well as geographically, and without the backing of a solid majority they were more likely to be sources of conflict than unity. Given that political groups had widely different views on the worthiness of candidates, the nature of national unity, what values or beliefs to inculcate and so forth, it is not surprising that only this small number was able to pass through Parliament – and some of them only with great difficulty.[10]

Economy remained another restrictive factor. After all, the size and quality of a monument ought to reflect not only the greatness of the man, the deed, or the concept so honoured, but also the status of the commissioner. National monuments had therefore to be the biggest and best, which also meant the most expensive, and restricting their number was a way of keeping down the total cost. In fact, the Italian state concentrated nearly all its resources in one single project, the huge monument in Rome dedicated to King Vittorio Emanuele and the unification of Italy (fig. 3). The magnitude of the investments in this one project cannot, however, be understood in a limited national perspective; this project was conceived for the international scene, for the 'noble contest among nations' to construct the highest and biggest monuments (the result of which we have already seen in fig. 2).

---

[10]   Berggren and Sjöstedt, 1996, esp. pp. 143 f (Minghetti) and 153 f (Depretis).

Fig. 3 – The monument dedicated to 'The Unification of Italy
and King Vittorio Emanuele', usually called the 'Vittoriano',
Rome 1885-1911.

The situation in Rome was peculiar since the city was not only the capital of Italy, but also the spiritual centre of the Catholic Church. For the Italian Government the situation was problematic, although not without its benefits. Having a hostile religious superpower locked up in one's backyard meant that there were few political shortcomings and mistakes, either national or international, that could not be attributed in some way to the machinations of the priests. A standard solution in situations of serious internal dissent was to provoke a crisis in relations with the Vatican and then use the spectre of clericalism to close the liberal ranks. On the other hand, the drawbacks were serious. One of them was the necessity to compete with the sculptural and architectural glories of Papal Rome. The problem was tackled in several ways; one was to confiscate and appropriate high-status buildings of the former regime, another to excavate and make visible as much as possible of pre-papal antiquity, while a third was to articulate post-papal liberal Rome as clearly as possible with new buildings and monuments.

The national monuments of this 'Third Rome', successor of the Rome of the Caesars and the Popes, were regarded as extremely important political statements (the concept of the 'Third Rome' was later taken over and modified by Fascism, as discussed in Steen Bo Frandsen's chapter). As such, the route from their proposition to their realisation is extremely well documented in parliamentary debates and in the extensive archival material of working committees. Moreover, all decisions, public competitions, constructions and inaugurations of monuments were extensively covered and hotly debated in the innumerable Italian newspapers and magazines. In the case of the monument dedicated to Vittorio Emanuele, for instance, more than 400 projects were judged and discussed during three successive competitions. In short, we have a wealth of good sources for the study of what the government regarded as 'monumentable' Italian history and how it ought to be represented, and also for what the opposition said and thought about these matters.[11]

To understand these discussions and their ultimate outcome – the monuments as they were finally realised – it is essential to keep in mind that the Italian state deemed itself so weak, its external and

---

[11] The *Vittoriano* is dealt with in many publications, of which Brice 1998 is not only the most recent but also probably the best. See also Berggren and Sjöstedt, 1996, pp. 285 f.

internal enemies so many, and the particularism of the provinces so strong that, to be able to hold itself together, it needed not only the symbolical charge of Rome, but also that of a monarch to fill the place of an ancient Roman emperor. It was the survival of the national project that made liberals from left to right subscribe to a standard version of the foundation myth. In this, the king was represented as both embodying and terminating the sacred national cause, while the heroes and champions of rival political currents were reduced to his mere adjutants. Figures like Giuseppe Garibaldi, Camillo Cavour, and even the intransigent republican Giuseppe Mazzini, while receiving their official recognition, were always to remain in the shadow of the *'Padre della Patria'*.

How this strategy worked when it came to monuments is shown by the two most spectacular national monuments in Rome, one dedicated to King Vittorio Emanuele and the other to Giuseppe Garibaldi. The *Vittoriano*, was situated on the Capitol Hill, the holiest place of ancient Rome. It can be described as a colossal assemblage illustrating all the various thoughts, concepts, persons and events that led to the unification of Italy, neatly structured according to the scheme outlined above, and duly terminating in the apotheosis of the king (fig. 3).[12] In the infinitely smaller, but still very sizeable, monument dedicated to Garibaldi, secondary figures, reliefs and inscriptions reflect a whole range of conflicting political aspects of the hero's deeds. Garibaldi's position *vis-à-vis* the king is acknowledged in various ways in the monument itself, as well as by its peripheral position on the top of the Gianicolo Hill, where he was placed to keep an eternal watch over the enemy in the Vatican (fig. 4).[13] In both these monuments, practically everyone could be sure to find a key for their own individual interpretation of the whole.

---

[12] The construction of the *Vittoriano* was begun in 1885; the inauguration took place in 1911. Berggren and Sjöstedt, 1996, p. 49; Brice, 1998.

[13] Berggren, 1994, p. 139; Berggren and Sjöstedt, 1996, esp. pp. 218 ff.

Fig. 4 – The monument dedicated to Giuseppe Garibaldi,
Rome 1884-1895.

How much of the available space on each of these monuments was assigned to each political faction and their respective versions of the national myth was determined by their relative weight in the actual balance of power. The same flexible system was also used for lesser monuments, but since the available space in these cases was too limited to allow partitioning, the tendency was to reduce the iconographical apparatus and instead reach some kind of tacit agreement on the number and size of the monuments allotted to the interested parties. It is here that the internal system of parliamentary regulation coincided with the functioning of the external control mechanisms of the state.

The political opposition as such was hardly ever allowed to erect monuments. The state bureaucracy controlled, either directly or indirectly, the issue of all the necessary permissions, and exerted various forms of pressure on monument committees to encourage them to purge their projects of subversive symbols and allusions and to conform to the official version of the national myth. In cases of resistance, the ultimate measure was to stop the project by taking it over, that is, by declaring it 'national' and expropriating its funds, or by adjudicating it illegal on some suitable pretext – usually that it was subversive and threatened the security of the state. The history of the monument to Mazzini in Rome provides a typical example of how the former method was used, while the fate of the monument planned for Guglielmo Oberdan illustrates the latter.[14]

Such measures did not, however, prevent the political antagonisms of the period from frequently being directed into monument projects. Critical views could be expressed in many indirect ways: they could, for example, be disguised as projects dedicated to historic characters of ambiguous interpretation, or to vague concepts such as patriotism and the nation. The real instigators could be hidden in large committees, while political resistance could be overcome by national or even international subscriptions (as in the case of Giordano Bruno).[15] Indeed, the capacity of monuments to capture public attention was so strong that the question of their final realisation could be wholly secondary, if it was considered at all. In order to put a question on the local or even national political agenda, it was often quite enough to launch a project (normally by starting a subscription).[16]

But the government, or rather the political groups that enjoyed dominance in the state machinery, did not restrict itself to prohibitive activities. It also supported hundreds, maybe thousands of municipal and private projects in various ways. Ministries often made substantial

---

[14] The Parliament 'nationalised' the Mazzini project in 1890, but the monument was erected only in 1949. Berggren and Sjöstedt, 1996, pp. 185 ff.
Guglielmo Oberdan tried to assassinate the Austrian emperor in Trieste 1882. Sentenced to death and executed, he immediately became the most popular martyr of Italian irredentism. Berggren and Sjöstedt, 1996, p. 103.

[15] Unverfehrt, 1981, pp. 315 ff. ; Berggren, 1991.

[16] Berggren and Sjöstedt, 1996, especially chapter 14.

contributions to private or semi-private initiatives, thereby solving the financial problems inherent in every monument project. Even if the sums were not always large, such contributions gave the projects an air of respectability and realisability that was important for the outcome of public subscriptions. After all, we must not forget that, despite the great number of existing monuments, the vast majority of projects failed.

There were also other forms of official support. Projects that fitted into the general scheme – or at least did not contradict it – and had the support of politically influential protectors, might benefit from other forms of official support. They could be exempted from tax, benefit from reduced price or even free material and transportation, the plot for the monument could be conceded free of charge, special laws could even be passed in Parliament, and the government could put pressure on provincial and municipal authorities to abandon resistance to monument projects or to further them, as the case may be. The mayor of Rome, for instance, was dismissed because of his refusal to comply with Prime Minister Crispi's wishes in the matter of the monument to Giordano Bruno.[17]

I have investigated these matters most closely in the case of Rome, but I consider that the general picture was much the same everywhere in Italy. The strong impetus to erect monuments came not from authorities trying to disseminate a centrally constructed vision of the national myth, but from various groups in society fighting for recognition and representation in public space. The state itself had neither the economic means nor the political unity required to embark on a large-scale programme of monument building. Instead, it used its resources to channel the tidal wave of municipal and private projects into forms that underpinned, or at least did not contradict, the official version of the national myth. A closer look at the entire inventory of Italian 19th century monuments would probably reveal that almost all of them were the result, both in terms of iconography and of financing, of the joint, or rather mixed, efforts of a number of agents. Thus, the overall governmental strategy for making Italians through monuments can be described as letting all geographical and political

---

[17] Berggren, 1991, 1993, 1996. The battle over what was probably the most contested monument of all times went on for more than 13 years (1876-1889). In a last desperate move, Pope Leo XIII threatened to move the Holy See from Rome if the monument was inaugurated.

factions have their monuments according to their own version of the national myth, just so long as it was kept within the officially approved framework.

The working of the system can be described as flexible and 'democratic', at least in comparison with what was to follow under the Fascist regime. During Fascism, the visual representation of national ideals in public spaces was monopolised by the party, but it brought no major change in the basic understanding of the political significance of monuments, only more control, co-ordination and standardisation. Just as Fascism took over the *Risorgimento* myth, rewrote parts of it and provided it with a new ending, it also took over many projects and ideas from the old regime. Indeed, in Rome it is difficult to find Fascist projects for monuments that had not already been contemplated and elaborated during the previous century. Let this serve to remind us once more that public monuments are never simple expressions of a particular moment, a particular place or a particular political party. Rather, they are the result of long processes in which past and present, tradition and modernity, artistic and political ideals, power relations, great ambitions and economic reality fuse together as a single composite.

CHAPTER 9

Representations of the American Nation in Architecture: The Case of the 1920s

Ron ROBIN

Introduction

This paper examines the architectural designs of American diplomatic edifices in the 1920s as officially ordained, yet culturally revealing representations of the American nation. In focusing on diplomatic edifices I have assumed that these structures are particularly charged versions of nationhood. As cultural and political products manufactured for foreign consumption, their symbolism is explicit and deliberately decipherable. At the same time, the embassy as symbol is not a monolithic creation. These structures are culturally negotiated attempts to produce a collective version of nationhood. Archival records reveal that the process of choosing a particular style was not based on the whim of any one person or bureaucracy. Neither tenacious federal officials nor ambitious politicians (and nor, for that matter, their constituents) controlled national symbolism abroad. The American national image as defined in these structures was characterised by jostling, infighting and negotiated settlements between various groups espousing different and sometime competing agendas.

I have chosen to analyse the 1920s because this was a period of significant cultural and political transition in the United States. Periods of transition usually generate concerted and explicit efforts to define the collective self. Within this context, figurative representations of the nation abroad proved to be particularly intriguing because an American presence in foreign lands was a highly contested issue. Contrary to popular opinion, the 1920s was not a period of isolationist retreat. Certainly, isolationism was quite pervasive in the America of the 1920s, but, at the same time, a series of conservative and ostensibly isolationist Republican presidents expanded the nation's international presence in an aggressive manner. The attempt to dissipate the tension between isolationism and globalism, between American exceptionalism and cosmopolitanism through the process of embassy building serves as the basis of the following analysis.

From a methodological point of view, the embassy construction project poses an intriguing problem. Government files, professional periodicals, and the memoirs of protagonists are replete with grand technical details; there is, however, no theoretical discourse. Unlike Britain and France, the United States did not develop an imperial school of architecture. My solution to this problem has been to evoke the symbiotic relations between domestic and foreign affairs. I intend to argue that domestic concerns and a self-centred, historically oriented cultural discourse had an overwhelming effect on these national symbols abroad.

In short, this is an exercise in the collapsing of distinctions. First, the distinction between time (conventional historical analysis) and space (spatial analysis), and secondly, the distinction between diplomatic history (preoccupation with the foreign) and cultural history (a predominant emphasis on the familiar). Moreover, I shall call into question the traditional boundaries separating history from other disciplines, while skirting the internal enclosures of the historical enterprise, in this case the peculiar institution of diplomatic history, which is all to often a history of near great men and their mediocre accomplishments.

Background

Prior to the First World War, the purchase or construction of embassy buildings was sporadic and practically non-existent. In the early 1920s, in response to the demands of the business community for greater governmental representation in the many new potential markets for American goods, the State Department requested and received a large congressional financial allocation for a diplomatic construction programme. By 1932, the United States owned property in 40 different overseas locations and the administration had requested an additional multi-year programme of funding in order to construct almost 100 new diplomatic outposts.[1]

Defining a respectable American image in foreign lands was not an easy process. To begin with, there were no pertinent role models. Monumental government architecture in the United States had not adapted to the changing times and federal architecture was mostly an unimaginative emulation of classicism. A further complication arose from the multiple and, at times, conflicting dimensions of America's ambitions abroad; there was no one pattern to the enterprise. Economically, the United States sought a variety of goals ranging from stark colonial exploitation and protectionism in its own hemisphere to the grand ideals of free trade in other parts of the world. Political goals were equally diverse, shifting intermittently from aggressive intervention in Latin America to altruistic and somewhat vague support for freedom and democracy in the world at large. These fluid concepts of empire hindered the search for a pertinent archetype of national symbolism abroad.

By the mid 1920s, ambitions and objectives abroad were becoming more coherent. 1926 marked a real turning point in official attitudes towards embassy buildings, with the establishment of the Foreign Service Building Commission (FSBC). The FSBC consisted of the secretaries of State, Treasury, and Commerce and ranking members of the Foreign Relations Committees of Congress. Their task was to select sites, decide on priorities, and devise an architectural policy for diplomatic edifices.[2] This body became the sole arbitrator of, and contractor for, diplomatic architecture.

Establishing Architectural Symbols of Nationhood

While still in its early stages, the FSBC articulated a series of master guidelines for the construction of embassies:

---

[1] United States Congress. House of Representatives. Committee on Foreign Affairs. Seventy-First Congress, *Hearings on H. R. 15774* (Washington, D. C., 1931); Letter from Frederick Larkin to Miss O. L. Nelson (April 4 1932), in State Department Records, Record Group 59, Decimal Files 124. 01, National Archives, Washington D. C. (Hereafter: R. G. 59)

[2] *New York Times,* February 18, 1926, 27; May 8, 1926, p. 6.

1) Avoidance of Opulence: Unwilling to upset critics of federal power in general, and American global policy in particular, the FSBC ruled out any form of ostentatious architecture. Prior to the establishment of the FSBC, the haphazard policy of embassy construction had produced a series of palatial structures. Unused to the new status of world leader, the federal government had set out to acquire and build diplomatic abodes that emulated the architectural strategies of other powers. The architecture did not focus on anything that was specifically American, and national greatness was expressed through architectural extravagance.[3] In such diverse corners of the globe as Spain, Chile, Mexico and Germany, the United States either acquired or constructed an array of palaces.[4]

The palatial approach to the diplomatic outposts of the early 1920s aroused predictable criticism at home. Sumptuous structures had obvious divisive social connotations; their patrons had been the Old World aristocracies, and to cultivate their tastes implied an acceptance of foreign mores and values. Luxurious edifices aroused associations of corruption, tyranny and dissolution rather than greatness, democracy, and progress. Moreover, rich architecture, like other luxuries, was the product of ageing societies; it forebode imminent decay. In addition, the traumatic events of the First World War suggested that extravagant opulence preceded national decline

2) Standardisation: The growing power of the federal government was reflected in the commission's aspirations for a standardised image of the nation. Instead of the haphazard process that had produced an eclectic jumble of strange architectural structures, ranging from palaces to a mid-western post office in Beijing, the FSBC demanded a collective and repetitive symbol of the nation.

3) Historicism: Of all possible strategies for representing the nation, the FSBC opted for a historical style. In part, the decision to identify a robust, forward-looking nation with a distant past was an acceptance of international conventions. Greatness in the international

---

[3] On the obsession with the architectural opulence of both great and second-rate powers see: U. S. House of Representatives. 64th Congress, Report No. 1332 Purchase of Embassy, Legation and Consular Buildings (Washington, D. C., 1917), pp. 4-7.

[4] See various reports in the *New York Times* on the acquisition of palaces for American diplomatic posts: March 22, 1922, p. 16; March 8, 1923, p. 9; January 1, 1926, p. 11; May 28, 1926, p. 21; July 16, 1926, p. 4.

arena was evoked through retrospective architecture. The mobilisation of history made particular sense given the volatile nature of the 1920s. Historical continuity – in this case, the transferral of architectural symbols from a nation's golden age to the present – implied endurance, stability, and strength, in short, all the qualities required during an age of confusing social change and unstable global arrangements. Moreover, the mobilisation of history served to disguise the sharp break with previous patterns of limited global designs and ambitions by suggesting continuity rather than rupture and evolution rather than revolution of American foreign policy.

Historicising the Nation

As for the choice of historical images, the records of the FSBC reveal a debate over two contending representations of the past; the plantation house and the little White House. The commission's first attempt to articulate a historical diplomatic style called for the planting of 'little White Houses all around the world.'[5] On a purely practical level, the White House was an ideal model for a functional embassy. This multi-purpose structure included an office wing and living quarters as well as a ceremonial section. Its architecture was considered 'a splendid example of that colonial type which is distinctively American.'[6] The White House was simple, easily copied, and uniquely American. The White House plan for foreign legations calmed anxieties about the apparent affinities between luxury and decadence, opulence and corruption, which had been raised during the era of palatial embassy procurement, prior to the establishment of the FSBC. The neo-classical design of the White House had terse yet monumental proportions; it avoided the visual richness and elaborate ornamentation that characterised the supposedly monumental structures of decadent societies. At the same time, the neo-classicism of the White House was not bound too rigidly to a levelling, indiscriminate democratic ideology. Indeed, its first great occupants had been patricians, even slave owners.

---

[5] *New York Times Magazine*, February 10, 1924, p. 15. The article attributes the idea of White House embassies to Senator Robert La Follette. This is a mistake, as all other material suggests that the idea was presented by Senator Porter. See for example 'White House For Tokio,' *American Architect*, cxviii (October 13, 1920), p. 484.

[6] *Ibid.*

Despite initially enthusiastic support for the executive mansion as embassy model, the FSBC abruptly abandoned plans for reproducing the White House as symbol of American political virtues. Nothing in the surviving records indicates why this model lost favour. One can only speculate that perhaps the committee's congressional members became wary of the political implications involved in adopting an archetype that lauded the virtues of the rival executive branch of government. All the same, applying the same philosophical reasoning for seeking a historical, uniquely American style, the commission remained loyal to its quest for a uniform, historical, and uniquely American embassy prototype. Instead of the White House, the FSBC chose the southern plantation mansion.[7]

Practically speaking, the adoption of the plantation house was a plausible plan because the commission sought first and foremost a residential structure; the need for office space was of secondary importance. Politically, one could argue in favour of the plantation house because the essence of American democracy had been formulated by country gentlemen from the south. Nevertheless, the choice of a southern model rather than a New England manor or a Far Western domicile requires an explanation. Southern architecture signified sectionalism, represented the spirit of secession, and conjured up memories of internal divisions that had brought the nation to the brink of self-destruction.

The surviving FSBC minutes are somewhat laconic and do not elaborate on the arguments in favour of the plantation manor, but upon examining the prevailing myths of contemporary American society, the attractiveness of the plantation house reveals itself to be quite compelling. To begin with, the essence of American democracy had emerged from the soil of this region. Secondly, a southern representation of the nation's spirit was appealing given the fact that, in foreign lands, the stereotypical assessment of Americans was often that of the predatory Yankee or the violent, irresponsible cowboy. One of the few positive stereotypes of American history in the early 20th century was the resurrected southern gentleman. The new century witnessed a massive sentimentalisation of the Old South. An urban and urbane American society selectively remembered plantation society as the epitome of a noble way of life rather than a vile setting

---

[7] 'Our Buildings in Foreign Countries', *American Foreign Service Journal*, 8 (February, 1931), pp. 51-53.

for human exploitation. This sentimentalisation of the plantation milieu, according to historian William Taylor, was an expression of widespread reservations concerning the restless mobility and aggressive materialism of contemporary society. Modern Americans developed pronounced longings for the antithesis of their self image, 'They longed for a class of men immune to acquisitiveness, indifferent to social ambition, and hostile to commercial life, cities, and secular progress.'[8] Alarmed by the impact of immigrants on American life, and disturbed by new and seemingly 'foreign' aspects of modern America, the nation's power wielders embarked on a nostalgic journey to a golden age where the principal destination was the mythical, innocent South of the *ante-bellum* years.

From the very beginning of the 20th century, American culture showed many signs of being enraptured by a sentimental version of the south. In literature this tendency was eloquently expressed in the works of Thomas Dixon. In his best-selling novels, *The Leopard's Spots* (1902) and *The Clansman* (1905), the southern domicile symbolised fundamental values of the American way that had supposedly originated in the south – order, permanence and a stability derived from close contact with the soil. Dixon was followed in the later years of the 1920s by a cast of 'Agrarian' writers, who discovered redeeming qualities for the entire nation in the innocent and noble agrarian south. The epitome of a healthy American society, according to this school of literature, lay in the Deep South, with its 'fair balance of aristocratic and democratic elements.' Donald Davidson, literary critic and articulate spokesman of the Agrarian movement in literature, stated that nowhere were the redeeming qualities of southerners more evident than in their architecture which 'was in excellent harmony with their milieu.' The old plantation houses, 'with their pillared porches, their simplicity of design, their sheltered groves, their walks bordered with boxwood shrubs', spelt order, grace, and unity and counterpoised contemporary complexity, philistinism and fragmentation.[9] This love affair with the plantation house was by no means restricted to literary circles. During this same period, suave New York moguls were employing America's foremost architects to build summer residences in the style of southern plantation houses.

---

[8]   Taylor, 1957, pp. 201, 334, 341.

[9]   Davidson quoted in Davenport, 1967, p. 61.

The uneven implementation of what was meant to be a universal policy suggests that the representation of the embassy as a plantation house was a sensitive political issue. The guidelines for a standardised style of embassies were, in actual fact, implemented selectively. By 1928, the FSBC had approved the construction of ten new legations, but for three of these, in Japan, Canada and France, the commission chose not to build plantation embassies. Plantation manors were planned for all of the other sites. Four of the buildings, all in Latin America, were cancelled – Lima in Peru; Managua in Nicaragua, Matanzas in Cuba and Panama City, Panama. The remaining three buildings were planned for what are nowadays called developing countries: Aden, China, and India.

The ostensible reason for diverting most resources for embassy construction to Central America and the 'Orient' was that 'health conditions were bad and European amenities non existent.'[10] Yet this explanation fails to suggest why the plantation style was so rigorously implemented in these regions. Similarity of climate was the most common reason given for reproducing the southern manor in these locations: irrespective of differences in climatic and sanitary conditions, the Asian and Latin American sites were all stigmatised as wilderness areas with vaguely tropical climates, for which plantation architecture was both politically and environmentally appropriate. The sketch of the Lima Embassy, for example, reveals the spurious nature of this argument. This embassy, according to State Department officials, was a faithful derivation of Mississippi plantation architecture, although the cool, arid, perpetually cloudy weather in Lima had nothing in common with the climactic conditions of the southern states of the US.

Using oppressive weather as a metaphor rather than an objective assessment of prevailing climatic conditions, the State Department effectively divided the world into two blocs. In the empires and the 'civilised' countries of the world, the United States did not use the southern colonial style, while in the 'uncivilised' corners of the globe a stereotypical tropical climate was invented in order to rationalise the condescending representations promoted by the American body politic. Regardless of climatic, topographical and cultural differences, the American government planned diplomatic replicas of the Old

---

[10]   *New York Times*, May 23, 1927, p. 10.

South in Asia and in the capital cities of Central and South American client states.[11]

Inadvertently or not, plantation architecture was an unambiguous reflection of American objectives in Latin America. The region often appeared to be an extension of the American south, in the sense that an American planter class dominated its economic structure. As for the unexploited regions of Asia, these were part of America's new frontier designs, figuring prominently in the economic and cultural expansionism of the period.

Due to the Great Depression, the construction of most plantation sites was never completed. Nevertheless, their architectural sketches and plans reveal much about their salient qualities as political artefacts, as well as the speciousness of the argument for the climatic appropriateness of these structures. The selective implementation of these southern-colonial prototypes illustrated the manner in which the State Department had sorted the world into two distinct diplomatic territories; countries where the United States merely intended to show the flag in a dignified fashion, and 'underdeveloped' regions of the world on which the United States had economic and/or territorial designs. In countries where the United States limited its objectives to a dignified symbolic presence, the State Department continued its policy of either purchasing or building palaces, in line with local architectural fashion. The use of southern colonial architecture in other parts of the world suggests that, rather than being approached as individual countries, the New World was considered virgin territory of insignificant cultural and political divisions upon which enterprising Americans could still make their mark without fear of arousing the wrath of any meaningful political entity.

By the 1930s, the plantation house model appeared to be losing favour. Once again, the changing mood and growing disillusionment with the plantation manor as symbol of the national self was reflected quite vividly in the literature of the times. Margaret Mitchell's epic saga of the south, *Gone With The Wind* (1936), ended dramatically with Scarlett O'Hara gazing at the charred ruins of Tara. The novels of William Faulkner, *The Sound and the Fury* (1929), and *Sanctuary*

---

[11]   Foreign Service Buildings Commission, *Report of the Progress on the Purchase of Sites and Construction of Buildings for the Foreign Service of the United States* (Washington, D. C., 1929), p. 19.

(1931), were scattered with descriptions of rotting, almost foetid, southern mansions. The cheerless plantation house in literature coincided with disenchantment with southern virtues in political circles. If the south represented anything, according to the new President, Franklin D. Roosevelt, it was the epitome of the infirmities of the nation. The south was the most economically backward and socially reactionary section of the country. There was, according to the newly elected President, a southern problem plaguing the United States.[12]

The plantation house as embassy model also lost favour for more diplomatic reasons. Dissenting voices claimed that these and other attempts at self-aggrandisement were counter-productive. James McDonald, the executive director of the Foreign Policy Association, warned that America's international relations were being jeopardised by the country's 'attitude of the superior helping the inferior'. 'As long as Americans continue to boast that they are different from and better than other nations', he added, 'they are sowing the seed of much ill feeling among other nations.'[13]

With the change of president in the early 1930s, and within the context of a new socio-economic period, the concept of the embassy as a little White House received new life. Despite the spectre of global conflict and economic turmoil, three little White Houses were constructed; in Yokohama, Japan (1932), Baghdad (1932) and Chungking (1942). The economic and political events of the 1930s and 1940s halted any further proliferation of embassies in general, many of which had been planned as White Houses.

The Significance of Embassy Construction in the 1920s

The embassy construction programme reveals certain important aspects of American foreign policy in the period following the First World War. To begin with, these activities took place under Republican presidents often remembered for their inactivity and incorrectly labelled as isolationists. Presidents Harding, Coolidge, and Hoover laid the foundations for using architecture as a tool of foreign policy. In the years following the Second World War, the federal government would initiate an unprecedented expansion of its political architecture

---

[12] Roosevelt quoted in Davenport, 1967, p. 92.
[13] *New York Times*, May 23, 1929, p. 24.

abroad, for which the fundamental rationale was derived from the experiences of the 1920s. Building on the precedent of plantation embassies, but employing a different strategy, embassy architecture in the 1950s and 1960s would be used as a tool for both defining and controlling the *Pax Americana*. In the post World War II period, US diplomatic edifices were mostly anti-historical and futuristic; montages of local decorative motifs given new life through the use of technological innovations. Here the search for legitimacy by tracing roots in the past was conspicuously absent, as was the celebration of rural democracy. The guiding light was provided by forward-looking modernisation rather than backward looking historicism.

The elements of this process had been elaborated during the 1920s. The necessary infrastructure of a political advisory board and a supervising bureaucracy were already firmly in place in these years and provided the basis for the expansion of the role of the State Department some 30 years later. The unassuming Republican administrations of the 1920s had quietly developed an important diplomatic mechanism for years to come.

The embassy construction programme also provided a fascinating reflection of how domestic politics and culture within the United States operated upon the formation of the country's foreign policy. The iconography chosen to represent the United States abroad was the continuation of a cultural discourse on federalism and sectionalism, the nature of American culture and the contribution of the south to the cultural framework of early 20th century America. Behind the seemingly single-minded pursuit of pure foreign policy objectives lay continuously shifting conflicts between competing cultural interests in the United States, between north and south, and between nostalgic isolationism and aggressive *realpolitik*. The inner tensions between change and continuity, and regionalism and federalism, accounted for much of the country's diplomatic symbolism during the inter-war years.

CHAPTER 10

The Baltic as Image and Illusion: The Construction of a Region between Europe and the Nation

BO STRÅTH

Throughout history, the Baltic has been a sea of conflicts and dividing lines. While this was especially evident during the Cold War, the dividing line that cut straight through the Baltic from north to south was in fact much older than the Cold War. It was in order to hide this and other expressions of power and political ambitions that the term 'Sea of Peace' was invented.

This concept expressed a Soviet vision of the 1950s and, like all visions, this one had an ambiguous and contradictory content. The concept of the Sea of Peace encompassed the notion of a Soviet *mare nostrum*, an inland sea for the exercise of Soviet power politics. As so often happened during the Cold War, in both the East and the West, the notion of the Baltic as a nuclear-free zone linked together the concepts of peace and power. The Baltic was to form a protective zone of peaceful understanding and trade, beyond the Cold War lines of conflict. The western view maintained that the Sea of Peace was nothing more than a mythical mask which the Soviet Union used to hide its power ambitions. According to this perspective, the concept of the Sea of Peace meant direct confrontation transformed into practical politics. The ambivalence of this concept was one of the ironies of the Cold War. As a meaningful concept it was a dead letter long before the end of that particular conflict, indeed, in the West it was discredited as early as the beginning of the 1950s, after which it became meaningful only as another example of Soviet hypocrisy.

After the fall of the Berlin Wall and the Iron Curtain in 1989, there was a great desire to reduce the vast quantities of weapons that had been amassed around the Sea of Peace and to transform the former geopolitical threats into new possibilities. In the euphoria of late autumn 1989, the vision of a sea that joined nations instead of dividing them began to take shape, the vision of a sea that conveyed peaceful trade and economic development rather than battle fleets. But the disarmament process also presented great difficulties within the project of western integration, since the fall of the Wall and the Iron Curtain reopened the 200 year-old question of what Europe is and what it is not. The new concept of Central Europe that was formed at that time expressed the hope of countries such as Poland, Czechoslovakia, and Hungary that they could move away from the concept of Eastern Europe which, since 1945, had always come under the Soviet sphere of influence. The events of late 1989 meant that Europe's eastern border had moved eastwards. But how far? Did Russia belong to Europe? It is clear that Gorbachev with his concept of 'the European House' was claiming that Russia was European, but west of the old Iron Curtain this was not so obvious.

In order to prevent this problem from provoking a relapse into the polarising tensions of the Cold War there arose the notion of the Baltic as a unifying alternative to the European integration process. This notion linked northern Germany's interest in promoting economic expansion and dynamism in areas where it had inherent advantages over the politically and economically dominant regions of the south, to Sweden's political interest in finding alternatives to the dominance of continental Europe, which, since the 1930s, had been experienced as a threat to the image of a Protestant and progressive Sweden (see my chapter on the construction of Swedish national identity). In the Swedish self-image, Europe was conservative, capitalist, and Catholic.[1] The notion of the Baltic offered a rhetorical alternative in the attempts to break down the popular resistance to Sweden's plans to join the European Community. Economic interests in Sweden and Germany saw the Baltic as the link that could connect them to the expanding Russian market. To put it succinctly, the end of the Cold War resulted in a redefinition of interests and a reassessment

---

[1]   Cf. Stråth, 1993.

of perspectives in light of new political and economic possibilities. For the first time in history these perspectives hinted at the possibility of a Sea of Peace in the actual meaning of the term. But as it turned out, this expression was utterly unviable as a guiding concept for the expression of these visions. It had been corrupted far too much to be recharged with a new and up-to-date content. A brand new concept had to be sought in order to express a new, peaceful Baltic vision, a vision that, unlike its predecessor, would not offer a contradiction to power but, although hidden, be *linked* to power, albeit economic and not military.

No one foresaw the events of 1989. Debates and theories within both history and the social sciences had all considered the Cold War to be a clear framework for foreseeing future events, and German reunification was just as unthinkable as the Soviet Empire's implosion. The consequences of the razing of the Wall and the fall of the Iron Curtain were decisive in provoking the widespread revision of debates and theories within political science. Amidst the general euphoria at the beginning of the 1990s, many academics came to believe that the lowest common denominator of this development was the dissolution of the entire modern state system. Economists rushed to support the political scientists. The former Soviet Empire became a giant laboratory for applied economics that would demonstrate that it was free market forces and not the state that was the factor responsible for development and prosperity and so illustrate how correct neo-liberal rhetoric had been.

The view that now came to be applied to the Baltic region was that of an entity where a period of some 500 years of centralised states was coming to an end, and where political legitimacy and authority were seen as progressively more dependent upon administrative levels beyond the centralised state. From this perspective, the increasingly predicted end of the nation-state would not automatically lead to the emergence of a strong 'supra-national' organisation like the EU, state-oriented on a new and higher level. Rather, it would produce ever more complex systems of administration and communication in which political power and legitimacy would be distributed among more and more levels.[2]

---

[2] See, for instance, Jann, 1993 and Gerner, 1990.

In this future scenario, parallels were drawn with medieval political structures in which the Pope had certain prerogatives, as did the emperor, the king, the feudal lord and the community. In this context, political authority shifted depending on the nature of the question, while in the classic centralised territorial state, which began to develop around 1500, only a single political authority was recognised. This analogy with the Middle Ages made it appear evident that post-1989 Europe was not about to give rise to a new centralised power to replace the one that had imploded. The historical and political rhetoric linked up nicely with the economic rhetoric, that claimed that the market, and not the state, was the relevant steering mechanism for a functioning economy. The emerging scholarly discourse spoke of the dispersal of power and the softening of the entire concept of sovereignty. 200 years of misguided European development, arising from the fateful linkage of the concepts of nation and state were coming to an end, and the social organisation of the Middle Ages offered the new model. The Holy Roman Empire became, *cum grano salis*, the intellectual leitmotif that replaced the French Revolution.

This intellectual current can only be understood against the background of the general euphoria at the beginning of the 1990s. The situation was revolutionary, in the sense that this concept has had since the French Revolution; suddenly everything was possible. But the euphoria that gave rise to new visions of the Baltic was short-lived. Towards the middle of the 1990s, the crisis of political legitimacy arising from the lack of control over the economy that had already been responsible for the collapse of the socialist state system, spread to western industrial nations. The epicentre of this crisis of legitimacy was the nation-state, in which political power was concentrated, but that could no longer guarantee prosperity as it had done previously. The conventions of state-centred social responsibility that had developed in the western industrial nations had, in the 1930s, after decades of social bargaining, found their solution: the state. Paradoxically, one of the manifestations of this crisis of legitimacy in the 1990s was the way the nation-state became ever more in demand and signs of populism and national introspection increased while, at the same time, it was proclaimed that the complex and uncontrollable social problems that had brought about and accelerated the crisis of legitimacy could only really be solved through international co-operation.

It was during this brief moment of euphoria around 1990, with the Middle Ages held up as the model for a new world, that the view of the Baltic changed.[3] If the Baltic had once been a region divided into spheres of influence founded upon power politics – and therefore too dangerous to touch – now the possibilities of the area were emphasised. The notion of a Sea of Peace was promoted, but naturally without using this corrupted term. Instead a metaphor was introduced that drew its orientation from the Middle Ages. When Schleswig-Holstein's Prime Minister, Björn Engholm, began to speak of the 'New Hansa', his source of inspiration was an idealised image of the medieval German trade organisation as a network of independent cities without a centre or hierarchy. Above the Hansa stood only the emperor who, for many questions, was far away. Björn Engholm's New Hansa was a sort of postmodernist notion of a trans-national, non-hierarchical, integrated network structure.[4] This net, stretched across the Baltic, was to draw together eastern, western, and northern Europe.

Historians developed the medieval metaphor and granted it scholarly legitimacy. They traced the development back to the time before the French Revolution, when Europe had supposedly gone off track, in order to create a better future.[5] Social science theorists shored up these thoughts with concepts such as 'policy network', 'community', 'civil society' (in contrast to the state), 'regionalisation' and the like. Policy networks supposedly developed from below as a response to the emerging problems that had remained unsolved under state rule. These networks were focal points for the pressure of organised interests and for defining regional problems. Social scientists assumed that given their quality as a 'modern' form of administration, networks would foster mutual understanding, consensus, trust, and co-operation. The scholarly discussion about networks and

---

[3] The vision of a new, and at the same time historically legitimised, Baltic emerged when the growing expectations for the nation-state community generated by the forces of globalisation were canalised in new directions in a form of by-pass operation.

[4] Cf. Jann, 1993.

[5] Cf. Gerner, 1990.

regionalisation went hand in glove with the political, medieval vision of a Baltic built around the Hansa.[6]

The Soviet myth of the Baltic as the 'Sea of Peace' encountered its neo-liberal double in the term 'New Hansa'. In the euphoria around 1990, which some optimists interpreted as the end of history, the Baltic was conjured up as a new category of community. The political attempts to create new communities from the material of the medieval myth were legitimised by scholars who increasingly turned their backs on the state while praising the potential of the market. The Hansa and an idealised version of the Middle Ages became the underlying concept in processes that were aimed at developing new identities and redefining interests.

The new Hansa and the new Baltic were intended to replace the concept of the Sea of Peace with the concept of the peaceful sea unified as a network. But what did they actually look like? What historical foundation did Björn Engholm's Hanseatic medieval myth have which enabled it to create political visions of the future? By myth, I mean a special kind of story about the past that symbolises the values of a group and legitimises their positions or claims. Myth is a slippery and ambiguous term, and the question of the possible truth or falsehood of these stories is never resolved, or rather, it is only resolved in cases when it is raised during the very period in which it is evoked. This is the case here, and therefore the truth content of this myth needs to be discussed briefly. With concepts such as 'historical foundation' and truth content we are dealing with relationships that are far more complex than the dichotomy between true or false. It is more a question of how alternative images with a trace of truth can be distilled from the historical sources. Such an alternative historical scenario can be sketched out for the Baltic without difficulty.

The spread of German cultural and economic activity around the Baltic began in the 12th century. *Plattdeutsch*, Lübeck artwork, and commercial families formed a tightly spun web. The German influence was also felt politically as the Teutonic Knights extended their influence across the Baltic region. Danish expansion plans in the same direction at the beginning of the 13th century were effectively stopped with the battle of Bornhoved in 1227. Albrecht of Mecklenburg

---

[6] For a discussion of the emergence of the regional discourse in the academic sphere, see Pichierri, forthcoming.

became King of Sweden in the second half of the 14th century and brought with him a considerable retinue of mercenaries and administrators. That is as far as Germanisation went. Albrecht's administration encountered resistance from the aristocracy, the church and the peasants; in other words, from all centres of power. Queen Margrethe of Denmark exploited this resistance and organised it politically and militarily. Albrecht's German forces were defeated on the battlefield in 1389 and the king was forced to withdraw home to Mecklenburg. From Rostock and Wismar a trade boycott was mounted against the Nordic nations, and pirate and freebooter activity was supported on the Baltic. The German pirates occupied Stockholm and raided the Swedish and Finnish coasts, lending their support to the Hansa in the Baltic in a conflict that had a clear German-Nordic dimension. The Kalmar Union of 1397 between Sweden (of which Finland was an integral part), Denmark, and Norway can be seen as a political counterblow aimed at the Hanseatic 'colonialism' in the north. This union, which lasted until 1521, was the political response of the Nordic powers to the German infiltration in culture, language, economics, administration, and politics. The idea of German and Nordic as elements of the *same* Germanic culture was transformed into a conflict between German and Nordic cultures. There thus developed a line in the southern Baltic that marked the division between north and south. Of course, this line ran in a different direction to that of the Cold War's east-west division, but the situation was much better characterised by this division than by the idea of a Hanseatic seamless web.

Strong political, economic and cultural forces acted upon the Nordic-German dividing line. The Nordic front in particular was not especially solid since the Kalmar Union was full of conflicts between potentates and was characterised by economic interests in ever-shifting constellations. There was no real question of an early form of German and Nordic national feelings that stood against one another. In parts of Sweden there soon developed dissatisfaction with the union's policy against the Hansa, which disrupted important commercial interests such as iron exports. The banner of rebellion was hoisted by Engelbrekt. The Hansa therefore not only had a unifying effect, but also a disrupting one. The same forces that drove the Nordic kingdoms together in a union also drove them apart. During the 16th century, the Hansa was an important power factor, playing a role in the increasing Danish-Swedish conflict, but this was to be the last time it would exert such an influence before it was finally dissolved.

This is a very different image of the Hansa metaphor from that which was described around 1990. Against the idealised view of the Baltic as a borderless region woven together through culture and commerce, one can juxtapose this image of a warlike Baltic, notorious for military conflicts, plundering and piracy, a *mare bellicus* as it were. Of course, this is not to say that the view in the 1990s was completely false and that a different, more 'truthful' one should be set up to replace it. We are dealing here with different descriptions of reality. Both images contain elements that have a basis in the sources. The truth depends on the particular perspective adopted. We are not talking about the era 'as it really was'. That reality is completely inaccessible in the sense that we cannot convey it to our present without at least attempting to translate it within the limits set by our contemporary language and symbols. In other words, the discussion is about *our* image of that era.

The idealised view of the Baltic as a borderless, rich and communicative body of water can be traced back even further than the Hansa. The same is also true for the opposite view of the warlike Baltic region, criss-crossed by dynastic, religious, and economic ambitions. The extensive body of historical writing on the Vikings has taken the Baltic as an important field of study, and the Viking era can, in many ways, be seen as a preliminary stage of the Hanseatic epoch. It is especially in reference to the Hansa that there has a emerged an idealisèd image of the Vikings as a people engaged in peaceful commerce as opposed to the conventional warlike view. It is debatable to what extent the Vikings' expansion across Europe should be seen as a consequence of peaceful trade or systematic plundering, but it is clear in any case that the idealised image is much too simple for both the Viking era and for the Hansa. This is an image that reflects the mood that prevailed when the image was recreated around 1990, not the time it is intended to describe.

The European trans-oceanic, political, and military expansion that began in the 1490s directed commercial interests more and more toward the Atlantic. This marked the end of the Baltic's golden age as the region lost importance in relative terms and Baltic trading became increasingly peripheral. But if Germany's economic and political penetration of the Baltic region to the north became less significant, its cultural and administrative influence continued; the introduction of Protestantism to the Nordic countries and the translation of the New Testament into the Scandinavian and Finnish languages were, of course, inspired by Luther; Gustav Vasa brought in German assistants to structure and develop a centralised state administration; and political reforms were introduced on the Saxon model. Laurentius Andrae, Olaus Petri, Conrad von Pyhy, and Georg Norman are some of the figures who personify this process of Germanisation. In this sense, we can speak of a significant continuity in German penetration after the formal dissolution of the Hansa. We can also speak of a network that linked the Baltic region together, although here it is important that we do not regard the content of these network relationships in purely idealistic terms, but consider also their political power context. German political and administrative support in the construction of a Swedish central power entailed a significant amount of exploitation in the context of centre-periphery relations.

There developed, superimposed on this German network across the Nordic countries, a new dividing line in the Baltic. The old division between the Nordic region and the Hansa was replaced by a new one between Sweden and Denmark. The power struggle over the control of the Baltic shifted from being a German-Nordic affair to an intra-Nordic affair, in keeping with the Baltic region's increasing commercial marginalisation. The region was therefore still marked by a dividing line, albeit of a different appearance and content, and in this, as well as in the presence of the interwoven networks, there was a clear element of continuity.

The Swedish-Danish conflict drew to a close during the 1600s, with the Swedes having gained the upper hand. One consequence of this was that the dividing line became less obvious. But even during the ensuing century or so, during which the Baltic can be described as practically a Swedish lake, the dividing line was still there beneath the surface. Karlskrona was founded in 1679 as a naval base on the border with Denmark. Swedish dominance was achieved through struggles against Russian, Polish, and Danish forces, and was in turn challenged by them, indicating that military and naval movements were just as important components of the Baltic as peaceful trade among the different parts of this region.

The Baltic had scarcely become a Swedish *mare nostrum* in the 17th century when new lines of conflict began to develop, this time produced by Russia's drive to the Baltic. The Russian alliance with the Poles and the Danes would, in 1720, finally and definitively crush Swedish sovereignty in the Baltic and, at the same time, activate the new dividing lines. The wars and subsequent peace settlements of 1741-1743, 1788-1790, and 1808-1809 reinforced these dividing lines even more. When, in the mid-18th century, Sweden began building the fortress of Sveaborg in Helsinki, directly across from the Russian fortress in Reval (Talinn) on the opposite shore of the Bay of Finland, the dividing line received a sort of symbolic representation. From 1809, when Finland went from being a part of Sweden to become a Russian grand duchy, this dividing line was reinforced yet again.

In the course of the 18th century, the Russian expansion into the Baltic region was increasingly complemented by a Prussian expansion in the same direction. For the first time since the Hansa, a formidable German military offensive was directed toward the Baltic (if one does not count Wallenstein and the Catholic League during the Thirty Years War in this category). The halt in German expansion during the Napoleonic Wars was only temporary and, after 1815, Russia and Prussia were the dominant powers in the Baltic. They were, at the same time, potential enemies around whom other states had to arrange themselves as best they could. The construction of a Scandinavian ideology, as well as the difficulties in transforming it into practical politics, are rooted in this new power situation that emerged after 1815.

Matti Klinge has shown what this development meant on the level of mentality in Sweden. From a mental image of a realm that ran east-west, there gradually emerged, through the Swedish experience of repression (in the Freudian sense) over the loss of Finland, a new identity-building north-south mental map.[7] This map fitted well with practical political realities, as Russia gradually came to be viewed as the prime threat to Sweden, just as Prussia would be seen as a threat to Denmark some years later.

In this respect, the 'politics of 1812' of Jean Baptiste Bernadotte, the successor to the Swedish throne, did not change very much at all. These politics resulted in an agreement with the Russian tsar when Sweden had relinquished its plans to re-conquer Finland. This agreement was met with a certain amount of surprise in Sweden, since

---

[7]   Klinge, 1983. The earlier east-west image encompassed the Sea of Åland and the Baltic as a Swedish lake that united the realm's central regions from Lake Mälaren westward around Stockholm to Åbo, Nyland, and Österbotten on the Finnish side, where the forest regions of Småland and Värmland in Sweden were just as peripheral as Savolaks and Lapland in Finland.

the expectation had been that the Napoleonic field marshal cum Swedish king (Karl XIV Johan, 1818-48) would in fact re-conquer Finland. Instead of Finland, Bernadotte asked for and received compensation in the west. Under the Treaty of Kiel of 1814, in the aftermath of the Napoleonic Wars, Norway was transferred from Denmark, which had supported Napoleon, and entered into a union with Sweden (1814-1905). The Baltic now divided more than it united. Even if the 'politics of 1812' and the Congress of Vienna in 1815 changed the geopolitical landscape and there were signs that the Baltic might develop into a sea of armed peace, there soon emerged new tensions, this time between Russia and Great Britain (that particular era's east-west conflict) that turned the Baltic into a focus for conflicting interests.

It was in an attempt to withdraw from these growing divisions that, in 1834, Karl XIV Johan declared that Sweden wished to be neutral. This was the first time that the term had been used in Swedish foreign policy. However, Swedish neutrality was not to be long-lived; it was forgotten as soon as the situation around Swedish waters began to seem less threatening, if only temporarily. Nor did Swedish neutrality have any effect in reducing the level of conflict among the major power interests. The Crimean War of 1854-6 also affected the Baltic, with the British-French fleet blasting away the Bomarsund fortress on Åland and bombarding the Finnish coast.

Prior to this, Prussia had, in its turn, increased the tensions in the Baltic region with its war of conquest against Denmark between 1848 and 1849. After the next Prussian attacks on Denmark in 1864, one could perceive two potential great powers in the region. At first Prussia and Russia formed something like an armed peace by co-ordinating a joint policy of suppressing Danish and Polish interests, but following the founding of the German Empire in 1871, there emerged the clear risk of a German-Russian conflict. Bismarck sought at all costs to avoid such a development through his policy of alliances, but during the 1890s, after his removal from power, this line of conflict developed even more visibly.

The leaders of the Nordic countries had to manoeuvre around this potential threat. When Denmark was attacked from the south, the Scandinavian countries, in the name of 'Scandinavianism', made an attempt to revive the medieval coalition against the Hansa. Scandinavianism became an ideology for repelling the Russian and German threats, but, all things considered, the German and Russian threats were too strong to bring about a Nordic coalition. In Sweden and Norway no one was prepared to die for Denmark. On the other hand, Sweden saw Russia as its greatest threat during the 19th century, but in Denmark no one was prepared to die for Sweden in a struggle against Russia. By no later than 1864, Scandinavianism had revealed itself to a bourgeois society as little more than a student fantasy which offered little alternative to brutal power politics.

The German-Russian tension was not reduced by French naval visits to Russia or by Germany's decision in 1864 to upgrade its fleet. Kiel and St. Petersburg were increasingly transformed into opposing symbols of naval military strength, and the Russification policy in Finland around 1900 must be seen in this context of German naval expansion. The imperial German-Russian negotiations on the high seas in 1905 and 1907 were aimed at masking the growing tensions. The same goal lay behind the Baltic exhibition in Malmö as late as 1914. This exhibition was characterised by the illusion of a Baltic ideology that could secure peace. During the World War I, the Baltic was a militarised and mined waterway, and it was only these mines that prevented a major naval battle.

The end of the war and the toppling of the Russian and German empires drastically reduced the military tensions in the region. It *could* have been seen as symbolic that it was the sailors of Kronstadt, near St. Petersburg, and Kiel who, with their uprisings, precipitated the fall of the imperial thrones, and for a brief historical moment, there was the possibility that a Sea of Peace might be created by the common sailors themselves. In the long run, however, other powers were much stronger. The promise of a Sea of Peace proved to be just as transient as it had been after the Napoleonic Wars. During the 1930s, the tensions in the region rose dramatically. In Sweden, the Social Democratic Foreign Minister, Richard Sandler, strove to set up a Nordic coalition in response to the growing sense of threat. He conceived of a joint Swedish-Finnish defence of the island of Åland which would have prevented either Germany or the Soviet Union from occupying it. Since it was in the interest of both great powers that neither should gain a foothold there, he considered that both would find the plan acceptable. However, the Nordic ideology proved to be just as flimsy when faced with the growing military threat as it had been in 1864. Stalin refused to accept Sandler's plan, and the Nordic governments allowed themselves be intimidated rather than rally together against the growth of military power in the Baltic. It would have been almost comical – had it not been so serious – when Denmark signed a non-aggression treaty with Germany, as if Denmark represented a military threat to the might of Germany. Within the Swedish government, Ernst Wigforss was especially opposed to all military co-operation among the Nordic nations. This was not the first time that a Swedish finance minister sank a Nordic coalition – in 1864 it had been J. A. Gripenstedt who had refused Swedish assistance to Denmark. Economic and political factors had demanded good relationships with the great powers in the Baltic region in the 1860s just as much as they did in the 1930s, but these economic and political dependencies had never constituted a peaceful network capable of preventing war.

During World War II, the Baltic was once again a theatre of operations. After the war, the demarcation line of the Cold War powers went straight through this Baltic. The vision of a Sea of Peace was projected onto a situation which was perceived as threatening, indeed, this was the very reason for its projection. The vision was a sign that the Baltic region was anything but as peaceful as it was depicted. Of course, one can point out that, in contrast to Central Europe where the forces of East and West stood facing one another directly, there was no Iron Curtain that passed through Sweden, and Finland lay between NATO and the Warsaw Pact. On the other hand, the presence of Russian submarines among Sweden's islands was a reminder that the neutral powers also stood in the shadow of the superpowers. It was not only Sweden and Finland, but also Denmark and Norway that contributed to the relative minimalising of the East-West confrontation in the Baltic region through their refusal to allow the stationing of nuclear weapons and foreign troops on their territory during peacetime. But these conditions could not hide the fact that, even without an Iron Curtain, the line of conflict through the Baltic was obvious.

This, as they say, is where we came in. We have come full circle to the starting point of this chapter: the myths of the Sea of Peace and the peaceful Hansa. The interesting thing about these myths is not only the visionary power they attempt to convey, but also the way they break with the long continuity of war and conflict in the Baltic region. If anything stands for continuity in this region, it is conflict rather than peace. In fact, it is this continuity of war and violence that has given rise to this alternative vision.

Was there nothing besides weapons and warfare in the Baltic? Is there not an historical basis for the peaceful visions too? How did peaceful pursuits relate to the military muscle-flexing in a long historical perspective over many centuries? These questions contain another one: Why has no one written a history of the Baltic on the model of Braudel's *The Mediterranean*? Braudel depicts the Mediterranean's long and durable structures, conveying the impression of the industrious cultivation of the land and the peaceful sharing of its fruits, despite the fact that since ancient times the Mediterranean has been characterised by a history just as belligerent as that of the Baltic. In Braudel's perspective, these conflict are consigned to the turbulent history of events that, in his *longue durée*, are no more than tiny ripples on the surface. In contrast to the hasty mobilisation of the Hansa by politicians, historians, and political scientists after 1989, which cannot help but look like some sort of historiographical grab bag, Braudel worked with a methodological thoroughness impermeable to the political events of the day, and this is the great value of his *Mediterranean*. In the Baltic there also existed, alongside the sea battles, networks between burghers and nobility that went beyond state authorities and represented longer and more durable structures beneath the warlike surface.[8] But a Braudelian *The Baltic* that addresses the structures of this region has yet to be written. All the same, the Mediterranean and the Baltic display certain interesting similarities. Both have gone from a role as a leading trade and production centre for Europe's economy to a marginal existence, and both are now seeking to create new meaning for themselves in the context of the globalisation process, a process that has seen the development of new identities and communities in an attempt to counteract the alienating effects of global culture and economy.

The construction of community in the Baltic region on the basis of the Hansa myth began to flounder after the initial euphoria at the beginning of the 1990s wore off. It became apparent that within the region there were great disparities in economic strength as well as in both physical and immaterial infrastructure. Apart from this, there were also great cultural differences. Three great Christian doctrines had taken root there over the course of time; Roman Catholicism in

---

[8]   See, for instance, Attman, 1946a and *ibid.,* 1946b.

Poland and Lithuania, Greek Orthodoxy in Russia, and Protestantism in varying forms in the Nordic countries, Germany, Estonia, and Latvia. The historical experiences of a warlike and violent development, in which Germany and Russia in particular have played important roles, have left deep wounds in the region. These wounds are still regularly reopened, giving rise to powerful aversions. Different cultural and economic experiences, enhanced by forced contact with other cultures, have led to the search for new identities in the wake of the events of 1989. These factors have acted centrifugally to propel different interest groups in different directions. This centrifugal force is intensified by factors that are much less present in, for example, the European Union. Not least, there are the communication difficulties exacerbated by ten different languages belonging to radically different linguistic groups; Slavic, Finno-Ungric, and Germanic. Among the other problems are the ethnic tensions in the Baltic countries, while the handling of the post-Soviet identity problem is difficult and contains the potential for conflict. The environmental problem in the form of contaminated soil and water, high risk sites like ex-Soviet nuclear reactors, and cross-border organised crime that has recently become extended to the smuggling of radioactive material, are some of the factors that have eroded the Hansa myth.

The Baltic discourse gradually transformed the Hansa myth and made it politically viable by expressing a functionalistic perspective through which different authorities could gradually seek and find a workable form of political co-operation within the region. Little by little, these co-operative networks were brought together, but this process was more the result of trying to solve everyday problems than the outcome of national policy. A functional co-operation appeared to be emerging around political issues such as economics and trade, security, the environment and culture.[9] Concrete co-operative projects and institutions reinforced this notion of pragmatic functionalism. The parallels between this point of view and emerging interpretations of the (Western) European integration process are obvious. But just as this new web of co-operative projects and institutions was taking form, the optimistic notion of impending economic expansion fuelled by growing Russian buying power began to fade. With the decline of expectations in the performance of the Russian market and in the

---

[9]   For this development, see Jann, 1993 pp. 191-192.

213

notion of a Russian civil society on the western model, so too the Baltic rhetoric and the Hansa myth started to disappear.

The Hansa metaphor was a unique expression of the attempt to combine two incompatible aspirations. First, there was the idea that Russia was to become part of the western modernisation process. The underlying thought was that this modernisation represented a sort of normal development in which Russia could also now participate by means of introducing a western-style civil society and a capitalist market. Abstractions such as market, network, and civil society took on concrete dimensions in this discourse. It was believed that this was something that could be introduced simply by copying what various economic theorists had suggested for western societies. None of the economists or social scientists who were writing these prescriptions ever questioned the role of cultural and historical pre-conditions in transcribing this 'standard development' model.

The second aspiration was that Russia should stand aside from European development. The Hansa metaphor sought to recreate the 200 year old borderline between Europe and the Other by pushing Russia further eastwards after the end of the Cold War. This borderline would then be transcended by linking it to abstractions such as the market, civil society, and networks. Russia should not be part of the European Union, but the borderline created from this standpoint should still be capable of being crossed with the help of the Hansa metaphor and the Baltic rhetoric. When, towards the end of the 1990s, it had become clear that Russia was not following the standard development model of economic and sociological theory, the border-line between Us and the Other began to look insurmountable, and the expectation that it could be transcended through networks and market arrangements vanished. Along with these expectations the Hansa metaphor vanished too. The familiar old borderline was still there.

MYTH AND MEMORY
IN THE CONSTRUCTION OF THE NATION

CHAPTER 11

The Emergence and Transformation
of Foundation Myths

Wolfgang KASCHUBA

On 23rd March, 1999, United States special envoy, Richard Holbrook, who had visited Belgrade in an attempt to negotiate a solution with Yugoslav President, Slobodan Milosevic, over the issue of autonomy for Kosovo, announced that talks had failed. The same day, NATO authorised air strikes in the Federal Republic of Yugoslavia. As this book goes to print, in early summer 1999, there is talk of peace, but for now the air strikes continue. The media reports on the conflict carry 'factual', technical features on missions flown, aircraft used and targets hit, they offer 'human' stories on the suffering of refugees or the 'reality' of life in Belgrade, and they carry political dispatches, outlining diplomatic initiatives, tensions within the NATO or the outrage of the opponents of the war. In a morass of moral ambiguity and contradiction, there have been attempts to simplify the issues surrounding the war by evoking 'morally unambiguous' history, a history that almost becomes parable. Thus, for example, President Bill Clinton, on the day air strikes were authorised, asked an audience if it would not have been better if we had listened to Churchill in the 1930s and stood up to Hitler, and this theme finds daily resonance in the use of the term 'genocide' in the Western press.

Apart from parallels with World War II, there is another conflict that has often been cited, not least in Western Europe and the United States as a means of explaining Serbian intransigence in the face of an intensive NATO bombing campaign that is now entering its third month. This is the Battle of Kosovopolje, the Blackbird Field, and, legend would have it, it took place on 28th June 1389. Serbian politicians like Milosevic, as well as Serbian historians and intellectuals, see this battle as marking the formative moment of the Serbian nation. They claim Kosovo, the site of the battle, to be ancestral Serbian territory and they quote the old legend that this region was the historical cradle of Serbian identity. The legend tells how, at the end of the 14th century, the Serbians lost the battle of Blackbird Field against the Turks, and that this event marked the end of the ancient Serbian state. But, at the same time, 1389 marked the birth of the myth of the Serbian national and ethnic community. From that point on, this community's historical heritage and destiny was to become a nation once more. And there can be no doubting the currency of the myth – on 28th June, 1998, Milosevic celebrated the 600th anniversary of this military loss but 'moral victory' in front of a massive audience.

This is a myth that, in the history of Serbia, 'ascribes' to Kosovo the role of the 'Serbian heart', making it fundamental for both Serbian identity and for its political geography. From the Serbian perspective, the symbolic dimension of Kosovo means there can be no autonomy for Albanian people in this region. This myth, derived from loss, becomes an expression of power and dominance, but its justification is founded upon the 'cultural' arguments of history and tradition.

We know for certain that the ancient Serbian state never existed in the form claimed by the myth because, from the Middle Ages, the region was made up of a multi-ethnic society rather than a real 'Serbian' dynastic regime. And we are even not quite sure whether this famous battle of 1389 on Blackbird Field really took place. But 'how it really was' is not the datum point of mythical arguments. Myths, and especially foundation myths, tell us legends and narratives of invented collective biographies. These biographies grant charisma and legitimacy to a 'common history', such as that of a nation-state, whose genealogy is then fixed in space and time by these foundation data. But these are data – names, places and meanings – that fuel our imaginations, but offer us no proof. They are sacred, and they are believed, and it is impossible to deny or to criticise them, because they operate as a kind of *Gesamtkunstwerk*. In other words, foundation myths are tightly woven fabrics of data and ideologies, of semantics and aesthetics, of values and practices. They represent extremely highly condensed cultural codifications that tell us 'quote me, use me, believe me, but don't ask me!', because myths discard their concrete temporal and spatial references and try to assume *universal* meaning.

I started this chapter with a concrete example of the use of foundation myths, because it is in concrete context and practice that construction and deconstruction become most interesting. On the other hand, general reflections on the theme of myths always seem to be rather redundant and elaborate, because it is through their 'glittering' and indeterminateness that myths come to 'live'. Despite this problem, I shall try to make some more general remarks in response to four simple questions. Why was it, or is it, politically necessary or fruitful to operate with foundation myths? What is the stuff or the substance of these myths? What kind of plausibility and logic do they offer? And what dimensions of social, political and cultural actions are legitimated by foundation myths, especially under today's 'post-modern' conditions?

Myth as Collective Representation

When discussing foundation myths we usually look at the history of national, regional, ethnic or religious landscapes of identity, where there seems to exist a 'common sense' of belonging to a larger social unit and of sharing an ongoing history. Normally, there exists a narrative describing how this unit and this history had to be 'made' (in E. P. Thompson's specific sense of 'making').[1] And normally there are also sufficient ideological, aesthetic and emotional figures and symbols to show us why and how foundation myths work as complex identification codes, and why they produce a kind of 'natural feeling' of being an inseparable part, a born member, of this 'community through history'. When we talk of 'myth', the precise meaning of the term we are using is 'construction'. It is not the dextrous building-up of a complicated framework of dates and texts, but is instead the obvious interpretation of common ideas which thereby convey the feeling and the security of 'identity', of being 'one of us'. This was the 'normal' process of mobilising national identity in the 19th and early 20th centuries. To draw again on my first example, the legend of Blackbird Field had already been used as a central theme and ideological tool during the Balkan Wars of 1902, providing an historical 'instruction' that legitimated the Serbian recovery of Kosovo.

---

[1]   Thompson, 1980 [1963].

This use of myths was the 'state of the art' in the 19th century and first half of the 20th century. Foundation myths were constructions of identity by means of images of national community, organised and institutionalised in the figure of the nation-state; Germanic tribes, the Battle of Hastings or Jeanne d'Arc. These were the legends that fuelled a national 'making and becoming' and that established the linkage between a more unstructured pre-history and a concentric national history. They also provided the bridge between national and ethnic concepts of origin. It fell to historians, intellectuals, painters and architects to develop and display this 'national decor'.

In the years following the Second World War, we began to trust in a more unmythical perception of the world. In placing trust in the principle of learning from history, foundation myths and national myths began to look like the tools of an outdated system of *Weltanschauung*. If there were other, new myths to take their place, then these, if anything, were the myths of regional cultures, of continental civilisations and of global humanity. But now, in the 1990s, this tranquil vision of foundation myths as a mere historical phenomenon is being troubled by a new perspective. Nationalist and ethnocentric movements grow all over the world, and the old model seems to provide the basis for contemporary ways to manage the politics of identity. The question we must ask, therefore, is whether we are witnessing a reversion to the old forms of nationalism, and whether myths today have the same functions and effects as they did yesterday.

There is a very interesting and complicated debate around this question, and it is a popularly held opinion that we are indeed witnessing a reversion to the old forms of nationalism. I will argue here, however, that this is, in fact, not the case. It is true that many of the keywords and topics in today's nationalist discourses sound similar to those in the past, but they are now used – and this is my point – in a profoundly different context. In the 18th and 19th centuries, national and ethnic foundation myths were intended to open up narrow feudal and local horizons. They were also formulated and constructed for aggressive, militaristic strategies of power. However, a central aim of these concepts of national mobilisation had always been the formation of a new, nation-wide system of social experience and identification that linked the local and the regional with the national or, in the terms of Max Weber, associated and socialised society.

Today, the strategy appears to work in the opposite direction. National identity still represents a space of history and memory, but we now seem to be witnessing a strategy of dramatising global processes and symbols. This involves the exclusion of social views and experiences that exist in a national framework, the redefinition of national communities and ethnic borders, and the organisation of social inclusion by means of cultural and, to a very large degree, ethnic exclusion. The European map has scarcely ever borne witness to such a landscape of borders and territories, of ethnic and religious domains, and of distinctive 'cultures' of majorities and minorities as it does in the 1990s. The difference between, the distance from and the contrast to the Other seem to be the most important qualities of collective feelings and identities in a context where they are confronted by strange and threatening external worlds, brought ever closer by images of worldwide migration and crisis. Meanwhile, on the 'inner' side, there is continuous pressure to perceive, think and act in common. The case of the former Yugoslavia offers a terrible example of this strategy which is not, however, an exclusively post-Communist one. It is a strategy of the politics of identity and the mutual effect of inclusion and exclusion in ethnic terms that employs historical arguments and murderous means. This strategy implies mass media construction of a horizon of mythical tales of origin and descent, of common language and religion, of culture and tradition, in short, of stories which ought to compose and represent a picture of history as a common past.

The headlines, and the topics of foundation myths, quote the language and symbols of the 19th century, but as a strategy of collective representation, the myth certainly indicates a very contemporary, modern or postmodern pattern of identity politics. Arguing against the *status quo* of social tension and emphasising the insecurity of political and cultural change, it tries to defend a common historical and organic identity against the global threat. More than real experience, it seems to be the discourse on 'globalisation' that is reactivating our need for images of concrete homelands and familiar horizons, of historical spaces and cultural roots. The vision of a boundless economy and cultural standardisation, and the fear of losing the local and the regional settings of life in a globalised world, combine to give the idea of the nation, or of European civilisation, the comforting aspect of an old friend. There must be an 'own' against this global Other, a hierarchy of orders and values, of borders and rooms that is capable of offering a horizon of individual as well as collective identity. Being a part of a whole, as a member of an ethnic group, a nation, or a civilisation, is like reinventing one's own place in the universe of history, a universe which seems to be more cosy than the so-called postmodern conditions. Maybe it is a kind of human need in postmodern times to rediscover one's place under one's own horizons, but maybe it is also necessary and fruitful if you want to control media, markets and minds somewhere down the line by means of (inter-)national strategies of economic and political power.

Commemoration Work, or the Art of Memory

Foundation myths set out to form themselves into 'history', but it is not history in general that is reflected and presented, but always history in its specific and numberless configurations of collective and national memories. This type of history is history in a real 'constructed' sense. It is the history that is organised in public and private memory structures, in architecture and monuments, in archives and museums, in books and films, in biographies and family stories and in commemorative rituals and ceremonies. It is thus a seen, heard, felt and believed history. It is a history inscribed in objects and readings that seem to reflect common historical experiences, or rather, a special type of experience that is available everywhere as 'our own' history. The directions for using this history are part of our everyday culture. Memory does not simply mean the substance of history: it is the practice of a socialised remembering, it is a culture and a cult of commemorations, in public spaces and private contexts alike. It is for this reason that the aesthetic quality of these rituals and acts of commemoration have a very high importance. The design of a monument, the arrangement of a ceremony, the style and rhythm of a memorial speech or the sound of funeral music or prayers are all ritualising elements that help us to learn how to feel compassion and how to become integrated. Commemorations work like an appeal for a pre-scientific experience of 'having been', of an old, remembered synthesis of contradictions, of a renewed consensus between past and present, mankind and nature. The myth of the French Revolution once symbolised the fulfilment of an unstructured past in a 'revolved' and restructured future, while the idea of dynastic traditions in Eastern Europe today tries to quote and imagine pictures and narratives of gravity and sublimity in a re-nationalised perspective.

Aesthetics as a 'style of reasoning' clarify and identify historical landscapes as one's own territory, as a part of a national, ethnic or regional heritage. They make one's own history present, and give it life. And to achieve this, memory needs a complex culture of memorials, national iconography and metaphors, whose signals have to evoke the correct semantics and feelings. If they do not, collective memories lose their orientation and function.

This is one reason why there is currently a great transformation of everyday aesthetics taking place in Eastern European countries. This is why, for example, socialist architecture in Moscow or Berlin (see, respectively, Andrei Zorin's and Beate Binder's chapters) is being destroyed or remodelled and reinterpreted to fit a modern or post-modern profile of urban space. History has to be restructured and re-invented before it can be transformed into a collective memory. This is a twofold process. On the one hand, it involves returning to national roots prior to the Communist era in order to find continuity, rearrange history in its 'natural' way and delete the Communist *intermezzo* as an 'unnatural' and erroneous historical episode. It is for this reason that the graves and bones of national heroes, both ancient and more recent, provoked such interest in Eastern European countries in the early 1990s and were re-established as places and figures in the reinvented landscape of national history. On the other hand, the process also involves a 'return to Europe', a search for models for national restructuring and modernisation, the adoption of Western types of consumer and civic cultures, and the acceptance of Western constitutions and laws. The Communist period, along with the decades that preceded it, are now remembered as moments outside European civilisation, moments of 'not belonging', of a second and secondary European continent. Emancipation from these historical burdens is achieved by rearranging history according to new aesthetic terms and emotional feelings. This is 'the art of memory'.

The New – Legitimated by the Old?

Of course, there are semantic marking points and symbolic border lines that limit the production and interpretation of foundation myths. Constructing tradition does not mean a kind of free-style, improvised history, rather, it requires the plausible linkage of historical data, allegories and images. The imagined community, as Benedict

Anderson characterised the nation, is not a fictional community.[2] It is both real and powerful, and it has learned how to use its historical and ideological options.

Plausibility therefore means the arrangement of historical data and social biographies to correspond to an acceptable and accepted common version, but plausibility is always linked to the question of time and context. At moments of change and crisis there seems to be a greater need for mythical and symbolical configurations of history and identity and for a renovation and rearrangement of the past. Anthropologists like Arnold van Gennep and, more recently, Victor Turner, have argued that a crisis of social values and meanings always provokes a greater production of symbols.[3] These are used to bridge the breaks and changes and to imagine historical continuities and traditions, thereby re-establishing or inventing common emotions and loyalties. The myth, we might say, is the topic and the ritual, it is the medium of this cultural crisis-management. Plausibility in this sense has to be understood as a psychological quality with a temporal dimension. It means wakening the feeling that we are once again remembering the right and essential topics of our history, topics which we had forgotten in our everyday routines, but which we have rediscovered as our heritage.

Continuity and tradition, authenticity and origin are the keywords in this sentimental review of our history and identity. They can give us new ways of imagining old securities by quoting political, ethnic, religious or mental horizons of history that seem to resonate as 'our own'. Today we need these new ceremonies and events, be they exhibitions, feasts, jubilees or commemorations, because they allow us to remember our history. When the new is legitimated and made sacred by the old, it requires, to borrow Eric Hobsbawn's term, the 'invention of tradition'.[4] It needs the flavour of myth and the speech of history, which is the speech of commemoration, of an emotional and aesthetic integration in a common language that tells us, 'we are those who belong together by destiny and history!' This means transforming individuals into a seemingly natural, organic unit. This means collective feeling.

---

[2]   Anderson, 1990.

[3]   van Gennep, 1980 and 1981; Turner, 1986 and 1995.

[4]   Hobsbawm and Ranger, 1983.

There are, of course, ironic breaks, like the 'origin game' of archaic images and foundation myths with its Etruscan and Gothic tribes, or Asterix and Obelix. But even this *bricolage* of genealogies, whether it is ironic or serious, does not remove the legitimacy of commemoration acts. Regained history has come to seem the best social representation for the future, but just as this history is a particular history, so the future is also particular and does not aim to create a global unity.

Initially, this prognosis may not appear to be very optimistic, but the vision of a European or global future should not necessarily imply the denigration or standardisation of models of identity. On the contrary, these visions should contain a wide spectrum of options on 'who we are' and 'how we are', in order that aggressive models of identity like nation and ethnic constructions are forced into competition with more open and informal models. Pitting myth against myth is one way to ease the political tensions of identity, of destroying concepts and ideologies of ethnic and cultural homogeneity and restoring the old European myth of enormous regional and cultural diversity in which multicultural identities in this informal sense are the norm.

But Legitimation for What?

From my point of view these are the two basic functions of foundation myths; to represent someone, and to legitimate something. Foundation myths represent a social group as a cultural and political unit, constituted by history and welded together by memory, and they legitimate purposes and ideas by drawing justification from an invented heritage. Often the idea that is legitimated is one of being culturally oppressed or threatened, and the purpose is to provoke a reaction and to provide an answer in the language of resistance and power. History provides foundation myths with their definitive proof, while they, in turn, provide history with the motives for social or military aggression. This is a form of purification and sacralisation of new tasks by the authority of old traditions and ideas. Old ideas, yes, but as I have argued above, in very new contexts. To return to the example of Kosovo, the myth of the battle on Blackbird Field provides the legend of the Serb's honourable but hopeless fight to protect Christianity and civilisation. This is a legend that told Europeans about the moral credits that history gave to the Serbs and which would have to be paid. From the Serbian point of view, these credits are a chapter of history that has to be written down in the European archive of commemorations. The events of the last months have meant, of course, that the memory and the debt due will be denied to the Serbian state, as it 'compels' Europe to turn upon itself. More than ever, to accept or to deny the myth of Blackbird Field is the confession of one's faith. It means belonging to a Serbian 'us' or to a strange 'them', to be brother or enemy.

This inherent mechanism of inclusion or exclusion is one of the main reasons that foundation myths demand our attention, for this mechanism is used to transform national or ethnic ideologies into structures of political power. Myth is rarely a monologue, and while there is almost no possibility for an internal discussion or counter-position, there is often scope for external dialogues. The Serbian myth of their 'historical' territory has long ago provoked Albanian legends and stories that are now providing, under Serbain military oppression, arguments and legitimations for military resistance. There is, therefore, also a battle of myths, but we should not forget that it is only in the space of the myth, in the minds and heads of the people, that these opponents are fighting from near equal positions. Is this equality in the space occupied by opposing myths not one more argument against the fundamentalist claims of national or ethnic groups that try to present their identities as, so to speak, 'anthropological' ones?

My own answer to this question would be 'yes', although I am not sure if this position is really 'politically correct'. Some time ago, when I first read Samuel Huntington's *The Clash of Civilizations*, it seemed to contain the typical confusion between cause and effect.[5] What he described seemed to me not to be a clash of civilisations, but a clash of foundation myths that, each in its own way, try to fundamentalise the origins of their culture and religion. But that is a long story, and Huntington told us only the very end.

---

[5]   Huntington, 1996.

CHAPTER 12

National Identity as Trauma:
The German Case[1]

Bernhard GIESEN

No construction of collective identity can entirely dispense with memory. Memory supports or even creates the assumption of stability that demarcates identity in distinction to the incessant change of the phenomenal world. Triumphant or traumatic, memory marks the centre of identity and sets up a horizon that delineates the space of possible pasts. Identity is constituted by the very conception of the past as traumatic or triumphant: trauma and triumph are liminal experiences of individual as well as of collective subjects. There is no way to imagine a land beyond the liminal horizons, but memory strives to reach out for it, to cope with it and to relate and adapt the movement of history to it. It can be spoken out or silenced, but it is always there, enabling us to represent and present the past as our history.

Both issues, memory as well as collective identity, have recently attracted increasing attention in debates among historians, sociologists, and literary critics. They reconstruct and deconstruct lost paradises and promised lands, the traumas of defeat and humiliation,

---

[1] This chapter is further developed in a larger article by Bernhard Giesen entitled 'Lost Paradise, Failed Revolution, Remembered Victims' in Neil J. Smelser and Jeffrey C. Alexander, eds, *Cultural Trauma*, published by University of California Press, 2000. The article was written during a fellowship at the Center for Advanced Study in the Behavioral Sciences at Stanford University, within the framework of the study group on Cultural Trauma which was established in the Center. The themes of the chapter are also developed in a book by Bernhard Giesen entitled *Triumph and Trauma*, University of California Press, 2000.

tales of founding heroes and triumphant liberations. But the trend of looking back on the past from an exclusive perspective and the preoccupation with challenges to identity have also been criticised for diverting attention from present problems and eroding the universalistic project of modernity.[2] This chapter, however, is based on a position that considers memory to be a path, and perhaps the only one, that leads toward a universalistic construction of national identity following the collapse of the great utopias and master narratives of modernity.

The historical paradigm case dealt with here is the construction of German national identity in the 19th and 20th centuries, with particular reference to the period after the Holocaust. Since the turn of the century, German national identity has been treated as the result of a *Sonderweg* to modernity, and this German exceptionalism, originally coined by German historians such as Meinecke, has been reaffirmed by recent publications pointing, although in a quite different way, to a primordial German national character that is seen as bound to the death camps.[3] Like other constructions of national identity, the thesis of German exceptionalism stresses Germany's uniqueness and inimitability in distinction to other nations. The Holocaust represents this uniqueness in an exemplary way and has to be regarded as the traumatic reference for German national identity after 1945. In this chapter, the discussion of identity will be patterned by the typological distinction between primordial, traditional, and universalistic constructions of collective identity.[4]

Primordial identities refer to sharp and exclusive boundaries based on natural distinctions; they imagine the outsider as a superior demon that cannot cross the boundary and never should. Traditional identities insist on continuity between past and present and are based on the routines and practices of local life worlds. Their boundaries are gradual transitions between inside and outside; in principle they can be crossed, but it takes time and a certain cautiousness to approach the traditional community. The outsider is treated as a stranger who is neither superior nor inferior but difficult to communicate with. In contrast to primordial and traditional communities, universalistic

---

[2]   Maier, 1993; J. Butler,1990; Gilroy, 1993.

[3]   Goldhagen, 1996.

[4]   Shils, 1981; Eisenstadt and Bernhard Giesen, 1995.

constructions open their boundaries for the inclusion of outsiders. Universalistic identities are based on the tension between the sacred and the mundane. They claim a special link between the community and the realm of the sacred and transcendental. They try to establish a radical discontinuity between the past and the future.

Social constructions of national identity are never unanimous, nor are the modes of remembering the past. Instead, they are prone to conflicts and subject to public debates. They vary according to the life world of the social carrier group and are transformed by the turnover of generations. Rituals can bridge the cleavages of political conflicts and public debates, but they can also sometimes provoke public controversies. Although the perspectives may shift, evaluations may differ, institutional arenas may vary and the rituals may change, constructions of national identity cannot escape from an orientation toward the past, a past that, whether traumatic or triumphant, does not pass away. Traumas and triumphs constitute the 'mythomotors' of national identity. They represent liminal experiences and ultimate horizons for the self-constitution of a collective subject, just as birth and death provide the ultimate horizon for the existential experience of the individual person. Only by reference to the undeniable fact of birth and the inescapable prospect of death is the individual able to construct an encompassing identity beyond shifting encounters and experiences. In a similar way, by referring to a past as a collective triumph or a collective trauma, contingent relationships between individual persons are transcended and forged into a collective identity. Triumphs are moments of 'effervescence', to use Durkheim's expression, or of 'charisma' and '*Verzauberung*' (enchantment) in Weber's terms. Even if the event that is recalled as a triumph was not experienced as an extraordinary moment at the time it occurred, the collective memory glorifies it and imagines it in retrospect as a moment of utmost intensity. It is this lack of awareness and con- sciousness that has to be coped in the ritual re-enactment of the triumph, in annual celebrations and through mythologisation and narration. The trauma is constructed according to a similar logic. Traumas remember a moment of violent intrusion or a collapse of meaning that the collective consciousness was unable to perceive or to grasp in its full importance when it happened. Only later on, after a period of latency, can it be remembered, worked through and spoken out. Both these imaginations of a collective origin, triumph as well as trauma, refer mostly to an act of violence that breaks down and reconstructs the social bond. Collective identity is never exclusively triumphant or traumatic; it is never based only on the imagined homogeneity of insiders or only on the otherness of excluded outsider; it is never driven only by Eros or only by Tanatos – it is always both, but the balance may be disturbed and the levels may differ.

The following remarks will outline a repertoire of German identities that respond to three predominantly traumatic moments of German history: the belated origin of the German nation-state, the lack of a successful revolution in Germany and – most importantly – the Holocaust.

Lost Paradises: Germany as *Naturnation*

Nations that cannot look back to a long political history as states, or that cannot ignore the discontinuities in their history, face special problems in constructing memories to support their identity. The emptiness or the evil of their recent history fosters an escape to a timeless mythical past in which culture and nature are merged and blended in harmony. This primordial unity of culture, nature, and community is usually considered to have been lost in the course of history – culture and community were alienated from their natural base, but the people kept a memory of their origins embedded in nature. Looking back to the primordial paradise fuels energies in present societies to overcome decadence, disease, artificiality and pollution, or it provides a claim on a homeland, thus bringing the community back to its natural roots. From this perspective, the continuity between the present and the remembered past is perceived as having been interrupted by a long history of alienation and opposition. Here, national identity is not constructed by reference to a recent historical past that is available in the form of witnesses' testimonies or written reports, but is formed by imagining a timeless past that is seen as the origin and source of identity, as the horizon of history, and as the ultimate goal, collective action.

Even more than other forms of memory, the representation of a lost paradise is a social construction of the present. It comes as no surprise that primordial conceptions of an ethnic identity resonated well with the new nations that emerged in Central and Eastern Europe in the 19th and 20th centuries. The old nation-states in Western Europe were not entirely immune to these primordial constructions of ethnic origins either, even if they could look back to a firmly established republican tradition. Indeed, France, as well as England and the Netherlands, all had their own myths of ethnic origins, their own racism and their own anti-Semitism, however, the pre-19th century roots of their political traditions prevented these primordial ideas from becoming anything more than influential intellectual heterodoxies.[5] In contrast to its western neighbours, the German national identity is frequently regarded as being founded upon natural or primordial structures.[6] Indeed, Germany may be considered the paradigm case of a latecomer to political modernisation and nation-state-building.[7] It was only in 1871 that – after centuries of fragmentation and division – the political mosaic of many small and two large princely states was replaced by the unified nation-state of Imperial Germany. Although the Austro-Hungarian Empire had been a major player in European politics for centuries, and Prussia had ascended in the 18th century to the status of a military superpower and a focal arena of European enlightenment, the German nation had been imagined as a cultural community rather than a political one. When the German nation-state was finally realised, however, the absence of Austria, an important element of the imagined German cultural community, meant that the new state was perceived as more of a political unit than a cultural one. But it was a political unit that lacked political institutions. This situation fostered the imagining and invention of primordial paradises.

These primordial constructions of a German identity are not immutable and nor are they invariably connected to the essence of the Germans; instead they result from a repertoire of societies' ideas about their relationship to nature as provided by history. Even nature, which is usually considered as objectively given, does not exist in a self-evident and socially unmediated way. Instead it is a cultural construction reflecting the particular setting of a society. Imagining the outside as a demonic threat that has to be fought or to be fled from; as a wilderness that requires taming and civilising; as a resource or a property that can be used and traded; as an object that can be investigated by the methods of science; as a bodily existence that is at risk of disease; and, finally, as a precious garden that has to be protected against pollution and destruction – all these conceptions hint at particular patterns of social interaction and community. Our idea of

---

[5]   Sternhell, 1996.

[6]   Brubaker, 1994; Giesen and Junge, 1991.

[7]   Plessner, 1992; Bendix, 1978; Hobsbawm, 1990.

nature reflects our own situation and our longing for a lost paradise in which culture is connected once more to nature.

The constructions of German national identity have been influenced by four different models relating nature to the social community. All of them emerged in situations of crisis and rapid change and focus on the theme of alienation from nature. In these models, nature is perceived as an issue of identity rather than a field of resources to be used and exploited. A discourse about purity and pollution supports these constructions of a lost paradise, although the level of this discourse varies from ambitious philosophical reasoning to trivial novels.

The German Romantics conceived of national identity in an ambitious philosophical way. It was considered as an inalienable natural individuality exempt from ordinary communication and from the changing tides of history. Responding to the trauma of the French occupation, the Romantic intellectuals discovered a sublime essence, that is, a national identity of the Germans concealed and hidden by layers of foreign influences. This identity could be disclosed and approached only from an aesthetic point of view – for example in contemplating medieval ruins, which in their very deterioration reunited and merged culture and nature.[8] Only art, or infinite longing that conveyed a radical distance from the realm of the ordinary and, above all, from the world of power and money, could provide access to the sublime primordial identity of the *Volk*. Particular rituals of discourse, like romantic irony and the exaltation of sentimental life (love, even craziness), reflected and reinforced the detachment from idle business and ordinary society and the orientation toward the sublime. This ambitious conception of national identity as the sublime, ineffable essence, set the stage for the subsequent imagining of German primordial identity, reducing *demos* to *ethnos* and politics to aesthetics.

In the second half of the 19th century the *völkische Bewegung* revived these romantic ideas in a trivialised way. Again, the movement was propelled by heterodox intellectuals who marked their distance from the centre of Imperial Germany. Like the Romantics, the *völkische* intellectuals, such as Dahn, Freitag, Lagarde and Langbehn, and their petit bourgeois audience, opposed the world of

---

8   Giesen, 1998.

art to the world of money. Instead of focusing on sublime essences, however, they had more tangible and earthly matters in mind. Between 1880 and 1910 Germany underwent a process of accelerated modernisation and mobilisation. Every third German changed residence, mostly from the rural areas to the expanding large cities. Germany became the leading military and industrial power on the continent, and even challenged Great Britain. The intellectuals of the *völkische Bewegung* reacted to the rapid social changes by depicting the idyllic life of free Germanic peasants and warriors, who were seen as sane, vigorous, and bound to the natural soil.

The lost ethnic paradise was contrasted to the decadent, unhealthy, and alienating world of the large cities. Criticism of modern decadence and disintegration was combined with a longing for a vanished primordial unity between body and land, blood and soil. Outside of intellectual circles, the attempt to shake off the decadence of modernity and the disruptive forces of industrialism led to particular forms of retreat and special patterns of ritual purification. New rural communities revived seemingly ancient Germanic forms of economy without money and worshiped the sun or other Germanic or natural deities; reform movements promoted vegetarian diets and so-called natural clothing; nudism gained followers and was practised with almost religious devotion; and youth movements like the *Wandervogel* sought to flee the cities and live in close contact with nature. Public discourse was preoccupied with sexual diseases and decadence, while the ambitious reform movements in music (personified by Wagner) and art *(Jugendstil)* gained widespread attention. All this was patterned by a discourse about purity and pollution that aimed at reconstructing indisputable boundaries in a society where traditional structures were blurred and dissolved.

In the third model, the merging of culture, community and nature was also based on a discourse about purity and pollution, but it was not moved by nostalgia for bygone folklore. Instead of pursuing the sublime, it was couched in the objectivist language of scientism. At its core was a quasi-scientific conception of racial differences. Distinctions between races had been quite common in intellectual discourse since the 18th century, but now they were based on biology instead of culture and were thoroughly medicalised.[9] At the end of the

---

[9] With reference to race, see also Sebastiani, 1999.

century, this new racism merged with anti-Semitism and the eugenic movement, and it attempted to organise societies according to the order of nature as revealed by science. Here, the recollection of lost paradises consists mainly of the statement of the primordial purity of the Germanic or Aryan race, which was endangered by migration and risked becoming lost in the increasing mixture of races.

The Nazi ideology blended this racism with elements of the *völkische* movement, particularly in the cult of the heroic warrior whose superiority and dominance over others was considered as natural, original and unalienated. Again, the everyday life of liberal capitalist democracies was seen as decadent and artificial and was contrasted with the natural harmony between the people and the land and with the primordial violence of the Germanic hero, a violence that invested the triumphant beast with sacred qualities.

A fourth model of a primordial harmony between nature and culture can be seen in the ideas of ecological fundamentalism, which has an extraordinary strong resonance in Germany (comparable to the wildlife protection movement in the US or the animal rights movements in Britain). Although the political orientation of its social carriers shifted from Right to Left, ecological fundamentalism clearly uses not only elements of Romanticism, but also motifs of anti-industrialism and radical 'retreatism' from the heritage of the *völkische Bewegung*. Evidently and understandably, any reference to this heritage is taboo in Germany. When Rudolph Bahro, one of the most interesting fundamentalist intellectuals, mentioned this heritage in an affirmative way, he provoked a public scandal and was immediately expelled from the Green Party.

German ecological fundamentalism pushed the contrast between past and present even further than the *völkische Bewegung*: it is not only the primordial purity of a particular nation that is at stake, but the fate of humankind in its entirety, and it is not only the primordial paradise of pre-industrial life, but nature itself that is endangered and jeopardised by industrial society. As in earlier imaginings of a lost paradise, nature is here considered as the non-malleable fundament of identity. It will decay and lose its order when subjected to exploitation and instrumental use. Again, these fundamentals of identity are approached mainly from an aesthetic point of view, but in a trivialised form. The romantic wilderness is intentionally produced and carefully preserved in the suburban gardens of the ecologically minded

Bildungsbürgertum, the most important supporters of the German Greens.

The striking continuities between 19th century and contemporary imaginations of a lost paradise should not, however, blur a very important difference: although local, regional and, occasionally, even national boundaries show up in the discourse of ecological fundamentalism (when, for instance, foreign plants and animals are banned from the territory because they 'pollute' the original ecosystem), the national coding of the lost paradise is, in this last model, clearly replaced by a global horizon. Ecological fundamentalism is a global movement and aims at a global scenario; national boundaries appear only as differences of sensitivity with respect to ecological issues.

Failed Revolutions:
Democracy Without a Triumphant Myth

More striking than these memories of a primordial paradise, however, are social rituals that try explicitly to revive the memory of a particular event in the historical past. These might take the form of days of remembrance and monuments, dates and places of memory visited and venerated by members of a community, pictures and narrations presenting the past for the following generations or the presentation of its relics in museums for the educated public. Even rituals that construct and continue a tradition emerge, not as effortless and evident remembrances of an unquestionably given past, but as a social constructions that may, in principle, be objected to, debated, and questioned. Outsiders do not have to share these conceptions of the past, and their presence in rituals of remembrance is often seen as disturbing or even offensive – it is our own past, and we consider ourselves sovereign with respect to our common memories.

This is especially true with respect to the triumphant memory of past victories and acts of liberation by which a political community construes its own origin. Liberation from foreign domination, the birthday of the ruler or the enactment of a national constitution, are ritually remembered and celebrated. Monuments recall the victories of the nation over its enemies, poems and anthems praise the great deeds of the sovereign or the liberation of the country, and public marches and rallies revive the triumphs of the past (on this theme, see also Arve Thorsen's chapter in this volume).

Even the seemingly unprecedented rituals of modern revolutionary movements that attempt to establish an entirely new society and set out, not to repeat the past, but to accelerate into an open and undetermined future – even these rituals are founded, consciously or unconsciously, on memories. The rhetoric of the great French Revolution recalled the republicanism of Roman antiquity, the European revolutions of the 19th century in turn took over the symbols of the French Revolution as well as the national traditions of citizenship and bourgeois self-consciousness, the Russian Revolution referred to the patterns of the preceding revolutions in the 19th century, and so on. After defeating the *Ancien Regime*, the revolution-aries strongly traditionalised their own historical success; the French as well as the American and the Russian Revolutions quickly spawned annual memorial celebrations.

Such highly elaborated rituals of remembering revolution are not mere folklore and remainders. Instead the triumphant memory of the revolution must be considered indispensable for the construction of a modern *demos*.[10] A nation is constituted as a sovereign political subject only if the people can imagine themselves as rebelling and rising against the personal regime of the prince. Hence, remembering the revolution provides the ritual basis for a democratic identity. In order to create such a triumphant collective memory of revolutions, even relatively harmless insurrections and upheavals are hailed as heroic actions – the famous seizure of the Bastille by a large street crowd liberated only a dozen non-political prisoners. Consequently the French king could write in his diary on the evening of *quatorze juillet*, 'today nothing.'

Indeed, it is not the factual political success, but the collective memory that constitutes the triumphant origin of a nation. Only in exceptional cases like the American, Russian or Chinese Revolutions can the uprising of the people really establish a continuous and uninterrupted new government. The French Revolutions of 1830 and 1871 failed in this respect, and, strictly speaking, even the great French Revolution of 1791 cannot be regarded as successful. But their factual success and their uninterrupted continuity are less important

---

[10]   Eisenstadt, 1999.

than the way they are perceived in cultural memory. The cultural memory of the French Revolution is marked by a deep divide between trauma and triumph that was at the core of French politics in the 19th century. The *gens de robe* and the upper *bourgeoisie* perceived the reign of the *Sans-culottes* between 1792 and 1793 as a trauma, whereas the *petite bourgeoisie* and the emerging working class remembered the revolution as the triumphant beginning of a republican tradition. This class coalition was the major carrier of the long-lasting Third Republic and could hence treat the return of the *Ancien Regime* as an interruption of its own successful tradition.

In contrast, the German revolutionary uprisings failed not only to establish a lasting regime, but also to engender a memory of a triumphant constitution of national identity. The short lived Weimar Republic and the Bonn Federal Republic were both the result of defeats in devastating wars that had claimed millions of victims. The beginnings of democracy were thus remembered as traumatic rather than triumphant. In this respect they continued a tradition of traumatic origins that had started in the first half of the 17th century with the devastating Thirty Years War. One third of the German population died in this confessional war, and the unity of the Holy Roman Empire of German nations, always fragile, was shattered into a multitude of princely states, the most important of which being Austria and Prussia. So it was that, while England and France emerged out of their bloody confessional wars as powerful nation-states based on the dominance of one confession, the same decision by the ruler to adopt monoconfessionalism, the same expulsion or repression of religious minorities, and the same legalist modernisation of the state, occurred in Germany on the level of small princely states.

Therefore, in 1848, the revolutionary constitution of a national *demos* was not framed by an existing nation-state that simply had to decapitate its ruler. On the contrary, it had to create the nation-state by itself. In a desperate attempt to make up ground on the western lead, the German Revolution of 1848 even considered establishing a national monarchy. It was therefore the creation and not the decapitation of a king that was debated as one of the solutions in the German parliament in Frankfurt. The radical Left opposed this return to monarchy, and instead suggested replacing the traditional rivalry between Prussia and Austria by embedding the German nation in a European conflict between the culture of the West (which included

Poland and Hungary) and the barbarism of the East, that is, Russia. A century later, new national mythologies would once more make reference to this opposition.

Overly burdened by the task of simultaneously establishing the state and forging the identity of the nation, the revolution of 1848 collapsed, and its radical continuation in Baden was crushed by Prussian troops. More important than its factual breakdown, however, was its failure to give rise to triumphant memories. Disappointed and traumatised by their political failure, the carriers of the revolution, the German *Bildungsbürgertum*, left the country or converted their former enthusiasm into cultural oblivion and even into contempt for the idea of revolution (see Marta Petrusewicz's chapter in this volume for a discussion of a similar phenomenon in the Kingdom of Two Sicilies after 1848). In contrast to 1848 and 1918, the wars of liberation against the Napoleonic occupation could well be regarded as a successful revolt of the people, and could have become a powerful foundation myth for the German national movement. Although its initial impact was limited, it nevertheless preluded the military defeat of the French Emperor some years later. The democratic potential of this movement faded away, however, in the course of the 19th century, and the final realisation of the German nation-state by Bismarck could dispense with any kind of democratic legitimation.

In imperial Germany, the myth of the wars of liberation fuelled hostility against the *Erbfeind Frankreich* rather than lent support to democratic constructions of identity, and this hostility was reinforced by defeat in World War I. It was therefore difficult to establish a connection between the first German democracy in 1918 and the revolution that had failed 70 years earlier. When the *Arbeiter und Soldaten* movement entered the stage in 1919 as a new carrier of the revolutionary project, the educated *bourgeoisie* refused to join the ranks of the revolutionaries – the class that had achieved 1848 felt that it had lost control over the project of revolution. The democratic uprising of *les classes dangereuses* did not give birth to a triumphant founding myth, but was, instead, held responsible for a military defeat (*'Im Felde unbesiegt...'*).

In addition to this change in the carrier group, the frightening example of the Russian Revolution, with its turmoil and chaos, deterred even Social Democrats from supporting a radical revolutionary course. Finally, the level of economic, social and even political modernisation which Germany had reached at the turn of the century alleviated the fundamental tension that is at the core of successful revolutions. Whereas in 1848, the lack of the nation-state prevented the revolutionary constitution of the *demos*, in 1918 it was the existence of a relatively modern state that deprived it of its thrust. The revolutionaries could only extend already existing institutions by establishing the right of women to vote, and seek to radicalise the revolutionary project according to the Russian example and opt for a global revolution – a turn that not only diminished its support, but also failed to construct a specifically German *demos*. The revolution collapsed and was remembered as a failed local rebellion instead of a triumphant uprising of the German people against reactionary imperial rule.

There was only one German 'revolution' that could lay claim to having established a new regime that endured for some years: national socialism. The Nazis – like the Italian Fascists before – presented and remembered their seizure of power as a *'völkische Revolution'*. They considered their regime as the reconstruction of the free German nation, constituting itself by violence and heroism, triumphantly rising over the forces of decadence, money and foreign repression. The Nazi Revolution claimed to reverse the defeat of World War I and to abolish 'the shame of Versailles'. Consequently, its rituals of remembrance focused on the triumphant rebirth of the nation out of the sacrificial death of the heroes of the past.[11] The rituals of the Nazi Revolution did not only remember the fallen soldiers of the World War I and the casualties of their own early years, but also reached back – especially towards the end of their rule – to the wars of liberation against the Napoleonic occupation (see, for example, the film *Kolberg*). Because of its close connection with Nazi cults, the memory of the wars of liberation disappeared with the collapse of the Third Reich. The very fact that the Nazis could claim that their regime was a revolutionary uprising of the people contaminated the idea of a triumphant self-constitution of the nation. This was particularly the case after the defeat of 1945, when a new democratic state was founded. The establishment of democracy from outside by the Allied forces ran counter to the conception of a people determining its own fate, empowering its own government and defining its own identity. Obviously, the new German democracy did not result from a revolu-

---

[11] Mosse, 1991.

tionary upheaval of the people, but was decreed by the Allied forces. Indeed, only a small part of the German population considered their military defeat to be a liberation from repressive rulers.

In spite of this shameful situation, the representatives of the new democratic Federal Republic tried to establish a people's foundation myth by concentrating on the actions of the German resistance against Nazi domination. The resistance of the students around the Scholls, of the Kreisauer Circle, and most prominently of the *coup d'état* of July 1944, was used as a substitute for a people's revolt against Nazi tyranny. In this way, the German nation, which – at least in the western Federal Republic – tried to enter the political arena as a sovereign democratic subject, could uphold an image of innocence. This image said that not all Germans had collaborated with, or tacitly accepted the criminal regime, indeed, more than this, the good people of Germany had been forced to keep their mouths shut by the Nazi tyrants.

In this construction of a substitute resistance, it was widely ignored that most of the heroes of the German resistance against Hitler (*e.g.*, Stauffenberg and Moltke) did not have democratic ideas in mind when they planned the new Germany to come following the successful overthrow of Nazi rule. It was also ignored that the good people of Germany had voted Hitler into power by democratic elections and that a majority of them had supported the Führer '*in Treue fest*', even when the prospect of military defeat was becoming real.

The Denial of the Trauma:
Nazi Demons and Timeless German Virtues

The defeat of 1945 and the disclosures that followed resulted in the most profound trauma of recent German history. First, there were the obvious and catastrophic German losses – more than ten million Germans lost their lives as soldiers on the battlefield, in prison camps, as casualties of the Allied bombing raids, or as victims of ethnic cleansing in the lost eastern provinces after the war; hundreds of thousands of women and girls were raped; twelve million refugees were displaced in the wake of the Russian invasion or expelled from their homes in the eastern provinces; and most German cities were devastated. All these experiences were traumatic in their own right, but as horrible as defeat and death in war may be, their atrocity would have been alleviated by the moral triumph of a collective project – a heroic war of liberation and independence, for example – that could have persisted even after a defeat and could have even earned the tacit respect of the victors. However, moral justification of the war was entirely and radically denied to the Germans. The aim, the form and the circumstances of the war were criminal and were labelled as such by the victors. The shame connected with the German name from then on was a matter of collective identity. The ultimate trauma of 1945 resulted not only from ruin and rape, death and defeat, but also from the sudden loss of self-respect and moral integrity. The utmost barbarism had taken place in the nation that had based its identity on *Kultur* and that could claim to have furthered and supported Jewish emancipation more than most of its European neighbours. The triumphant notion of a German *Kulturnation* was replaced by the traumatising disclosure of the Holocaust. As Adorno wrote, faced with Auschwitz, there was no place left for poems.[12]

Traumas result from a sudden, unmediated inversion of inside and outside, good and evil, security and destruction. In the Freudian tradition they are defined as violent events that, at the time they occurred, were ignored or disregarded – the individual mind cannot perceive the possibility of its own death.[13] In a similar way, collective consciousness tends to reject any perception of the actions of its own community as barbaric in the moment when the barbaric violence occurs. Therefore collective traumas, too, require a time of latency before they can be acted out, spoken about, and worked through. Postwar Germany responded to the disclosure of the Holocaust by an 'inability to mourn' or a 'communicative silence'.[14] Nobody could bear to look at the victims. *Hitlerjungen* could detach themselves from their former involvement and consider it a mistake born of immaturity, but adults who had devoted the most formative and active years of their lives to a movement whose members now had to consider themselves as collaborators in a mass murder could not repair their ruined moral identity even if they had been ready to confess their guilt. There would be no second chance, life was spoilt. The trauma is insurmountable; as a moral subject the person is dead. He or she can only remain mute, look away, turn to other issues, and hope that nobody will ask the wrong questions. It was thus a tacitly

---

[12]   Adorno, 1992.

[13]   Caruth, 1996, pp. 60 ff.

[14]   These expressions come, respectively, from Mitscherlich, 1994 and Lübbe, 1981.

assumed coalition of silence that provided the first national identity after the war. Everyone assumed that the others, too, had supported the Nazi regime and would therefore agree to remain silent about their common shame. No one mentioned his or her relationship to the Holocaust in informal communication, even if they had only been involved as bystanders of history who had never known exactly what was happening (this muteness and silence concerning the Holocaust contrasted with vivid informal communication about other aspects of the war: the escapes from the eastern *Heimat*, the nights in the bomb shelters, and the struggle on the *Ostfront* during the last month of the Third Reich). There was a moral numbness with respect to the horror, and very few spoke of their responsibility as bystanders, collaborators or party members. If those who had been enthusiastic followers of National Socialism could not avoid the unspeakable issue in informal conversations among Germans, they could sometimes only cope with the trauma of total defeat and their involvement in the horror by simply denying obvious facts: they considered the documentary evidence to be faked by the Allied forces. Others tried to separate the programme of National Socialism from its realisation, or insisted that *'der Führer'* did not know about the Holocaust. The vast majority, however, maintained that they had not known anything about the mass murders or that they had been too concerned with mere survival to care about the monstrous rumours. *'Wir wussten von nichts...'*

Most of the horrors certainly were concealed from the German public.[15] But even if the Holocaust was declared to be *'Geheime Reichssache'*, tens of thousands of Germans participated, rumours were spread, and questions could have been asked even by those who were not directly involved in the deportation and killing. Whether deliberately or inadvertently, most Germans avoided focussing their attention on the disappearance of the Jews from public life. They did not want to get involved in piercing moral questions out of fear, negligence or resentment. In this way, what was later to become the crucial challenge for the German self-consciousness was removed to the diffuse and dim periphery of awareness and perception. In some

---

[15] Himmler's famous Posen address to the SS leaders shows his attempt to hide the genocide from the German public; the members of the *Sondereinheiten* had strict orders to keep the terrible secret (Laqueur), the foreign governments did not respond to the secret reports about the Holocaust because they did not believe it, and even the people in the Ghetto of Lodz did not know their fate some weeks before their deportation to the death camps. Cf. Laqueur, 1996; Diner, 1995.

respects, the silencing of the past after 1945 continued the ignorance and disregard prior to this date.

The coalition of silence was not limited to informal communication in intimate spheres, shielded from public control. It also left its traces on the political rhetoric of Germany's public discourse.[16] The German chancellor Adenauer mentioned the Holocaust only rarely in official speeches. On the few occasions that he did address the Holocaust, he referred to it in the passive mode as 'the immense suffering of the Jewish people', thus avoiding making reference to the perpetrators. The judaeocide was, of course, not denied, but it ranked among other losses, like fallen soldiers and refugees *(Vertriebenen)* who had lost their *Heimat*. Instead of mentioning the crimes directly, the political rhetoric referred to the events as the 'dark times of the recent past', the 'time of unfathomable barbarism' or the 'catastrophe of German history'. The crimes and their perpetrators were thus removed into a realm of unreal nightmares beyond conception and description. Like the period of latency in the case of an individual trauma, the Holocaust was removed from the collective consciousness and shifted to the level of haunting dreams which occasionally found their way to cultural representations. For example, popular movies about Doctor Mabuse, who used men like string puppets in order to commit horrible crimes, hinted at the collective nightmare but never uttered aloud its direst reference.

Not everyone, however, consented to the coalition of silence. Some intellectuals raised their voices and posed the inconvenient question, 'where have you been, Adam?' (Böll). Some situations required an explanation to outside observers, to schoolchildren, foreigners, and those Germans who never supported the Nazi regime. Faced with these outside observers who could not be co-opted into the coalition of silence, Germans required a new exculpatory narrative. Postwar Germany constructed this narrative by primordialising the opposition between oppressors and the people. In this narrative, the Nazi rulers, and Hitler in particular, were depicted as insane barbarians, as wild beasts, as satanic seducers who had approached the good and innocent German people from outside and deprived them of their common sense like a drug, a disease, or a diabolic obsession. The criminal domination was represented as inescapable and fatal, whereas

---

[16]   Dubiel, 1999; Herf, 1997.

the people were imagined as seduced into blindness, unsuspicious and completely ignorant of the atrocities of genocide. Demonisation of Nazi rule removed the nation from the realm of moral responsibility and culpability, while intoxication, seduction, and blindness allowed Germans to regard the German nation as the true victim of Nazism.

In this new exculpatory narrative, primordialisation was again used to exclude the outsider, but its direction was radically reversed: before 1945 anti-Semitism rejected Jews as poisonous demons secretly invading and seducing the German nation. Now the same primordial exclusion and its rituals of purification and decoupling (*Abspaltung*) turned on the Nazis themselves. Hitler, once the charismatic redeemer and saviour of Germany, was converted into a devil, a crazy epileptic, a monster, the immense misfortune of German history, an alien demon seducing the innocent German people. This pattern of radical conversion was given its most extreme form by Nazis who tried to change their personal identity. They assumed new names and, after several years, re-emerged in public life as faithful and respected democrats, supporting social democracy and assuming important public offices before their concealed identities as SS officers were disclosed.[17]

Faced with the collective trauma, even public communication in postwar Germany insisted on the strict separation of the few unquestionably criminal perpetrators from the majority of seduced citizens and soldiers. Of course, the position of the boundary was debatable. The Social Democrats, in their oppositional role, were keener to include a larger group of higher officials into the circle of perpetrators and in particular targeted Globke, the previous commentator of the *Rassengesetze*, who had become a member of the government. In contrast, the chancellor, Adenauer – himself unquestionably an anti-Nazi – and his conservative coalition insisted that, although the criminal perpetrators should be punished, there should be no distinction between the two large classes of Germans: those with blemishes and those without.[18] Sometimes even leading generals of the *Wehrmacht* who had been sentenced to prison were included in the community of abused people.[19] Despite dissent and

---

[17] Leggewie, 1998.

[18] Dubiel, 1999.

[19] See H. J. Merkatz in the parliamentary debate 8.11.1950 'Männer wie Manstein und Kesselring und andere, die in Landsberg und Werl einsitzen, diese Männer

debate, most politicians of the new democracy agreed with the denial of the collective guilt of all Germans and supported the new narrative of demonisation. The parliamentary debates about denazification, wearing military decorations in public, parole for mass murderers, the end of prosecutions for Nazi crimes, and even about the Auschwitz trial in the early 1960s, were aimed at demarcating a clear boundary between the majority of normal and 'decent' Germans on the one side, and the few criminal Nazi monsters on the other.[20] This demarcation not only allowed for a new construction of national identity, but stressed, by expulsion and oblivion, the radical newness of the political system and the departure from totalitarian rule. Expelling the condemned perpetrators from civil society and ending prosecutions for newly discovered Nazi crimes simply represented two different aspects of the same drive to get rid of the past.

The law court was the institutional arena where the demarcation was staged, ritually constructed, and re-affirmed. Although the imprisonment of Nazi criminals at Landsberg and the related trials was still much criticised by the conservative Right in the early 1950s, there was no way to avoid the trials if discontinuity between past and present was to be constructed. Here, the roles of the accused perpetrators and the accusing public, represented by the prosecutor, were strictly separated, just as the rules of law on the one hand, and the criminal action on the other, were clearly distinguished. Both these oppositions supported the demarcation between an innocent nation and treacherous criminals.

Denying any collective responsibility, the ritual of trials confined the question of guilt strictly to individual acts, in particular with respect to formal decisions within organisations. But even if it was beyond any doubt that crimes were committed, the perpetrators tried to relativise their guilt by referring to the inescapable nature of military orders: *Befehlsnotstand*. Even the commanders of Auschwitz and Treblinka tried to present themselves as acting strictly within their formal competencies. They emphasised that they had never participated personally in cruelties (this was a lie). Acts of cruelty,

---

und wir, wir sind doch eines. Wir haben doch das mitzutragen, was man stellvertretend für uns auferlegt' cited in Frei, 1996, p. 202.

[20] Dubiel, 1999. This demarcation was even shared by some Jews, such as Victor Klemperer, cf. Klemperer 1995.

they argued, were committed by subordinate *Kapos* from Ukraine, Lithuania, and Poland. In passing the blame, they adapted their contempt for the Slavic *Untermenschen* to the new situation.

Demarcating the perpetrators and denying one's own involvement and guilt was not only the Federal Republic's way of coping with the past. It was also used in the new socialist German Democratic Republic, where the founding myth of the new state focused upon the idea that the repressed German people, assisted by the glorious Red Army, had succeeded in overthrowing the Fascist regime. The boundary between the past and present was declared to be radical and insurmountable, '*der neue sozialistische Mensch*', the new socialist human being, had nothing in common with Hitlerism and Fascism. Any traces of continuity between past and present were shifted across the border to the 'revanchist and fascist' FRG in the west. The Federal Republic, indeed, could not deny being the legal successor of the Nazi state, because it had to provide a legal basis for the citizenship of refugees and for its claim to represent Germany in its entirety. The new, socialist GDR considered the Federal Republic as a Fascist society in bourgeois disguise. This demarcation between the good, anti-Fascist and socialist east, and the fascist and capitalist west was also used to deny any responsibility to the survivors of the Holocaust – hence no restitutions and reparations were paid. The public rituals of the GDR focused upon the Fascist barbarism of the past and the heroism of the anti-Fascist resistance, while the judaeocide was rarely mentioned. Based on the anti-Fascist ideology and the constitutional rupture between past and present, the politics of the GDR occasionally even took an anti-Semitic turn: the Stalinist wave of purges in the early 50s were centred upon Jewish communists like Paul Merker and Leo Zuckermann who, after returning from exile in the west, had tried to merge anti-Fascism and socialism in the new Germany. Like leading Jewish members of the Communist Parties in Hungary, Poland and Czechoslovakia, they too were accused of 'cosmopolitan-ism' and secret espionage in collaboration with imperialist and bourgeois forces.[21]

In a similar and even more self assured way, Austria also tried to rid itself of its Nazi past. The foundation myth of the Second Austrian Republic was one of victimisation. It turned the '*Anschluß*' of 1938 into a military occupation by foreign forces, and tried to position itself

---

[21] Herf, 1997.

among liberated nations like Czechoslovakia, the Netherlands and Denmark. Here, too, responsibility and guilt for the Holocaust was simply pushed across the border and the perpetrators were defined as non-Austrian outsiders, while the Austrians were seen as the innocent victims. And here, too, decoupling the new nation from the history of the perpetrators weakened its alertness with respect to new manifestations of anti-Semitism.

But the thrust to shift the guilt across the border and to turn collaboration into victimisation was not limited to German-speaking nations. Italy rapidly forgot its Fascist complicity with Nazi Germany and presented itself as a nation of resistance heroism, and the Flemish, Slovakian and Croatian participation in the *shoah* was blurred because they were parts of new nation-states that emerged out of anti-Nazi resistance movements.

In conclusion, it is interesting to note that the process of coping with a traumatic past by expelling the perpetrators was once more acted out in Germany, half a century after the Holocaust: the 'de-Stasification' that took place in the former GDR after German unification in the early 1990s shows a striking similarity to the de-Nazification of the late forties. Again the issue was to demarcate the line between the perpetrators and the majority of the decent Germans who had suffered from repressive rule, but this time it was even more difficult to turn the filthy greyish web of collaboration into a clear-cut black and white picture of guilt and innocence: almost a third of the entire population had been involved in Stasi activities, and the system of surveillance and control had expanded during four decades to reach a degree of perfection the Gestapo had never achieved.

CHAPTER 13

(Re)creative Myths and Constructed History: The Case of Poland

Ewa DOMAŃSKA

My chapter follows the line of a critique of scientism in Western historical thought. It is a product of a scepticism toward disciplinary history, which was always and still is a powerful instrument of ideological manipulation. In this chapter, I put the problem of community in terms of 'becoming' or growing rather than of 'being constructed'. I am interested here in the concept of *palingenesis* – the process of beginning again, of a new genesis – especially because I regard the present time as *kairos*, 'the right time', a special moment in world history for making decisions that will be crucial for the future.

This paper refers also to an ethical turn in historical thought that, in a sense, comes back to R. G. Collingwood's idea of history as human self-knowledge. Thinking about our past might help us in our search for ourselves and the meaning of life insofar as we consider history as a literary genre that originates from the most powerful myth – the myth of searching for a lost identity (Northrop Frye).

A Post-Mythical and Post-Scientific Understanding of Myth

In order to study myths, one has to have courage, erudition, a certain naivety, and a drop of desperation. The literature on myths is enormous, but most of the methodologies used for the study of myth, be they sociological, symbolist, psychoanalytical, structuralist,

249

Marxist, and so on, approach myth from a functionalist perspective and seek to determine its uses and misuses in pragmatic terms. Theorists of history have a great interest in myths, which are understood as epistemological principles, since historical writing plays an important role in supporting myths. Thus, according to Jerzy Topolski, the history of historiography is a story about the continuous creation of myths and the attempts of historians to dissolve them.[1] But such an understanding of myths refers to an abstract knowledge about the past that pushes us farther and farther away from reality. Interest in those myths that are latently contained in historical narratives is another sign of a textualist and constructivist approach to history that makes us realise how wide the gap is between the 'historical past' and the 'real past'. Marie-Laure Ryan suggests differences among three types of discourse; science, fiction, and myth. She argues that if the conflict between myth and science is to be resolved, we need to distinguish among four ways of understanding myth: '1) as authoritative, inspired, community-defining, literal-truths (the fundamentalist mode); 2) as authoritative, inspired, community-defining but potentially figural truths (the mainstream religion mode); 3) as literary truth, offering one source of inspiration among many others; and 4) as fictional truth, forming entertaining narratives about imaginary worlds.' Ryan claims that communities that still have certain myths embodied in their cultural systems have to decide whether, 'to accept the fundamentalist view and reject science altogether; start an "alternative science" to support their liberal belief in myth; accept both myth and science but establish a hierarchy when the two come in conflict; or adopt myth to science by opting for the figural interpretation.'[2]

Following Ryan, I would prefer to consider myth as a mode of discourse that contributes to the foundation of culture. One might also presuppose that myths are specific kinds of memories, a reservoir of 'cultural genes' that preserve the basic features or archetypes of a given culture. I am not inclined to see history (considered as a science) and myth as opposed to each other. Myth and science can be seen as complementary modes of grasping a common reality. We might consider the category of the 'non-historical' as applying to the

---

[1] Topolski, 1997 (on theoretical consideration on the concepts of fundamental myths, see pp. 97-108).

[2] Ryan, 1998, p. 827.

present, like Walter Benjamin's 'now-time' (*Jetztzeit*), the time of 'becoming', a dimension of time pregnant with chances and possibilities. This is the religious time of *kairos*, which offers a possibility of 'fulfillment'. The 'now-time' marks a moment of fullness in which a historian, or 'prophetic critic', after Deborah J. Haynes, would be able to focus on the potentiality of the present to become a future different from any past. Such a 'new' kind of scholar would foretell the future. S/he would carefully examine the present and indicate possible results of present actions, and in so doing would also voice collective fears and hopes.[3] By repeating, indicating and quoting certain ideas, motives, symbols and metaphors that circulate in a given community or culture, the 'prophetic critic' would act as a powerful 'vehicle' of cultural (mythic) memory that would help to transcend the present cultural stage and expand the 'horizon of expectations' of a given community. One of his/her tasks would be to diagnose the present in such a way as to help this community to concentrate on those actions that might extend its 'space of experience'.

The fact that we return to a discussion of myths today can be seen as an effect of an identity crisis, as an outcome of the problem caused by the decline of the nation-state, the present attempt to unify Europe, and a critique of history as the predominant approach to the past. Perhaps we have had enough of historical determinism or the 'deification of history' and enough of the historicism and relativism that it has caused. I believe that this is especially the case in Poland, where the demand for a point of reference that is beyond history is quite explicit among young people, who seem to be searching for a perspective that does not depend on history. Michel Foucault's definition of history (*'l'histoire c'est le discours du pouvoir'*), together with Emmanuel Lévinas' claim that history is part of a Western philosophy of violence appear, after a long period of Communist official state historiography, to be very persuasive. Thus, certain questions inevitably arise: can we still trust history, or better, can we still trust historians? What is history for? Can we still believe that we can learn something from history (or rather, from historians)? These questions are particularly relevant to Poland, where the official (state) historiography has been depreciated and devalued. Rebuilding a faith in history would largely be made possible by re-establishing

---

[3]   Cf. Haynes, 1997, pp. 173 and 193.

the ethics of the historian. This would mean the historian assuming the role of a responsible intellectual who is thrown into the world that s/he wants to understand, rather than that of a hero of science who seeks knowledge in order to control and rule the world.

This criticism of history as ideology is accompanied by the search for an alternative approach to the past. Indeed, all the humanities seem to be searching for a principle capable of providing a transcultural image of society. But what category might be able to offer an integrated (or 'defragmented'?) image of a human being? We see a fervent interest in the 'Other' and otherness, and a search for an idiom of translation that would permit us to understand other people(s) and other cultures. We thus observe attention shifting from time to space (or, in the case of time, from *chronos* to *kairos*), from word to image, from *logos* to *eros/caritas*, from 'cause and effect' reasoning to metaphorical or relational thinking, and from logic to rhetoric or poetics. From this perspective, our interest in myth can be seen as a reaction to the modern world view based on Science, Logic and Reason, a reaction that provides a place where our lost humanity might be rediscovered. Myth is a space where the desired integration of the 'cubist' individual might be achieved, where the pre-modern relations between individuals, between the individual and nature, and between the individual and the Absolute might be rediscovered. But the question remains: is it possible to find a myth that would be 'everybody's story'?

The voices of past Others remind us that history is one of many possible approaches to the past, that it is a specifically Western, Eurocentric, imperialistic, masculinist and therefore ideologically biased vision of time. However, in Europe we are so obsessed by history that we tend to identify history with the past. 'Epistemophilia', to use Melanie Klein's expression, is indeed closely connected with 'historiophilia'.

Although myth is still a very suspect way of dealing with the past, it does resemble primitive, pre-civilised and atavistic thinking, and as such perhaps represents an alternative way of perceiving the limitations of a civilised way of thinking. Myth allows us to see how a historical way of viewing the past obscures what we have had to give up in order to enter history. Myth returns to the order of phantasms and reveals the unconscious master narratives (to use Fredric

252

Jameson's idea) that inform our historical consciousness.[4] Myth gives access to our repressed history, and history is our repressed myth. In fact, when historians decided to attack myth and expel it from history, they actually undermined the most important basis for our approach to the past. To set history against myth, that is, to separate history from myth, enfeebles both, for it is myth that protects and saves fundamental features of a given community's cultural *ego*. When history defines a community's 'space of experience', it deprives this community of any basis for hope which could revise and enlarge its 'horizon of expectations'. To rebuild a community means to regenerate its morality, to re-establish its ethical foundation that has been shattered by the collision of its expectations with brutal reality. When dealing with myths, historians tend to make them banal and treat them as expressions of a pathological condition of consciousness. They seem to forget the healing value of mythical belief: myth does what love does – it revives hope.

Thus, if we agree that myth is an expression of the deepest level of history, we can ask whether there are any myths that exist above or beyond everything that separates history from myth.

Polish Baroque and Romanticism: Two Sources of 'Polishness'

There are two epochs in Poland's past during which the 'essence' of Polishness is supposed to have been manifested. These periods are referred to in terms of the pleasure and pain principle.[5] The first epoch, characterised by the pleasure principle, was the 16th and 17th centuries, and was considered the Golden Age of Polish culture. The

---

[4] Cf. Jameson, 1981, p. 180.

[5] Among many available publications on Polish history, I would recommend the following overviews: Davis, 1981; Mączak and Samsonowicz, 1985; Olszer, 1981; Halicz, 1982; Fiszman, 1988; Fedorowicz, 1982; Tazbir, 1988 and 1973; Wandycz, 1974.
On Polish literature in general, see: Miłosz, 1969. As regards particular literary works that participated in the creation of Polish national myths, see for example: Kochanowski, 1928; Micheovo, 1581; Mickiewicz, 1968; Mickiewicz, 1989; Pasek, 1978.
On Polish myths, see: Barszczewska-Krupa, 1996; Byrnes, 1997; Król, 1986 (in Polish); *Mity i stereotypy*, 1991; Molik, 1998; Pekacz, 1995; Walicki, 1982, 1983, 1991.

battle of Vienna (1683), with the famous victory of Jan III Sobieski over the Turks, was the last successful battle of the Noble Republic of Poland and there followed a period of slow decline. From 1772, Poland was partitioned among Prussia, Russia, and Austria, and in 1795 finally disappeared from the map of Europe for a period of 150 years. The second epoch that supposedly manifested the essence of Polishness (this time characterised by the pain principle) was the period of Romanticism in the 19th century. This was a period of humiliation, rebellion and uprising, conspiracy, dreams of independence and of the rebirth of the Polish State.

It was in the 16th and 17th centuries that the belief in the uniqueness, exceptionality and individuality of the Polish nobility found its fullest expression. This belief was sustained by two myths; that of the origin of the Polish nobility in ancient Sarmatia, and that of Poland's continuity with the Roman Empire. Poland was considered to be *antemurale christianitatis* (the bulwark of Christendom). It was the shield of Europe, and Poles regarded themselves as a chosen nation whose mission was to defend Europe from heretics, pagans, and barbarians. The nobility of Poland's purpose was manifested in an image of itself as a country without religious conflict, a country of tolerance, a 'land without stakes' (that is, a community that did not burn heretics). Poland was also an exceptional case as regards its political system, which was called 'noble democracy'. This system was governed by the principle of the 'Golden Freedom' of the nobility and, after 1573, was headed by an elective king who 'rules but does not govern'. What is more, the prosperity of the Polish economy, based especially on grain production and grain trade, promoted the idea of Poland as the 'Great Mill' of Europe. Poland was a Catholic country, and to be a true Pole meant to be Roman Catholic. A crucial element in religious life was the cult of Holy Mary, connected especially with the monastery of Jasna Góra at Częstochowa, home to the miraculous icon of the Black Madonna, crowned as the 'Queen of Poland'.

Frank Ankersmit claims that Western historical consciousness originated in the traumatic experience of certain historical events.[6] This idea could be linked to a common belief that history is fascinating for 'unhappy nations'. I am inclined to argue that Polish historical consciousness, burdened by Romanticism, was based on and

---

[6] Cf. Ankersmit, 1999.

supported by traumatic events. In the case of Poland, it is this fragment of its history that 'hurts', in Jameson's sense of the term. Polish culture is a 'wound culture', that is, it is founded upon the experiences of trauma, suffering, victimisation and melancholy. The Polish 'psychic reality', as a response to this trauma, is manifested in its fundamental myths.

In the 19th century, the age of partitions, passionate Romanticism empowered a distinct kind of Polish messianism. The greatest Polish poets – the national prophets – Mickiewicz, Krasiński, and Słowacki, called Poland, the nation without a state, 'the Christ of Nations'. Poles would sacrifice themselves for Freedom, Honour and God, and this sacrifice was not just for their own freedom, it was 'for your freedom and ours'. Poland's destiny was to be the leader of oppressed Slavic nations while, at the same time, protecting Europe from despotism, materialism, and atheism. The geographical situation of Poland, its location in Europe between the two great powers of Germany and Russia, the sense of the uniqueness of the Polish nation, and the belief that Poland was a bulwark of Christendom, informed Polish messianism or, in other words, the belief in the historical mission of Poland. I consider that Polish messianism is one of the deepest convictions governing the way Poles think about themselves, their country and their sense of meaningful existence.

A clear continuity in the collective consciousness as regards the messianistic role of Poland is manifested in the aura that is associated with Poland entering the European Union. In May 1998, the Polish Embassy in Brussels was officially opened. In the main hall there is a huge painting (4 x 3.40 metres) by Franciszek Starowieyski. This work refers to the myth of the rape of Europa by Zeus. It represents a naked woman (Europa), sitting on a 'techno-bull' that kidnaps another woman (Poland), who is surrounded by a nimbus. The caption of the painting is, 'Polonia divina rapta per Europa profana', however, according to Paweł Dobrowolski (the spokesman of the Polish Ministry of Foreign Affairs), the title of the painting is, 'Poland being absorbed by Europe'.[7] This controversial allegory is interpreted in two ways: either as Europe, profane, bereft of values and lacking any element of spirituality and depth, absorbing and degrading Poland,

---

[7]   Information according to articles: Szymańska-Barginon and Spalińska, 1998, p. 5 and Spalińska, 1998, p. 8.

which was originally divine and pure; or as Poland kidnapped, but sacrificing herself in order to save the continent.

Despite the ambiguities in the interpretation of this painting, it is clear that in this representation of Poland we have a resurrection of one of the most powerful Polish myths, that of messianism, the idea of the Poles as a chosen nation and Poland as the *antemurale christianitatis*. Juxtaposed with this messianism, there is also a representation of demonism in the form of the 'black myth of the West'. Looking at Starowieyski's painting, one might say that 'the final combat' over the vision of the future will take place not between history and myth, but between two powerful myths: a futuristic myth that comes with consumerism and has nothing to do with national messianism; and a past-oriented, national myth that supports tradition and the eternal Polish values. I would argue, however, that the roots of this myth of messianism go deeper and touch yet another level – the myth (or archetype) of the victim.

The Myth of the Victim: Between Dionysus and Jesus

For Poles, the motifs of the decline and rebirth of Poland, of a chain of life, death and palingenesis or resurrection, are not ways of thinking about their past and present. Instead, they are the motifs that define a destiny, embodied in the historical events of the 19th and 20th centuries, they are the symbols of a sacramental drama that unfolds at the deepest level of national existence. Since the cycles of military defeat, political partition, liberation and rebirth have been regularly repeated in Poland's history, this cyclical pattern has come to form a kind of archetype or 'master narrative' that enlivens the Polish people and defines their historical identity. In terms of Eliade's conception of 'the myth of the eternal return', Poles regard as normal the experience of cyclical catastrophe. Death is viewed not only as inevitable for individual human beings, but as desirable for the nation's periodic renewal and revitalisation.

From the beginning of the 19th century, there has been a deeply rooted conviction in the Polish consciousness that each generation has to give its blood to the Homeland and that such a sacrifice is a necessary condition for the rebirth of the country. This belief was once so strong that, after a series of events, occurring roughly every 15 years and including the November Uprising (1831), the People's Spring (1848), and the January Uprising (1863), Otto von Bismarck expressed his surprise when nothing happened around 1880. When we look at the calendar of historical events that took place later, we see a chain of sacrificial generations: 1905 and the Revolution in Russian Poland; 1914 to 1918/21 with World War I, the Silesian Uprisings, the Great Polish Uprising and the Polish – Soviet War; 1939 to 1945 with World War II and the Warsaw Uprising; 1956 and the revolt of workers in Poznan; 1970 and the revolt of workers in the Baltic cities; and finally, 1981 and the massacre of workers in Silesia under martial law. There is also a belief that the battle for a free Poland is not yet finished, since there was no blood spilled in the 1990s. The 'Velvet Revolution' did not fulfil this criterion because where there is no blood, there is no catharsis, and consequently there can be no rebirth.

The Polish literary critic Maria Janion observes that Poles have a feeling of living in the midst of some existential enigma in which they are fated to stumble, be led astray, and be betrayed and cheated (by reality itself).[8] While having this rich tradition of failures, Poles have never accepted the view that these defeats were fiascos (or rather, they were fiascos on a political level, but they supported the spirit of the nation). The defence of Poland in October 1939, when Polish cavalry charged German tanks (as the myth would have it), and the Warsaw Uprising, have become the stuff of legend, but Poles relive them as moments of pathos in the tragedy of their history. They see themselves as tragic heroes, and failure is the existential experience necessary for the recognition of the tragedy of being.[9]

The category of 'victim' is a key concept in order to understand the Polish approach to Poland's history. Polishness is manifested in the myth of the victim and his/her tragedy. Because Poland is traditionally compared to the Christ of the Passion, it is easy to say that Polish history simply replicates the story of Christ's sacrifice, and certainly the Polish history of the modern period conduces to a Christian-type valuation of suffering as a blessing. But a consideration of Poland's past would reveal that there are many elements of Dionysian paganism in Polish consciousness and that, after a thousand years of belonging to Christendom, Poland's Christianisation is still a kind of unfinished project. By this I mean that the Polish world view tends as much towards pagan notions of the tragic as it does towards

---

[8] Cf. Janion, 1998, p. 256.

[9] *Ibid.*, p. 265.

Christian notions of redemption. This means that defeat and death for a noble cause are in themselves redemptive, having ritual values of ontological transformation, and are not merely the means of attaining life after death. Poles have had many tragic reversals in the past, but the sufferings caused by those events did not humiliate so much as inspire them. In this sense, suffering has had a cathartic value. The motives for suffering and victimisation are connected as much with a Greek Dionysus as a Christian Jesus, indeed, I would claim that when the myth of sacrifice is analysed on the basis of Polish consciousness, it becomes a place where Christianity and paganism, and religion and myth come together. On one hand, suffering feeds history, but on the other, it allows history to deviate from linearity, causality and change.

Analysing the Polish attitude toward the past, one might claim that while the general history of Poland from the Romantic perspective could be connected with the paradigm of Christ's passion, the nation's famous 'martyrs' are closer to the paradigm of Dionysus's suffering in as much as they are more ecstatic and have an element of mystical ontological metamorphosis. Janion points out that, although Poland has traditionally been represented as 'the Christ of Nations', it sometimes appears as a phantasm, a demonic force or a cruel and bloodthirsty vampire. The Polish motherland needs blood in order to survive and regenerate. Poles bitten by her went mad, as happened, for instance, to Tadeusz Rejtan who, trying to stop the Polish Parliament from ratifying the first partition in 1773, rent his clothes and threw himself on the floor shouting, 'kill me, stamp on me, but do not kill my Homeland' (seven years later he committed suicide). Thus, we may speak of 'Polish Rejtanism', a kind of patriotic madness. Hence, Janion claims, we are dealing with a kind of vampiric patriotism that reveals demonic powers we all possess.[10] The 'homeland' requires a kind of revenge for its martyrdom that extends far beyond the limits of Christian charity and reaches back to Dionysian mysteries.

Conclusion: The Myth of Searching

Northrop Frye pointed out that, beyond cultural heritage alone, there has to be some psychological heritage that links the European tradition with the traditions of other cultures. He introduces the concept of a 'mythological universe' which is a reservoir of beliefs

---

[10]   Cf. Janion, 1991.

developed from basic existential dilemmas. Like Frye, I would argue that history and myth (considered as literary genres) have their source in the myth of the search for lost identity, and that this myth lies at the centre of the 'mythological universe' common to different cultures.[11] Therefore a search for the ego of a culture is like a vocation or calling for a given community, and the history of its culture would be a kind of self-reading and self-writing in order to return to a 'unity', to the Hegelian notion of a thing in and of itself. One might also claim that the current 'ethical turn' in the human sciences is another sign of the embodiment of the myth of the lost identity, where the fragmented subject returns on the ground of ethics.

---

[11] Cf. Frye, 1982, p. XVIII.

Polish Myths

THE GOLDEN AGE AND SARMATISM (16th-17th centuries)		ROMANTICISM (19th century)	
		MESSIANISM	INSURRECTION MYTH
Genealogical myths of nobility: Continuity between Roman Empire and the Polish Commonwealth	Poland – the 'GREAT MILL'	Christological myth Poland – 'the Christ of Nations'	Tyrtean myth *Pro patria mori*, death for Homeland
Cult of the 'GOLDEN FREEDOM': Noble Democracy, (*liberum veto*), nation=nobility (ethos of nobility)	Myth of Polish tolerance: country of religious tolerance ('land without stakes')	'For your freedom and ours': (panslavism), Poland, leader of the conquered Slavic nations	Pole-conspirator (martyr, loser, 'desperado', tragic hero
Catholic Poland (Pole=Catholic), *Polonia semper fidelis*	*ANTEMURALE CHRISTIANITATIS* The Bulwark of Christendom (Poland a shield of Europe; pagans and heretics)	*Antemurale* Myth of the West (Western debt to Poland; belief in Western aid)	Cult of insurrection veterans
Myth of the Domestic and the Alien: (Polishness=positive, alien=negative; alien because of language, religion and culture)	Poland as a chosen nation: Historical mission of Poland, spreading civilisation in the East		Figure of noble traitor (*wallenrodyzm*: morality and history)
			'Black myth of the West' (Consumerist and uprooted West, bereft of values)
Manor house: symbol of Polishness Sarmatian ideal of natural life	MARIAN CULT (Holy Mary – Queen of Poland; The Black Madonna of Częstochowa)	Polish Mother	
Polish Baroque (coffin portrait)			
National megalomania (national superiority complex)		(suffering–death–sacrifice: elements of the mission)	
Scapular with an image of Holy Mary-mansion-worldliness		Grave–cross–death–resurrection	
SARMATIAN NOBLEMAN		INSURGENT–CONSPIRATOR	

The above table offers a schematic representation of the main myths that have contributed to Polish identity at one time or another. At present, the basic problem of the Polish approach to Poland's past is the myth of lost Polishness. Poles turn back and look for an archetypal Eden in which Poland had existed in its 'original state' before being expelled from this garden by the tragedy of war and the sin of Communism. They therefore want to re-create this innocent state of the nation (myth) and to reconstruct the world before the fall (history). The Solidarity movement distanced itself from the People's Republic and wanted to return to the tradition of the Second Polish Republic that had come into being in 1918 after the long period of partitions.

This desire to bring back the past manifested itself in gestures such as referring to Polish constitutions of that period, rebuilding the tradition of political parties and organisations, reintroducing national symbols (principally the crowned eagle), encouraging the admiration of politicians (Piłsudski's cult), and so on.

After 1989, it appears that this return to the imaginary Eden is impossible, not so much because of the changes in the political situation, but mainly because the nation whose existence was supported by these myths no longer exists.

Living in a democratic, liberal and tolerant country, we have suddenly discovered that not all Poles are Catholic (or that our faith is superficial), that we have minorities that want to speak with their own voices, and that the stereotype of the 'Polish mother' is now being undermined by a vigorous feminist movement. Faced with these changes, one might say that the fundamental Polish myths are constructs or concepts that functioned in a specific way in the epoch of the nation-state and that they were embodied in a historiographical discourse that allowed them to be manipulated for different political agendas. It suddenly seems that all the constructs that made up the skeleton of the way the Poles thought about the past (nation, state, history, gender, race etc.), as well as the myths that supported them, have become 'dead metaphors'.

Poles have realised that they are speaking a 'dead language', a language for a world that no longer exists. They are also coming close to admitting that wounds in the Polish soul cannot be healed by a return to the 'Golden Age' and that they can no longer believe in the utopia of the wonderful future originating in the past. In the social consciousness there has to re-emerge a belief in the possibility of a 'new beginning', but this must be a 'new beginning' in a new world, not in the old one. Thus, the concepts of palingenesis, with its god, Dionysus, and 'now-time' seem to be more powerful at present than the concept of resurrection as manifested in the Christ paradigm and the concept of historical time based on eschatological progress.

CHAPTER 14

The Creative Fear: Fascism, Anti-Semitism, Democracy and the Foundation of the People's Democracy in Hungary

Péter APOR

Introduction

When the traveller arrives in the Hungarian village of Kunmadaras, one of the first things he or she notices is the town hall, in front of which stands a memorial to the victims of the First World War. On the other side of the square, which was once the market, there is a newly-erected monument to the soldiers and civilians who died in the Second World War. Should the traveller turn around, on the other side of the street he or she will see a black plaque with an inscription dedicated to the victims of the pogrom in Kunmadaras 1946. However, the memory of this event is still ambiguous. The memorial to these Jewish victims is set beside a more glorious memory in the form of a column that reminds the visitor of the 750th anniversary of the arrival of the Cumanians (*kun* is Cumanian in Hungarian) in Hungary. Moreover, the monument to the Second World War immortalises only the non-Jewish victims. The heavy burden of remembering is embedded history.

The trials that followed the pogrom in Kunmadaras represented a crucial event in the disappearance of democracy in post-war Hungary. During the first years of peace, one particular notion of democracy came to dominate all other interpretations among the newly-emerged

263

political elite. This notion was based upon the idea of a strong, centralised state that was authorised to defend the people from its enemies. The genesis of this concept was closely related to the formation of the memory of fascism and the war. The pogrom trial in Kunmadaras was one of the first events where the concepts of fascism, anti-Semitism and democracy merged into a mythical unity. This chapter analyses this process through two particular trials. The first ended with the sentencing of a local school teacher as a fascist war criminal, and this sentence had in turn a very strong impact upon the judgement in the second trial in which the pogrom itself was interpreted.

Prologue: The Trial of the Village Teacher

János Nagy was the village teacher of Kunmadras. From 1929, he had also been a trainer of the *levente* youth, who, under the Horthy regime, were intended to become soldiers in the Hungarian army. In 1945, Nagy was found guilty of being a war criminal and participating in fascist activity. Subsequently, the National Council of the People's Tribunals overturned this judgement on the grounds that it had not been made according to the appropriate regulations. A second trial was therefore set to be held in the village of Karcag on 20th May, 1946. Nagy's trial divided the population of Kunmadras. For many of them it was not acceptable; Nagy was a respected member of the community, and they did not regard him as a fascist. In addition, he was a Calvinist teacher, a religious denomination shared by 84% of the population. There were, however, some witnesses who insisted on testifying against Nagy, including the secretaries of the local Communist and Social Democrat Parties, Ferenc Takács and Ferenc Wurczel. Both of them recalled that at Nagy's first trial the crowd had been led by the youth of Kunmadaras, and had behaved unbearably, demonstrating at the teacher's side and cursing the People's Tribunal, with the result that the atmosphere had become hostile towards the judge.

On the day of the second trial, a crowd of approximately 300 people accompanied Nagy on his way towards the neighbouring village of Karcag. The tension increased when the villagers arrived at the edge of the village, where they were informed of the regulation that only five persons per party could enter the courtroom. Then negotiations started between the representatives of the crowd and the police, with the result that 50 persons were allowed to join the trial audience. The people of Kunmadaras, however, were dissatisfied with this proposal and decided not to go. Moreover, they did not permit Nagy to participate in his trial, despite his asking his followers to allow him go. According to several statements, the crowd became angry when they tried to enter Karcag in defiance of the police forces blocking the road. Their anger was made worse by the police firing warning shots into the air, but they were persuaded to return to their village, disappointed at the failure of their action. There they gathered in the building of the Trade Corporation in order to prepare a petition to the Minister of Justice. Recalling this tense situation, several witnesses claimed that they had heard Zsigmond Tóth, the first defendant in the post-pogrom trial, making anti-Semitic statements and claiming that the Jews must be struck dead by all means since it was thanks to them that the people could not enter the court-room. He called upon the crowd not to give trade to Jewish shops.[1]

The Pogrom Trial

The day after these events, on 21st May 1946, a riot broke out against the Jews of Kunmadaras. Three people were killed, and several more were beaten.[2] The pogrom had been preceded by an intense campaign against black-marketeers, who were considered to be enemies of the economic recovery since their activity was seen as the main cause of the shortages that threatened the rebuilding of the country. However, for the villagers the abstract notion of the speculators was inconceivable, whereas the figure of the Jew was strongly connected with trading activities in popular knowledge. Most of the Jews who had survived the Holocaust had opened their shops immediately on returning to their birthplace, and as a result they stored relatively large amounts of goods in their houses. This phenomenon was absolutely incomprehensible to the peasants, who conceived of the post-war privation as a condition shared by everyone. Many of them thus understood the campaign against black-marketers as a call to take steps against Jewish merchants, although their conception differed greatly to that of Nazi racist theory. Other than

---

[1] Budapest Főváros Levéltára (Budapest City Archives; hereafter BFL) V 56032/1

[2] The most detailed reconstruction is Vörös, 1994, pp. 69-80.

this, the sources provide no hint of previous provocation for the events.

The trial was an exceptional one since it occurred at the Special Council of Five, part of the People's Tribunal that was set up in order to try persons who were accused of committing crimes against democracy and the republican system. In this case, the court of competent jurisdiction was the Special Council of Five of Budapest and thus the trial took place in that city in late June 1946. All the principal defendants were found guilty of leading a movement that had had as its aim the overthrow of both the republic and democracy. At first sight, it may seem surprising to declare a violent action against Jewish merchants a conspiracy against the system of the state, but nevertheless, the sentence stated unambiguously that 'the fall of state order was inevitable if similar such demonstrations became frequent for whatever reason.'[3] How was it possible to interpret the pogrom in Kunmadaras in this way?

The trial was regarded as extremely important by the Communists, with the result that the party intervened into the process immediately. Originally, the Communist Attorney General looked to having the defendants tried as swiftly as possible, and therefore assigned the Summary Court of the County of Szolnok as the court of competent jurisdiction. The Attorney General then changed his opinion and passed the issue to the People's Tribunal of Budapest. However this move had to include the modification of the charge, which was in the Attorney General's power, since the Summary Court had the right to sentence only common criminals while the People's Tribunal tried political cases. It should be noted that although the People's Tribunals were influenced by the left, they cannot, in 1946, be regarded as Communist institutions. The courts consisted of five members, each of whom was delegated by a party of the Hungarian National Front for Independence.[4] The aspirations of these workers' parties saw them encourage the nomination of judges whom they believed would represent justice appropriately.

What was this justice? What were the events in Kunmadaras? The aim of this part of the chapter is to examine how the interpretation of the People's Tribunal was formed. The text of the trial will be

---

[3]   BFL V 56032/2 the sentence, p. 58.

[4]   On the organisation of the Hungarian People's Courts see Tibor, 1979.

analysed and, as an additional source, the dissent of the chairman of the court of the first instance will be incorporated. The latter was written as a protest against the mitigating sentence of the National Council of the People's Tribunals, and perhaps therefore expresses more clearly the standpoint of the court.

There were 59 defendants in all, but the greatest importance was given to the first three. Of these, the first, Zsigmond Tóth, was born in Bratislava (Pozsony) in 1920. He was a citizen of Czechoslovakia who had been expelled from the country according to the Czechoslovak policy of collectively classifying the Hungarian minority population as war criminals. The second defendant was called Gergely Takács, and was the secretary of the local organisation of the Smallholders Party. He was born in 1899, in Balmazújváros, but had lived in Kunmadras for many years. Takács was one of the leading members of the local community and he had occupied various posts in the local administration between the wars. The third defendant was János Nagy, whom we have already met. He was born in Kunmadaras in 1903, had scarcely ever left the village, and knew Gergely Takács from pre-war times. The others defendants were local villagers, and in fact it had been these people who had physically assaulted the Jews.[5]

The judge knew of János Nagy's Fascist past from his previous trial. It thus came about that the People's Tribunal of Budapest generated certain assumptions about the identity of the teacher, according to which his actions were judged. Thus the attempt to obstruct the trial of Nagy could be understood as the crowd trying to save a fascist criminal from lawful punishment. Nagy's initiative to gather the crowd in the building of the Trade Corporation in order to prepare a petition to the Minister of Justice was interpreted as his realisation that if the crowd had dispersed, all of its influence would have been lost. Consequently, according to this logic, he was responsible for the fact that the people did not go home peacefully, but became caught up in an anti-Semitic demonstration. Finally, Nagy's idea was described as the definite basis for further terror actions. The fact that he had stayed at home passively during the whole assault on the Jews was transformed into a crime, on the grounds that he had not tried to prevent the people, and especially his former pupils, from

---

[5]   BFL V 56032/1

attacking the Jews, in spite of the fact that, as a teacher, he had had considerable authority.[6]

Since the teacher was regarded as the central figure in the movement, the other actors were expected to demonstrate the same identity. The facts gained their meaning in the narrative assigned to them by the People's Tribunal, which in turn was articulated according to the prescribed narrative identity of Nagy. Closed institutions, as far as possible, maintain the validity of the identities produced by them, and the trial worked as an institution in this sense. It not only showed fascists, it also produced fascism through prescribed identities while using the narrative as a means to fill particular experiences with significance.[7] The judgement dealt with the events of the assault on the Jews in a ten-page document describing in minute detail the particular acts. It started its narrative with the events around dawn on 21st March. Two of the participants visited Zsigmond Tóth in his apartment. Tóth first buckled on his dagger and then all three of them went to the market square, which was already full of stall holders and buyers from the village as well as from other parts of the region. According to the judgement, the pogrom started after Tóth, convinced that the size of the crowd and the general atmosphere were appropriate, took up the slogan, 'Well, now it's time to start the dance!' The People's Tribunal stated that the villagers had realised that Tóth was calling upon them to assault and kill the Jews. Since the judgement was able to indicate one precise moment as a starting point and then followed the course of the crowd from one Jew to another, it implied that the riot in Kunmadaras had been an organised event.[8]

What is more, the judge made this opinion explicit by consistently using the word 'organised'. Listing the events of the morning the document stated that, 'At about eleven o'clock in the morning the organised crowd reached József Kohn's house in which he also has his shop.' The actions of the villagers are made to appear consciously co-ordinated: Kohn and his wife tried to escape using the back gate, but there they ran into one of the participants who forced them to return to

---

[6]   BFL V 56032/2, the sentence p. 60.

[7]   BFL V 56032/1; Goffman, 1968, pp. 159-86. On the narrative see also: Braun, 1995 and the English summary, Braun 1994.

[8]   BFL V-56032/2 on pp. 45-46 of the sentence.

the house where they were beaten by the others.[9] Another victim tried to hide himself away in a wagon at the railway station but was soon discovered and ordered to come out. The judgement argued that the only way the crowd could have found him was if he had been observed during his flight by certain people who had later called the others to the station. It concluded that the aforementioned scene proved that the pogrom in Kunmadaras, 'occurred in an organised way, systematically, and it was known and carried out by a great part of the people.'[10] The shouts of the crowd only confirmed this: 'Come down, bloody Jew, none of you will escape!'. Having beaten their victim, the crowd, 'advancing and operating systematically' proceeded towards the house of another Jew.

If the pogrom was an organised action of the villagers, then somebody had to be responsible for this organisation. According to the judgement, the first direct organiser of the movement was Zsigmond Tóth, who had voiced the phrase that had signified the start of the attack. However, he had begun his action much earlier, when the villagers gathered to go to the neighbouring village of Karcag in order to take part in the Nagy's trial on the day before the pogrom. At the edge of that village the crowd had been told by some people from Karcag that two children had been lost. The judge stated that at this point Tóth realised that this was the right time for him. He immediately began to claim that the children must have been taken by the Jews. He also added that similar events had taken place in Slovakia, and that several Jews had been strung up on street lamps as a result. He stated, pointing at the dagger that hung from his belt, that this weapon had been also used against the Jews in Slovakia. In addition, he moved through the people, whispering in people's ears, and his words provoked an anti-Jewish atmosphere among the villagers. The judgement argued that Tóth had been waiting for this opportunity and had prepared himself well,

It could not be said how long he had been waiting for this propitious occasion, but he was well-prepared which is shown by the fact that he systematically engaged in this activity with all his might

---

[9] BFL V-56032/2 p. 50.
[10] BFL V-56032/2 p. 52.

and competence, and did not rest until he had heated the passion of the crowd to a sufficient degree to provoke the events of the day after.[11]

Tóth pursued his activity throughout the day, inciting the people against the Jews. He prepared the atmosphere by mentioning that he had several tough friends who were also ready to set Kunmadaras to rights. He called upon the crowd to be present in great number in the market square on the following day since something would happen, 'probably, a Jew-baiting'.[12] In this way, the People's Tribunal transformed the spontaneous violence against the Jewish merchants into an organised fascist pogrom. The theme was immediately taken up by the press. One newspaper asked, 'who prepared the pogrom of Kunmadaras?'[13] Another stated that the population of the village organised a classic pogrom, scuffle and blood-bath.[14] The local newspaper referred to the events in the same way, claiming that the villagers organised a pogrom after returning home from Karcag.[15]

The judgement additionally proved that János Nagy and Gergely Takács had also been responsible for the assault on the Jews. It was stated that they knew that the atmosphere among the people had become anti-Semitic, but rather than acting to combat it, they assisted in planning the pogrom. They acted consciously, asserted the judgement, and, given their intelligence, they would have been able to predict the way the events would go. In the subsequent parts of the judgement, reasons were given why the other participants were also guilty. The Tribunal was convinced that Tóth had known that what he had done had been influenced by the spirit of fascism, and moreover, that what the actions of the crowd would constitute a fascist-like movement. He had known that inciting against the Jews was a fascist deed, and this fact was clear to the most primitive villager as well.

One of the court's main pieces of evidence that showed that the villagers in Kunmadaras had organised a pogrom was the fact that they had held a meeting after their unsuccessful excursion to Nagy's trial. The judgement argued that when the villagers found that they could not enter the court, they returned home and decided to gather in

---

[11] BFL V-56032/2 pp. 40-41.

[12] BFL V-56032/2 p. 44.

[13] *Szabad Nép* (hereafter *SZN*) (May 27, 1946), p. 3.

[14] *Képes Figyelő* 2 (May 25, 1946), p. 5.

[15] *TV* (February 13, 1947), p. 4.

the hall of the Trade Corporation of Kunmadaras in order to write a petition to the Minister of Justice on Nagy's behalf. The judgement stated that the atmosphere of the meeting had been characterised by hatred against the People's Tribunal. When Gergely Takács learned from a participant that somebody had rung the police in Karcag in order to prevent the crowd from entering the village, he had immediately claimed that this was undoubtedly the action of the Jews. Takács then suggested forcing the witnesses for the prosecution to withdraw their evidence. Thus the crowd waited for Ferenc Takács, one of the witnesses (not to be confused with Gergely Takács, one of the defendants) and pelted him with stones as he returned home by cart. The judgement stated that by that time, they had been persuaded that the Jews had obstructed the trial, as evidenced by the way they cursed Ferenc Takács and his wife, 'Wait till we catch you, bloody democrats, henchmen of the Jew People's Tribunal, Jewish henchmen, there will be no trial now!'[16] Later, the witness was led to the meeting in the hall of the Trade Corporation, where the crowd wanted to beat him and, according to the judgement, only the intervention of the local police saved his life. One of the witnesses recalled that the reason for the aggression had been that Ferenc Takács had been a secretary of the Communist Party, while another claimed that the crowd had wanted to beat Takács because he had shot at them. A participant at the meeting asserted that a person who shot at his Hungarian brothers ought to be hanged, arguing that, 'It is a disgrace that *even* you try to shoot me. Was it not enough that the Austrians and the Germans shot our people?' The crowd accused the witnesses for the prosecution of preventing them from taking part in the trial.

A few villagers started to identify the witnesses of the prosecution with the Jews and to imagine a Jewish conspiracy underpinning the events, 'We are going to drag Wurczel the Jew from his house. We will finish off the bloody Jew because he called the police in Karcag when we wanted to demonstrate!'[17] A group of villagers then went to the house of Ferenc Wurczel, the second witness for the prosecution, and forced him to go with them to the Trade Corporation hall, but on the way he was attacked by the crowd and seriously beaten. The

---

[16] BFL V 56032/2 p. 43.

[17] V 56032/1

judgement was convinced that he was assaulted primarily because of his Jewish origin.[18]

What thoroughly convinced the People's Tribunal that the case had been an anti-Semitic conspiracy was that Zsigmond Tóth had stated that he had learned that the Jews would try to carry off János Nagy from his house at night, and had therefore decided to keep watch on it. Tóth became an active participant in gathering support for the petition on behalf of Nagy, and undertook to deliver it to the capital.[19] The judgement thus saw an organised conspiracy planned by three anti-Semites in order, first, to achieve the release of one of their number and humiliate the People's Tribunal, and secondly, to organise a pogrom. The judgement considered Tóth's anti-Semitic activity and Nagy and Takács's movement against the People's Tribunal as being connected. When Zsigmond Tóth incited the people against the Jews, Gergely Takács joined in the activity claiming that, 'it's time to get rid of those who sponge off the Hungarian people.'[20] As a result, the crowd, already excited by previous events, turned against the Jews. The judgement did not suggest that there had been a direct connection between Tóth and Takács, but it placed them on the same level as anti-Semite demagogues. On the other hand, by proving that all three defendants were anti-Semites, the crowd action to obtain the release of Nagy could be regarded as anti-Semitic agitation. The judgement made this explicit when it stated clearly that both Takács and Nagy 'have anti-Semitic emotions.'[21]

By perceiving the people as a fascist mob, all of their acts became fascist activities. Thus, for example, after the pogrom the representatives of the local parties gathered and issued a declaration that the Jews and Ferenc Takács, the most important witness of the prosecution, would have to leave the village. The People's Tribunal understood this as a fascist action against democracy, since it combined anti-Semitic elements with an attack against a person 'who is truly faithful to the ideas of the people's democracy.'[22] This perspective gave anti-Semitism a new function; it ceased to be a crime

---

[18]   V 56032/2, sentence, p. 44, p. 59.

[19]   V 56032/2 pp. 44-5.

[20]   V 56032/2 p. 41.

[21]   V 56032/2 p. 37.

[22]   V 56032/2 p. 56.

for which the defendants had to be called to account and became instead the indicator of fascism. The inevitable concomitant phenomenon of every fascist action was anti-Semitism, as implied in the following statement;

> As a natural, obvious and inevitable outcome of the fascist, anti-state character of the whole movement, the action that was originally directed solely against the power of the state, the People's Tribunal and the state institutions that ordered the arrest, turned against the Jews under the guidance of Zsigmond Tóth and Gergely Takács.[23]

If fascists always organise anti-Semitic pogroms and these are always committed by fascists, then clearly the People's Tribunal equated fascism with anti-Semitism and *vice versa*. The inevitable result of this was that any anti-Jewish action was seen as being directed against the democratic system. According to this logic, the Chairman of the Court argued that the events in Kunmadaras were not a Jewish matter, but concerned the order of the whole Hungarian state.[24] The court argued that the movement that had been initiated by János Nagy, organised by him and Gergely Takács, and pursued by Zsigmond Tóth, had resulted in the Jews and the witnesses for the prosecution losing their right to live without fear, to enjoy security of the person and to exercise their civil and property rights. One man had been robbed by two swineherds who called on him to, 'Give us your money, that Jewish mother of yours!' When the crowd broke into the house of another Jewish merchant, they carried off all his meat, and one of them even stole a pot in which to take it home. Episodes like this served as evidence that Kunmadaras had experienced a fascist-like terror and that the state authority had collapsed as a result. In this way, the events in Kunmadaras ceased to be a Jewish issue. Although beating and killing Jews (or any other group) is obviously an anti-democratic action, the sentence made reference to them only to prove the presence of fascism.

In a situation where the notion of democracy required an absolutely new form of public discourse, one that was based mainly upon the sense of being threatened, fascism was produced as the enemy, and in this way, democracy could be identified with the struggle against fascism. In the 13th century, when the Eucharist started to occupy a

---

[23]   V 56032/1, the dissent of the chairman of the Court

[24]   V 56032/1, the dissent of the chairman of the Court

central position in Christian ceremonies, this ceremony was repre-sented as more potent and more capable of working miracles than other rituals. The Eucharist was considered a sacrament that was able to defend itself from its enemies, and it was the Jews, often referred to in official church discourse as the murders of Christ, who were involved in this process. A new narrative emerged about Jewish abuse and desecration of the holy host that usually ended with a miracle saving the Eucharist. However, these accusations were not only about demonstrating that the Jews were enemies of Christianity, but were also intended to provide evidence of both the vulnerability and the miraculous power of the host. The Jews played a crucial role in confirming the qualities and existence of the Eucharist and, more than this, they were fundamental requirements for the foundation of that entity.[25]

A very similar process took place with the notion of democracy in Hungary. In March 1946, the National Assembly accepted Act VII, which concerned the protection of the democratic system and the republic and which contained the definition of several political crimes. In a situation where Hungarian democracy defined itself as young, and therefore defenceless, and where fascism had proved its opposition to democracy during the war, the representatives of the Assembly considered penal sentences an effective and necessary measure against those who sought to damage the system. This was explained in the reasoning of the act:

> The penal defence of the order of the state is an obligation of the first rank for every country. The effective penal defence of the state cannot be lacking in a system based on democratic principles, but least of all a state like Hungary that is rising again after the Second World War and the Arrow Cross – German devastation. Our democratic system can look back on only one year of development, while the republican form of the state has been realised only recently. Regarding these conditions, the attacks against the Hungarian democratic system and state form are of even greater account since they substantially endanger the existence of the state, the development of the life of the society and, together with them, the place of the Hungarian people among the democratic nations.[26]

The act therefore regarded that every attack aimed at the overthrow of the democratic system and the republican form of the state should

---

[25] Rubin, 1993.

[26] Tibor, 1979, pp. 19-20.

be seriously punished. The reasoning of the act clearly indicated that its purpose was to prevent the recurrence of fascist-like, anti-state activities. The trial of the pogrom in Kunmadaras was the first case to be tried on the basis of this new act.

The position of the political left in Hungary was reflected in a speech delivered by one of their representatives in parliament: 'Is the government aware that one of the concomitant phenomena of fascism, anti-Semitism, has appeared again in certain parts of the country? [...] What is the government ready to do in order to nip in the bud this reactionism disguised in such a manner?'[27] This is a very interesting argument, because it reveals the left's way of thinking about anti-Semitism. According to this perspective, anti-Semitism related exclusive to fascism. The Hungarian Communist Party was omnipresent in the country, and presented itself as knowing about every event that happened in Hungary. It was therefore inevitable that the Hungarian Communist Party had its explanation immediately to hand. After the pogroms, the Central Board of the party (*Központi Vezetőség*) arranged a conference where the issue of the anti-Semitic events was on the agenda. The party considered this issue so important that Mátyás Rákosi, the Secretary-General himself, delivered a speech on the subject. He listed all the pogroms he knew, beginning with a case at Ózd. 'We have enquired into things there', concluded the Secretary-General, 'and obviously we have found traces of fascism [...]'[28] Then he introduced the murder of a police officer in Szentes and stated that, 'We have checked on things and have found fascist threads leading to Budapest'. He also spoke about suspicious connections with Budapest with respect to a pogrom in Békéscsaba. Rákosi then interpreted a case in Miskolc as a pogrom that had happened after an anti-Semitic provocation during a political meeting. He argued that 'numerous fascist people from Miskolc and the neighbourhood' had joined the participants of the gathering. He was convinced that it was a well prepared provocation since it had succeeded in paralysing the economic life of the region (nobody had gone to work during the pogrom), it had presented the Communist Party as anti-Semitic, and it had dealt the police a heavy blow. He closed his speech with a supposition that 'a central fascist organisation has a part to play in this.'

---

[27] Vörös, 1994, p. 77.

[28] 'A miskolci pogrom...' with the preface of Éva Standeisky, 1990, pp. 78-86.

The People's Tribunal also shared this view that fascism was the enemy of democracy and that fascist actions were capable of over-throwing any kind of democratic system. The judgement effectively argued that the inherent characteristics showed the real nature of particular actions. Thus, fascist deeds and movements naturally opposed the notion of democracy, and since fascism could prevail only after the death of democracy, it aspired to destroy the democratic order.[29] The chairman of the court argued that fascist activity offered the same threat to the Hungarian Republic as it had to the Weimar Republic, which had been overthrown by Hitler's fascists. It was therefore logical for the People's Tribunal that in Kunmadar the events had been nothing other than old fascists appearing and acting again. The judgement claimed that Gergely Takács had been the election agent of an Arrow Cross member of parliament and that later he had been appointed sergeant by Szálasi during the last days of the war in Germany, while János Nagy had personally trained his followers for fascism.

Not only did old fascists reappear, but the whole village reverted to the age of fascism, to 1944. The chairman evoked one scene as follows, 'Ernő Weinberger's family are lying bloody in the ditch and the crowd is carrying off fat, bacon, and other goods in stock. The atmosphere of 1944 is complete.'[30] He considered that disorder in Kunmadaras had become absolute and only the deportation wagons had been missing. According to these statements, the events in Kunmadaras were the fascist re-enactment of their attack on Hungarian democracy.

A historical trial makes history internal, that is to say, it persona-lises it, transforming the historical narrative into personal experiences. A trial is a drama where social reality is constituted, reproduced and re-enacted.[31] In the pogrom trial in Kunmadaras the judgement evoked history, connecting the defendants to the fascists of World War II:

A rare smile appeared on the faces of the organisers and leaders of the movement. What they wanted was realised; the village of Kunmadaras went back on the cart of time to the fascist and Arrow Cross era of 1944,

---

[29]   BFL V 56032/2, sentence, pp. 59-60.
[30]   V 56032/1, the dissent of the chairman of the court
[31]   Hariman,1990, pp. 1-16.

and certain of its inhabitants acted as the fascist and Arrow Cross scoundrels of that time.[32]

For the People's Tribunal, the events in Kunmadaras recalled particular events of the Second World War. In the process of interpretation, a direct relationship between Nazi pogroms and the Jew-baiting in Kunmadaras was established, and during the hearing, certain memories emerged in the minds of the judges. Since the People's Tribunal recognised the actors of its narrative in the people of the village, the interpretation could be presented in a form that was comprehensible for the participants of the trial. Personal relations and emotions emerged that decreased the distance between history and memory. The historical interpretation endeavoured to encompass the personal memories that were collected in the court. The fact of gathering all the memories in one space thus operated as a memorial that aimed to materialise personal memories in historical notions. The trial was a site of memory or properly a site of remembering history.[33]

In this sense, memory is never innocent, neutral or independent of other aspects of its environment, for there are always certain consequences that are interrelated to its context. The trial can be described as a memorial since it attempted to remind the participants of particular events. The process established historical continuity between Nazism and the anti-Jewish riot of Kunmadaras in order to demonstrate the continuation of fascism. Through this representation, the enemies of post-war fascism could present themselves as the heirs of an anti-fascist past, or speak about their past as the anti-fascist past. Since fascism opposes democratic systems, the adversaries fascism could show themselves to be perpetual fighters for democracy. Thus, the emergence of the new democratic state of Hungary could be explained, not as the result of the collapse of the pre-war regime, but as a constant and continuing anti-fascist struggle. As a consequence, only those who could prove their anti-fascist past, and gain the credentials of a person with a democratic mentality could present themselves as propagators of the new democracy.[34]

---

[32]   BFL V 56032/2, sentence, p. 46.

[33]   The term 'sites of memory' is the translation of Pierre Nora's original French *Les Lieux de mémoire* by Marc Roudebush. Nora, 1989.

[34]   Young, 1993, pp. 11-5; Knapp, 1989, pp. 123-149.

This narrative produced a new concept of democracy, and the evocation of history served as a means to establish its meaning. This new form of memory can be seen, for example, when the defendants were reminded that their crimes had not been directed against the Jews, but against the state which they declared to be theirs. The court asked several witnesses for their opinion of the democratic system. All of them replied that for them the new system was more advantageous than the old one. Defending themselves they had not only to prove that they had not assaulted Jews, but that they were not enemies of democracy. One defendant argued that, 'When a father is looking for his child and, in so doing, is dragged into an excited crowd, he meets none of the criteria required for prosecution under the act that aims at the defence of the democratic system.'[35]

Of the three main defendants, János Nagy referred to his democratic way of thinking and his actions which were always in favour of the people. He explained how he had wanted to leave his post as *levente* trainer in 1941 and help the persecuted Jews. He also argued that he has turned towards the democratic parties with his petition, and that therefore his purpose could not be the overthrow of democracy. Gergely Takács called attention to the democratic political behaviour he had demonstrated in the past. In 1930 he had joined the Social Democratic Party in Debrecen, for which he had been dismissed from his job. He organised the Social Democratic Party section in Balmazújváros in 1932, and as a result was beaten by the police to such a degree that he had needed three weeks to recover. He subsequently became an object of police surveillance. Even Zsigmond Tóth presented his anti-fascist past, claiming that he had been a partisan in Slovakia.

The chairman of the court stated that after the crowd had arrived back in Kunmadaras, there had been an event of fascist-like terror that had led to the fall of the state's authority. This fall had been preceded by the demonstrators' attack on the police in Karcag. According to this interpretation, in Kunmadaras on 21st May, 1946, it was the Arrow Cross terror of 1944 that prevailed rather than the authority of the state.[36] This interpretation added a new aspect to the concept of democracy, which came to be equated with the institutions and structures of the state. From this moment, the security of democracy

---

[35]   BFL V56032/2

[36]   BFL V 56032/1, the dissent of the chairman of the court

could be taken to mean the defence of the state's authority. In this case in the People's Tribunal, democracy came to equate for the first time to the notion of the people's democracy. The concept of the democratic system formulated during the trial laid great stress on the role of the state as the guardian of the people against their enemies. For the birth of the Hungarian People's Democracy, it was crucial that the post-war system should find fascist conspirators and present them as the greatest threat. Thus it was the regime itself that produced fascists. The People's Tribunal defined the anti-Jewish riot in Kunmadaras as a fascist conspiracy. This statement identified fascism with anti-Semitism and provided a means by which the authorities could find their enemies. From this point on, the manifestation of anti-Semitism made fascist conspiracies immediately recognisable. This connection made it possible for the system, which defined itself as a young democracy under threat from fascism, to demonstrate the historical continuity of fascism and so present the regime as the authentic heir of the anti-fascist struggle. In turn, this meant that, since the state authority was seen to be taking measures against fascism, it could be conceived as a democracy.

CHAPTER 15

A *Nazione Mancata*: The Construction of the *Mezzogiorno* After 1848

Marta PETRUSEWICZ

The *Mezzogiorno* as Italy's Negative Foundation Myth

It is one of Italy's famous paradoxes that at the same moment that political unity of the country was proclaimed in 1861, the profound absence of cultural unity was realised. The Italian people, as the Neapolitan historian Guido De Ruggiero was to observe, were not an organic unity. After centuries of division, this was hardly surprising, nor was it necessarily negative. However, in a very short time this lack of unity was construed as a 'dualism' between North and South with the consequent 'failure' of Italy. And, in another quick conceptual turn corresponding roughly to the war against *brigandage* (1862-5), the *Mezzogiorno* alone became both the main cause and the most visible sign of the nation's failure to 'happen'. Promoted to a synonym for the failure of the Risorgimento, for a *nazione mancata*, the *Mezzogiorno* has become, understandably, one of the most powerful and long-lasting representations in modern Italian history, filled with political and symbolic implications.

A concept endowed with such a symbolic power cannot but be nebulous. The *Mezzogiorno* is not a geographical expression, because the boundaries that separate it from 'the North' are fluid and uncertain, and it includes the *isole*, some of which, like Sardinia, fall geographically somewhere in the centre of the country. It is not an historical heritage of the Kingdom of Two Sicilies, for Sardinia was never part of that state, while some of the former kingdom's lands now belong to the centre. But the very question 'what actually is the *Mezzogiorno?*' can be posed only by an outsider. Within Italy's cultural and historical borders, the *Mezzogiorno* simply exists.

Within these borders, the *Mezzogiorno* is synonymous with 'the South', which in turn is simply the *alter* of 'the North'. When 'the North' historically stands for the Kingdom of Sardinia and the Savoyas, 'the South' stands for the Kingdom of Two Sicilies and the Bourbons. When 'the North' stands for urbanisation and industrialisation, 'the South' represents peasant culture. When 'the North' produces machines, manufactured goods, services, know-how, with a skilled and unionised work-force, 'the South' produces foodstuffs and raw materials and supplies a cheap and docile labour force. When 'the North' of the Longobard tradition belongs to Western Europe, the 'South' stands for the Mediterranean civilisation of the Greeks and the Arabs. When 'the North' is shown in iconography through its civic architecture, 'the South' is symbolised by the permanently erupting Vesuvius. 'The North' is reason, 'the South' is passion. And so on.

It is this relation of *alterity* that provides the *Mezzogiorno* with an existence. By the same token, of course, it also creates 'the North', which would be meaningless without it ('North' of what?). But this obvious symmetry is far from being acknowledged by the majority of scholars, politicians and the media, progressives and conservatives alike. Quite the contrary, all the negative ideological charge of the *alterity* is turned against the *Mezzogiorno*, which is consistently described by a limited number of clearly recognisable and negative terms: poverty and structural economic backwardness; unemployment, but also under-population; wrong relationship with the state, whether by scarcity or by excess (as in the recent work of Robert Putnam[1]); a semi-feudal society, with no modern bourgeoisie and a weak middle class subordinated to the interests of old barons or newer political notables; an irrational society lacking all the Weberian 'spirits' of association, of enterprise, of co-operation; a world of anthropological peculiarities such as familism, always amoral, like in the famous formulation by Edward Banfield, individualism (always possessive), factionalism, clientelism, and, occasionally, an innate propensity to

---

[1]   Putnam, 1993.

crime.[2] A society incapable of organising for a *true* class struggle, but inclined, instead, to rebellion, always primitive (as in the well known study by Eric Hobsbawm) and often criminal.[3]

Significantly, the terms often associated with the *Mezzogiorno*, along with particularities and extraordinariness, are those indicating an insufficiency or an outright absence, a *mancanza*. The idea of *mancanza* is central to many modern progressive interpretations of Italian history, from Piero Gobetti to Antonio Gramsci, and refers to opportunities missed and to things that might have happened and did not.[4] The *Risorgimento* itself is seen as a *rivoluzione mancata*, a missing revolution, one that never happened, with dire consequences for the future of the country. In such an interpretative context, the *mancanze* of the *Mezzogiorno* are not only deficiencies and absences, but outright failures that build up into a multi-layered narrative; they prevent 'the South' from progressing (development *mancato*), they drag 'the North' into 'the South's' failure by draining the former's resources, they lead to a growing gap between 'the North' and 'the South', and, finally, they contribute to the failure of the central state. The variety of concrete and complex difficulties associated with the *Mezzogiorno* are thus all subsumed into one global failure – Italy's national problem, or the so-called 'Southern Question'. At the final level of this multi-layered narrative, the *Mezzogiorno* stands for the failure of Italy to realise the historical project of the *Risorgimento*; the failure of the nation to become one, undivided and indivisible. The *Mezzogiorno* is the symbol of, and bears the responsibility for, a *nazione mancata*.

Who Invented the *Mezzogiorno*?

The obvious question that arises is, who 'constructed' the *Mezzogiorno* in these globalising terms? How did different, and often discordant descriptions and analyses of the politics, economy, society and culture of the Kingdom of Two Sicilies come to constitute one uniform representation of a mega-failure? Conventional wisdom has it that the Southern Question arose after the Unification, when the

---

[2]   Banfield, 1958.

[3]   Hobsbawm, 1965 [1959].

[4]   Gobetti, 1964, pp. 33-35; Gramsci, 1975, pp. 1766-67.

conditions for alterity with the North were created. In fact, this chronology is accepted both by the 19th century 'founding fathers' of the Question, like Pasquale Villari, Leopoldo Franchetti and Sidney Sonnino, and by modern day students of representation such as Nelson Moe and John Dickie.[5] The latter see the rhetoric of the Southern Question and all the accompanying stereotypes as coming mainly from the North, with the southerners assuming the role of accomplices in spreading this representation.

Yet, if one listens to the southern voices of the mid-19th century, from letters and memoirs to political journalism and pamphlets, one discovers that all the elements necessary to construct the global negative image of the *Mezzogiorno* were already there, in place, by the time of the Unification, with the full arsenal of negative terms, the Dantesque and the medical languages, the *imagerie* of *barbarie* and primitiveness. Two important implications follow. First, that the authorship of this lexicon belongs not to the northerners, who limited themselves to adopting it, but to the southerners themselves, and secondly, that the representation was constructed before the Unification and, by 1861, it was largely accomplished. It is these two issues – the authorship and the periodisation of the *Mezzogiorno* – that are the topics of this chapter.

My argument runs roughly as follows. During the half century preceding the revolutions of 1848, the Neapolitan *intelligentsia* had laboured strenuously to reform state and society, to enlarge citizenship and to modernise the nation. In this process, it constituted itself in a modern political and civil subject, an embryo of a modern nation, or 'almost a nation', *quasi una nazione*, in the words of Eleonora Fonseca Pimentel.[6] This modernisation project collapsed, dramatically and definitively in 1848, and its embittered heroes, from prison and exile, set out to assign the blame. It was precisely as an outcome of this defeat and disappointment that, in the decade that followed, a new representation of the *Mezzogiorno* emerged in which impossibility and failure became central and constitutive parts.

In order to see the novelty of the post-1848 representation of the *Mezzogiorno* we must discuss what the image was before 1848, and in

---

[5] Villari, 1878; Franchetti and Sonnino, 1974 [originally *La Sicilia nel 1876*. First published in 1877]; Moe, 1992; Dickie, 1992.

[6] Croce, 1925, pp. 174-175.

order to understand how bitter the disappointment was after 1848, we must see the promise of the preceding decades. For this reason, disproportionate attention in this chapter is devoted to the situation in the Kingdom of Two Sicilies before the revolution. The protagonist of this story is the Neapolitan *intelligentsia*. In a way, it is the story of a generation, the generation of 1848, which was made up of people who came of age and were active during the Restoration and who fought and otherwise participated in the 'great banquet' of 1848, to use Francesco Mastriani's nostalgic term.[7] The term *'intelligentsia'* is freely borrowed from its proper Russian and Eastern European context and is used here to signify a social stratum that was culturally homogenous, educated and united by a certain set of values. It includes the intellectuals of the opposition, revolutionary or otherwise, as well as, more broadly, all those who thought critically and independently and whose public action, however practical, was guided primarily by ideological choices. I use here the noncommittal term 'stratum' rather than 'class' to stress that what held this group together were, above all, bonds of consciousness, critical thought and moral passion. All the same, there undoubtedly existed a class character to the Neapolitan *'intelligentsia'*; though by no means all noble, they came mostly from the 'land,' – the gentry, the clergy and the professions – rarely from the artisan class and almost never from the peasantry.

The Making of the *Quasi Nazione*

The genealogy of the 'forty-eighters' goes back to the Enlightenment. The general climate that prevailed in the country during the second half of the 18th century was propitious to both the ideological temper of this generation and its impact on the world. The Kingdom of Two Sicilies, independent from Spain since 1734, was the largest of the Italian states. It was governed stably by a single dynasty (that had rapidly become 'neapolitanised'), and had an autonomous foreign policy, a strong position *vis-à-vis* the Papacy and vast commercial opportunities opening up to it. Its rulers, Don Carlos and his son Ferdinand, attempted wide-reaching reforms, from the reorganisation of finances, taxation and the prison system to the *Cassa Sacra* land reform that involved the expropriation of the Church's

---

[7]   Mastriani, 1994 [1863], p. 164.

wealth and the curtailing of baronial privileges. They created a modern cadastral system, reorganised the *annona* (the system of grain reserves), negotiated a Concordat and expelled the Jesuits. They patronised culture, built the splendid San Carlo theatre and sponsored the discovery of Paestum and the first archaeological excavations at Herculanium. Intellectuals thrived in this environment – their opinions were sought, their approval courted, and critical writings were tolerated as long as they did not question the institution of dynastic monarchy. The ailing University of Naples was revamped, and the first chair of political economy in continental Europe, which went to the noted economist, Antonio Genovesi, was established there. It was a period of intellectual giants, and the writings of Genovesi, Galante, Broggia, Galiani and Palmieri made the Neapolitan Enlightenment famous throughout Europe. The inspirational teachings of these masters triggered a movement of moral and institutional innovation that was concerned with public good and capable of political agency, and this, in turn, gave birth to the stratum that we might call the 'proto-*intelligentsia*', the grandparents of the 19th century *intelligentsia*. It was this stratum that Eleonora de Fonseca Pimentel – poet, journalist and political activist – had in mind when she spoke of the emergence of '*quasi una nuova nazione*'. Passionate believers in the religion of Reason and Humanity, dedicated to the *patria* and full of *amor di patria*, these public intellectuals were the harshest critics of the backwardness of the country and the evils that hampered its progress, and they felt confident that their critique would fuel and direct the monarch's reformist drive.

The end of the century marked a turning point. With the political context abruptly altered by the advent of the French Revolution and the attendant regicide, the honeymoon between the intellectuals and the dynasty came to an end. The reforms were abandoned and even reversed, and the intellectuals were ostracised and persecuted. There followed a turbulent period from 1799 to 1815, marked by revolution, civil war, foreign rule and more than one defeat. Eleonora Fonseca Pimentel was executed in 1799 along with other members of the *quasi-nazione* who had fostered and joined the revolution, served the short-lived and unhappy Partenopean Republic and had finally fallen victim to the mob's rage and Ferdinand's vicious vengeance. In 1806 those who survived joined the French kings, Joseph and then Murat, who had been installed in Naples by Napoleon's troops, and lent them support in their modernising effort. In 1815, after that 'happy decade', came the Restoration.

The Restoration as Humus for Reform

The Restoration, all things considered, did not offer barren soil for reform action. It is important to point out that, although absolutist, the Restoration regime had a character of its own; it was both different from the *Ancien Regime* and infinitely milder and less vengeful than the first Restoration of 1799. *De facto*, upon their return to the throne, the Bourbons acknowledged the irreversibility of the changes that had taken place in the *Weltanschauung* and in the institutions of the country during the period 1799-1815. They did not attempt to restore feudalism, and maintained most of the administrative and institutional structure and the appointments of Murat's period. Freedom of the press and freedom of expression was relatively extensive, although it was punctuated by periods of aggressive censorship. King Ferdinand I returned as a reactionary but not a fanatic and, more like Louis XVIII than Charles X, continued to favour at least some form of modernisation. The revolution of 1820 – mobilised through the networks of the *Carboneria* and free-masonry, led by the veterans of '99 and the Napoleonic armies, with the Spanish *(sic!)* constitution of 1812 hastily granted and then taken back – would have appeared almost as a classical theatrical classical interlude had it not been for the executions and the exiles. Francis I's reign was uneventful, but the ascent of Ferdinand II to the throne in 1830 seemed to announce change. In tune with the vigorous cohort of modern young absolute monarchs coming to the thrones of European at that time, he seemed serious about modernising the state and society. He granted an amnesty and allowed the exiles to return, carried out an 'administrative revolution' and encouraged the development of industry and banking by initiating the construction of railways. The following two decades marked a period of maturation, of civil society, reformist awareness and political action.

It was during these decades that the Neapolitan *intelligentsia* came of age. Far from falling into the languor and desolation that Vincenzo Cuoco feared, it used the experience acquired in the revolutionary years to clarify its modernising project and to free itself from the 'passivity' of the past, from that political and intellectual dependency on foreign ideas and universalist prescription that Cuoco so brilliantly analysed in his *Essay on the Neapolitan Revolution of 1799*.[8] Without rejecting the *problematique* of their enlightened masters, the new *intelligentsia* challenged the universalism of the recipes offered for economic and political development, and criticised the universalist contempt for native customs and institutions, and its remoteness from popular sentiment. They found inspiration in their Neapolitan forebear Giambattista Vico, who had taught that different societies should be taken on their own terms rather than in terms of universal categories. Like their contemporaries in other countries, younger intellectuals were under the spell of Romanticism. In addition to the usual exaltations and soul-searching, the influence of Romanticism inspired them to search for local traditions, local economic 'vocations' and the 'spirit' of local territories, the *genii loci*. They initiated programmes of local action, making use of new regional forms of sociability and communication such as associations and journals, while distancing themselves from free-masonry which was becoming old and *passé*. The emphasis on 'localism' helped mobilise and form an opinion in the provinces that gradually enlarged, organised and inhabited a new 'civic' space.'

The *intelligentsia*'s main bone of contention with the throne remained the questions of the constitution and representative government. No modern nation could exist, they claimed, without political participation for people like themselves, and if citizenship was not gradually extended to those who were excluded. This conflict unfolded through a succession of promises and negotiations, concessions and abrogations. In the meantime, however, this *intelligentsia* set to work on extending the bases of a nation through reform and education. Their new *raison d'être* became the modernisation of the state and the system of governance, the rationalisation of the economy, and the encouragement of literacy, social reform and structural improvements with the aim of helping the *plebs* turn themselves into a *popolo*.

The Culture of the Restoration

The cultural climate of the 1830s and 40s was lively. Naples swarmed with 'liberal' students, who came from all parts of the country. The prestige of the university had declined, but a multitude of new

---

[8]   Cuoco, 1998 [Milan, 1800].

public and private schools, institutes and academies thrived. Many of these schools were run by the most illustrious members of the Neapolitan *intelligentsia* such as the literary scholar Francesco De Sanctis, the economist Antonio Scialoia, the historian Francesco Trinchera and the jurist Pasquale Stanislao Mancini. Years later, in his autobiographical reminiscences *La giovinezza*, De Sanctis painted an extraordinary portrait of the free, liberal and original nature of private education in Naples in that period. His own school, self-governed in the spirit of Proudhon-like anarchy, was a 'small self-contained society, without rules, without discipline, without any authority of command, moved by sentiments of duty, value, and reciprocal respect.'[9] All these institutes actively sought out talented provincial youth and attracted them with fellowships, free admissions and competitive 'incentive awards'. While upper-class provincial youth had always gone to Naples to study, now, in Pasquale Villari's words, 'students were flowing in thousands', and many of them were the offspring of provincial gentry, lawyers and even, occasionally, artisans.[10] In addition to traditional disciplines such as law, medicine, military arts and philosophy, there were new, popular ones such as Italian, political economy, history, engineering and architecture. The students were pervaded by the Romantic spirit, engrossed in all that was fantastic and sentimental, and attentive to all 'rumours' from Lombardy.

The world of fine arts was also thriving. Naples swarmed with artists, art students, visitors and distinguished foreigners. New schools and 'revolutionary' Romantics successfully challenged the domination of the classicist Academy of Fine Arts. The Court actively patronised artists through exhibitions and royal commissions, and in 1825, Francesco I instituted an annual exhibition modelled on the French *salons*. Private patronage followed the royal example, purchasing from art students and offering commissions and fellowships.

Even in the provinces life seemed less monotonous. The *Carbonari,* daring, radical, anti-clerical and anti-Bourbon, were the heroes of the provincial youth. The Romantic mood was overwhelming, and young people in the provinces read Madame de Staël, Walter Scott and Alessandro Manzoni, wrote and published their own intensely

---

[9]   De Sanctis, 1961 [1888], p. 293 (translation MP).

[10]   Villari, 1878; De Sanctis, 1898, p. 336.

Romantic work in a growing number of reviews. Their output not only included poems, ballads, tragedies and novellas, but also history, folklore, popular traditions, *rumanze, impressioni*, archaeology, new philosophy and psychology. There too an important role was played by boarding schools and *collegi*, part of the university system, and by many private schools of law in towns and cities. There was much theatre, with a long opera season and a shorter drama season. Young members of the elite travelled in Italy and Europe and, in the course of these *bildung* tours met exiles, political opposition, foreign and Italian intellectuals and artists.

In Naples and the provinces alike, the salons, known as *case*, held in patrician houses, played a very important role in defining and spreading the reformers' ideas. There, the elites' patronage was at its best. Many, like *casa* De Thomasis, *casa* Poerio and *casa* Ricciardi counted scholars and authors among the family members. Politics were everywhere, but they were always mediated by culture. The *case* were generically liberal, the artists were liberal, but obliged to the regime for its favours, while the students were more radical. The political passion was there, and would manifest itself in 1848 when the schools took to the streets, and the *case* expressed their support for parliaments and governments. For the time being, the youngest were the most impatient, associating themselves with the *Carboneria* and becoming involved in conspiracies. These activities often led to arrests, trials, imprisonment, exile and even, occasionally, executions. Repression, however, was neither continuous nor universal. In 'normal' times there was room to express ideas and opinions. Local press flourished and non-Neapolitan journals and reviews also circulated widely. New legal journals promoted the new juridical culture and literary reviews flourished. Associations, professional organisations and political and literary movements all published some kind of periodical literature. One of the most influential journals, *Il Progresso delle scienze, delle lettere, delle arti*, was founded in 1832 and was edited for some time by Giuseppe Ricciardi, son of Murat's Minister of Justice, a republican, mazzinian, free-thinker, and the would-be president of the splinter republican government formed in Cosenza in 1848. Liberal and pluralistic, his journal favoured a diversity of approaches and accommodated four political generations and political views, ranging from the radical republicanism of Ricciardi himself to the conservative municipalism of Luigi Blanch.

There were also several left-wing journals, expressing republican, radical, democratic and anti-capitalist views.

There was a broad and general interest in things economic. In addition to the Tuscan *Giornale Agrario* and the Milanese *Annali Universali di Statistica*, there circulated widely *Il Gran Sasso d'Italia*, which was founded and directed in Abruzzi by Ignazio Rozzi, agronomist and professor of agriculture and was mostly dedicated to social and economic problems, *Annali della Calabria Citeriore*, founded and directed in Cosenza by Luigi Maria Greco, a lucid conservative social critic, and *Giornale di Statistica*, founded in 1835 in Palermo by two brilliant young liberal economists, Francesco Ferrara and Emerico Amari. Even institutional and establishment-sponsored publications such as the governmental *Giornale del Regno delle Due Sicilie*, were used in a creative way and were often critical of their mother-institutions. The most influential of the institutional publications was the government-funded *Annali civili del Regno delle Due Sicilie*, founded in 1833 by a group of young journalists close to the established reformist circles. The *Annali* counted among its collaborators some of the best and most influential writers, civil servants and administrators of the period, and it co-ordinated the efforts of various economic and cultural associations. Even a part of the clergy became a vehicle for the modernising discourse. Many provincial priests were active members of economic societies, contributors to economic journals, teachers in agrarian academies and schools and active promoters of innovation and agrarian improvement. Some seminaries established schools of practical agronomy for the education of the peasantry.

Probably the most important indication of, and at the same time, breeding ground for, the growing civil society was the new associationism, radically different from the tradition of secret societies and free-masonry. Among the variety of associations, it is worth giving special attention to the economic societies, both because of their diffusion and because they transformed government instruments into autonomous *loci* of critical discourse. Economic societies, instituted by Murat and revamped by Ferdinand I, flourished in the 1830s and 40s. With 14 of them on mainland Italy and a couple in Sicily, they constituted the largest network of their kind in the Italian Peninsula. They gathered and disseminated information and statistics, promoted mechanisation and experimentation and stimulated innovation and rationalisation by means of exhibitions, fairs, competitions and awards. They promoted both vocational and general education by establishing agricultural schools at various levels by setting up model teaching farms and experimental gardens and providing scholarships for poor students. Their networks involved a significant number of people; each society counted approximately 200 members, ordinary, honorary and corresponding, but their plenary *sedute* were attended by the entire local elite, as well as by delegates from other associations and visiting scholars and celebrities. They, in turn, sent delegates to Italian scientific congresses and other trans-peninsular and international meetings. Moreover, in a variety of *comizi*, or meetings in smaller towns, these societies brought together the local middle class – professionals, entrepreneurial farmers and artisans – with landowners, judges, civil servants, and university professors, thus facilitating both a certain interaction among the classes and the dissemination of ideas. The influence of the economic societies was extended by means of their periodical publications, which numbered some twenty journals ranging from annual to bimonthly, and from economic to literary-agrarian, with, in addition, a growing number of more popular forms of literature such as manuals, textbooks, almanacs, calendars, and 'agrarian catechisms'. The target of these publications ranged from barely literate peasants, to small property owners and medium-sized landowners engaged in specialised production.

The Representation of the *Mezzogiorno*

All these different *loci* of growing civil society contributed to the construction of a common discourse. Economic and political debates found their way into all journals, national and local alike. Literary reviews published long articles on political economy and statistics, while economic journals published articles on literature, the spirit of times and the psychology of the senses. All journals eagerly participated in debates on language and dialect and reviewed grammars and dictionaries.

The overall common concern was the global condition of the Kingdom. There is a representation of the state of the country that emerges from these texts that is, at one and the same time, pessimistic and optimistic. Having adopted the imperative of progress and the 'European' criteria for its measurement, the modernisers treated the conditions of 'development' and 'backwardness' not as dichotomous oppositions, but as different relative positions on a material and temporal *continuum*. Accordingly, they viewed the Two Sicilies as a backward country in comparison with those 'ahead' of it, like Great Britain, France, the United States, Lombardy, Tuscany and Prussia, but more or less at the same point as Ireland, and ahead of Russia and Poland. As it stood, the kingdom faced numerous problems, but progress was regarded as possible.

Among the problems, the first and foremost was considered to be the agrarian system. Making use of antiquated crops, methods and instruments, restricted by ill-defined and confused property relations, resistant to innovation, and increasingly wasteful, inefficient and irrational, it was regarded as holding back the whole economy. The conditions of industry and manufacturing were hardly considered better. Enterprises established during the *decade* were struggling to survive, while new ones encountered numerous obstacles. The kingdom shipped out raw materials – something deplored by the modernisers – not only because its erroneous customs policies favored the export of 'primary products', but also because there existed no local processing industries. The state of the transport infrastructure was pitiful since the old Roman and French roads were deteriorating and there were too few canals. The almost total absence of banks and credit institutions, especially outside the city of Naples, discouraged investment and enterprise. The *Banco delle Due Sicilie*, although praised for some innovative policies, devoted most of its activity to financing public works and the *annona*. Last but not least, the country was haunted by the 'social question', by which was meant the issue of the general condition of the peasantry, including poverty, poor health, insecurity of land tenure and contracts and widespread illiteracy.

The modernisers agreed, however, that some progress had been made and that more was likely. First and foremost, feudalism, the former archenemy of progress, had been abolished in 1806. Moreover, the prospects were not poor since the country was endowed with natural resources and a steadily growing population. They also considered that the government was doing the right thing by modernising institutions, loosening tariff regulations and building railways and factories. Most importantly, the country was participating in the *Zeitgeist* of progress, so compelling at that time. The modernisers considered that further remedies were needed and agreed on the importance of two; education and good government. In fact, the education reform engaged the best intellects of the period, from Vincenzo Cuoco to Francesco De Sanctis, while the 'administrative revolution' of the 1830s occupied the best legal scholars such as Pasquale Stanislao Mancini, Matteo De Augustinis and Giuseppe De Thomasis, who advocated local autonomy and communal self-administration. But there were many other problems that begged solutions: What role should the government play in furthering progress? What was the utility and impact of public works? Should land be further privatised and to what degree? How rapid and widespread should industrialisation be? What were the comparative advantages of centralised control versus municipal autonomy? Was total freedom of trade appropriate for a 'latecomer'?

To sum up, the image of the kingdom that emerges from the debates of the modernisers was not too bleak. The 'retardation' was severe and 'catching-up' would require energy and effort, but neither was paralysing. The double image of a country at once backward and modernising appears in the art of the period; along with the traditional rural landscapes with bare-footed peasants in front of their huts, we find modern industrial landscapes such as Silvano Fergola's railways, stations and iron suspension bridges, and Giuseppe De Nittis' and Luigi Fergola's industrial landscapes with factory chimneys.

Reformist activism carried out in the various *loci* of civil society contributed to the forging of cultural cohesion among the *intelligentsia* and encouraged this society to start extending its boundaries. Some ties were established with the *popolo minuto* of the cities and even with the peasantry, as Enrica Di Ciommo has recently argued.[11] By 1848, the Neapolitan *intelligentsia* felt strong enough to demand its share in the government of the country.

1848: The Revolution

In January 1848, revolution started in Sicily, and broke out soon after in Naples. The Sicilian uprising was 'nationalist', with strong separatist demands, while the Neapolitan one was 'urban' like those in Paris, Vienna and Berlin. But although there were differences between these two revolutions, they were both 'modern' and formed part of the European wave. Indeed, they both had more in common with other

---

[11]   Di Ciommo, 1993, pp. 298-299.

contemporary European revolutions than with the previous uprisings of 1799 and 1820. The 'revolution' of 1799 had been a Jacobin and republican attempt to turn French invasion into a liberation. That of 1820 had been dominated by middle-aged men, veterans of '99, soldiers and administrators of the *decennio*, imbued with 18th century rationalistic and classical culture and mobilised through the network of the *Carboneria* and free-masonry. The 1848 revolution was, *vice versa*, a revolution of the youth, pervaded by Romantic culture. The streets of Naples were crowded with the pupils of De Sanctis, Puoti and Scialoia, who manned the barricades, full of ideas learned from Hegel, Chateaubriand, de Staël, Lamartine, Hugo, as well as Colletta, Berchet and Gioberti. Certainly it was a revolution of the intellectuals, with the limits pointed out by Lewis Namier, but it was also a revolution of all, of the nation.[12] Or so it appeared. 'Each honest heart joined the festive banquet', wrote the novelist Francesco Mastriani, and among the revolutionaries numbered intellectuals and students, artisans and peasants and returning exiles.[13] The air of Naples was excited and festive and, the theatres having been shut, the unemployed singers sang popular and revolutionary songs in the streets. 'I always recall that spring of 1848', reminisced Giuseppe Sodano, former monk, writer and historian and, in 1848, the president of the 'Club of Progress', 'Those unforgettable days when we were free. Those who did not see these days, never saw anything truly great and sublime.'[14]

The revolution quickly fulfilled the dreams of the reformers; with a constitution and parliaments the kingdom finally joined the community of civilised nations. New Sicilian and Neapolitan governments and legislatures were made up of spokesmen and representatives of the progressive *intelligentsia* like Carlo Poerio, Luigi Dragonetti, Antonio Scialoia, Francesco Ferrara and the brothers Michele and Emerico Amari. The new central government formed in April and headed by the historian Carlo Troya was composed of the most respected moderate liberal critics of the old regime, active contributors to the nation-making discourse who were endowed with years of public experience. Troya himself was a conservative, but Luigi Dragonetti (Foreign Affairs) and jurist Raffaele Conforti (Internal Affairs) were democrats, while Paolo

---

[12] Namier. 1946.

[13] Mastriani, 1994 [1863], p. 164.

[14] Zenobi, 1959, p. 92

Emilio Imbriani (Public Education) and Antonio Scialoia (Agriculture, Industry and Commerce), were confirmed liberals. Although moderate, the government was sincerely opposed to absolutism and determined to carry out reforms. It granted amnesty for all political offences, abolished the Ministry of Police, took responsibility for popular education away from the bishops, and instituted schools in even the smallest villages.

The mood prevailing in the continental kingdom was conciliatory and moderate (Sicily's story is different since, by April, the island had *de facto* seceded). Neither the new government nor the public were republican or rabidly anti-Bourbon. With the exception of a few committed republicans, the revolutionaries felt that a constitutional monarchy was the best guarantee of the stability that was necessary to promote progress and that the Bourbons and Ferdinand could perform the task. Peasant movements were less frightening than in 1799 and certainly less hostile to the liberals. The elections of 18th April confirmed the nation's commitment to the revolution, gaining the support of liberals and radicals alike.

The events of 15th May, the dynamics of which remain an enigma, did not divide the nation as the June Days did in Paris. In the French capital the great divide was class, with the workers on one side and the National Guard, bourgeoisie, students and *provinceaux* on the other. On 15th May in Naples, the National Guard, the bourgeoisie, the students, the artisans and the peasants were all on the same side, and the 'nation' defended the revolution in the streets and on the barricades. In a sort of reverse evocation of 1799, the provinces rushed to the defence of the government, with the Calabrians conspicuous in their costumes on the streets of Naples. On the other side, the treacherous king stood alone.

Following this confrontation, the conciliatory mood was over. Exasperated by calls for armed insurrection and for the abolition of the monarchy, Ferdinand dissolved the parliament, called new elections with limited suffrage, and arrested and expelled the radicals and the democrats. As in France, parts of the rural districts defended the revolution; in Calabria the resistance, led by radical members of parliament who had fled Naples, lasted into the autumn. The elections were held in November and, despite the restricted suffrage, once again returned many revolutionaries, confirming the nation's commitment to the revolution. There then followed the *spergiuro*; in March 1849, Ferdinand dissolved the parliament and abrogated the constitution.

If the revolution was indeed an examination of maturity for the *quasi nazione*, the result seemed positive. It is impossible to say, given the present state of research, how vast was the actual patriotic consensus and how genuine was the popular participation in 1848. However, many of the revolutionary leaders, including moderates, felt that the revolution was indeed fought by the enlarged nation – the *intelligentsia* joined by the youth, the bourgeoisie, a part of the aristocracy, and an element of the *basso popolo*. It was the strength of this revolutionary alliance, the awareness, as De Sanctis wrote, that the 'cry of the few had an accomplice in the sentiment of an entire *popolo* ready to rise', that forced Ferdinand to offer concessions.[15] The feasibility of such an alliance was regarded as proof that, during the fifty years since 1799, the *Mezzogiorno* had partaken fully in the European process of political and civil growth, with the liberal groups shedding their dependency on French ideas and evolving from secret societies into modern forms of associationism, and the *plebe*, no more ignorant or superstitious than other peoples of Europe, growing and maturing into a *popolo*. 'Those Calabrians', wrote de Sanctis, 'who then [1799] shouted death to the liberals, in '48 raised the first cry of freedom in Europe.'[16]

Defeat and Repression

When considered in a wider European context, the defeat of the Neapolitan revolution does not come as a surprise. Like the revolutions, the counter-revolutions were part of a general European wave, and just as at the beginning of 1848 no government could resist, by late 1849, no uprising could. However, unlike rulers of other countries (like France, Piedmont, Prussia or even Austria) who had experienced revolution but had nonetheless maintained some of the novelties introduced in 1848, the king of Two Sicilies reacted with vicious repression and the abandonment of all modernisation projects.

The repression was both heavy and vindictive. A bloody terror swept through the rebellious provinces, especially Calabria, and there

---

[15] De Sanctis, 1898 [1855] (translation MP).

[16] *Ibid.* p. 190. (translation MP).

were obsessive mass arrests, intimidation, assassinations, endless trials and heavy prison sentences. Summed up, this repression turned out to be less bloody and less spectacular than in 1799 since, for example, death sentences were rarely followed by executions, but it lasted much longer and was much more pervasive and widespread. While show trials were going on in Naples, thousands were arrested and tried throughout the country. Ferdinand resurrected the Ministry of Police and instituted a police state, to punish and control. 'Loyal subjects' were encouraged to inform on their friends and colleagues and spies infested the provinces in search of revolutionary groups. Endless checks were run on the political, religious and moral conduct of candidates for government-related jobs. Office bearers in all forms of associations were required to swear under oath that they did not, had not and would never belong to any secret society. Mere police reports, unsupported by legal referral, were sufficient to list some 300,000 people as *attendibili* and ban them from all civil service posts and many other jobs, including that of lawyer, university professor and even the director of the excavations at Pompeii. This number represented almost half of all the literate population of the kingdom!

But it was not only people that Ferdinand II wanted to control, but also ideas and goods, indeed anything that recalled the liberal efforts. Strict censorship was introduced, both by civil and ecclesiastical authorities, prohibitive custom duty was imposed on imported books and protective barriers on imports and exports were raised far beyond any real or supposed economic requirement. The king made a political choice of seclusion; as one writer put it, he erected his own 'Chinese Wall' around his kingdom.[17]

The results of Ferdinand's efforts were predictable. Even the most cautious reforms were abandoned, and he treated even his own ministers' recommendations for reforms as subversive. Public works were all but dropped, public health deteriorated, education reverted to the Church, which was also to provide whatever social services it deemed necessary. Many public projects, such as statistical record keeping, were abandoned because the administration was short of personnel due to the number of *attendibili* excluded from these posts. Nearly half of the state expenditure in 1854 was devoted to the army. Entrepreneurial energies were stifled, trade diminished and the

---

[17]   The reference to the 'Chinese Wall' was first used by Giuseppe La Farina. Cf. Mastriani,1994 [1863], pp. 11-12.

economy grew stagnant. Foreign investors shunned this police state, whose reputation had reached its lowest point. As always, some social groups were better off, principally the police, the army, the higher echelons of the Church and, to some degree, the peasantry, but the general impact of these measures was profoundly damaging to civil society.

Among the victims of repression, it was the *intelligentsia* who occupied the place of honour. The *crème de la crème*, from radicals to moderate liberals, from republicans to monarchists, from members of secret societies to members of government and parliaments, found themselves in prison. Huge show trials were held in Naples, and among the accused stood the members of *Unità italiana*, the '44' with Scialoia and Spaventa and the '40 defaulters' as well as the followers of Carlo Poerio. Hundreds more trials, spectacular on a smaller scale, were held in the provinces. Penalties were exemplary; death (maintained for the absent and usually commuted to perpetuity for the detained), irons or life imprisonment. The horror of these prisons would become proverbial when, in 1851, the whole of Europe read about them in William Gladstone's *Two Letters to the Earl of Aberdeen*.[18] In addition, the property of the prisoners was confiscated, making the lives of their families miserable and assistance to the prisoners virtually impossible.

The repression resulted in the largest number of exiles in the country's history, and their number grew still more when some life sentences were commuted to deportation. By the mid-1850s, a significant proportion of the *quasi nation* found itself outside the borders of the country. Once abroad, some joined struggles for freedom elsewhere, while others settled into the life of an exile in Piedmont, Tuscany, France, Switzerland or Great Britain, plotting, waiting and hoping for the moment of return. Those members of the *intelligentsia* who were not imprisoned or exiled went into, to use an anachronism, 'internal exile'. Often, they had little choice, for listed as *attendibili*, they were forcibly removed from public life. In other cases they wanted to escape the subservience that public life required, and even a conservative like Luigi Maria Greco preferred withdrawal into the *Accademia Cosentina* to a 'police job'. Civil society shrank rapidly; most of the journals that had flourished in the previous

---

[18]   Gladstone, 1851.

decades folded or were closed by the censor, and the meetings of learned societies became abstract and boring. With the exception of a few prominent intellectuals who collaborated with the crown, a few 'loyal' scholars who denounced the 'errors and fallacies of Mr. Gladstone', and some rabid reactionaries who rejoiced at the return of the Christian order, the 'nation' stood silent or kept to neutral subjects.

The Birth of the *Mezzogiorno*

As often happens, in the first moments the repression actually seemed to help consolidate the identity of the national revolutionary alliance. With the repression, the regime revealed its 'true', brutal face, creating an unbridgeable gap between 'us' and 'them', between the 'nation' and the 'Bourbon'. The repression cut across class barriers and, in jails, brought together intellectuals and artisans, noblemen and peasants, with '*popolani* and bourgeoisie locked to the same chain' as De Sanctis wrote.[19] The intellectuals were thrilled by instances of popular resistance, and the *popolani* were proud of being political prisoners. The show trials popularised the ideas under indictment and won them the support and admiration of European opinion. Even the horrors of the prisons were worth bearing when William Gladstone, after a visit to Carlo Poerio and Michele Pironti, turned them into a powerful indictment of the Bourbon regime, 'the negation of God elevated to the method of government.'

In his 1851 introduction to the Italian translation of Gladstone's *Letters,* Giuseppe Massari spoke of the 'great battle of civilisation against *barbarie*, of reason against ignorance, of virtue against vice, of innocence against calumny.'[20] It must be noted that the terms '*barbarie*', 'ignorance', 'vice' and 'calumny' apply here exclusively to the Bourbon government, the 'great battle' is one against tyranny. The country, on the other hand, differs from its government in that it represents civilisation, reason, virtue and innocence. Full of human and natural resources, it is inhabited by a *popolo* which is strong and generous. The *intelligentsia*, revolutionaries and moderates alike were convinced that the gap between the country and the government was

---

[19] F. De Sanctis, 1898 [1855], p. 194.

[20] Giuseppe Massari, 'Il Signore Gladstone ed il governo napoletano. Raccolta di scritti intorno alla questione napoletana.' Introduction to Gladstone, 1851, p. 11.

actually an abyss from which deliverance was bound to come. In 1849, Ricciardi re-launched his credo in an *iniziativa meridionale*, a Southern initiative, by which a powerful popular insurrection would deliver from tyranny not only the country, but the whole of Italy.

In the longer term, however, the effects of repression and disappointment became deeply destructive. It was the third time in half a century that the South had lost a significant proportion of its *intelligentsia*, and this time the 'blood-letting' was particularly massive and long-lasting. With the passage of time, internal discord grew, not only among the exiles, but also between them and the 'internal exiles', as well as among the prisoners. Increasingly bitter and impotent, the *intelligentsia* was waiting for something to happen, for the Southern initiative to manifest itself, for the *popolo* to rise and bring about the collapse of the 'rotten body of tyranny that keeps it prisoner'. But the *popolo* showed no sign of rising, nor was the regime about to collapse. For years, prisoners and exiles placed their hopes in every conspiracy, every assassination attempt, every insubordination that might unleash a general uprising, and each time they were disappointed. The cholera epidemics in 1854 were not followed by popular unrest, as had happened in 1837. The king, following his policy of seclusion, refused to become involved in the Crimean War. The 1856 plans for a military expedition under the command of Luciano Murat to land on the Neapolitan coast fell through. The 1857 *programma d'azione* that Luigi Settembrini and Silvio Spaventa addressed from prison to the *partiti meridionali*, the parties of the South, met with no reaction. Lastly, and this was the final blow, came the 1857 tragedy of Sapri in the province of Salerno, where an expedition of 300 young revolutionaries under the leadership of Carlo Pisacane was massacred by peasants. Anger and despair were growing. In a letter of 1852 from prison, Settembrini screamed out his anger against 'this *popolo*, or rather this *volgo* filled with ricotta' and his despair that nothing could ever deliver this '*terra sventurata*', this misfortunate land.[21] In this significant inversion, the *popolo* once again became *volgo*, while the land became *sventurata*.

Why did the *popolo* not rise? This question, repeated over and over, could have been an occasion to reflect on the strengths as well as the weaknesses and shortcomings of the 1848 revolution, and to

---

[21]   Settembrini, 1962, p. 81.

evaluate the reality of the liberal revolutionary alliance, the internal cohesion of the *quasi nation* and its ties with the *popolo*. The opportunity was largely wasted, however, because disappointment and resentment dominated the debates, often turning analysis into blame and reciprocal recrimination. Already, in this early phase of the debate some *topoi* of the future representation of the *Mezzogiorno* began to appear. 'Our country is a deeply infirm body that has no vital force left to make a recovery by itself', writes Scialoia from prison in 1850. His '18 months of experience' of revolution and government had convinced him that 'abject vices and deep corruption, for centuries the affliction of our society [...] have totally destroyed in it logic, morality and common sense.' Faithful to its sad, inveterate tradition, the government encouraged these evils, considering them indispensable conditions for its own existence. 'Thus,' he concludes, 'at least for this generation, I have no hope whatever of better fortune.'[22]

By the mid-1850s this form of discourse had become prevalent. Its most blunt formulation came from the pen of Francesco Trinchera – historian, protagonist of '48 and exile – in his 1855 pamphlet entitled *La quistione napoletana*.[23] The occasion was significant; part of the *intelligentsia*, mostly exiles, had announced their support for Luciano Murat, one of the former king's sons, to take the throne of Naples. The idea was not in itself new, but the support from former republicans and radicals was. It implied a positive assessment of Joachin Murat's government of reforms, order and modernity. More importantly, it meant favouring an immediate authoritarian solution over the hope for the country's autonomous action, a preference that sounded ominous in the context of growing Bonapartism. Francesco Trinchera, a committed murattist, posed the question quite bluntly: did the Neapolitan liberals have enough strength to deliver themselves from the yoke of this 'most vicious of governments'? His answer was unambiguously negative: they did not have sufficient strength, and for that reason they needed a 'strong hand' from outside. But Trinchera goes much further in his indictment, thus penning the blueprint for the language of the Southern Question. Not only did the Neapolitan *intelligentsia* lack the strength to undertake an action now, they had never had this potential. He regarded the paralysis of Neapolitan

---

22 Alatri, 1956, pp. 149, 156, 161 (translation MP).

23 *La Quistione Napoletana* appeared anonymously, but the authorship was immediately attributed to Francesco Trinchera. Trinchera di Ostumi, 1855.

society not only as the outcome of the symbiosis between the barbaric dynasty and the degenerated plebs, but *also* as the result of the vagueness and abstraction of the dreamy *intelligentsia*. Taken together he considered these factors to be responsible for the dreadful state of the country.

Trinchera's language is significative. The government, 'brutal' and 'savage', 'tortures', 'poisons' and 'corrupts' the entire nation. It made the country into a 'desert' in both civil and institutional terms, such that there was no sign of 'civilised life, no useful institution, [...] no public or private education, no roads, [...] no commerce, no industry, [...]'. This desert is inhabited by a 'degenerate' *popolo*, immersed in superstition (they believed in *'jettatura*, in *fascino*, in magic, wizards, witches and witchcraft, in dreams, and in the miracle of the blood of San Gennaro'). This was a cruel and violent people, who 'delight in murder and robbery, who know no law or God, and who have long lost any notion of good and evil.' Along with this people, there lived an *intelligentsia* that was intellectually naive, having had its thought 'blocked' by years of 'religious and political tyranny'. The members of this *intelligentsia* were 'removed from the real world', dreaming of a government that, rooted in virtue, could never be formed 'in the midst of a horde of savages.' They were great individuals, the best men in the country, educated, moral and heroic, but they were impotent against this 'despotism, immobile and inflexible as the fate of the ancients, that reposes upon a large inert mass.' There had never existed any alliance between the *intelligentsia* and the *popolo*, as the latter was too degenerate to even understand freedom, let alone 'desire it, and die for it and with it.'[24] The unbridgeable gap is indeed there, but it is the one that lies between the dreamy and impotent *intelligentsia* on the one side and despotism and the masses locked in a deadly embrace on the other.

Thus, by 1855, both the lexicon and all the main *topoi* of the *Mezzogiorno* were in place: the infirmity of the country that has lost its *elan vitale*; the centuries-old nature of its condition; the degeneration and deep moral corruption of the *popolo*; its sinister symbiosis with the regime; the unbridgeable gap between the *popolo* and the *intelligentsia*; and, as a consequence, the impossibility of an autonomous recovery of the South. Years before the Southern

---

[24]   *Ibid.,* pp. 26-30 (translation MP).

Question was officially called into existence as a national problem, the *Mezzogiorno* already stood for failure.

A Postscript to the *Nazione Mancata*

We still need to ponder briefly the question of how this reversal in the opinion of the Southern *intelligentsia* came about. Why did they, after so many decades engaged in reforming and modernising their country and in building the enlarged national alliance, end up constructing the very *Mezzogiorno* that they had been the first to mistrust, reject and despise? After all, the experience of disillusionment and despair after the failures of 1848 and 1849 was shared by all European revolutionaries and reformers, and all regarded the components of the drama as discredited, be it the rulers who broke their promises, the proletariat that proved cowardly, inefficient and ill-organised, the bourgeoisie that showed itself enamoured mainly with its privileges and its wealth, or the intellectuals who turned out to be divisive, alienated and impotently 'chatty'. What then was so particular about the disappointments of the southern *intelligentsia* that provoked such a generalised, long lasting and exceptionally bitter reaction?

The answer, I think, is twofold: the particularly tenacious character of the last Bourbon regime, combined with the double nature of the *intelligentsia*'s defeat. By the mid- and late 1850s, a gradual reconciliation was beginning to take place in Europe. The France of Napoleon III, the Austria of Franz Joseph and the Piedmont of Vittorio Emmanuel II were hardly the regimes liberals and democrats had dreamt of, but nonetheless, the revolutions had left some positive traces everywhere, some seeds of modernity that were likely to germinate – a suffrage, a statute or a constitution, some national or civil rights, some social legislation. Even in Russia, where there had been no revolutionary uprising in 1848 and where the most oppressive autocrat had ruled for 30 years, the ascent of Alexander II in 1855 bore the promise of reform. The Kingdom of Two Sicilies stood alone among large countries in its blind commitment to repression and self-seclusion.

As for the *intelligentsia*, it was forced to question its own past efforts at making itself into a modern nation and forging a modern national alliance with the *popolo*. We have to return briefly to

Eleonora Fonseca Pimentel's idea of a *quasi nazione*, a nation in the making in the late 18th century. As Eric Hobsbawm argued, there is no inevitability in the number of nations that emerge, especially during the most intense period of modern nation-making from the late 18th to the mid-19th century.[25] In fact, there was nothing *sui generis* about the emerging Neapolitan *quasi nation*. As Benedict Anderson brilliantly demonstrated, in the early stages of the construction of the national community, two identities can coexist in a national elite; an old one, composed of language, culture and religion, and a new, modern one, made up essentially of citizenship, and engaged in inventing new traditions to share.[26] In fact, the pre-1848 southern *intelligentsia* remained strongly Italian in cultural terms, even while they were busy building a new, enlarged Neapolitan nation. The prerequisites for nation-making were there: a modern sovereign state endowed with a rational bureaucratic structure; clearly established and uncontested borders; a stable *national* dynasty; and a political monarchical order accepted in principle (though in need of serious reform). The choice of myth-making material was available as well: the *Brutii* and the *Enotri*; the Magna Greece; Frederick II's modern state; and the Sicilian *Vespri*. Neapolitan cultural identity, though not linguistic, had its sources in the landscape, the *genius loci* popularised by the Romantics, and in the quintessentially *rational* character of the culture. Finally, there were founding fathers; first and foremost, the 'national' historian and philosopher Giambattista Vico, followed by other 18th century intellectual giants such as Pietro Giannone and Antonio Genovesi, and by the luminaries of the Enlightenment. And there were the martyrs of '99.

Now all this was gone. The Bourbons turned into pure barbarians and could never again be expected to reform, to work with the *intelligentsia*, or to lead the Italian peninsula towards a confederation. The culture of the country turned obscurantist and superstitious. The *intelligentsia* either disappeared or became subservient to the power. And the *popolo* reverted to the condition of *plebe* and *volgo*. The nation-making effort failed entirely, the *Mezzogiorno* was a *nazione mancata*, and there was nothing to be done.

---

[25] Hobsbawm, 1990.

[26] Anderson, 1991.

Challenging Israel's Foundation Myths: The Constitution of a Constructive Mythology?

Ilan PAPPE

Introduction

I would like to begin by demonstrating the difficulties that face historians who wish to promote and implement a deconstructive/ reconstructive approach to Israel's foundation myths. Generally speaking, the introduction of a new sceptical and critical approach to foundation myths or, more precisely, the *idea* of this new approach, was welcomed in the Israeli academic world. That was until it was suggested that this approach could be employed as a tool to analyse Israel's own historiography, for this meant analysing it as mythology, and worse, analysing its historians as either myth constructors or myth perpetuators. This idea of historians becoming the object of their own study was rejected with particular vehemence: more than merely unprofessional, it was considered as tantamount to an act of treason.[1]

I encountered a different set of problems when I developed an educational approach for the study and teaching of the history of the

---

[1] This sort of language was used in several conferences, and appears in articles collected after one of these conferences. See for instance Ahronson, 1997. By 'Sociological Context', Ahronson means the genealogical tree to which the 'new historians' belong; a succession of self-hating Jews.

conflict in Palestine at high school and university undergraduate level. This programme, which I described as 'the way to a bridging narrative', was based on the assumption that common consent on past events provides a far more useful, functional and moral position than a segregated, nationalist quest to find out 'what had really happened' in the past. Common consent is achieved by assigning equal status to the two conflicting national narratives (or the two mythologies represented in academic discourse). This parity is not the outcome of scientific research, rather it is achieved by giving equal respect and legitimacy to both narratives, by granting the two narratives equal legitimacy.

Here lies another difficulty involved in introducing a relativist or even a post-modernist approach to the history of the Palestinian conflict. In the case of Israel, one is immediately faced with the requirement to prove that this approach also has validity in the case of the Holocaust. There is probably no need to elaborate on the problems associated with attributing legitimacy to the narrative of the Other in this terrible chapter of Europe's history.[2]

The belief in the particularity of Israel's history leaves little room for manoeuvre; on the one hand, there is the treatment of Israel's historiography of its national myths as *sui generis*, immune from deconstruction, and, on the other, there is the shadow cast on a deconstructive approach to historiography by the *sui generis* of the Holocaust. Given this, I suggest, as a kind of a methodological and epistemological introduction to this chapter, two qualifications to the multi-narrative approach.

The first of these qualifications is that, in the era of nationalism, historians dealing with the past of their own nation face a difficult task in liberating themselves from their own foundation myths. This is particularly true for historians working in the context of a national conflict where history serves as a tool for consolidating one's own collective memory while destroying that of the Other. In cases such as these, the line between mythology and historiography becomes completely blurred. Amongst those who preserve the foundation myths one not only finds politicians and educators, but also, of course, academics. The professional qualifications of these academics determine the form in which the mythology is represented, as well as

---

[2]   White, 1995.

the means employed to sustain it. In historical contexts such as this, mainstream historiography rejects *a priori* a critical approach to mythology. At the same time, however, it tends to employ a 'discourse of proof' in order to create the impression that the validity of the foundation myths has been proved by 'scientific', that is, 'objective' historical research.[3]

Societies caught in national conflicts can be defined as 'tense' societies, while those in non-conflictual situations can be termed 'relaxed'. Historians in 'tense' societies have a tendency to hide behind the banner of positivism and empiricism much more than their colleagues in 'relaxed' societies. They claim to work in the service of science, while, more than any other group of historians, they are, in fact, working in the service of the nation. But they have chosen an impossible, or even, as Hans George Gadamer puts it, futile, mission.[4] Academics dealing with the experience of their own societies are unable to divorce themselves from their national interpretation of the present and the future. In 'tense' societies, material in mainstream historiography is almost always arranged in a pattern that not only corresponds to the master narrative of the nation, but also echoes its discourse and reflects its mythological literary genre. In the case of the Palestinian conflict, this is exemplified by the use of a discourse of redemption on the part of the Israelis and a discourse of catastrophe on the part of the Palestinians. These two national historiographies are loaded with these society's images of the self and the outside, with all their distortions and prejudices.

The outcome of academic research in 'tense' societies (and this is also the case for their political propaganda and educational curricula) is the vigorous propagation of shared conventions of discourse and even, surprisingly, of conventional devices of story telling (the narrative) that are imposed on the past. In short, subjective history, which demonstrates the multiplicity of possible and legitimate historical narratives, has never been a more fitting description than in the case of historians reconstructing their own past within the context of an on-going conflict. The irony is, of course, that it is often in these situations of on-going conflict that claims to scientific objectivity and 'truth' are voiced with greatest determination and frequency. The

---

[3] For 'discourse of proof' see Thompson, 1981, p. 407.

[4] Gadamar, 1975.

deconstructive effort in such cases is directed towards finding a bridging narrative. In other words, historians aspire to *agree* on what happened in the past, rather than seeing themselves as belonging to a community of 'truth seekers' who can *know* what had happened in the past.

The second qualification to our multi-narrative approach must therefore be that, while the principal question of the validity of a multi-narrative approach to history remains open, it is easier in the context of 'tense' societies to assert that the acceptance of the 'legitimate' co-existence of several narratives is unavoidable. Moreover, these narratives are determined by the 'tense' present, which prevents professional historians from escaping from their collective memories or personal ideologies. Historians can thus act in one of two ways: either as preservers of mythologies that have the effect of concretising divisions in their society's relations with internal and external Others, or as conciliators, producing evidence that promotes non-violent and even peaceful co-existence with these Others. From this perspective, historians are asked to question the functionality of historiography rather than its validity.

The Particularities of the Case Study

In the 1980s, a group of Israeli revisionist historians produced a new historiographical picture of the birth of the state. They made three claims. First, they asserted that their scholarly research had pushed them closer to the Palestinian national narrative. Secondly, they claimed that the foundation myths in Israel have played a negative role in contemporary Israeli society and should therefore be replaced. The positivists among these revisionist historians argued that these myths were obsolete, since they told a false story, while the more relativist historians declared the myths redundant since they served a negative function, that is, they supported an exclusive society that now needed to open up and become inclusive. They recommended a search for myths of coexistence, or rather, myths of inclusion, that would replace the segregative or exclusionary ones. Both groups of historians, positivists and relativists alike, noted that in any case these foundation myths were socially and culturally eroded.

The revisionists' third claim was that, contrary to Israel's self-image and, to a degree, also contrary to its external image, Israeli professional historians writing on their country's past were totally committed to Zionist ideology. Their positivist methodology and their concern for minutia, which often resulted in uninspiring microhistories, made it more difficult to uncover the hidden hand of ideology. But in the 1970s, the doyens of the profession, like high priests, were allowed to summarise these technohistorical works into macrohistorical analyses. This made it easier to discern the 'academic' scaffolding in the construction of the mythology and to identify the master narrative in its historiographical form.

The challenge to the foundation myths, in both its popular and academic forms, focused on the year 1948. This was a miraculous year in the Israeli collective memory, but a catastrophic one in the Palestinian collective memory. In the mythologies of both these societies, this was a formative year in the construction of their collective patterns of behaviour, and even in the formulation of their moral codes. It is this, together with the declassification of the archival material for 1948 and the emergence of a more radical orientation among Israeli scholars, that has led to what is called 'the new history of 1948', and the emergence of the 'new historians'.[5]

The 'new historians' undermined some of Israel's key foundation myths. There was the myth of 'the few against the many', of the Israeli David defeating an Arab Goliath, that bred a collective and elitist perception of invincibility. This was connected with another myth, the myth of 'Israel on the eve of annihilation' during the 1948 war. The image of the Jewish community in Palestine finding itself in conditions similar to those existing in Europe on the eve of the Holocaust has been incorporated in Israeli propaganda ever since. It was the main content of the external image Israel had been trying to construct, and it has worked most effectively in the United States.[6] The third myth was the most sensitive, since it touched upon the realm of principles and morality. This was the myth of the 'voluntary flight of the Palestinians from Palestine'. The undermining of the credibility of this myth by the 'new historians' not only brought them closer to the Palestinian version of events, but it placed the blame for the Palestinian refugee problem squarely on Israel. In a more implicit manner, it revealed the possibility of a national mythology covering up Israeli war crimes, namely the 'ethnic cleansing' of Palestine in

---

[5]   Pappe, 1995.
[6]   Pappe, 1998, pp. 14-16.

1948.[7] The last myth which was undermined by the 'new historians' was that of 'Israel the peace-loving nation', and its complimentary negative image or myth of 'Arab intransigence'.

How, if at all, have these myths been demolished? The answer depends upon the scholarly paradigm. Within a positivist context, it was a matter of exposing the previous generation of historians as a community of deceivers, and proposing instead a 'true' version of what had happened in 1948. From a more relativist perspective, the demolition of these myths was an ideological struggle, not a matter of true or false history. But even this approach is only relativist to a point. The removal of the Palestinian presence as a result of the establishment of the state of Israel is not a debatable fact in this historiographical discussion, and even the number of people massacred, deported and so on is not a source of serious divide. Nobody questions that these events took place, rather, it is the explanation of these deeds and their moral evaluation that is at the centre of the debate.

The crux of this debate is about language and the way it is used to describe the deed. The options are either a neutral language – the one that has been used up until now by Israeli historians – or a charged one, which is used by the 'new historians'. An example of the former would be a description such as 'the transformation of the human geography in the war of 1948'[8], while the 'new historians' might talk about the 'Zionist ethnic cleansing of Palestine in 1948'. However, the court historians do not always use a neutral language in order to disguise unpleasant chapters in Israel's history. Sometimes a very poetic discourse is employed in the service of the national cause, and this in turn is challenged by a very prosaic approach. This point can probably be better understood if we examine some of the topics that are now at the centre of the historiographical debate in Israel. These relate to the essence of Zionism, Zionism and the Holocaust, and the early years of the state (the 1950s). When court historians in Israel want to circumvent the colonial nature of the Zionist project, they talk about the 'redemption of the land of Israel', while revisionist historians call this 'the takeover of Palestinian land' (Palestinian historians call it 'the violation of the land'). To give another example, Zionist historians use the term *Aliyya* – ascent – when describing the Jewish

---

[7] A chapter covered in Morris, 1988.

[8] Artzi, 1992.

immigration to Palestine from 1882 onwards. Revisionist historians prefer the terms 'invasion' and 'colonisation' as adjectives to describe the Zionist project in Palestine.

In some cases it is necessary, therefore, to deconstruct the euphemistic discourse which has become a shield for national mythologies. Thus, while mainstream historians describe the 'purely defensive' means by which the Jewish community consolidated its control over Palestine, in the vocabulary of the revisionist historians these same methods are described as 'uprooting' and 'expulsion'. In general, 'pure' and 'defensive' are adjectives that are attached to the most violent actions committed by 'our' side against the 'enemy'. The same actions, when committed by the enemy, are described as 'brutal', 'callous' and 'inhuman'.

The 'new history' elicited two kinds of response from the historiographical establishment in Israel. The first was to depict the revisionists as mythologisers themselves, with an explicit suggestion that their professionalism was suspect. A later response was to absorb minor corrections into the master narrative on the basis of the new works, without undermining the narrative's major parameters. As we can see, positivism and ideology were therefore intermittently employed in the defence of the foundation myths. Foundation myths are also under attack among Palestinians historians, but with less force.[9] The contemporary agenda is far more important then the interpretation of the past, and hence the deconstruction of exclusionary myths, and the reconstruction of new, inclusive ones, is conducted by an alliance of intellectuals and more powerful agents of societal change.

In the case of both societies, these alliances are still a minority voice, but their position is attractive and therefore they have the potential to cxpand. In order to be more successful, they need to maintain their multi-narrative approach, not only for the sake of legitimising the Other's otherness and narrative, but also in order to include the various groups that constitute the fabric of each society. This is most evident in the case of Israel, where new historians who deal with the chronology of disadvantaged groups such as women,

---

[9]   In two different articles, two leading Palestinian intellectuals have dealt most successfully with the denial of the Holocaust among Palestinians. See Bishara, 1995 and Said, 1997.

Palestinians, Orthodox Jews and Oriental Jews, have been able to provide a historical explanation for the contemporary fragmentation of Israel. They have also been able to make a case for the diversification of the nation's master narrative, a narrative that has accorded a marginal role to women and Orthodox and Oriental Jews, and has totally erased the Israeli Arabs as legitimate partners in the state of Israel.

Such an act of diversification, from a radical, or even humanist historiographical perspective, aims at substituting insularity with openness, ethnocentricity with multiculturalism and so on. In short, it cares for the individual and his or her rights. But does such a process always end there? Does deconstruction always breed diversification? As the case of Israel shows, the end result was not the denationa-lisation of the past or of society, but rather the emergence of collective memories corresponding to autonomous and particular forms of localism and ethnocentricity that replaced the master narrative and broke its control over the memories of these groups. The main lesson so far from this intellectual exercise is that challenging a dominant national master narrative does not create an alternative master narrative, but instead atomises and fragments the master-story. Most of the group stories that are produced in this process still, in essence, justify violence, ethnocentricity, insularity and other tendencies that work against coexistence.

This conclusion may have a bearing on a more general discussion about 'European identity'. If the formation of a European community, or the construction of a supra-national identity are meant to be alternatives to ethnic and national identities, then there is a risk that, once liberated from their state or nation-state frameworks, these identities will become still more fragmented. And yet this seems to be the right way. Even in the case of Israel, the polarisation and fragmentation caused by the act of deconstruction seems preferable to the dictatorship and hegemony of the master narrative. This new development has promoted a historical reconstruction inspired by a universal, humanist agenda and has provided a counter-position to insular ethnocentricity. It is a challenge that leads to a *Kulturkampf*, and it is at the heart of the struggle necessary to build, with the help of historiography, a mythology of inclusion and coexistence.

CHAPTER 16B

Two Cheers for the New Historians: A Critique of Israel's Post-Nationalists

Ron ROBIN

Israel's new historians, a cohort of critical intellectuals bent on deconstructing the foundation myths of the nation-state, are prominent members of the Israeli historical guild. Disaffection with the nation-state and its myths, a concern for multiculturalism, and a rejection of positivism are now central components of the historical discourse throughout most of the western world. Their self-portraits suggest, however, that they are unaware of their mainstream status. Their rise to positions of prominence within academia and the public arena is invariably presented in very romantic terms. The recurring autobiographical sketches of the new historians describe a group of maverick intellectuals who, against all odds and at deep personal cost, have forced an unwilling establishment to confront the speciousness of its 'myths', its duplicitous values and its pseudo-scientific frameworks. The new historians, according to the common narrative, are truth seekers in a world of mobilised intellectuals.

This romantic portrayal is quite problematic. To begin with, immaculate conceptions are not common occurrences in academia. The thriving presence of new historians in our midst suggests that they are flesh and blood of the establishment itself. We are all aware of the numerous tools available for removing unwanted opinions from the precincts of science. The politics of journals, the selective mechanism of tenure and the fashioning of research profiles are common tools for governing the practices of normal science. There is, of course, no doubt that challenging the foundation myths of a society still suffering from perceptions of existential dangers required courage and the willingness to confront adversity, yet the very fact that the new historians have not been banished to some academic purgatory or worse, suggests that the paradigms of the new historians are not as antithetical as its advocates suggest. We should not forget that the academic estate, the target of their criticism, is their primary sponsor.

The depiction of new historians as being at the cutting edge of new methodology is, moreover, in need of qualification. Under this very broad nomenclature we find a collection of odd bedfellows, ranging from the deconstructivist work of Ilan Pappe to the painstaking archival studies of Benny Morris.[1] Thus, positing the new historians as a counterforce to the positivist work of mainstream historians is only partially correct. The common denominator linking the various new historians is not methodology but politics. As Pappe disarmingly admits, the new historians are not bearers of a some new scientific discovery, they are bearers of alternative myths. Their main task has been to uncover the speciousness of the scientific claims of the Zionist state's so-called 'court historians'. Instead of presenting an alternative truth, Pappe explains, the new historians plead relativism. The truth is not theirs to find. Instead they prefer the 'multi-narrative' approach. Legitimising the voice of the Other of course has important methodological ramifications. It is, however, first and foremost a political gesture.

In this brief glance at the new historians, I intend to suggest an alternative explanation for the current resonance of new history in Israel.

Rethinking Zionism

The major target of the new historians is the Zionist movement, which they describe as part of the great European imperial enterprise. The Jewish settler society appears as a colonial venture, not unlike those of European countries in the Americas. Zionists in Palestine are fundamentally portrayed as Orientalists, afflicted by condescending myths and pernicious attitudes with respect to the indigent inhabitants of the region. This model for understanding the Zionist enterprise is, however, somewhat shaky. To begin with, one might argue that the

---

[1] See, for example, Morris, 1988.

new historians are in fact Occidentalists, unwilling to entertain the nuances and the sometimes major differences between various forms of expansion and movement, both in Palestine and elsewhere. All shapes and forms of expansionism are given the common label of colonialism.

Gadi Taub, one of the major critics of the new historians, draws our attention to the fact that Jews in Palestine do not fit the typical model of the colonialist. Moreover, the portrayal of Zionism as a hegemonic and unchanging movement afflicted by Orientalism is in itself a form of Occidentalism. In actual fact, there is little consensus over the meaning of Zionism. Under the rubric of Zionism lies a diversity of competing paradigms, ranging from cosmopolitan visions of socialism to an exclusive conquest of the land.

From a purely intellectual perspective, the new historian's form of inquiry presents certain problems. The idea that all narratives are equally applicable undermines much of the academic enterprise. If history is merely narrative, we cannot expect to discover the scientifically verifiable version of the past. The most that the professional historian can hope is to forge a broad consensus on past events by legitimising all competing and conflicting narratives. There is no truthful version, only the superficial plausibility of the dominant paradigm.

The Demise of the Nation-State, Great Men and Great Ideas

In the final analysis, the growing prominence of the new historians is tied to a general disaffection with the nation-state. A cursory glance at Israeli politics and society suggests that significant elements of this society find little of value in the classical model of the nation-state. As far as the country's minority groups are concerned, such disaffection needs little elaboration. Pan-Arabism, Islamic fundamentalism and other transnational movements have eclipsed the well-worn formula of 'two nations, two states'. However, Israel's ostensible Jewish majority has also discarded the nation-state. The rising number of non-Zionist, mostly ultra-religious, members of parliament is the most evident indicator of this general disaffection with the nation-state. Moreover, the sheer number of political parties represented in parliament – at the last count fifteen – is evidence of a narcissism of difference that has transformed what once appeared to be a monolithic community into a series of jealous encampments. Zionism, while still part of the political discourse, has proven to be an unconvincing rallying point. Ethnic difference, religious schisms, and ceaseless harping about micro-exclusiveness has eclipsed the Zionist paradigm.

It is, therefore, a culture of differences that has provided the basis for the rise of the new historians. By clearing the ground of Zionist hegemony, the new historians have allowed a thousand micro-narratives to bloom. However, it is clear that this enterprise would not have been possible without the presence of a willing and appreciative audience. The New historians have also thrived due to the fading attraction of great men and great ideas. 'No man is a hero to his valet' wrote Hegel in his *Philosophy of History*. The demise of the great man was, Hegel amplified, 'not because the former is no hero, but because the latter is a valet.' The historian, in the case the critical historian of Zionism, 'looks at the historical figure and sees only a person.' It is our familiarity with the founding fathers of the Zionist movement that breeds contempt, for scrutinising the hero from close quarters inevitable makes us more familiar with his or her private habits and compulsions.

The Meaning of the New Historians

There is no doubt that the new historians have initiated a crucial debate. The deconstruction of the Zionist narrative has forced us, as a society, to bring to the forefront a discussion concerning moral obligations to take heed of the proverbial Other. Now that Israeli society seems no longer to be living under the threat of existential external dangers, we have the moral obligation to extend our moral universe beyond the borders of tribe, language, religion and nation. But this does not mean that the post-national discourse should discard the nation state as a useless, even pernicious vehicle for social involvement. Loosening the bonds of the nation-state is likely to encourage results no less pernicious, for it is the institutions and myths which are under attack that enable individuals to form civic identities and obligations to their fellow citizens and, eventually, beyond. Class identity, which lies at the core of the new historians' vision, is no less mythic, no less imagined than the myths they have set their sights on destroying. The Zionist myth that provides the foundation for the Israeli nation-state is far more complex than the new historians would lead us to believe. The resonance of the new historians' discourses is evidence of the need to question continuously national and religions delimitations. But, whatever its defects, the nation-state at least perpetuates a moral responsibility to a community that far surpasses the alternatives inherent in the discourse of the new historians. The dissolution of the nation-state promises to unleash antagonisms far more destructive and uncontrollable.

Nationalism, be it the Israeli version or any other, is a fiction that requires the suspension of belief. However, the notion that there is a viable alternative to this social construction of reality has proven, time and time again, to be significantly more lethal.

CHAPTER 17

In Search of a New Identity: Visions of Past and Present in Post-Communist Russia

Andrei ZORIN

Present-day Russia is a survivor country that is searching for itself after a cluster of major collapses; economic, ideological, territorial and institutional. The country that emerged after the revolution of 1991 found itself enclosed by borders it had never had, with a political regime and economic system it had never experienced, and without any coherent vision of its own past, present or future. This newly emerged country had to reinvent for itself a history and mythology. It is a characteristic of revolutionary societies that such attempts are generally doomed to failure. The historical myths and customs that might provide any sort of political consensus are lacking. The main elements of national identity – a foundation myth and a holiday celebrating it, a flag and anthem, the legitimacy of government, and even borders, are not taken for granted, but rather serve to fuel major political debate. It is important to realise, however, that political conflict *per se* does not prevent or inhibit a sense of community and shared destiny. Indeed, political debate and disagreement draw together a society through shared experiences, and this is what happens in most election campaigns, for example. The problem in Russia was rather the clumsiness of the attempts to establish a foundation myth and a national holiday.

There can be no doubt that this situation offers extremely fertile ground for all sorts of projects for national ideologies and national identities. The most famous, and at the same time the most notorious such attempt, was made by the group of advisers to President Yeltsin after the presidential elections of 1996. The strategy of this exceptionally successful election campaign was to construct a coalition against the danger of Communist restoration, which was presented as representing a divisive threat rather than a unifying force. The outcome of the elections confirmed the resonance of the call to search for unifying values that lie deeper than the purely political level, and this in turn led to the formation of a team of experts assigned with the task of forging a new national ideology. For perfectly understandable reasons the project collapsed after only a very short time; brainstorming sessions is not a suitable technology for providing new national myths and identities. The group was dissolved after six months with nothing to show for their efforts other than a collection of press articles discussing their endeavours.

However, recent years have seen two very important attempts to create new national myths, each with their own vision of the past and, importantly, the future of Russia. The first of these emerged in the course of spontaneous political action; the popular resistance to the putsch of August 1991. The second was launched during the public holiday of 1997 to mark Moscow's 850th anniversary. During these events, one of which was a social cataclysm, the other a holiday ritual, one could see the emergence of two alternative 'maps of problematic social reality and matrices for the creation of collective conscience', as Clifford Geertz defined ideology.[1] No doubt, the quality of symbolic map drawn by ideology is determined by the possibilities it offers to users to orient themselves in the space it opens up, and of course the way in which a social entity develops, be it a professional group or a whole country, is deeply influenced by the map it has in its possession. The strength of ideological metaphor lies in its capacity to grasp an apparent reality and produce new meanings and thus influence the dynamics of historic events.

When considering the attempted neo-Communist putsch of 19th to 21st August, 1991, we must take into consideration many parameters of this historic drama, including the logic of the economic develop-ment of the country, the collision of social forces, institutional crisis, undercover political intrigues, the personal qualities of the leading actors and, of course, the morphology of revolutionary forces

---

[1]   Geertz, 1973, p. 220.

described by de Tocqueville. All the same, the cultural and symbolic dimension also played a substantial role. I think it would be proper to remind the reader of the course of the main events.

On 19th August, 1991, central television and radio stations announced that the president of the USSR, Mikhail Gorbachev, was unable to perform his duties for health reasons and explained that his power had been transferred to the State Emergency Committee (GKChP). Censorship was introduced and tanks were brought onto the Moscow streets. However, the government of the Russian Federation, led by President Yeltsin, defied this decision and thousands of Muscovites gathered around the building of the Russian Government to protect it against possible military attack. After two days of deliberations, the emergency committee, terrified by the scale of possible human losses, gave up, and this moment marked the end not only of the Communist regime in the USSR, but also of the USSR itself. During that handful of days, several square miles in the centre of Moscow witnessed the representation of the struggle between two systems which had been described many times by both Soviet and anti-Soviet propaganda. It is important to mention that the building that housed both the government and the parliament of the Russian Federation at that time is traditionally referred to as 'the White House'. Throughout the post-war period, the Kremlin and the White House – this time the American one – synecdochally representing the corresponding superpowers, were the main protagonists of the 'final' historical battle. Paradoxically, in August 1991, the White House on Krasnopresnenskaya embankment played the role of its elder American brother.

It is worth mentioning the functional emblems employed by both sides in the course of these events. The Kremlin had at its disposal the same attributes of power which it had shown the world throughout the Soviet era. There were the tanks, which had been demonstrated as the main weapon of Soviet geopolitics in Hungary in 1956, in Czechoslovakia in 1968 and on many other occasions. There were the canons of Russian classical art, that had always served as the symbol of continuity between Russian history and Communist power and had helped to veil the political discontinuity. For the entire day of 19th August, all television channels transmitted Tchaikovsky's 'Swan Lake' instead of the news programmes, which had been censored. Finally, the authority of the Kremlin was represented by a totally illegitimate body of collective government – the notorious GKChP, that resembled, in functional terms, the old, omnipotent politburo of the Communist Party. However, the leaders of the GKChP made a important and symbolic communicative blunder. While the politburo traditionally functioned behind a wall of secrecy, the State Emergency Committee made the decision to appeared in public, participating in a live press-conference. Their poor performance, and the general demystification of illegitimate power marked the beginning of the collapse of the coup.[2]

On the other hand, the defenders of the White House had at their disposal a nationally elected president and parliament, and considered their civil disobedience in the face of GKChP orders as an act of political self-constitution ('We the people...'). Minor details of the event, such as the non-stop rock concert and the distribution of free imported cigarettes, only added support to an idealised image of the USA as the highest expression of the concept of the civilised world which had been elaborated by the whole culture of anti-Communist protest. Crowds surrounding the building felt that, apart from defending their legally elected government, they were also protecting their individual human dignity in the face of the bureaucratic state and, no less important, the ideals of democracy and the free-market. It would not be an exaggeration to say that the barricades around the White House were viewed by the crowd as the ultimate frontier of the 'civilised world'. The most frequently repeated slogan during these days,'Russia, Yeltsin and Freedom', served as a prototype of the synthesis of non-imperial patriotism, legalism, and individualism which was promoted as the ideology of a new Russian state.

The outcome of the events of the summer of 1991 was decided when the tanks were 'suffocated' in the crowd, having proved themselves to be useless against the nation. The myth of 19th to 21st August was the regeneration myth, the myth of the people finally realising their right to freedom, overcoming totalitarian tyranny and joining the rest of the world, which was waiting to generously welcome them into the family of democratic nations.

An analysis of why this model ultimately failed would take us too far from the theme of this chapter, however 19th August did not prove to be popular enough to serve as a real foundation myth and so

---

[2]   See Freidin and Televorot, 1995.

represent the symbolic dawn of the newly formed country. Disappointment in the reforms rapidly set in, and the absence of nostalgic associations made this event unacceptable as a national holiday to the majority of the population. Even the liberal intellectuals who view themselves as committed supporters of the reforms tend to downplay the dimensions of the August Revolution. The main theme of television broadcasts and newspaper articles commemorating the events of August 1991 is, 'That was the day when we were all deceived'. The only semi-official celebration connected with this events is the so-called day of the national flag on 22nd August, when skateboarders are permitted to skate in Red Square during a rock concert.

The 12th of June, which was chosen by the leadership of the Russian Federation as the proper date for a national holiday, failed even more miserably. As a result, the majority of the Russian population is blissfully unaware that what they are celebrating on the 12th of June is the day of Russia's independence, chosen as the Foundation Day by the new authorities. Generally, the best reply one can hope for from any Russian citizen quizzed on the significance of the day is that this was the day in 1991 of the first elections for the Russian Presidency. This answer is definitely wrong, as the elections themselves were specially arranged on the 12th of June to mark the first anniversary of the declaration of Russian sovereignty, adopted by the first Congress of the People's Deputies of the Russian Federation. This fact is now deliberately downplayed by either end of Russia's present-day political spectrum. Both the government and the Communist opposition, which regards this day not a holiday but as a day of national tragedy, are reluctant to mention the fact that Russia's independence was launched by the Communist majority of the Congress which was later dissolved by Yeltsin. What is even more important is that this foundation act did not presuppose Russian independence at all, but in fact meant the radical increase of the power and prerogatives of the Russian government within the Soviet Union.

The level of confusion about this holiday can be seen clearly in the ceremonial events used to mark it. These events most usually combine the excessive use of the word 'Russia', and seek to appeal to Russian patriotism through elements of religious ritual combined with the aesthetics of a traditional party concert. The most striking example was the ending of the 1994 ceremony in the Kremlin Palace of

Congress when, after the performances of a female folk dancing group and a military chorus, a religious icon was brought onto the stage. The audience, made up mostly of the members of the old Communist elite, had no idea how it should react, and finally the whole hall stood up and broke into a round of applause. An even more convincing piece of evidence for the failure of this day is that a considerable part of the population militantly opposes this new holiday. The editorial of the main opposition newspaper said of the 12th of June, 'This day is not a holiday. It is the day of our sorrow, the day of mourning, the day of weeping'.[3]

Russia therefore could not lay claim to any real holidays, a situation which spoke eloquently of the degree of the citizens' uncertainty about their own country. As Paul Ricoeur put it, 're-enactment of the founding events is a fundamental ideological act. There is an element of a repetition of the origin [...] Can we imagine a community without the celebration of its own birth in more or less mythical terms?'[4] This situation in Russia was due in part to the lack of the traditional continuity that is necessary for effective celebration, in part to the lack of confidence in the overall political arrangement established by the government, but it was due in most part to the absence of a coherent vision of the country's national identity with which to underpin the celebrations. Or at least, this was the case before 5th to 7th September, 1997, when Moscow celebrated its 850th anniversary. This was the first truly national holiday in many decades. It is estimated, and I can testify to these figures, that more than three million people took to the streets to celebrate. The last time Moscow had seen such crowds was in 1953, when thousands of people were crushed during Stalin's funeral.

Traditionally, the choice of the day for national celebration is defined by the national foundation myth. This myth usually sees the creation of a cosmos, in opposition to the chaos that reigned before this moment. When American people celebrate Independence Day, they assume that the time before independence was a sort of a dark age from which a nation gloriously emerged on the 4th of July. During the imperial period in Russia, the main holiday was the day the ruling monarch's accession to the throne. This accession was made to mark

---

[3]   *Sovetskaia Rossia* (Soviet Russia), 1998, June 10.

[4]   Ricoeur, 1984, pp. 261-262.

the beginning of the new era, advising the royal subjects to forget the previous reign. The ideological message of the celebration of the October Bolshevik Revolution during the Soviet period was the same. This division between cosmos and chaos is not only true of political holidays, but also of religious ones. When one celebrates Christmas or Easter, one presumes that the time before Christ, or the time before his resurrection, has ended. The holy day divides the time in two, and rejects one part of it.

By choosing the foundation of the city as the day of the national holiday, this rejection is, in fact, minimised. Nothing is rejected in its celebration, rather, it simply provides an incentive to other localities to search for their own foundation myths. And the wave of local celebrations is now spreading all over Russia. Historically, the anniversary of Moscow is a completely invented date, since nobody knows when Moscow was actually founded. The first mention of Moscow in historical documents was dated April, but it was decided that the celebrations should take place in September. This did not seem to matter; nobody really cared about history, mythology was much more important.

During the anniversary festivities, the unfortunate history of Russia, full of tragic experience and horrible human loss, was somehow transformed into an uninterrupted Golden Age. We saw several theatrical representations of a national history which was shown to consist exclusively of 'good guys'. The old Russian princes were good guys, and Moscow's mayor even came to the celebration wearing the costume of an old Russian prince. Moscow tsars, who beheaded those princes and transformed feudal Russia into an absolute monarchy, were also good guys, especially Ivan the Terrible. His image was projected on the wall of the Moscow State University during the laser show by French composer and engineer Jean-Michel Jarre. Peter the Great, who hated Moscow and switched the capital to St. Petersburg hoping never to come back was also a good guy, and a monument was erected to him in Moscow and officially opened during the celebration. The Petersburg emperors were also very nice. The Communists who overthrew these emperors and shot the last of them and his family were also okay. Indeed, during the celebration television was filled with neo-Soviet retro, songs about Lenin, Stalin and friendly meetings in Moscow during the good old Communist days. After all this, it came as no surprise to learn that the democrats who ousted the Communists were also very nice. The festivities were officially sponsored by President Yeltsin, and appropriate honours were presented to him during the ceremony. Everything was fine, and it always had been. There were no contradictions between different historical periods and historical heroes.

One can point to what seems to be the same traits in the European tradition, where there are neighbouring monuments to Charles I and Cromwell, or neighbouring streets named after Robespierre and Louis XVI. In Europe, this sort of proximity means the acceptance of the drama of history and of mutual forgiveness, but this way of celebrating in the new Russia meant exactly the opposite. The message it contained was to forget the drama of history. Many new 'old' churches, including the biggest cathedral in the city, the Cathedral of Christ the Saviour, were constructed in Moscow to replace those demolished by the Communists. These brand new cathedrals are intended to look exactly like their predecessors, which were built between the 16th and 19th centuries. The ideological goal of this reconstruction was to create the illusion that the demolition never took place. We must believe that these buildings were always present, and that no harm ever befell them.

One of the interesting results of this extremely intensive rebuilding *ex nihilo* is that the real historical buildings and sites lose their authenticity and uniqueness. When, in Red Square, which is the historical centre of Moscow, we see these newly erected 16th and 17th century churches, we begin to doubt whether the Kremlin and St Basil's Cathedral have really been here since the 16th century and to suspect that they too were also recently built by Moscow's mayor. In this way, history loses its narrative logic. Eventually, when history has been purged of bad guys, it ceases to exist and becomes an assemblage of historical relics, a collection of beautiful things from the past that can only serve as decoration for some kind of performance. In a way, the 'new' Red Square and other 'old-new' parts of Moscow became a gigantic installation made specifically for festivities, although they might remain for a while after the party's over.

As mentioned above, the Moscow State University, which is the largest symbol of Stalinist Russia and is depicted on many Moscow postcards, was used as a screen for Jean-Michel Jarre's laser projection. The building became a part of the installation. In the same way, the Kremlin wall became a mere theatre backdrop for the performance of 'Our Old Capital', the major ballet staged by the famous producer Andrei Mihalkov-Konchalovski, a former celebrity of the Soviet cinema who now lives in the United States.

It is interesting to follow the functional changes that have occurred in Moscow's two most important squares; Red Square, which used to be the symbol of the imperial might of the Soviet superpower, the place of military parades, of soldiers, tanks and rockets, and, nearby, the Manezhnaya, the largest square in Moscow, an enormous empty place that, during *perestroika*, became the centre of social activity. Now Red Square is confined by its brand-new 'ancient' gates, and it is impossible to ride a tank on it. Similarly, the Maneznaya, once the symbol of the nation brought back to political life and the scene of massive demonstrations, is completely occupied by the building of the new Moscow trade centre.

It is significant that the symbol of the new era is a trade centre. But this trade centre does not tower over the city like its counterpart in New York. It is built under the city, like the Stalinist metro stations, symbolising a new proletariat culture, and it is constructed and decorated in a historical manner. The lowest level is loosely styled upon 17th century Moscow architecture, the middle level upon the styles of the 18th and 19th centuries, the upper level belongs to the 20th century, while the composition is crowned by a cupola, the traditional symbol of Russian architecture. History is used as a decoration for trade, which is the new way of life. No more imperial might, no more mass demonstrations, and no more political activity – the nation, tired of its imperial responsibilities and political storms, can relax.

One of the most typical, and at the same time most grotesque reconstructions was that of the Neglinka River. This river once flowed through the centre of Moscow, before it was directed into the drainage system and disappeared from the surface. Now one can see a sort of pseudo-Neglinka, a river decorated with tiny bronze sculptures of animals from Russian folk tales. When these monuments were built, there were many who objected that these strange creatures were too close to the eternal fire at the grave of the unknown soldier, yet, at the same time, nobody can actually say why they should not be so close. The wars are over, we won all of them, and now it's time for relaxation and recreation.

The main day of the festivities was marked by an enormous procession that made its way across the city. It was lead by the mayor, followed by the representatives of the different districts of Moscow, then those from the different regions and provinces of Russia. Then came the elephants and the Scottish bagpipers. In Imperial Rome, processions such as these represented the different parts of the world conquered by the imperial might of Rome. In Moscow which, as we know, is the third Rome, this procession had a different meaning. We saw all the countries of the world sending us their goods.

The festivities demonstrated that the consumer society had arrived in Russia, but it was legitimated by the history of the Russian empire, and by the religion of the Eastern Orthodox church. At the end of the celebrations the mayor gave his speech, addressing the patriarch and the president who were present at the ceremony, but the final word was left to Russia's most famous pop singer, Alla Pugatshova, the Russian Madonna. For this event, she played both Madonnas, the American singer and the original one. After the Mayor's speech she arrived on stage in a snow-white dress, leading a small child, and sang a song in which Moscow was called a prophet and the Messiah. After that she blessed the audience, making a cross with her hand, and the fireworks began. It was, without doubt, the triumph of bad taste, but at the same time it was also a liberation from the totalitarian tyranny of the grand style. This second myth enacted during the celebrations can be termed the reconciliation myth. In this myth, the country, torn apart, reconciles itself with everything in its past and present, including the horrors of wars and mass annihilation. However historically false and even cynical this vision may seem, it is successful in helping to alleviate historic pain and humiliation. All the same, there was a difficulty that emerged in the aftermath of the celebration, for while the holidays proved enormously successful in uniting the Muscovites, it provoked total indifference and even animosity in the provincial cities and towns. Russia, a country suffering enormous hardships, was irritated to see its capital celebrating its successful entrance into the consumption era.

So, the search for a new national identity and ideology is bound to continue. New myths are in the pipeline, and it is certain that they will not only shape Russia's vision of itself, but also its historic, political and social future.

CHAPTER 18

Foundation Myths at Work: National Day Celebrations in France, Germany and Norway in a Comparative Perspective

Arve THORSEN

What can the historian learn from three national day celebrations? The intention of this chapter is to highlight the value of analysing such celebrations from a comparative perspective in the framework of research on national ideology and nation-building. The focus of this study is the instrumentalisation and reception of the respective national foundation myths, and the key theme is the concept of friction and opposition as elements of political processes.

The historiography of national day celebrations is fairly young, although the number of studies is already relatively high. However, the focus of most of these studies has been the introduction and implementation of the celebrations. In the interest of defending the constructive dimension of the national integration processes, many historians, like Eric Hobsbawm, have concentrated on how and why the celebrations were introduced.[1] The focus has seldom been put on the chances of survival of these creations. Nevertheless, it is a fact that the European national day celebrations, despite the similarity of the general intentions of the elites responsible for their construction, did not share the same resonance and popularity. They therefore made different contributions the processes of national integration in their

---

[1] Hobsbawm and Ranger, 1983.

respective homelands. Their common task was to operate in the field of national opinion, to gather and to unite, and their challenge was to establish and maintain links between a defined national project and this opinion. Historians have always played an important role in the implementation of the foundation myths that have provided the legitimisation for these celebrations, eagerly consecrating elements of their research to the strengthening of these myths, and thus serving as valuable allies for the groups deciding and defending the dates of national day celebrations. The challenge to the contemporary historian is therefore the revelation of the reasons why some of these celebrations myths succeeded while others did not.

It is against this general background that a comparative approach is both fruitful and instructive. By comparing the celebrations and the discussions around them, using not only the celebrations as such, but also their *dates* as objects of comparison within a limited time frame, we can go beyond the ideographic description of important aspects of the *status quo* in national integration processes. By considering the frictions that occurred commonly and those that did not, we would also seem to get closer to understanding the mechanisms of success and failure.

The approach chosen in this chapter is derived from the conclusions of a three-year study of national day celebrations.[2] This study found that the different ideologically, confessionally and socially defined groups which it analysed all tended to relate, not to one, but to three objects in their own approach to the national day. First, there was the date, and the event referred to as the birth of the nation. The celebrations were seen as mobilisations for or against whatever was declared the national foundation myth. We will call this the historical, or rather the *mythical* dimension of the celebrations. Secondly, there was the form given to the celebration, the face accorded to the nation in the rituals that took place. The celebration was seen as an attempt to capture the nation's soul, visualising what the organisers and supporters regarded as the keystone of their national heritage. We will refer to this as the *symbolic* dimension. Thirdly, there was the government, which laid claim to represent, or rather fill the space of the nation and its heritage. Quite often, the celebrations were seen as tools in the hands of the sitting government and were interpreted in a political perspective. The evaluation of each

---

[2]   Thorsen, 1997.

celebration might therefore vary according to the ideological basis of the governing elite and to more general changes in the political landscape. We will call this the *political* dimension of the celebrations. Of course, the three were interwoven, and different groups put different emphasis on each aspect in approaching and assessing the celebration. It was, however, when the celebrations were in question that these aspects were most often referred to.

We will employ the word 'dialogue' for each of the three dimensions of the object of the celebrations. The term seems quite suitable, because the celebrations examined in this chapter turn out not to be *monologues* by the governments in power at the time, but three parallel *dialogues*, with the triple object as one interlocutor and the national opinion, in all its variations, as the other. The question to be asked – and, hopefully, answered – is if and how these dialogues succeeded, and what these celebrations can tell us about why this was so.

We will focus primarily on the form of each of the three celebrations as it was around the turn of the century, trying, however, to find features that were significant for the respective nation-building processes. What can this triple approach teach us about the projects in question, their foundation myths and their ability to unite and to gather the nation? In the following, I will first treat the three case studies separately, then draw conclusions along national and more general lines. The first case study is the 14th of July in Paris, the second is Sedan Day in Berlin, while the last is the celebration of the Norwegian National Day on the 17th of May.

The 14th of July: Reflector and Catalyst of National Convergence

Around the turn of the century, the 14th of July was still a *pomme de discorde* in France, that is, an object of much national-ideological debate. As the German historian Monika Flacke puts it, France was a nation of divided memory, and indeed, few dates in French history could provoke such inflammatory rhetoric as the French national day. There were historians in both camps, instrumentalising their research for one side or the other.[3] Yet the date of this annual national

---

[3]   In this struggle over the myth of the Bastille and its fall, a multitude of different interpretations were available to suit every political approach to both the

celebration was never to change, and it has gradually gathered support from most of the political camps in Republican France. It has proven to be highly integrative, despite its inherent potential for division. The study of this celebration and its resonance, from 1895 to 1905 (a very tormented time for the French Republic) helps to explain why this should be. Even in this period of national distress, or perhaps *especially* then, the integrative force of this national celebration was apparent, and was manifest in the flexibility and pluralism of the three dialogues.

The first dialogue, the historical or mythical, was of course rich in arguments and criticisms. These criticisms were interminable, but very different in their resonance. The most significant opponents of the 14th of July as the mythologised *'naissance de liberté'*, the birth of freedom, were the Catholic right-wing movements and their press. A good example of the latter was the paper *la Croix*, which was the best-selling of all Catholic newspapers in the period, and which never hid its contempt for the historical underpinnings of the celebration.[4] The 14th of July was ungodly and unworthy of the glory of France, it claimed. It was savage, an annual apotheosis of anarchy. It was the shameful memory of civil war and national division. Even convinced Republican organs, such as the centre-right newspaper *le Figaro*, gave their restrained approval to such an interpretation, especially after historians had weakened the Republican myth by referring to the realities of the incidents that had originally taken place, at a time when the celebration was enjoying little support.[5] The biggest socialist

---

Republican regime and the national day as such. Around the turn of the century, newspapers critical of the choice of date would use historians and their research for their purpose, denouncing the myth of the Bastille as false, dangerous or hypocritical. See Bois, 1990. The clashes over this myth have also been well described by Amalvi, 1984. Furthermore, the myth and its history have been comprehensively presented in a catalogue published by Deutsches Historisches Museum in Berlin, 1998. See the article by Danny Trom: 'Die Gespaltene Erinnerung'.

[4]   This newspaper was part of the publishing house *La bonne presse* and was very traditional and conservative, if not reactionary in its approach to French history and society in general. For more about this newspaper: see Bellanger, 1972.

[5]   *Le Figaro* was, in 1896-7 becoming rather sceptical as to the choice of the date. In an article on 15th July, 1897, it claimed that now, after the historians had revealed the truths about the 14th of July, there was not even a mythical reason for keeping this date as the national day of France: 'Il n'y a donc pas de raison, même mystique, pour maintenir notre fête nationale et républicaine à la date incommode

newspaper, the *Petite République* showed equal contempt for the celebration, but from an entirely different perspective. The 14th of July was hypocritical, it argued, because it was the historical victory of the *people*, whose commemoration had ironically been chosen to mark the birthday celebration of an oppressive bourgeois regime that had itself become a new Bastille.[6] For its part, the centre-left press, such as *Le Temps*, steadfastly defended the date though, *le Temps* added, one could question the historical importance originally accorded to it. However, the paper argued that a people does not choose as a symbol the actual historical fact, but rather the legend that it has generated.[7] The 14th of July was undeniably the 'the symbol of the principles of liberty, equality and fraternity' and, the paper added, some time in the future when the Republican regime was in danger its opponents would see the force which this legend had acquired.[8] For now, however, the Republicans were not alert and the 14th of July lived peacefully, as a latent day of mobilisation for the Republican forces. The columnist of *le Temps* would be proved largely correct in his conviction a few years later when, in 1900, the Dreyfus affair and the *antidreyfusard* right-wing movement threaten the Republican regime with a *coup d'état*. The brief conclusion that we can draw for the mythical dimension of the 14th of July is that it did divide opinion, and that it especially alienated the forces of the Right.

---

du 14 juillet'. It continued: 'de grâce, que l'on renonce à ce 14 juillet, à cette ripaille malsaine, à cette solennité sans grandeur, à cette apothéose de l'anarchie. Il est temps de reléguer au musée des horreurs poncives cette date sinistre qui n'est en somme, selon la belle expression de Gambetta, qu'un "haillon de guerre civile"' This attitude, however, turned out not to be very long-lived. In 1900, the newspaper would praise the day for its ability to gather French opinion and celebrate the nation, giving place to 'la concorde, la paix et le patriotisme. Dans tout Paris, en un mot, c'est un débordement de joie exubérant. La foule s'amuse.' *Le Figaro* 15/7 1900.

[6]   *La Petite République* 18/7 1897. The newspaper continued by encouraging its readers and all others to take back the revolutionary tradition: 'reprendre la tradition révolutionnaire et faire passer dans la réalité des choses, cette fameuse devise: "Liberté, Egalité, Fraternité", qui ne fut jusqu'à présent qu'une lamentable duperie.'

[7]   *Le Temps* 15-16/7 1897.

[8]   'Symbole des principes de liberté, d'égalité, de fraternité démocratique.' *Le Temps* 15-16/7 1896.

The same is not the case for the *content* of the celebration. The Republican *tricolore* was widely accepted, as was, for the most part, the national anthem, the *'Marseillaise'*, although the right-wing, determined to remain distant from this spirit, did not mention this element of integration in their rhetoric. They also either neglected the annual city balls, which were generally very popular, or chose only to mention those that had been poorly attended. What the right-wing could not ignore, however, was the *revue* or military parade. This gigantic annual demonstration of French military strength, a symbol of the hope of future military glory and revenge over Germany, the victor of Sedan, managed to win over even the most convinced enemies of the regime and its national day. It did so because it could convince the right-wing, who regarded the army as its ally in the battle against the parliamentary Republic, that it could appropriate this part of the celebration as its own. Whereas the partisans of the centre-left regime cried, *'Vive la République'*, supporters of the right-wing cried, *'Vive l'armée'*. This was a distinction that became most evident during the Dreyfus affair. All the same, the parade was unquestionably an integral part of the Republic's self-celebration. It was skilfully designed to include even the enemies of the date, as the French historian Jean-Pierre Bois has shown.[9] It was in this event that the date and the nation seem to have most strongly and convincingly revealed their force and potential for integration. There were groups that felt attached to this part of the celebration who were strongly opposed to both the mythical dimension of the day and the universal Republican values attached to it by the defenders of the regime. In the military parade they had found *their* part of the celebration, but, paradoxically, it was also the part most cherished by their opponents. *La Croix* could, in retrospect, analyse the survival of the 14th of July celebrations in the following way:

But gradually, contempt or simply indifference eliminated the speeches and parades that marked the date, and the parade turned the celebration into a military event that unites all Frenchmen in the same patriotic fervour. One no longer saw the date, one saw only the celebration.[10]

---

[9] Bois, 1990.

[10] 'Mais peu à peu, la réprobation ou simplement l'indifférence ont éliminé les déclamations et les parades qui rappellaient la date, et la revue a fait de la fête une

For all camps, the *revue* represented the climax of the day, clearly reflecting the *flexibility* of the French symbolic dialogue. The military parade provided a face for the nation that gathered even the conservative Right, more particularist and exclusionary in their national ideology than the other groups. This display was the embodiment of the cult of state and military power. It was a celebration of the territory and the glory, not of the regime, but of the nation, *la France*. The men behind this celebration had been very aware of the competing dimensions of French national or patriotic thought. An analysis of the celebration and the rhetoric that surrounded it at the turn of last century seems to prove that they were correct in their appraisal of the situation: despite its inherent potential for division, the *revue* managed to serve as a reference around which the nation could gather. The symbolic dialogue was therefore very much a success.

The *political* dimension of the celebration was also something of which all were acutely aware. The day had been introduced as the Republicans' day of mobilisation, and the fact that this was still the case at the end of the 19th century was, as we have seen, not denied by defenders of the celebration such as *le Temps*. The inherent political dimension, the fact that this was the celebration of a parliamentary regime with allies on the Left certainly contributed to the right-wing's contempt for the celebration, a contempt that only grew in this period. The Right would not consent to a celebration with these political connotations. Their opposition was hardened still more by the secular identity of the regime, which the Right saw reflected in a godless celebration. On this side of the political spectrum, there was no room for flexibility in the dialogue.

This, however, was not true for the Socialist camps on the left. Generally, the regime was the object of much socialist criticism in this period. As we have seen, in 1895 *La Petite République* wrote ironically about the celebration, claiming that the regime had adopted the old revolutionary symbols and the *tricolore* as hypocritical representations of a government that was far from understanding the meaning of the revolutionary heritage. The paper's columnist stated that the Left was dreaming of the fall of this regime, while searching

---

fête militaire qui réunit tous les Francais dans le même élan de patriotisme. On n'a plus vu la date, on n'a plus vu que la fête.' *La Croix*, 14.07.1905.

inspiration in the commemoration of the fall of the Bastille. For the time being, the old trinity, *Liberté, Egalité, Fraternité*, was nothing but a provocative joke. There was only contempt and sarcastic distance, therefore, from the side of the moderate Socialists. This was to change however, and in the rhetorical shift of *La Petite République* during the Dreyfus affair, we seem to find a new flexibility in the political dialogue surrounding this celebration. Furthermore, the strong links between the Republican regime and important elements of the Socialist camp were revealed. In the midst of the Dreyfus affair, when the parliamentary Republican regime was threatened by the right-wing, the Socialist organ came to regard the regime in a positive light and it enthusiastically defended the strategy of the '*défense républicaine*' of Prime Minister Waldeck-Rousseau. When the French Republic was threatened, it announced that the '*patrimoine humaine*', the human patrimony, was at risk.[11] Some years earlier, the same newspaper had printed unenthusiastic reports of the military parade, but this was no longer the case. Class struggle and the defence of the Republic combined to produce a heartful '*vive la république*' from the Socialist benches of the Longchamp tribunes. On the 14th of July, 1900, the Socialists sang both the *Marseillaise* and the *Internationale* at Longchamp, mixing internationalist thought with national pride.[12] The political situation had forced the Socialists to reveal their political passion and recognise their link with the regime – the legacy of the French Revolution. While the Right saw nothing of their national ideology in all this, the French socialists found *their* French nation in the Republican ideology, the Republican symbolism and the declaration of human rights. This, they claimed, was *patriotisme modeste*, as opposed to the other form or patriotism, which was vulgar and aggressive. Military parades alone could not appeal to this modest patriotism, but the mythical dimension of the 14th of July, connected to a universalism that was complementary to the internationalism of the workers' movement, certainly could.[13]

---

[11] *La Petite République* 13/7 1899.

[12] *Le Temps* 15-16/7 1900.

[13] The content of this patriotism was defended most eagerly and eloquently by Jean Jaurès, who found a typical representative of this patriotic tradition in the figure of the Republican historian Jules Michelet. During the Michelet centennial in 1898, which intentionally coincided with the celebration of the 14th of July, *La Petite République* printed on its front page a long homage to Michelet by Jaurès. He first stated that Michelet had never really been one of them, being, after all, a bourgeois

These three dialogues of the French national day celebration around the turn of the century reveal interesting aspects of French national integration. Maurice Agulhon has concluded that, up to 1914, there was a movement of slow convergence taking place between *les Deux France* in the period of the Third Republic.[14] The national-ideological dialogue around the 14th of July would appear to reveal some of the mechanisms behind this movement. The background and content of the 14th of July celebration may not have been accepted by one and all, but an analysis of the three dialogues shows that it contained elements which everybody could cherish and identify with. Despite its historical and ideological connotations, it gathered the nation. The 14th of July was a melting pot of French patriotism, and as such was a valuable utensil for national integration. This is the story of a national myth that could not in itself unite, but that managed to do so, indirectly but forcefully, through the actions of the organisers of the celebration.

Sedan Day: The Failure of a Myth and an Idea

In Germany, the story of the national day was very different. An analysis of the so-called Sedan Day tells us that the sense of the celebration as it was conceived, as well as its outcome and function, were diametrically different to those of the 14th of July. Whereas the 14th of July gathered where it could have created division, Sedan Day managed to divide where it could have united. I say 'could have united' because it deliberately alienated large groups who, while feeling German, were stigmatised as *Vaterlandslos*, people without a

---

thinker. Nevertheless, he continued, it was the duty of good socialists to celebrate this anniversary along with the others (a sumptuous celebration, organised by the authorities, took place in the Panthéon, with all the notables of the Republican regime present). This was so, Jaurès argued, because of the universal dimension of Michelet's patriotism: In his numerous works he had not only praised 'la grande âme de la patrie', 'the great soul of the nation', but also 'l'amour pour toute l'humanité', 'the love for all humanity'. Jaurès concluded, 'for him, France existed wherever humanity was great. The French soul is a rapid fire which burns on the highest peaks', 'La France est pour lui partout où l'humanité est grande. L'âme francaise est comme un feu rapide qui se pose sur tous les sommets.' *La Petite République* 16/7 1898.

[14] Agulhon, 1995.

fatherland. To elaborate this further, let us examine the three dialogues of the celebration.

Considering the mythical or historical dialogue, Sedan Day was the annual commemoration of the victory at Sedan and the capitulation of Napoleon III, the German arch-enemy, in 1870.[15] This day was celebrated as the birth of the German nation. On this day, the rhetoric of the celebration announced, the German community had found the strength to gather and unite against a common enemy. This victory was given distinctly theological connotations; it was the intervention of God in world history, the moment where he revealed his preferential love for the German people. This interpretation of the battle had originally been conceived by the first German emperor Wilhelm I and then became the official version of German historio-graphy. The mythical sense of this celebration was particularistic rather than universal, with a constant focus on German virtues and God's love for the German people. In a church service in Berlin in 1895, the priest stated that victory at the Battle of Sedan had been given to the German people by God's grace, 'He has given us a wonderful victory. A victory in which we clearly recognise his hand.'[16] Furthermore, the celebration was distinctly antidemocratic in its form. The ideology of the day was authoritarian and linked to the veneration of the army as the creators of Imperial Germany.[17]

From the beginning, this celebration had few enemies on the Right – this *was* the celebration of the German Right. On the other hand, it had a mythical content that did not appeal to the forced of the centre-left such as the Social Democrats and Liberals. The Social Democratic newspaper *Vorwärts* called the day a celebration of chauvinism, hatred and bourgeois militarism. On this point there were no grounds for compromise, no flexibility in the rhetorics of the day. The ideology of the Sedan commemoration, *Vorwärts* claimed, was

---

[15] Several German historians have analysed the Sedan Day, especially the idea behind it and the way it was implemented. Among the most important contributions have been Schieder, 1961, in which he included a collection of the most important sources for the study of the celebration; Lehmann, 1966 and Schellack, 1990.

[16] 'Er hat uns einen herrlichen Sieg gegeben. Einen Sieg, in dem wir deutlich seine Hand erkennen ' *Kreuzzeitung* 2/9 1895.

[17] This was very evident in the first conservative newspaper of the Kaiserreich, *Kreuzzeitung*, which was an enthusiastic defender of the celebration. Thorsen, 1997, p. 71.

'*Mordspatriotismus*', the patriotism of murder.[18] Nor was there anything likely to win over the centre-left opposition in the content of the celebration. On the contrary, on this day, the supporters of universal, liberal democratic patriotism were defined as non-Germans, unwilling to devote themselves to an imperial manifestation of God's mercy. All the same, the centre-left made it clear that even the most energetic opponents of the celebration *felt* national. In 1895, the Social Democratic representative Ignaz Auer argued that he, and those of a like mind, were not essentially unpatriotic, but that they were forced to be because supporters of political reforms and the modernisation of the political system were denied the right to call themselves patriots.[19] The national flag, a black, white and red tricolour banner, was not recognised by this group; theirs was the old 'black, red, and yellow' from 1848, their year of patriotic reference. There was no room for this flag in the celebration and, as if this was not enough, the left-wing movements, though explicitly non-revolutionary, saw themselves condemned as such by the spokesmen of the right-wing and by the emperor himself.[20] In short, in Berlin as in

---

[18] The party newspaper of the German social democrats was uncompromising and intransigent in its opposition to Sedan Day. It claimed not only that the day was a celebration of militarism, but that it was, equally, a homage to hatred. Demonstrating their distance to what they considered the belligerent content of the day, the party sent a telegram to their socialist comrades in Paris: 'Am 25. Jahrestag der Schlacht von Sedan, als Protest gegen Krieg und Chauvinismus, den französischen Genossen Gruss und handschlag. Hoch die Völkersolidarität!' *Vorwärts* 3/9 1895.

[19] *Vorwärts* 5/9 1895.

[20] Wilhelm II's speech, given during the *paradedîner* on 2 September, 1895, is one of the best illustrations of the way the emperor contributed towards poisoning the political debate by revealing his contempt for social democracy, and thus legitimising strong anti-socialist and, tendentiously, anti-democratic currents. Reacting to some recent articles printed in *Vorwärts*, in which the newspaper mocked the day and its contents, and especially the way in which the emperor tried to canonise his own grandfather, Wilhelm I, the hero of Sedan, the emperor made the following outburst: 'Doch in die hohe, grosse Festfreude schlägt ein Ton hinein, der wahrhaftig nicht dazu gehört: Eine Ratte von Menschen nicht werth, den Namen Deutscher zu tragen, wagt es, die uns heilige Person des allverehrten Kaisers in den Staub zu ziehen. Möge das gesamte Volk in sich die Kraft finden, diese unerhörten Angriffe zurückzuweisen! Geschieht es nicht, nun denn, so rufe ich Sie, um der hochverrätigen Schaar zu mehren, um einen Kampf zu führen, der

Paris, there were *two* nations with two distinct perspectives on the national day celebration. In Berlin, however, there was nothing in the celebration that could appeal to its opponents, there was no space given to competing or alternative versions of patriotism. While the 14th of July could offer the ambiguity of a set of rival but complementary conceptions of the nation, Sedan Day remained uncompromising and monolithic. The organisers and thinkers behind the celebration had nothing but contempt for people whose conception of what it meant to be German differed from that promoted by the Sedan celebration. The day had only one message; either you are with us or you are against us.

This aspect becomes even clearer when one considers the political dimension of the celebration. On this level too there was no flexibility or dynamism in this microcosm of the national spirit. The reason for this is evident; Imperial Germany was, and would remain, a national project of the Right. At the same time, the trend in the elections of the period was the growth of support for the Liberal Democrats among the electorate. Berlin was the city where this trend was clearest. Around 70% of the city's electorate at that time was voting for political parties whose ideologies lay to the left of Sedan Day.[21] At the same time, however, the German *Kriegerbund*, the group most active in celebrating the day, started to exclude Social Democratic members, labelling them as enemies of the national community. They began to interpret and promote the celebration as a mobilisation against the country's democratic forces.[22] It is indicative that Sedan Day had never been declared a national day by any democratic assembly, as had been the case in Paris in 1880. The date had been introduced by those who moved in circles loyal to the conservative-authoritarian regime without any recourse to the *Reichstag*, the German parliament, and the supporters of Sedan Day continued to feel themselves to be above the opinion of this institution. Their Germany was a non-pluralist, anti-democratic one, where 'Germanness' was defined through the readiness of the *Untertanen* to subject themselves to the national will, a will that emanated from forces close to the emperor

---

uns befreit von solchen Elementen' *Schultheiss Europäischer Geschichtskalender*, 1896.

[21] See Ribbe, 1990.

[22] The new paragraph in the *Kriegerbund*'s articles of association was: '§7: Jede Person kann aufgenommen werden, die sich eines unbescholtenen Rufes erfreut und sich nicht zur Sozialdemokratie bekennt'. *Parole* 6/9 1905.

and the military and that was tied to the Christian faith. The political dialogue associated with Sedan Day, like the mythical and symbolic dialogues, was rigid and unforgiving. The supporters and opponents of Sedan Day remained entrenched in their positions in the battlefield of national ideology. In other words, it was a dialogue in which one party felt above discussion and would accept no response but acclamation. Their intention was not to engage in dialogue, but to hold a monologue in which their right to speak was accorded by their unconditional national and Christian devotion. In this, Sedan Day may be interpreted as a forceful demonstration of a spiritualisation of politics that was, and would remain, a scourge to the German nation. This spiritualisation was, in many ways, the fruit of a tradition of national thought that would accept no universal dimension of 'Germanness' and that rejected citizenship as the definition of nationality. This was a tradition with a very weak civic dimension. Instead, it mingled theology and national thought, with the result that the theological bipolarity of heaven and hell, of good and bad, was transferred to national ideology and national politics. A national ideology such as this could not integrate the German people who were, in fact, not nearly as servile as the organisers of Sedan Day would have wished. It is important to add that those who participated in Sedan Day did *not* embody Germany, and the choice of the date as the national day for certain groups within the nation-state cannot be interpreted as an authoritarian culture *uniting* the German nation. In fact, the celebration eventually disappeared, but the tradition that it had represented remained and, significantly, Germany never established any unifying national day celebration, since there was no date that could bridge the divides within the German nation-state. In an article on Sedan Day in 1898, the left-wing liberal, Friedrich Dernburg, stated that the time had not yet arrived when Germany could celebrate a common national day and that this was a symptom of a national sickness:

> When we succeed in understanding each other better in the field of politics, across classes, estates and confessions, when the social levelling takes its course, when a common culture has been extended, then the

national day can be celebrated every day. The fact that we do not have it for the time being is a symptom of this people's disease.[23]

With respect to their common mission to unite and gather, we can easily draw the conclusion that while the 14th of July was a success in this respect, Sedan Day was not; it was a *failure* as a tool of national integration.[24]

The 17th of May: The Story of a Uniting Myth

The history of the Norwegian national day is very different to that of Sedan Day, indeed, it is the history of a national cathedral. The 17th of May is a construction that always has, and still does tower above all other dates in the national calendar. In this respect, it has perhaps proven more successful in its mission than even the 14th of July, which has, despite its historically proven ability to gather and unite, become a rather passionless, sclerotic ritual. Today, Norway's national day has little political content, being unanimously regarded as *the* celebration, with Christmas Eve as its only real competitor. I will here concentrate on the historical role that this day has had as a tool of national integration. Most Norwegians regard the day as eternally

---

[23] 'Wenn es uns gelingt, uns zwischen Klassen, Ständen und Konfessionen besser politisch zu verständigen, wenn der soziale Ausgleich fortschreitet, wenn der Boden gemeinsamer Kultur sich verbreitet hat; dann wird das Nationalfest jeden Tag gefeiert werden können. Dass wir es zur Zeit nicht haben können, das ist das Symptom der Volkskrankheit.' *Berliner Tageblatt* 3/9 1898.

[24] The American historian Alon Confino, has recently demonstrated the degree to which the emnities associated with the celebration also restricted its popularity in the south-western parts of Germany. Confino's focus is on the confessional antagonisms which were tied to the celebration from the very beginning. He shows how in Württemberg, the secular experience of peaceful coexistence between Catholics and Protestants made it difficult to embrace the Sedan celebrations, which were originally introduced by anti-Catholic Protestant forces and which had had, since the *Kulturkampf* of the 1870s, an anti-Catholic undertone in most German regions. Confino, 1997. In the period of this study, the rather lukewarm attitude toward the celebration in Catholic circles was indicated by short comments during the debate of 1900 after the Franco-German military cooperation in China that year, about whether to keep the celebration or not. The newspaper of the Catholic *Zentrum* laconically stated: 'Was uns Katholiken anlangt, so würden wir der Sedanfeier, wenn sie für immer abgeschafft werden sollte, keine Thräne nachweinen. Wir haben es im "Kulturkampf" erlebt, welche Spitze der Sedanfeier gegen uns gegeben wurde. Artete dieselbe an manchen Orten doch zu einem regelrechten Hass gegen die katholiken aus.' *Germania* 25.08.1900.

uniting and an event that has never been marked by political conflict. This is, however, the lucky outcome of a process that was in fact full of friction. The 17th of May has, in the past, contained an element of both national unification and political diversity. In other words, it has not always or exclusively been a cathedral. It has also been a barricade, and it is in this respect that it resembles the French national celebration in its history. This tension between integration and political conflict has been important in giving the celebration the central position that it now occupies in Norway.

The 17th of May was and is called the nation's birthday, and the incident referred to as marking this birth was the signing of the Norwegian constitution, an event that took place on 17th May, 1814.[25] The constitution was written during the brief vacuum between the Danish defeat in the Napoleonic wars, and the new union era that started in November of the same year. The union with Denmark had been dissolved during the peace negotiations in Kiel, and Norway was technically handed over to Sweden, whose monarch, Carl Johan, had been on the winning side in the war. The months that followed were effectively used to gain the greatest possible degree of freedom in the eventual union. This task was assumed by an assembly of representatives from all of Norway's regions at the manor of Eidsvoll, north of Oslo, and resulted in the signing of the constitution. A huge painting immortalising this event still hangs in the *Storting*, the Norwegian parliament, and Falsen, the head of the assembly, is portrayed on the 1000 kroner banknote. These assembled representatives were the 'heroes of Eidsvoll' or the 'men of Eidsvoll', as they are still called, and their action is the fundamental national myth of the Kingdom of Norway. The most important role in the implementation of both the myth and its celebration has undoubtedly been played by the historian and poet Henrik Wergeland. In his work, the day of the signing of the Eidsvoll constitution marked the turning point of Norwegian history, the rebirth of the nation. It was, he claimed, 'the most special and salvationary of all the days that God had let shine over the mountains of Norway'. In entering this moral league, the

---

[25] The catalogue from the Deutsches Historisches Museum (see above) has recently dedicated an article to the 17th of May, written by Robert Bohn.

Norwegian people were 'linked to all free peoples and to those who expected similar freedom'.[26]

For its survival and success, the myth has had the immense advantage of uniting most Norwegians. It appealed to left-wing circles, finding in the constitutional heritage – the most democratic of its time – an origin and a source of inspiration. It appealed to the right-wing through its monarchism and the system of checks and balances between king and parliament. And it appealed to adherents of cultural identity by providing political instruments for the cultural or national community. This plasticity of the mythical dimension has proved to be a decisive advantage for the celebration, since all camps in Norwegian politics could agree on the value of the Eidsvoll heritage. There was no authoritarian military or bellicose dimension that could alienate liberals and left-wingers, as was the case in Germany, and there was no bloody popular revolt that could repel the Right, as had happened in France. The mythical dimension of the celebration, in short, was quite idyllic. Political struggles concerning the day usually took the form of a perpetual discussion over which political group was the true defender or heir of the Eidsvoll legacy. We may already conclude, therefore, that the starting point of the celebration, its potential to fulfil its noble mission, was rather promising, since it faced no competing national foundation myth.

How then did this affect the symbolic dimension of the celebration? The 17th of May had a national and integrative dimension that was connected to unifying rituals, but it also had a *political* dimension, and the tension, or rather the recognised and respected frontier between these dimensions is the characteristic feature of the symbolic dialogue associated with this day.[27] If we consider the time period corresponding to the other two case studies, the years from 1895 to 1905 were characterised by a transition from division to national unity. The catalyst of this transition was the relationship with Sweden, the union partner, and the discussions concerning Norway's future. In very simple terms, these discussions took place between the supporters of a moderate pro-union policy and those of a radically national policy who advocated the full dissolution of the union. The symbols used in this battle were two competing national flags. The

---

[26] Quoted by Storsveen, 1997.

[27] On the content of the celebration in this period, see the outstanding analysis by Bjørgen, 1997.

one hoisted by the left-wing, the anti-unionists and radical democrats, was referred to as the 'pure' Norwegian flag, and this is the flag that is still in use. The other was pejoratively called the 'herring salad', a particularly colourful version of the Norwegian flag that included the Swedish colours in the upper-left hand corner. This was the flag of the right-wing, and was considered to represent a compromise between national autonomy and respect for the union. From 1844, there had been an annual parade, known as the Citizens' Parade, which took place on the 17th of May. In the strain generated in the discussions between the right – and left-wing, with the latter skilfully linking the issue to a programme of extended suffrage, the parade split in two. Each of these marches was headed by the respective flag, and each pretended to be truly national and the rightful heir of the men of Eidsvoll. The discussions could sometimes be bitter and sarcastic, and the national day celebration without doubt came to reflect political divisions in Norwegian society. Hildegunn Bjørgen has adapted the old formula of Ernest Renan in characterising this aspect of the celebration: it was an annual – not a daily – plebiscite.[28] Eventually, the 'pure' flag and its defenders were to win, and in 1905 Norway withdrew from the union to become completely independent for the first time since the 14th century. After a referendum, a new royal family was imported (from Denmark) and the era of independence began.

So there was a distinct political dimension to the celebration that was directly linked to the celebration's symbolic dialogue. However, the political dimension never overshadowed the principal ritual of integration associated with the day. This ritual was not one of the many church services, nor was it one of the private celebrations that took place all over the capital in the evening; the climax of the celebration was, and still is, the children's parade. As strong as the political divisions might have been around the turn of the century, this parade, which brought together all the school children of Oslo to march along a prescribed route through the centre of the city accompanied by their school orchestras, was protected from political division. Certainly, there were parents who wanted their children to carry the national flag of their preference in the parade, but all

---

[28]   Bjørgen, 1997.

spectators, irrespective of political allegiances, agreed that the parade was a pretty sight and provided the highlight of the day.

In a comparative perspective, the importance assigned to this event made it Oslo's equivalent to the military parade in Paris. Furthermore, it was regarded as the most valuable ritual from a national-didactic perspective. It was the ritual in which the nation became a single entity, with both participants and spectators united in this national communion. As different as the two parades were – in Paris there were horse-drawn gun carriages and soldiers and officers in colourful uniforms, while in Oslo there were children from all classes, marching through the streets in their best clothes – the folkloric value was the same and, in both rituals, the fundamental sense was the consecration of the individual to the national community. It is important to realise that the children in Oslo did not stroll around in the streets nonchalantly waving their colourful flags – rather, they piously marched through the city, behind the banners of their schools. On their way to their objective, the royal castle, they passed the parliament and statues of national heroes. This was a national ritual of socialisation in which the teacher took the place of the French officers, where the school banners took the place of military standards and where children with national flags played the role of the infantry.

Comparative Remarks

In this juxtaposition of the national rituals in Paris and Oslo, we seem to see two successful variations on a common theme of national integration. Indeed, in both cases the three dialogues seem to have demonstrated the same flexibility. In celebrating the myth, the visual representation of the nation contained integrative forces that worked in several different, even opposite, directions. All the same, national unity in a European superpower with a strong militarist tradition, and in a young, small, and rather heterogeneous nation-state with no glorious military achievements or goals, had to be created along different lines.

The two rituals seem to reveal basic differences between the two nations, differences that derived from national history and that gave rise to two distinctly different national collective commitments. France, the nation of 1792, combined in the military parade and the Republican cry of '*Liberté, Egalité, Fraternité*', the defence of national territory and glory and the universalist heritage of the French

Revolution. The outcome was a cocktail of national pride, strength and international importance that was eventually to prove agreeable to most political groups in the country. The military parade became a national symbol, or rather a national communion. In Norway, the children's parade, the most integrative ritual of the national day, reflected a tendency that the Czech historian Miroslav Hroch has called the nationalism of the small nation-state, that is, a national ideology that has been formed by a period of opposition to a stronger power, and that has stylised the justness of its cause and the will to embrace its youth and innocence as its national identity.[29] In both these celebrations, however, there also seems to have been a very strong civic dimension.[30]

What then of parallels between the 17th of May and Germany's 2nd of September? There were certainly similarities, especially in the content, and one of the most important was the place accorded to Christian thought. In Norway as in Germany, the influence on the national ideology of Christianity, and Lutheranism in particular, has been significant; the national flag is, after all, undeniably a cross. There were countless church services that took place on the 17th of May in which priests praised national unity, and hymns and the national anthem were sung. There were, however, distinct differences in the instrumentalisation of Christianity. First, religion in Oslo, unlike Berlin, was not politicised. Secondly, Christian virtues and individual devotion were not seen as a *sine qua non* of Norwegian national identity by the protagonists and organisers of the celebration. The key to understanding this difference seems to be the strong civic dimension of the celebration that was present on all levels and seems to have characterised all dialogues that took place on the day; the myth, its form and its political dimension. Despite a long national tradition of conformism, the outcome was the general acceptance of

---

[29] Hroch, 1996, p. 25. Here he describes 'the auto-stylisation of "national character" into that of a peace-loving, non-aggressive nation, which would only protect what belongs to it.'

[30] The Norwegian historian Øystein Sørensen has concluded that 'civic' nationalism in Norway has had an ideological hegemony in the nation's history. He refers to this tradition as the 'French' tendency, as opposed to a an ethnic, 'German' one, adding that while these are 'ideal' types, they are useful for placing most nationalisms within a set of theoretical parametres. See Sørensen 1993/95.

plurality within the national community, with space given to both unity and diversity.

In this context, Sedan Day is an interesting and informative demonstration of the difficulties involved in an ethnic – in the sense of essentially particularistic – national ideology adapting to a changing world. The three dimensions of Sedan Day were less and less appropriate in a society characterised by rapid secularisation and the rise of liberal democratic ideologies linked to a pluralistic world. In its mythical background, the celebration was doomed to alienate opponents of a militaristic society and national project that has been realised by a 'revolution from above' rather than through popular participation. Its form was destined to disenchant democrats and non-Christians, while its political backing meant that it was eventually condemned to be regarded as a political rather than a national celebration. In its uncompromising Christian conformity it could not gather and unite, but only alienate.

Germany remained a deeply divided society until the outbreak of the World War I in 1914, when *Burgfrieden* was declared and the stress of the conflict united the community. Was this the outcome of popular militarism? This could be argued, and is certainly the opinion of many historians. For a researcher on national ideology however, it is equally evidence that there existed a national identity *beyond* that of Sedan Day, but which the celebration had been unable to capture in peace time. This identity tended to define itself through citizenship and not by the standards formulated by the supporters of the Sedan Day celebration. This was the *civic* dimension of national identity, and it was a dimension that the celebration had tended to neglect. Sedan Day demonstrates how a national celebration was capable of dividing a nation, and how deep this division could be if measures were not taken to integrate even those sceptical of the event and the myth it celebrated. The *Burgfrieden* could not hide the widespread conviction that a new, alternative Germany had to be shaped. The constitution of this new Germany was written during the World War I, but unfortunately for the German nation, the spirit of Sedan Day did not die. Its legacy of monolithic national ideology and its contempt for democratic civic traditions did not disappear.

CHAPTER 19

Remembering the Second World War in Denmark: The Impact of Politics, Ideology and Generation

Mette ZØLNER

This chapter considers the various ways in which the history of the Second World War is remembered in Denmark.[1] From the outset it is important to point out that the aim is not to clarify different phases in the development of what one might call the predominant or public memory of this period in Denmark. Instead, this chapter considers the diverse collective memories of the Second World War that have co-existed in Denmark through the 1980s and 1990s. Moreover, my analysis does not problematise the relation between these collective memories and history in the Rankian sense of '*wie es eigenlich gewesen*'.

Collective memory will be conceived of as the result of a selective process of remembering and forgetting the past, but rather than focusing on the outcome of this process, this chapter will raise the question of how to better understand the selective processes of remembering. That is, how to understand why a certain group remembers the past in one way rather than another?

[1] This is a revised version of the paper 'Danish Memories of the Second World War', which was presented at the Europe University Institute, Florence in November 1998. I am grateful for all comments which have helped substantially to improve the paper, and in particular for the comments from Professor Bo Stråth and Niels Arne Sørensen.

The French sociologist Maurice Halbwachs argued that man's memory of the past is affected by the present and that collective memory is therefore essentially a reconstruction of the past in the light of the present. Moreover, Halbwachs pointed out that a collective memory needs to be fed continuously from collective sources, and that collective memory only exists when there is a group that remembers.[2] This is the point of departure of this chapter which, with the aim of understanding the selective process of remembering, will look at how different groups remember in the light of their own present. In particular, the chapter will investigate how their generational belonging, their political ideas, and their political use of history influence the way in which they remember the Second World War.[3]

This focus on the collective memories of well-defined groups of people will also take the national context into account. That is, the social construction of a collective memory will be conceived of as a dynamic interaction between its social carriers (*i.e.* generational belonging and political mobilisation), the situational context in which the collective memory is constructed (*i.e.* competing memories of the past, deliberate attempts at influencing, and political opponents) and, finally, deep-rooted ideas/images/myths of the national community in question or, to put it another way, the constraining and enabling effects of prevailing images of a national community.[4]

Danish Identity and Memory

Why is it interesting to look at Denmark and its memories of the Second World War when studying collective memories? What are the deep-rooted images of the Danish nation, and in which way do they constrain or enable memories of the Second World War?

Comparatively, scholarly literature on Danish identity is limited, and one can observe a broad consensus concerning the way in which to describe the Danish self-image. The history of Danish nation building is the reduction of the middle-range empire in the Baltic Sea to a small nation that was remarkably homogenous in terms of

---

[2] 'Toute mémoire collective a pour support un groupe limité dans l'espace et le temps' Halbwachs, 1997 [1925], p. 137.

[3] Generational belonging, in the sense of Mannheim, 1952.

[4] Zølner, 1999.

language, culture and religion. The Danish historian Uffe Østergård has illustrated how this territorial reduction led to a national self-image of being small, innocent and human in opposition to aggressivity, nationalism, imperialism and pride, which were considered to be negative characteristics of larger neighbouring countries, and in particular of Germany.[5]

If one can speak about prevailing national memories of the Second World War, then they are, to a large extent, shaped by this self-image.[6] According to this memory, Denmark's policy of neutrality was infringed when it was occupied by Germany on 9th April 1940, and the country was therefore considered to have fallen victim of the Nazi regime. The Danish policy of collaboration until 1943 was presented as the only way for a small and neutral country to avoid total destruction. Moreover, the internal resistance movement and the exceptionally successful action to rescue the Danish Jews were sufficient reasons to be proud of domestic values and convictions as well as for being recognised as being part of the Allied effort.[7] In this prevailing memory, Nazism symbolises the evil and the bad, everything that is non-Danish. Moreover, when commemorating the end of the Second World War, Danes celebrate the liberation of

---

[5] Østergård, 1984, 1991, 1992, 1993.

[6] The celebration of the Danish liberation in 1995, and the recent book by Bryld & Warring (1998), have clearly illustrated that there is not one consensus on the Second World War in Denmark, but several that compete with one another. However, they all relate to a very particular self-image of innocence and unity.

[7] In October 1943, in the days before the German occupying forces started to arrest the Jewish population in Denmark, the majority of Jews were successfully shipped to Sweden.
In 1995, the Danish historian H. Poulsen described the Danish Occupation in the following way: 'We collaborated politically with the occupying power, achieved conditions that, in comparison to other countries which were occupied by Germany, were good and relatively free. Then we got a resistance movement at half price and, finally, without ever being involved in the war, we were accepted as having fought on the side of the Allies. This was the result of a strange relationship between the occupying power, the Danish government, and the resistance.' ('Vi samarbejdede politisk med besættelsesmagten, fik først de bedste og frieste levevilkår i det besatte Europa, dernæst en modstandsbevægelse til halv pris og blev til slut allieret uden at komme i krig. Det blev det samlede facit af et ejendommeligt sam – og modspil mellem de tre hovedkræfter: besættelsesmagten, den danske stat og modstandsbevægelsen'. Poulsen, 1995, p. 17.

Denmark (5th May, 1945) rather than the victory over Nazism.[8] Bryld and Warring argue that the prevailing public memory of the occupation has been co-ordinated by a national patriotic interpretation. Like the political and economic elites that collaborated with the occupying forces in France, Belgium and Holland, the Danish elites desperately needed a 'patriotic memory' with which to unite their nation in the subsequent Cold War period. Thus Danish memory downplayed the division between the politicians and the emerging resistance in the first years of the occupation (that is, in the period of political collaboration between 1940 and 1943), while its focal point became the resistance against the Germans, whether it was 'passive', in the form of the collaboration government, or 'active'. Although the resistance movement tried to challenge this memory in the post-war years, it gained growing consensus and, during the 1960s and 1970s 'it became increasingly difficult to identify elements of dissent, at least in the public discourse of commemoration'.[9]

Yet, the specificity of the Danish example is less the content of this memory than the fact that it has remained almost unchallenged. Or rather, despite the fact that the work of several scholars has moderated the deeds of the Danes by presenting less glorious sides of Danish activities during the war, the prevailing memory remains, to a surprising degree, shaped by the image of Denmark as small, innocent and human, whether this is the self-image of the Danes or the image of 'foreigners' from the 'outside'.[10]

---

[8] Pedersen, 1995. Pedersen has argued that despite a heated public debate there was a relative consensus on celebrating the 50th anniversary of the Second World War as a national event, namely as the liberation of Denmark from the German occupying forces. Instead, the public debate on the issue was directed at the way in which to do so, and concentrated particularly on the 'Sculpture for Peace 1995' (Fredsskuptur 1995), which consisted of a laser beam that, on the evening of 4th May (the day of the liberation message) was to be projected along the coast of Jutland and across the Danish-German border.

[9] Bryld & Warring, 1998, p. 555.

[10] Gammelgaard, 1981; Kreth & Mogensen, 1995; H. U. Petersen, 1987 and 1993; Sjöberg, 1993; Warring, 1994. According to Bryld & Warring, 1998, p. 558, the 'fruits of research had a very limited impact upon the content or form of public commemoration. Thus the narrative of national unity is maintained still today in public commemorations and in the Liberation Museum which is supported by the State'.

Two examples can briefly illustrate this point. On the occasion of the 50th anniversary of the end of the Second World War, an exhibition was held at the University of Pennsylvania to commemorate the rescue of the Jews. In this action, which took place in October 1943, 7,000 Jews escaped by ship from occupied Denmark to neutral Sweden.[11] The exhibition was entitled 'Resistance and Rescue: Denmark's response to the Holocaust', and the former Danish Minster for Foreign Affairs, Uffe Ellemann-Jensen, delivered a lecture on the question 'Is History Repeating Itself in the New Europe? How do we ensure freedom and security for all?' These titles, and the way in which the exhibition was presented on the Internet indicated that the image of Denmark abroad remained that of the small, innocent and human nation.[12] Denmark was presented as an example of how to actively fight racial discrimination and how to protect fellow citizens against persecution. Thus, next to the photos of Gilleleje, a small, idyllic and peaceful fishing harbour north of Copenhagen where the community was said to have 'traditionally' proven their 'strong sense of solidarity', one can read the following text:

> [the photographer Judy Ellis Glickman] evokes the people and the scenes involved in this dangerous rescue operation. In 1943, the Danish people conspired against their Nazi occupiers in support of their fellow citizens and other Jewish refugees within their borders. Large numbers of the persecuted population were ferried across the North Sea to safe havens in Sweden.

Thus, Denmark and the Danish way of confronting Nazism were being recalled as an example of how Nazism was resisted in a peaceful and human way. Conversely, what seems to have been forgotten were the conditions that had rendered the Danish rescue action so successful; the particular nature of the peaceful occupation of Denmark, the geographical proximity of the neutral Sweden, and the relatively small number of Jews.[13] Moreover, this glorious memory

---

[11] The exhibition was held from 19th August to 1st October, 1995, and it was co-organised by the University of Pennsylvania, the 'Thanks to Scandinavia Foundation', and the 'Interfaith Council on the Holocaust'.

[12] See www. upenn. edu/ARG/archive/R&R2. html

[13] In their analysis of the rescue action in October 1943, Kreth & Mogensen, 1995, point to a number of elements that help to explain its success. Before 1st October 1943, the German Chief Officer leaked information on the planned action to the Danish authorities who in turn warned the Jewish minority. Moreover, after that

overlooks the fact that, in the 1930s, the restrictive refugee policy of Denmark had discouraged, if not physically prevented, Jews and other persecuted groups from seeking protection from Nazism in Denmark.[14] Whereas the 'human' rescue action had saved the lives of fellow citizens in 1943, the Danish refugee policy had failed to shelter the refugees fleeing Hitler in the 1930s. This seems, however, to have been forgotten by the exhibition, which only commemorated the 'human' element of the Danish response to the Holocaust.

This image of being small, innocent and human when confronting Nazism also prevails within Denmark.[15] This was illustrated by the fact that, in 1998, the Danish company F. L. Smidt claimed reimbursement for the loss of an enterprise in Estland, which had been nationalised at the end of the Second World War by the Soviet Union. This firm had benefited from forced labour from concentration camp prisoners during the war, but this fact did not prevent the Danish Minister for Foreign Affairs from raising the issue of F. L. Smidt's claim in Estland. This was particularly surprising since, at the same time elsewhere in Europe, survivors from concentration camps and their heirs were claiming indemnities from life insurance companies and Swiss banks with some degree of success. The fact that the victims were remembered and compensated elsewhere in Europe did not discourage F. L. Smidt and the Danish Ministry for Foreign Affairs from jointly presenting their claims to the Estonian authorities.

This raises the question of why the Danish memory was so much out of touch with what happened elsewhere in Europe. My argument

---

date the occupying forces did not only abstain from stopping the fishing boats ferrying the refugees to Sweden, but they also accepted the lenient way in which the Danish authorities judged those who were arrested for assisting the Jews. Thus, some Danes were likely to have known that they were not risking their lives and, moreover, since the Danish police did not intervene, and in some cases even actively assisted the Jews, the rescue action appeared to be legal in the eyes of many Danes. In addition, fishermen and others, who ferried the refugees to Sweden, did not do so free of charge. Finally, by Autumn 1943, the unpopularity of the occupying power had increased, the collaboration policy had ended, and by this date it was clear that Sweden was ready to receive the refugees.

[14] H. U. Petersen, 1987 and 1993; Sjöberg, 1993.

[15] This image has also shaped the way in which colonial history was written. Olwig Fog, 1994, and Brimnes, 1992, brilliantly show that although European history was rewritten in the perspective of decolonisation, this happened comparatively late in Denmark.

is that one element that can help us to understand this was the Danish self-image, which has coined a memory that is, to a large extent, positive. Another factor is that this memory had not been challenged by the victims of the war as had happened, for example, in France where Jewish associations sought justice throughout the 1980s and 1990s.

Despite this predominantly positive memory, there were differing memories of the Second World War in Denmark in the 1980s and 1990s. If one looks at the way in which the history of the war is used in the Danish debate on immigration and refugees, the Danish case becomes particularly interesting, especially when considered in comparison to that of France for example. Instead of impeding discourses against immigration, the Danish memory of the Second World War was actively used by groups that fought to make Danish immigration and refugee policy more restrictive. In the remainder of this chapter, I will analyse two grassroots associations, New Era and the Danish Association, as examples of how the Danish history of the Second World War was used as arguments against Danish refugee and immigration policy.[16] Conversely, discourses in favour of protecting the rights of immigrants and refugees refrained from using the Danish history of the Second World War. For example, the Danish rescue of the Jews was not used in the way in which it was in the exhibition at the University of Pennsylvania discussed above, nor was the restrictive refugee policy in the late 1930s evoked as an example of how the lack of protection for persecuted people could have disastrous human consequences. The Young Anarchists will be analysed as an example of this position.[17]

Before analysing what these groups remembered and how they used the Danish history of the Second World War, I will stress the fact that these groups were situated outside established political parties and organisations, and neither they, nor their members were in any way representative in Denmark, nor are they likely to become so. I will therefore analyse them as particularly interesting examples of how collective memories of the Second World War emerged and were used

---

[16] This is the author's translation of 'Tidehverv' and 'Den Danske Forening'. Translations of quotations from books or interviews have likewise been made by the author.

[17] This is the author's translation of 'De Autonome'.

in the political debate on immigration and Danish identity in the 1980s and 1990s.

New Era and the Danish Association: Remembering the Danes' Fight for National Independence

Both the Danish Association and New Era disputed prevailing ideas on immigration and national identity, criticising them for presenting non-Danish views. New Era had originally emerged as a reaction against a theological interpretation in the 1920s.[18] When, however, Søren Krarup took over the leadership of this association in 1988, he used the journal of New Era in his political fight to restrict the legislation on immigration and refugees and to preserve Danish 'national identity'.[19] Krarup had initiated this political fight in autumn 1986 when he founded the 'Committee against the Refugee Law' *(Komiteen imod Flygtningeloven)*. The Danish Association, founded in 1987 by a group of journalists inspired by Krarup's writings, had a similar aim. Subsequently, Krarup and his supporters became directly involved in the activities of the Danish Association.

The activities of New Era and the Danish Association were mainly informative. They claimed that the political establishment concealed the real number of foreigners in Denmark and the implications of their presence. Their objective was to inform the Danish people about the 'real' situation, which represented a danger for the nation. These associations held that the Danish people widely shared their opinions. Furthermore, these information activities were aimed at legitimising national feelings, since they claimed that the political establishment delegitimized such feelings by equating national sentiments with racism. Thus, until the people could once again express their opinion, New Era and the Danish Association saw their role as that of speaking on behalf of the 'silent majority' *(det tavse flertal)*. This brief description illustrates that these associations considered Denmark to be governed by a political establishment that did not respect the legitimate desire of the people to remain Danish and, moreover, ac-

---

[18] New Era consists of a journal and an annual summer meeting. Membership is not possible, and one can only subscribe to their journal. New Era rejects being called a 'movement' or an 'association'. Nevertheless, for convenience, I will refer to New Era as an 'association'.

[19] Rydal, 1988; Bramming, 1993; Hageneier, 1989; Møllenbach Larsen, 1982.

cused them of being racist. This conception of Denmark is reflected in the associations' memory of the Danish history of the Second World War. In 1995, the President of the Danish Association, Ole Hasselbalch, wrote a booklet entitled *The Fight of Opinions (Opinionskampen 1933-45)*, which argued that in the 1930s indifference and the belief in peace in western democracies constituted indirect support for Nazism. This was also claimed to be the result of Danish policy, particularly during the first years of the German occupation of Denmark. According to Hasselbalch, the Danish political elites actively supported Nazism through their policy of non-confrontation and peace. Moreover, this elite betrayed the Danish population twice; first by collaborating with the occupying forces, and secondly, at the end of the war, by penalising those who, encouraged by the government, had enrolled in the *Frikorps Danmark* to fight on the side of Germany. Hasselbalch's presentation summed up the memory which one finds in the journals of the Danish Association and New Era. It is also the memory found in the writings of Krarup who explicitly expressed it in the following way:

> In reality, the Resistance was first of all a fight against the policy of collaboration – against the national defeatism and the politicians' readiness to let everything go, even that which can never be lost. [...] The Resistance was faithful to Danish history. The politicians failed to be so.[20]

The Second World War was recalled as a fight to preserve Danish sovereignty and identity when the political establishment had betrayed the Danish people. The crimes of Nazism, and the Holocaust in particular, are hardly mentioned, nor is the Danish rescue of the Jews in October 1943. Only the German refugees in the post-war period are mentioned by Krarup, who presents the Danish reception of these refugees as an example of a good 'refugee policy', since their stay was temporary.[21] Why did New Era and the Danish Association recall the occupation of Denmark during the war years when campaigning

---

[20] Krarup, 1998, pp. 47-51, 'Modstandskampen havde jo i virkeligheden i første række været en kamp imod samarbejdspolitikken – imod den nationale selvopgivelse, imod defaitismen og politikernes redebonhed til at sælge alt, selv det mest umistelige, for at slippe nemt om ved tilværelsen [...] Modstands-bevægelsen havde været tro mod Danmarks historie. Politikerne havde svigtet den'.

[21] Krarup, 1998.

against refugee policy in the 1980s and 1990s? In his introduction to 'The Fight of Opinions', Hasselbalch gave the following reason:

> At a time when the generation which is to be thanked for the happy ending 50 years ago is about to disappear, with the result that the national memory is reduced to the official writing of history, we need to retain what actually happened. The story is therefore told to the young people today. They belong to a generation that will have to bear the burden of the 'multiethnic' experiment that is forced upon us, but they are being presented with a version of the Second World War that aims at blurring the reality and ensuring that also they comply.[22]

In other words, Hasselbalch held that remembering the past was a way to avoid repetition, that is, to prevent similar and even more 'irremediable catastrophes' than the German occupation in 1940 from happening. In journals and writings the Danish Association explicitly compared the internal resistance movement during the war with the fight against refugee and immigration policy in the 1980s and 1990s. The historical link to the resistance fighters was established by stressing the presence of several former resistance fighters within the New Era and the Danish Association. Krarup, for example, quoted the well-known resistance fighter Toldstrup as having said, 'The occupation taught me how important it is that the old generation supports the young one. You can count on me.'[23] The journal of the Danish Association, *'Danskeren'*, printed several interviews with resistance fighters and the president, Hasselbalch, wrote the following about the old people who were members or supporters of the association:

> Old people are often better. People who in the war came to experience torture during interrogation by the GESTAPO know the importance of Danish culture. The old are stable and they are not tempted by well-

---

22 'På et tidspunkt, hvor den genertaion, der var årsag til, at det for 50 år siden endte godt, er ved at forsvinde, så at kun det taknemmelige papir står tilbage som grundlag for den folkelige erindring, er der derfor anledning til at fastholde, hvad der skete. Fortællingen er rettet til de unge i dag – altså den generation, der kommer til at bære byrden ved det 'multietniske' eksperiment, vi nu kastes ud i, men som overdænges med en version af begivenhederne før og under 2. verdenskrig, som er indrettet på at tilsløre virkeligheden og få også dem til at affinde sig'. Hasselbalch, 1995.

23 'Jeg ved fra besættelsen hvad det betyder, at de ældre bakker de yngre op. Du kan regne med mig' Krarup, 1987, p. 29.

spoken people. Moreover, they are not afraid that humanitarian people will speak badly of them.[24]

The analogy with the resistance movement was also constructed through the use of vocabulary. When publishing its report on its activities during the first five years of its existence, the Danish Association used the title 'The Five Cruel Years', immediately establishing associations with the German occupation from 1940 to 1945.[25] The fund that partly financed the activities of the Danish Association was named, 'The Danish Fund of 5th May 1995', commemorating the 50th anniversary of Danish liberation.[26] In his book *The Will to Resist* (*'Viljen til modstand'*), Hasselbalch described the Danish Association as consisting of a growing number of people who, with the support of the population, acted in secret against the establishment, which he labelled the 'national betrayers' (*landsforræderne*). The anti-racists associated with the Young Anarchists are labelled 'red Nazis' (*rødnazisterne*), while their violent attempt to block the meetings of the Danish Association was compared with the situation in Germany during the 1920s:

> Suddenly, they were there, a group of around thirty [...]. The atmosphere, the brutality, the rude shouts and the obscenity reminded us of the horrors of the past. We were faced with brutal violence. And, just as in the 1920s in Germany, the police did not have the force to intervene. Therefore, we have to warn our members [...]. Though the criminals pretend to be 'anti-racists', their violence reveals their true nature. The historical similarities are evident.[27]

---

[24] 'Gamle jerntanter er ofte bedst. Folk, der under krigen prøvede at blive hængt op med hovedet nedad i GESTAPO's afhøringslokaler, er klar over, hvad dansk kultur er [...] De gamle er vandtætte og falder ikke i fristelse eller for veltalende folk. De gamle er heller ikke bange for, hvad menneskevenlige politikere siger om dem' Hasselbalch, 1990, p. 23.

[25] 'De Fem forbandede år'; Danskeren, no. 5, 1992.

[26] 'Den Danske Forenings styrelse administrerer Danmarksfonden af 5. Maj 1995, der er en kampfond, hvis midler anvendes i overensstemmeles med DDF's formålsbestemmelse til at sikre danskernes ret til en tilværelse på egne præmisser her i landet. Fonden er opbygget på grundlag af testamentariske og andre gaver'. Danskeren, 1995.

[27] 'Pludselig stod de der, en flok, der var vel 30. [...] Hele stemningen, råheden, korpsånden, de gjaldende råb og de vulgære slagord bragte mindelser frem om fortidens rædsler. Vi står over for den afstumpede bandevold. Og politiet magter

Krarup, the president of New Era, made similar analogies in his books:

Soon we felt as if it was a meeting of the Danish Freedom Council *(Frihedsrådet)*. It was the persecution by the political establishment and by the media that made us feel illegal in a way that reminded us of life during the occupation. I did not colour my hair, nor did I wear sunglasses when I left Seem [the town in which he lives] in the direction of Fyn, but we had kept quiet about the meeting and we arrived discretely from east, north and west.[28]
Anton Jensen came from Skive. He became a main figure in the Resistance. My parents worked with him in the last years of the occupation, and I came to know him in the 1980s when we met in another resistance struggle.[29]

Presenting themselves as the 'new resistance fighters' served several objectives. The most obvious was that the resistance fighters, who initially had been few and whose actions had been rejected by the Danish authorities, eventually achieved national glory for having fought for Denmark and freedom. From this comparison it followed that, like the first resistance fighters, the members of the Danish Association and the circle around New Era were the first among the Danish people to understand the danger and oppose it. In other words, just as the resistance fighters were rejected by the establishment and treated like criminals before finally gaining respect and glory, the combatants against immigration would have to endure rejection before being recognised for their work. And once again, it would be the 'people' who would have to force the establishment to change policy. Thus, the self-image of these groups as the new resistance promised a

---

tilsyneladende ikke at gribe ind, som i det demokratiske Tyskland i tyverne. Derfor advarer vi vore medlemmer. [...] For selv om bøllerne kalder sig "anti-racister", taler volden sit tydelige sprog. De historiske ligheder springer i øjnene'. Danskeren, no. 1, 1990, p. 4.

[28] 'Vi følte det snart som om "Frihedsrådet" holdt møde. Den forfølgelse, vi var ude for fra det officielle Danmarks side, påtvang os en følelse af illegalitet, der ledte tanken hen på tilværelsen under besættelsen. Jeg farvede ikke mit hår og iførte mig ikke solbriller, da jeg kørte fra Seem ad hovedvej 1 over den ny Lillebæltsbro til Fyn, men vi havde tiet med, hvor vi trådte sammen, og ankom i al ubemærkethed fra øst, nord og vest til mødestedet', Krarup, 1987, p. 59.

[29] 'Toldassistent Anton Jensen i Skive. Han blev en hovedskikkelse i modstands-kampen. Mine forældre arbejdede sammen med ham i besættelsens sidste år, og selv kom jeg til at opleve ham i 1980'erne, da vi mødtes i en anden modstands-kamp'. Krarup, 1998, p. 41.

glorious future, which made it easier to cope with their present marginalisation. Furthermore, to present themselves as the inheritors of the resistance served to shelter them from accusations of racism and against any comparison with Nazism that ideas of 'national sentiments' might have provoked in post-war Denmark.[30] Finally, the resistance also symbolised positive national feelings and remembering it contributed to legitimise these feelings.

We can therefore conclude that the two associations recalled the Second World War in a way that justified their own ideas and activities. Remembrance appears to have been deliberately guided by their political aim of legitimising anti-immigrant ideas and national sentiment. This raises the question of whether the only reason New Era and the Danish Association recalled the Second World War was that they could put it to use in their favour? In other words, why did they use history at all in a political debate in the 1980s and 1990s? An examination of their political convictions as well as their generational belonging will help us to answer this question.

The members of both associations are concerned with Denmark and national identity. Moreover, in several interviews with the author, leading figures even explicitly declared themselves to be nationalist. They are conservative, in the sense that they value the preservation of tradition and define their main opponent to be the '68 generation, which in fact belongs to the same age-group as the leading members of New Era and the Danish Association. From their perspective, the '68 generation symbolises the decline of both family values and respect for national traditions and culture.[31] The fact that the leading members of the two associations can generally be described as conservative and nationalist makes their use of the Second World War understandable, because, from their perspective, the war represents the last legitimate national struggle.

In addition, when looking at the generational belonging of the founders and leading figures in the two associations, one observes that they belong to two generations that have autobiographical memories

---

[30]   The fact that New Era and the Danish Association tend to criticise the Danish political establishment, rather than blaming the refugees and immigrants explicitly, is also a way of circumventing accusations of racism.

[31]   Krarup, 1998; several interviewees.

of the occupation or of the immediate post-war years.[32] Some of the founding members belonged to a generation that had actually participated in the resistance, and indeed, some had participated personally in the movement. Among these former resistance fighters one finds, for example, W. Krarup and Toldstrup, both of whom had belonged to the fraction within the resistance that was particularly nationalist and conservative and that formed a network that remained in place for several decades after the liberation.[33] They had mobilised as much against the 'co-operation government' as against the German occupying forces, on the basis that it was 'morally' wrong of the former to have attempted to protect the population from the consequences of the war.[34] On the basis of available sources it has not been possible to determine whether these former resistance fighters participated actively in the work of the associations or whether they served only to consolidate the image of these associations as a new resistance.

Members from the second generation took over the leadership of the Danish Association and New Era in the late 1980s. They had been born in 1930s and early 1940s and they can be characterised as 'children' of the Second World War, in the sense that they were children either during the occupation or in the years immediately after.[35] Though they were too young to have participated in war-time activities, their autobiographical memory is likely to retain the talk of parents and family. This was particularly the case for the leading members of New Era, including S. Krarup and his cousin Langballe, whose parents were former resistance fighters. Krarup's parents had been active in the national conservative branch of the Resistance and had been forced to go into hiding in December 1944. At the time Krarup was still a young child (he was born in 1937) and was unaware of the activities of his parents:

> [when describing how British pilots were hidden in one part of the house while his parents had to house German soldiers in the other part.] My parents had to make sure that they did not meet. The British pilots could only come out at night. We were only children and we never met them

---

[32] Halbwachs, 1987.

[33] Bjørgo, 1994, pp. 3-34.

[34] Bramming, 1993, p. 64.

[35] Søren Krarup, (1938), his cousin Langballe (1939), and Niels Carl Lilleør (1935). Around the same age are Krarup's sister Majken Frost, his brother Sten Krarup, and Sten O. B. Vedstesen.

and we got to know nothing about it. This was probably prudent, since we were friends with the old German soldiers, who showed us pictures of their children [...].[36]

The occupation has been a recurrent theme in Krarup's writings from his first book published in 1960 to his latest book from 1998.[37] In this last book, he acknowledged the fundamental role that the Second World War had played for his understanding of politics. Indeed, whether he is speaking about the Denmark joining the EC in 1973, the '68 generation, or the reforms of the educational programmes in the 1970s, he makes comparisons with the occupation of Denmark and refers to what he considers to have been the main problem at the time; the elite's lack of understanding of, and respect for, the Danish people.

The available documentation cannot confirm whether the second generation of the Danish Association had similar personal memories, but they certainly belonged to the same age group. The President of the Danish Association, Ole Hasselbalch, was born in 1944 and, like Krarup, he used the division between the 'people' and the 'elite' to account for a multitude of political events and debates since the Second World War.

In this discussion I have referred to the fact that the members of these associations have claimed to have been unfairly accused of Nazism because of their nationalism and their position in the debate on immigration. One member described this in the following way:

Well, it is the fear of being accused of racism. It is the 'opinion Mafia' represented by the press which has meant that any criticism of foreigners [...] if you speak negatively about foreigners or simply about a foreign culture, then you are immediately considered to be a racist and a horrible nationalist. Well, being nationalist today almost implies being Nazi. This is the way the debate is in Denmark today. The debate is not free. People are whispering. Even those who completely agree with me are whisper-

---

[36] '[...] det gjaldt for mine forældre om at holde tungen lige i munden og de forskellige kategorier adskilt. De engelske flyvere måtte kun vise sig om natten. Vi børn så dem aldrig og fik intet at vide, hvad der sikkert var godt, for vi var venner med de gamle tyske soldater, som viste os billeder af deres børn, og som vi udvekslede påskeæg med'. Krarup, 1998, p. 43.

[37] Harald Jensen og hans tid, 1960, Tres års Danmarkshistorie. I min levetid, 1998.

ing. They know that many share their opinions, but they don't say it loudly...[38]

I will not question whether this description corresponds to the way in which members of these organisations were actually treated by the Danish public. Rather, I will examine one group among their opponents, the Young Anarchists, who have unambiguously accused the Danish Association of being Nazi and fascist. The aim is to demonstrate that a certain generational belonging and political conviction might result in no or hardly any memory of the Danish history of the Second World War.

Young Anarchists:
Remembering the War against Nazism

The Autonomous Movement emerged from the vast and diverse BZ movement that, from 1981 to 1986, occupied empty houses that had been earmarked for demolition as a part of the renovation of old residential districts in Copenhagen. Once their demands for 'youth houses' had been partially satisfied their activism declined, however, in 1991, a demonstration against racism and neo-Nazism brought together the Young Anarchists in a new fight.

In this new context, the principal activity of the Young Anarchists was to prevent groups such as the Danish Association and neo-Nazi splinter groups from exercising their freedom of expression. To do so, the Young Anarchist did not evoke anti-racist legislation as other organisations did, but simply obstructed their opponents' political meetings by making noise or throwing stones, rotten eggs, and toma-toes at the participants. Their justification for using these 'violent' means was that they considered it impossible to tolerate ideologies that express hatred and intolerance. What the Young Anarchists retained from the Second World War was precisely the fact that 'violence' was used to fight Nazism, arguing that, 'Today nobody would dream of questioning the Danish resistance fighters' right to do what they did. But during the occupation the newspapers accused them of being criminals and terrorists.'[39]

---

[38] Author's interview with a member of the Danish Association, September 1996.

[39] '[when justifying their use of violence] Der er heller ingen i dag, der kunne drømme om at sætte spørgsmålstegn ved den danske modstandsbevægelses ret til at gøre,

Just as New Era and the Danish Association remembered the Second World War in order to justify their own disputed points of view, the Young Anarchists evoked events that legitimised their own use of violence. However, the above quotation is one of the rare references to the Danish history of the Second World War that one finds in their writings. Although the Young Anarchists persistently used the terms Nazism and fascism, they did so without referring to the historical context of these ideologies. Consequently, in their discourse Nazism became decoupled from its history and was used instead to symbolise opinions which the Young Anarchist refuted. According to an illustration in their journal, reproduced below (fig. 5), these opinions were held by the main political parties (the Progress Party, Danish People's Party, Liberals, Conservatives, Social Democrats and Radicals) and by the major newspapers *(Jyllandsposten, Ekstra-Bladet* and *BT)* and television stations. To greater or lesser degrees, they were all considered to be Nazi.

---

som de gjorde. Men under besættelsen kaldte aviserne dem ballademagere, terrorister og voldsmænd' De Autonome 1994, p. 44.

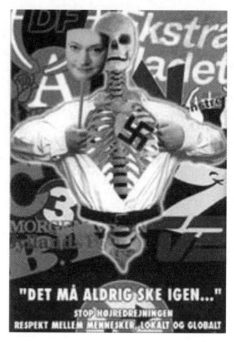

Fig. 5 – '"Never Let it Happen Again..." Stop the right turn. Respect for all people, locally and globally', Propaganda, no 11, Winter 1997/98.

This raises the question of why the Young Anarchists did not go beyond a symbolic use of Nazi references that merely served to discredit their opponents as being evil and bad. Why did they simply not refute the historical arguments of their opponents, and why did they themselves not use historical examples more explicitly to argue for protecting the rights of immigrants and refugees, by pointing to, for example, the disastrous human consequences of the restrictive Danish refugee policy in the 1930s?

A first element in understanding the lack of the use of history is found in the following answer to the direct question of what the Second World War signified for this participant in the Young Anarchists:

Well, for me the Second World War was first of all Fascist, [...]. But once I heard a skinhead saying that if he had lived during the Second World War he would probably have become a resistance fighter, because he wanted to preserve Denmark the way it was. But I do not think that one should in all circumstances fight for Denmark. One would of course fight against the Second World War and the ideas which Hitler represented [...], But at that time, the resistance was more than anything nationalist. [...] Well, for me the words associated with the Second World War are imperialism and nationalism.[40]

Thus, rather than a fight against Nazism, the Young Anarchists remember the resistance as a fight for the preservation of Denmark. They do not think that one should have fought a national fight then any more than one should now, when this has become the fight of their political opponents. Moreover, they consider nationality to be of little significance, and even to be negative. National belonging is arbitrary and meaningless, and they feel they have more in common with young people in other countries who share their own political convictions than with Danes who do not.[41] For example, in their writings there are hardly any references to Danish events or political groups, but rather there are references to those with whom they identify, such as the Bader Meinhof group, liberation movements against capitalism and imperialism in the developing world, and the BZ movements in Germany and Holland. They define their activities as being part of an 'international riot'.[42]It is not, however, only Denmark and its history that are almost absent in their discourse, but history and tradition in general. For example, although they are declared anarchists, they never refer to the origins of anarchism or to its historical development. Rather than the past, it is the future that appears to be important:

> Well history, I don't know, I think that the Vikings were rather interesting, but it is not because I have anything in common with Vikings. How can one have anything in common with people who lived before oneself. So, I suppose that I look a bit more into the future than to the past.[43]

Considering nationality and history to be irrelevant, the Young Anarchists are little inclined to look back or even to consider the historically-grounded arguments of their opponents. Moreover, they

---

[40] Interview with the author, June 1996.

[41] De Autonome 1994.

[42] 'internationalt oprør', De Autonome 1994, p. 16.

[43] Interview with the author, June 1996.

define their movement by its drive to construct a *'new* way of life'. They claim to have no model of reference, either ideological or historical, which they want to apply or promote, preferring to believe that each individual has the right to set the principles for his or her own life and that no one has the right to decide for others:

> We always stress that we have no perfect solution. We do not have any plan in front of us that tells us how things should be. And it would also be frightening if we had. The idea in all this is that everybody will participate in defining the principles.[44]

Certain elements, however, indicate that the absence of history is not only explained by their ideological conviction but also by a limited knowledge of Danish culture and of history in general. When asked whether they sang when demonstrating, an interviewee declared that some activists did indeed insist upon singing but that she did not understand why.[45] Moreover, the following account illustrates that, when they wished to sing at a demonstration against the presence of Nazi organisations in Denmark in 1994, they did not know one of the most familiar Danish songs: 'Then the debate was opened when the chairman from the Young Anarchists asked for a "singer who could lead *It has Recently Rained* because we would like to sing it, but we don't know it ourselves"'.[46] Unfortunately, the documentation does not indicate whether the Young Anarchists had in mind the traditional words to the song or those written by Ottosen in 1880 as an encouragement to the Danes who had lived under German rule since the defeat in 1864. The latter version, which praised the survival of Danish culture and belonging despite German repression, became a theme, an *opmuntrende samlingsmærke*, for the Danish resistance during the occupation.[47] It would have been interesting to know whether the Young Anarchists knew about the two different versions of the song and in particular if they had been aware of the significance of this melody during the Second World War. If they did, one may assume that they chose it specifically as a symbol of their fight against

---

[44] Interview with the author, September 1996.

[45] Interview with the author, June 1996.

[46] 'Så var det ordet blev givet frit – efter at ordstyren fra De Autonome havde efterlyst 'en sangerinde, der kan synge for til denne her "Det har nylig regnet" for den vil vi altså godt synge, men vi kan ikke selv' (Kasthol, C. in an article entitled 'Når gaden bestemmer' ('When the Street Decides'). Politiken, 10 October, 1994.

[47] Borup Jensen, 1992, p. 356.

Nazism, but since they did not know the words, it might be assumed that they were not aware of the strong national feelings which they expressed, feelings which, in any case, the Young Anarchists rejected.

On the basis of their age, one can assume that the Young Anarchists' schooling is likely to have provided them with a less thorough socialisation into Danish history and tradition than previous generations. Attending primary school (that is, from age seven to 16) in the 1970s and early 1980s, they had followed the modified school programme in which 'knowledge' and 'chronological history tea-ching' were downplayed and the main priority was given to 'learning how to learn'. Bryld and Warring have noted that, unlike public com-memorations, some school books published from between 1984 and 1993 incorporated insights derived from research in the 1970s. As a result, these newer school books gave a more nuanced and critical description of the occupation than earlier books had done. However, Bryld and Warring conclude that, 'it is difficult to estimate the significance of these changes because history teaching in the curri-culum for primary schools was quantitatively reduced during the same period'.[48] Additionally, due to the age of the members one may assume that, unlike the school days of former generations, those of the Young Anarchists did not start with singing a selection from the Danish song treasury, nor did they learn songs by heart.

Finally, in the Denmark of the 1970s and early 1980s in which they grew up, the occupation was no longer a 'common experience', and the celebration of the national liberation on 5th May enjoyed scarcely any popular support. In his article on the history of the com-memoration of liberation day, the Danish historian N.A. Sørensen argues that by the 1960s attitudes to the commemoration already indicated that the occupation was no longer a common experience and that the memory had not been transmitted to new generations for whom 1940-5 represented a chapter of history that had little, if any, significance for the present. For the youth of the late 1960s and early 1970s, the resistance no longer symbolised the fight for freedom, rather it was the Vietnam War that symbolised this fight and USA that infringed freedom.[49]

---

[48]   Bryld and Warring 1998, p. 558.

[49]   Sørensen, 1995.

This short analysis of the Young Anarchists, their ideological convictions and their generational belonging indicates a number of points. First, unlike their opponents, they do not consider national belonging and the past to be of any importance and they are consequently less inclined to make political use of the national history. Secondly, they grew up in a country in which the memory of the occupation was growing weak and, unlike their opponents, there is nothing to indicate that the Young Anarchists had learnt about the occupation through their parents or grandparents. In other words, the occupation of Denmark is likely to be a chapter of history which, due to school reforms, they were taught less thoroughly than their parents and in less patriotic terms.

Conclusion

This analysis of two memories of the Second World War and of their social carriers can contribute to our understanding of why different groups of people remember the past in different ways.

In the discourse of the Young Anarchists as well as in that of the Danish Association and New Era, the prevailing national image of Nazism was as non-Danish. Both groups used this image to discredit the political establishment and to show that the opinions of their political opponents were bad, evil and unworthy of discussion. They therefore apply elements of the prevailing national memory even as they criticise it. Specifically, the Danish Association and New Era challenge the memory of national unity by arguing that during the occupation the political establishment had directly and indirectly supported Nazism. On their side, the Young Anarchists reject the history of the occupation as being 'nationalist'. In other words, both sides use the prevailing national memory selectively, remembering the 'history' that supports their political arguments. Thus, whereas the Danish Association and New Era evoke the first years of the occupation to illustrate that 'elites had always collaborated with foreigners against the wish of the people', the Young Anarchists retain that Nazism justified the use of violent means.

The analysis also points to the fact that political ideology and the instrumental use of history are not sufficient in themselves to understand the way the Second World War has been remembered, since it leaves open the question of why Young Anarchists did not evoke historical events that could have supported their anti-racist fight, and why New Era and the Danish Association picked the Second World War rather than another period of Danish history. In this chapter I have argued that elements such as generational belonging and political convictions were determinant in shaping what the groups remembered, if they remembered at all. The fact that members of the Danish Association and New Era belonged to the war generation or the immediate post-war generation implied that they had autobiographical memories of the period, and consequently the Second World War was likely to be present in their mind in a different way than other events in Danish history. In contrast, belonging to a post-'68 generation, the Second World War was unlikely to represent any personal memories for the Young Anarchists. In addition, we may assume that the Young Anarchists had less extensive knowledge of history in general and that, in any case, they were little inclined to turn to history due to their political conviction that the present and the future were of more importance. Conversely, being nationalists and conservatives, history and national traditions were essential for the leading members of the Danish Association and New Era.

CHAPTER 20

Poverty, Neutrality and Welfare: Three Key Concepts in the Modern Foundation Myth of Sweden

Bo Stråth

Collective memory and collective oblivion are shaped in the framework of a mythic matrix, or, to use Hayden White's term, by a plot.[1] But the reverse is also the case; myth constructs collective memory and oblivion. Memory and myth are mutually reinforcing entities. The plot, within the framework of which emerge feelings of belonging and shared destiny, is made up of ideas of primordiality, sacrality (in either religious or in 'secularised' versions) and civility (subjectivity and citizenship in a sphere outside the state). The sociologist Shmuel Eisenstadt sees the variety in modernity (what he calls 'multiple modernities') as an expression of different sets of relationships between these three elements.[2] The aim of this chapter is to investigate how these elements – primordiality, sacrality and civility – interacted to form the plot in the case of Sweden.

In the 17th century, the plot of the Swedish self-image invoked a glorious past and Lutheran Protestantism (Gustavus Adolphus was depicted as the Nordic Lion battling against papism). After the military defeats in the 18th century, this combination of primordiality and sacrality was gradually transformed into a shape that emphasised

---

[1] White, 1974.

[2] Eisenstadt, 1999.

poverty and contentedness as the new forms of primordiality (cf. the idea of pleasure and pain used to describe Poland's past in Ewa Domańska's chapter, and the idea of Danish smallness in Mette Zølner's chapter. In the Danish case, it should also be observed how the idea of smallness went hand in hand with a certain xenophobia). The carriers of this poverty and contentedness were the *folket*, that is, the people, the peasants. In the early 19th century the adoration of the independent ('free') peasant, who enjoyed local self-determination, connected a remote past to a national romantic present and developed a new combination of primordiality and civility. Later on, in the context of the social protest movements (*'folkrörelserna'*: 'temperance', 'revivalism' and 'social justice and equality'), and in order to provide the roots that would legitimate the claims for democracy, the peasant primordiality was combined with sacrality. This saw state church Lutheranism mixed with free church revivalist Calvinism, which emphasised the connection of the individual with the divine rather than that of the church hierarchy. This combination resulted in the dismantling of the hierarchy within the structure of the state church. The image of 'the people' assumed individualistic and egalitarian dimensions, while the programmes of the popular protest movements contained obvious elements of social solidarity. This combination of primordiality and sacrality spilled over into a civil sphere through rhetoric on social justice and equality.

During the Cold War, and in the context of Keynesian views on the governance of economies, the plot of poverty, contentedness, and Protestant moralism emerged in a particular configuration which was referred to as 'the Swedish model'. Subsequently, concepts like neutrality, welfare, and 'the world' (rather than 'Europe'), 'international' (rather than 'European'), and 'UN' (rather than 'EC') were added as elements of the self-image.

The Gothic Past

Sweden, like so many other dynastically ruled states in medieval Europe, staked its claim to be the oldest state in the world, that is to say, in Europe. At the council in Basle in 1434, the Swedish representative, Bishop Nicolaus Ragvaldi, claimed, in a dispute with Spain, that Sweden was the oldest state. Both Ragvaldi and his Spanish counterpart referred to the (Visi)Gothic heritage of their respective states. This mythical field was further cultivated in 16th century Sweden by Johannes Magnus. During the reign of Gustavus II Adolphus, King of Sweden from 1611 to 1632, the Gothic rhetoric developed into a veritable campaign for a Gothic heritage. This *göticism* served as a royal propaganda instrument in the build-up of Swedish military power and for the claim to the Baltic as a *mare nostrum*. Archaeology and excavation of burial mounds supported the promotion of Gothic ideology and the proclamation of a grandiose past. Through this Gothic rhetoric, and in the panegyric delirium produced by the military success in the Thirty Years War – a delirium that was to last half a century – *göticism* came to mean the adoration of honour and virtue independent of Christian morals. *Göticism* has been described as 'a kind of homespun classicism, naive and cogent'.[3] It represented national self-assertion produced through the merging of the Gothic language with classicism by means of locating the origin of the antique world in *Norden*, the North. The poet Georg Stiernhielm and the runic scholar Johannes Bureus gave fresh life to obsolete vocabulary and expressions and launched a programme for the replacement of words borrowed from German and, more recently, French by Swedish terms. Poets were to devote themselves to writing about national heroic themes in a language in which foreign 'glitter' was replaced by vigorous and pithy Norse vocabulary. This linguistic puritanism had its equivalent in other Western European countries at this time; in Dutch and German speaking areas for example. However, in Sweden this puritanism was linked to the theory of *Norden* as an original cultural home. According to the view already established during antiquity, the Scythians belonged to the descendants of Japhet, Noah's son, and, Stiernhielm argued, the offspring of Japhet were those who had best maintained the antediluvian language. So it was that the theory was developed that Northeners were mentioned as the first among the Scythians. The patriotic speculations on this Gothic heritage culminated with the *magnum opus* by the Uppsala professor, Olof Rudbeck. The first volume of his *Atlantis* was published in 1679, but the work was still unfinished when he died in 1702. With arguments based on diligent study of both ancient authors and newly discovered Icelandic literature, Rudbeck drew far-reaching conclusions about Swedish antiquity. Plato's Atlantis was identical with the realm of the Goths, the king's castle had been situated in Old Uppsala, and it was from there that the gods of antique culture had

---

[3] Lindroth, 1955.

emigrated. As Sten Lindroth puts it, Rudbeck's 'patriotic gospel meant that he appropriated the whole Greek and Roman culture and provided it with a Swedish label'.[4]

The Swedish position as a great power crumbled away during a 90-year period that started in 1718, when the warrior king, Charles XII, was felled on the battlefield by a bullet perhaps fired from his own ranks, and culminated in 1809, when Russia conquered Finland. The loss of Finland was dramatic, since the central part of Finland, along the Baltic, had been considered to be as integral a part of Sweden as the central areas around Stockholm, while the Finnish periphery had been no more peripheral than the Swedish one. For this reason, the geographical orientation of Sweden had been understood in east-west rather than north-south terms.[5] From 1809 on, a new mental map was gradually projected along an imagined north-south axis. Mentally, the loss of Finland was coped with in terms of the motto 'reconquer Finland within Sweden's borders'.[6] In this therapy for the political consolidation of the smaller state, a glorious past was invoked ever more strongly. In 1811, patriotic intellectuals, each with a greater or lesser degree of Romanticism, founded an association based on imagined Gothic values and rites, the *Götiska Förbundet*. Gothic heritage and rhetoric were reactivated, after having been largely overlooked during the political and military decline and the emerging Enlightenment discourse of the 18th century. In this new context, the Gothic myth merged with the Viking myth in the poets' construction of a collective memory.

A glorious past was proclaimed and commemorated, and while this past was situated on the other side of the calamitous period of great power, it was also, through the Viking dimension, closer to the early 19th century than the legendary era of the Great Migration, when the Goths, linked to biblical events like the Flood, had emerged along with the Scythians and other mythical people. The Vikings made the myth appear more concrete, as did the peasant figure, *odalbonden*, who, particularly in the writings of historian and poet Erik Gustaf Geijer, ascended from a dim past. The peasants in Sweden had constituted a separate diet estate since the 15th century, and in the

---

[4]   *Ibid.* Cf. for a discussion of *göticism* Henningsen, 1997 and Hillebrecht, 1997.

[5]   Klinge, 1983. For a critical discussion of Klinge's thesis, see Nordin, 1998.

[6]   '*Återerövra Finland inom Sveriges gränser*'. Bishop and poet Esaias Tegnér in the poem 'Svea' 1810.

historiographical tradition that had become established by the 19th century they were the carriers of national freedom and equality. The peasants were the core of the *folk*, not as a passive crowd, but as the incarnation and manifestation of the general will. The free peasants were historically derived from the Viking Age and a mystical past in which, when they met at the *thing*, they were not only free but equal. There was a clear continuity with this idea when the Social Democrats redefined themselves as a *folk* party rather than as a class party in the 1930s. The free and equal peasant became a trope that represented a progressive historical force much more than the bourgeoisie did, as the Marxist scheme suggested. Progression in the Swedish foundation mythology went from the peasants to the workers.[7]

In the adoration of the Goths, attention was paid both to past greatness and to power, and peasant freedom was invoked. One of the leading figures in the Gothic association was Erik Gustaf Geijer who, in the first issue of the journal of the association, published a whole series of Gothic poems like 'The Viking', '*Odalbonden*', 'The Last Warrior', and 'The Last Poet'. There were others who were more conservative, like the bishop Esaias Tegnér, and the peasant rhetoric bridged the gap between liberal and conservative world views. The history writers (rather than historians) Nils Henrik Sjöborg and Magnus Bruzelius, also belonged to the association, and Bruzelius wrote the most widely used history schoolbook of the time. Through the association an influential group of patriotic individuals was able to kindle an interest in the romantic history of ancient Norse mythology in a much broader section of society than antiquarian research had ever done through runology and the archeology of burial mounds during the 17th century. A network of bonds of friendship and family ties linked the members of the association with almost the entire social group which, among the three million inhabitants of this poor and isolated nation, was the carrier of Swedish cultural life.

The superimposition and the overlapping of the memories of the Goths and of the Vikings through the figure of the peasant was a rather harmless and inoffensive instrument by which to build up collective self-confidence after 1809 without indulging in expansive dreams of revenge. The great power period was certainly present in the collective memory, but it was consigned to a less prominent

---

[7] Cf. Sørensen and Stråth, 1997, pp. 7-8.

position in a past almost as dim as that of the Vikings. Tegnér's ode of 1818 for the centenary commemoration of the death of Charles XII ('King Charles, the Young Hero') offers a good illustration of this. The Gothic escapism long survived the doomsday atmosphere of 1809, and only disappeared after World War I (when the Gothic and ancient Norse myths moved abroad and experienced a period of greatness in the context of Nordic studies at German universities). The strength of the national romanticism among the many schoolchildren who were raised on Gothic history in elementary school should not be underestimated (elementary school became compulsory under a law of 1814). Nor was the image of a glorious past only communicated through the school system – it also found an outlet through an expanding public sphere based on literature, journals and newspapers. In the 19th century, the collective memory, which earlier had had the court circles and the administration of central government as its main constructor and the pulpits of the Lutheran State Church as its primary distributor, obtained more refined methods for this construction and mediation.[8] The means for both sending and receiving elements of the collective memory were expanded, and interaction became more intense.

After the 1850s, however, other things came to the forefront of the popular interest, including emigration ships to America, temperance lodges, revivalist meetings and trade unions. When, at the end of the 19th century, the nation was once more mobilised on the basis of primordial images for the purpose of internal consolidation, it was not because of a loss of land as had happened in 1809, but because of the performance of a competing identity category; that of class. Both the myth of the past and the content of historical romanticism changed.

The Transformation of the Old Foundation Myth: From Power to Poverty

During the second half of the 19th century, the aim that had emerged from the French Revolution to break down social structures based on privileges of birth and replace them with social structures based on ideas of universal rights and principles of equality and freedom, were transformed into nationalism and nation-building in the context of competition in world markets. Everywhere, the language

---

[8]   Cf. Stråth, 1988.

used for societal discourse became increasingly aggressive, and the Darwinian theory of human evolution was adapted into a view of the condition of societies. The idea of peaceful competition and the view that the division of labour would lead to greater efficiency and economic wealth were transformed into the images of a struggle in the world markets, where only the fittest survived. This transformation not only meant the development of customs barriers and trade protection where, a few decades earlier, universal free trade had been seen as the source of the wealth of nations, it also saw the emergence of population politics in order to provide a strong military and physical basis for this competition. In all this, the nation came increasingly to be regarded as being at risk, and it was therefore considered that it should be reinforced. By the end of the 19th century, with growing signs of class awareness among industrial workers, the ruling elites began to perceive a threat not only from competing nations, but also from within. So it was that the concept of nation was mobilised against the concept of class.

During this phase of nation building, the period of great power was dusted down and assigned a more prominent place in the collective memory of a glorious past. The earlier basis for this memory, the Goths and the Vikings, now receded into the background, although it was still present. The peasant figure as the carrier of the *folk* idea remained to a notable degree. The rewriting of Swedish history took the expansionist warrior kings Gustavus II Adolphus and Charles XII as its point of departure, and in particular, their violent deaths on the battlefield were commemorated. The 6th of November 1632 in Lützen and the 30th of November 1718 in Fredrikshald became national dates and *lieux de mémoires* located outside Sweden. Monumental paintings of the funeral processions of the hero kings were made. What had started in an early national romantic framework with the centenary of the death of Charles XII in 1818, gathered momentum during the second half of the 19th century having received an impetus in 1868 with the unveiling of J. P. Molin's statue of Charles XII in the Kungsträdgården in Stockholm.[9]

---

[9] The debate about the historical role of Charles XII began 13 years after his death with Voltaire who, in the 60 French editions of *Histoire de Charles XII, roi de Suède* published between 1731 and 1778, under permanent revision by the author, established the view of the king as both a source of virtue and the root of Sweden's misfortunes. See von Proschwitz, 1997. Professor Sven Lagerbring of Lund, the

The Polish uprising against Russia in 1863 promoted latent revanchist feelings in Sweden and was enthusiastically supported. In this context there also emerged a kind of Charles XII renaissance.[10] Russia was presented as a large reactionary power and a threat to Sweden, and in this way, an old trope in the Swedish demarcation between Us and the Other – Russia as the sworn enemy and great danger – received fresh support. This trope was intensified around the turn of the century when Sven Hedin wrote his cautionary *Varningsord* against the Russians, whom he described as cruel and unreliable. In 1917, Gustavus Vasa's and Charles XII's Muscovites became Bolsheviks and the Russophobia was transformed into socialist horror. This view of the Russians went hand in hand with calls for the state to give more money to the army.[11]

It is important to note that this view that bound together Charles XII and Russia was not universally shared, but, on the contrary, provoked political conflict. In the wake of the Charles XII renaissance, the liberals, who were interested in Sweden's economic development, asked themselves why the king who had done more damage than any other to his country should be so elevated. In his *Svenska bilder*, published in 1886, Carl Snoilsky described the hardships experienced by the Swedish people during the reign of Charles XII and explained how the king had deceived them.[12] The Charles XII renaissance made a significant advance in the 1890s when, with Harald Hjärne as leading ideologist, the king began to receive a more positive historiographical treatment and was depicted as a great statesman who had understood the Eastern European question better than anybody else. Despite this, however, the negative view still remained as a counter discourse. These two poles were represented in the writings of Verner von Heidenstam and August Strindberg. In his overview of the Caroline period, Heidenstam emphasised the positive aspects of the suffering of a people,

---

most prominent Swedish historian of the 18th century, developed the same ambiguous view, coupling admiration of the hero with criticism of the political consequences of his war adventures. Erik Gustaf Geijer was much more critical in his judgement than Bishop Tegnér with his heroic poem in 1818. Anders Fryxell, outside the academic establishment but with great influence on the Swedes' concept of history, shared this critical position.

[10] Oredsson, 1999.

[11] Bohman, 1997.

[12] Oredsson, 1999, pp. 286-287.

presenting poverty as a key to national dignity. His imaginative vision of poverty and suffering corresponded with the view of military officers and professional historians who cultivated the hero motif, not least within the Charles XII association *Karolinska Förbundet*, which was established in 1910. On the other hand, August Strindberg, in his animated dispute with von Heidenstam and Sven Hedin, described Charles XII as uptight, autocratic and power-mad. The conflicting views on the king, already established between Tegnér and Geijer (see footnote 9), now took on much heavier political implications, and one's view on his historical role revealed whether one's sympathies lay with the political right or left. Strindberg became the hero of the Social Democrats and the liberal left, whereas the Conservatives had von Heidenstam and Hedin as their idols. In the 1960s and 1970s the debate faded away for some years, but in the 1980s and the 1990s, Charles XII has been resurrected yet again as a symbol of resistance against foreigners and immigrants.[13]

Rather than glorious victories, it was the violent death of two kings that was sublimated into a heroic past worth remembering in situations of political conflict[14] (although this was much less the case for Gustavus Adolphus).[15] Schools and the system of compulsory military service were two of the most important instruments in the production and maintenance of a collective memory based on the dignity that arose from death and defeat. These structures were supported by professional historians who, in a discourse that had started in the 1870s or even earlier, debated why Sweden had ever embarked on its expansionist politics under these two kings who had incessantly extended the frontiers of the realm. Their conquest of new territories had always been in the vain hope of finally establishing

---

[13]   *Ibid.* pp 288-299. Cf. concerning the view on Charles XII, Hildebrand, 1955 and Björck, 1946.

[14]   For the national fund-raising drive for the statue of Charles XII in Stockholm, and for a monument in Duved in memory of the tragic retreat by the Caroline soldiers under Karl Gustav Armfelt after the death of Charles XII in Fredrikshald, see Ellenius, 1971, pp. 105-110.

[15]   Gustavus Adolphus, as the victor of Protestantism, was much less contested in his worship than the warrior king. In his resistance against 'papism', he stood out as an icon of the Lutheran state church establishment, while, even if not a hero, he was at least a respectable figure in the Social Democratic and revivalist free church history view, given their demarcation of a Catholic, capitalist and conservative Europe (see below).

'security'.[16] This development of military power had taken place in the name of defence and in order to protect the 'true' religious belief which was felt to be threatened by dangerous Others: the papists in the case of Gustavus Adolphus, and the Orthodox Russians for Charles XII. The historians did not only discuss the enigmatic contradiction inherent in expansionist politics motivated by security and defence, (one question they toyed with was where or if Charles XII should have stopped his Russian campaign in order to avoid his final defeat), but they also studied the domestic consolidation that took place at the time and that was based on an efficient system of tax collection and the organisation of the peasants into a feared army. This discourse, which received an important input from the work of C. T. Odhner in the 1870s, continued as a main theme in academic history research and teaching up to the 1950s. The fact that from the 1920s, the source-critical positivistic Weibull School attacked the conservatively-oriented writing of history that had prevailed up to this time, only served to reinforce this theme.[17] When this academic discourse penetrated society in the form of an established collective memory by means of schools, military traditions, monuments and commemoration days, an image of Sweden emerged in which the people were seen as disciplined, contented, diligent and industrious. Charles XII, the Spartan warrior king, was supported by his loyal, determined and patient subjects, who endured terrible suffering. The image of Lutheran State Church Protestantism as a pure and genuine belief was established against the dubious values of the Catholic Church. This Protestant image was reinforced rather than disturbed when the Lutheran State Church establishment was attacked by the popular movements, *folkrörelserna*, whose social protest was based on claims for temperance, individual religious independence and revivalism without state and clergy (the free churches). They also called for

---

[16]   A key factor in these processes is the translation of professional, academic history writing into school books and other media, which can be seen as a depository for political rhetoric and for public debate in general in which interpretative frameworks are provided. The relationships between professional and popularised history should not be understood as a one-way connection, but as an interaction. Historians not only provide material for the debate, they also react sensitively to the themes which the debate sets. Although basically mutually confirming and reinforcing, the relationships between professional and popularised histories are exposed to strains and mutation in periods of experienced crisis.

[17]   For a historiographical survey of the debate, see Rosén, 1961, pp. 355, 513-515, 680-681, 690-692, 701-702, 709-710.

social justice (in the shape of the labour movement), which they derived from ideas of egalitarian and individualistic peasant mythology.

Literature also contributed to the establishment of this memory trope in which poverty became a virtue. When C. L .J. Almqvist wrote about the importance of Swedish poverty or von Heidenstam wrote about Charles XII's warriors, this was a construction of the nation that saw greatness and dignity in poverty and defeat. The people not only obeyed their ruler, they were actively loyal while maintaining their peasant independence.[18]

The emerging collective memory of the period of great power evoked discipline and self-control based on authoritarian rule rather than military revenge, and the suffering caused by the wars and the allocation of resources to the military in general were sublimated into a national epos. This transformation of the great power trope from strength to poverty was underpinned by the fact that one million Swedes sought to escape poverty through emigration to North America in the hundred years preceding the 1920s (out of a population of 3.5 million in 1850 and 5 million in 1900). Rather than political fundamentalism and chiliastic hopes, the trope promoted political pragmatism and escapism of a physical kind.

Artur Hazelius, who established the *Nordiska museet* (Nordic museum) and the adjoining open-air museum park at Skansen, was one of the 19th century pioneers in the creation of this history which combined kings and great artists with peasant culture. The peasant culture which was recreated in his museums became a model for a desirable national Swedish identity in demarcation to the treadmills of industrial society. This reshaping of an archaic past, which was supported by Viktor Rydberg in his criticism of industrial society, made a deep impression on the labour movement. However, this early incorporation of a peasant past into the Social Democratic view of history was not uncontested. Strindberg, who had initially been very positive regarding the Nordic Museum and Skansen, soon became very critical of this homage to peasant culture that reinforced the Swedish national feeling but repressed the condition of the industrial workers. It was Strinberg who drew attention to the controversial questions of what cultural heritage should be preserved and

---

[18]   Sørensen and Stråth, 1997, p. 14.

commemorated and what history should be remembered. Paradoxically, the disputes around these questions had a unifying effect, and, during the period from the 1880s to the 1930s, produced the sense of a shared arena for political conflict and the resolution of problems. These feelings of simultaneous conflict and participation, which one might describe as a form of collective identity, promoted the development of institutions where political conflict could be expressed, debated and resolved.

During this struggle over the assignation of meaning and content to the *folk* concept, the great power trope remained an important source for the collective memory. The Conservatives paid more attention to Charles XII, who experienced a veritable renaissance, while the political Left saw historical examples provided by the thrifty housekeeping figures and state-building projects of Charles XII's father, Charles XI and Gustavus Vasa, who confiscated property from the nobility (although a Conservative ideologist like Rudolf Kjellén also saw in Gustavus Vasa a good example of a state builder). The Social Democrats incorporated rebels against the authorities such as Engelbrekt and Nils Dacke in their arsenal. But this conflict over where to place the historical emphasis only served to strengthened the image; the thrust of the collective memory was a historical heritage of thriftiness, contentedness and harshness. In this memory, peasant independence went hand in hand with royal authoritarian rule, power with poverty, and honour with defeat. It was a contradictory but, nonetheless, a consistent memory, which could be approached and memorised from very different political positions. The political struggle over what the precise historical heritage should be moulded together the memory and produced social cohesion.

In the 1880s, when signs of working class awareness were becoming obvious, and in the 1890s, when the class language became more intensive, the great power trope was activated in order to defend the 'nation' against 'class'. In reaction to the experienced threat from the working class, conservative ideologists and political scientists suggested national socialism as an integrative alternative to the divisiveness of class-struggle socialism. In this formulation, Sweden should be like a home for the people: so it was that the *folkhemmet* metaphor was born. What followed was a political struggle over two or three decades between the Conservatives and the Social Democrats over how to fill the *folk* concept with content and what form of socialism should mould the *folkhemmet* (although the Conservatives soon dissociated themselves from the concept of socialism as such). Finally, in the 1930s, the Social Democrats emerged as the strongest group in this struggle. By this point they were retreating still further from the class concept and, through the appropriation of the *folk* concept, they became a people's party rather than a class party.[19]

The Interwar Period:
The Protestant Demarcation to Europe

For a short period after World War I, political dynamics were generated much more from utopias produced by the Russian Revolution and the collapse of three Empires than from history. Utopia was projected into the future rather than derived from the past, and the idea that history had a direction resembled the ideas of 1789, but seen from a new perspective. This draft outline of the future incorporated international co-operation and peace guaranteed by free and independent nations and the League of Nations. The Swedish Social Democrats, who now emerged for the first time as a serious alternative for government, were very active in the development of this optimistic scenario, and Sweden was seen as an active player in this European/international scene. On the other side, the Conservatives, in the wake of the German collapse and the rise of the Soviet Union, argued for strict neutrality based on a strong army. The old line of division, originating in the 19th century, between the Conservative view of neutrality linked to a strong army, and the Social Democrats' view of neutrality linked to disarmament was obvious, although now it was in the context of the stability provided by the League of Nations. The new element in the content of the neutrality concept came from the idea of international collective security. Neutrality had first been established as an option for Swedish foreign policy in 1834. The Social Democrats' neutrality of the 1920s was a kind of collective neutrality without weapons, with the prospect that the collective order, maintained through police intervention, would prevent dissidents from using arms in international conflicts. The expectations invested in the League of Nations by the Social Democrats were considerable. Arthur Engberg, editor-in-chief of *Arbetet*, and frequent Swedish delegate to the League of Nations, helped to spread this view through numerous editorials and articles in

---

[19]   Stråth, 1996, pp. 72-85.

his Social Democratic newspaper. The very idea of the League of Nation was, according to Engberg, to organise international relations under a 'state organism, an international state', which, step by step, would expand and strengthen its authority in relation to the member states with the aim of bringing order to the anarchistic conditions prevailing in international society. In this, the spokesman of the Social Democrats not only came close to Jean Monnet's vision when the European Coal and Steel Community was created a quarter of a century later, after yet another World War, but also to the old trope of memory where peasants and *folk*, and freedom and equality, went hand in hand with state authority. From the Social Democrat perspective, the League of Nations should be an organisation with full powers to guarantee the observance of international law, while they regarded the Swedish state as an instrument for progressive politics.[20]

This attempt to fill the national trope with international content was invalidated by developments in world politics. The 1930s smothered any expectations of a peaceful world, as Sweden's geographical location in the intersection between Germany and the Soviet Union began to look increasingly ominous. In this context of uncertainty, the building of a mental demarcation to this threatening development began. National consolidation once more became the theme, just as it had after 1809 and again after 1905, when Norway had split from its union with Sweden. In the self-image that emerged, *folk* and *folkhem* were again key concepts, but, in contrast to the beginning of the century, it was now the Social Democrats who defined these terms and gave them political content, appropriating and redesigning the social conservative concept of *folkhemmet*. In this new formulation, there was no real patriarchal authority in the home of the people, rather, they ruled over themselves in an egalitarian order. The *folkhemmet* concept had a deep sounding-board in Swedish political culture, a sounding-board formed by the old trope which, as we have seen, had been particularly developed at the beginning of the 19th century, and again during the identity-building of the 1890s. It was a national, romantic construction of identity founded upon free peasants, Protestantism, and popular and patriotic warrior kings fighting for the defence of the distinctive Swedish character. In the 1930s the contrast with continental Catholic culture was increasingly emphasised as the dreams of the League of Nations faded away.

---

[20] Stråth, 1993, pp. 189-192.

As opposed to the development of continental European countries, the Swedish labour movement voiced no strong dissent towards religion and church. Early on, religion had been taken off the political agenda and assigned to the private sphere. This step facilitated coalition building between the labour movement and other popular (mainly temperance and revivalist) movements during the formulation of social protest in the second half of the 19th century. This situation was, in a way, reminiscent of the religious low and free church embedding of the British working class in the same period. In the 1910s and 1920s, Social Democratic ideology builders transformed a policy of 'crushing the Lutheran State Church' into one of bringing it under political control. In this context, 'political control' meant Social Democratic control because, as a state church, it had been under constant political control since the Reformation in the 16th century. In practice, this meant that the teaching of liberal theology at universities was politically guaranteed and the government had a responsibility for the appointment of bishops and clergymen.

This church policy was supported by the construction of a Catholic threat. Arthur Engberg, one of the most pre-eminent spokesmen for international co-operation within the framework of the League of Nations in the 1920s, became possibly the most ardent builder of a barrier against Catholicism in the 1930s. Drawing on the national romantic narration and the great power trope of power and poverty, he warned in numerous articles against the spread of an expansive Catholic church unconstrained by any form of political control. In a Lutheran State Church under political control he saw a guarantee against Catholic 'lust for power' and the instrument to make 'the nation invulnerable to the weapons of papism'. In a parliamentary debate in 1930, Engberg, who was to become Social Democratic Minister for Church and Education a few years later, built a wall between the Swedish/Lutheran 'Us' and the Catholic 'Other': 'I prefer an iron-like closed Swedish state church system on the pattern we have, to the order of things we would experience if Catholicism were allowed to throw its weight about in our country.'[21]

---

[21] Misgeld, 1983a and b, 1990; Beltzén and Beltzén, 1973; Bo Stråth 'The Social Democratic State Church Policy in Sweden in the 20th Century'. Paper for the 8th Soviet Russian-Swedish history symposium in Moscow 8-14 October, 1991. Cf. Stråth, 1993, pp. 209-212.

In the contrast Engberg tried to achieve, he connected the description of Swedishness to the *folk* concept. The Swedish *folk* culture and the Swedish *folk* church would, through the representatives of the state authority who were ultimately responsible for church policy, ward off any tendency towards Catholicism within the church. Like the *folkhemmet* concept, which was initially a socially conservative concept, but was finally appropriated by the Social Democrats, the *folk* church was a concept which had been launched in the 1910s by conservative reform tendencies in the state church in an attempt to throw off growing criticism of the church's social insensitivity, but was then appropriated for Social Democratic purposes. The coming to power of the Social Democrats in the 1930s is usually referred to as a major political break, but, through the *folk* concept and the collective memory it transmitted, there was, in fact, considerable historical continuity and 'Swedishness'.

It is difficult to explain why Catholicism was wheeled out as a threat in this development. There did not appear to be, for example, any significant threat of social and religious protest from the popular movement (*folkrörelse*) in the 1930s. As a threat, Catholicism cannot have been more than a creation of the imagination. However, as a rhetorical referent to emphasise Swedishness, and as a linguistic tool in the political struggle over religious and cultural power, the Catholic threat was effective. Dangerous Catholicism was set off against the Swedish cultural heritage, guaranteed by Social Democratic politics. And this approach made a long-lasting impression, not least in the puritan revivalist environments of the popular movements. When, for instance, the Parliament debated legislation on freedom of religion in 1951, MPs belonging to the free church movement (revivalism was gradually institutionalised in free churches in opposition to the state church) considered the foundation of monasteries by 'the papists' as presenting almost as serious a threat to freedom of religion as secularisation and de-Christianisation.[22]

Although Social Democratic leaders in the interwar period like Hjalmar Branting, Richard Sandler and Arthur Engberg, were, *per se*, Europe-oriented in their cultural view, and several of them spoke English, German and French fluently (Engberg was also skilled in Latin and Greek), the image of a Catholic threat activated in the 1930s contained obvious elements of xenophobia *vis-à-vis* continental

---

[22]   Stråth, 1993, p. 211.

Europe. This foreign threat served a purpose. The parliamentary red-green coalition between the Social Democrats and the Farmers' Party that emerged as a political response to the Great Depression has often been cited as evidence of how peaceful the transformation of Swedish society was. This may be true in international comparison, however, Swedish society was, in fact, very polarised around 1930, and the labour market was one of the most strike-prone in the whole industrial world. The election campaign of 1928, when the Social Democrats were accused of planning to introduce a Soviet-type economy and to open the doors to the Soviet Union (the so-called 'Cossack election'), was but one of the expressions of this social polarisation. Another had a more tragic outcome: in 1931, military troops were ordered to prevent a demonstration in Ådalen in northern Sweden in support of striking sawmill workers. They fired on the peaceful march and killed five people.

The shootings in Ådalen provoked national shock, which opened the way for a situation of political compromises and social depolarisation in which the Social Democrats were able to assume a leading role by redesigning and reactivating the *folk* concept. The parliamentary compromise between the Social Democrats and the farmers in 1932 (*'kohandeln'*), and the compromise in the labour market between the employers and the trade unions in 1938 (The Saltsjöbaden Agreement), were expressions of new feelings of social responsibility and cohesion, outcomes of a national shock therapy. The mental demarcation of the image of a Catholic, capitalistic and conservative Europe also contributed to this construction of national community. The century-old Russian threat did not disappear, but it did recede into the shadow of the Capitalist-Catholic Other. At the end of the 1930s, Germany and the Soviet Union represented much more immediate military threats of course, but during the Cold War, the Communist threat was again mixed with the Catholic-Capitalist demarcation of continental Europe.

There is certainly continuity between this development and the Conservative design of *folkhem* and national socialism at the turn of the last century, but this continuity does not take the form of a smooth evolution. The line of continuity is discernible only *ex post*, and challenges and alternative developments were always present. The efforts to produce community in an ever more dangerous world situation triggered not only processes of collective memory, where homage was paid to a glorious Protestant peasant past based on the inter-weaving of power and poverty, but also processes of collective oblivion. The echo of the gunfire in Ådalen faded away and was replaced on the agenda by the *kohandeln* and Saltsjöbaden. Only in the 1970s, when the 'model' established in the 1930s experienced its first real credibility crisis was Ådalen incorporated into schoolbooks as a kind of historical *caveat* for what can happen when the social community splits up.[23]

The threat of the Catholic Other still remained after World War II, and served as the negative opposite to the Swedish development model which, during the 1950s and the 1960s, came increasingly to be regarded as unique. Catholicism represented the European Other, characterised by the prevalence of *Berührungsangst*.[24] The contrast between Catholic, capitalistic, and conservative Europe and Protestant, progressive and Social Democratic Sweden was obvious in the debate in the 1960s over Sweden's position with respect to the EC. In the most extreme Social Democratic rejections of the European project, the EC was described as a collection of states characterised by a more primitive social organisation than Sweden. Gunnar Myrdal was one of the three authors of a book that contained this very message. This book argued that Sweden had nothing to gain from membership of the EC. A nation as small as Sweden, or even smaller, was entirely capable of governing itself so long as it existed as a living communion (*'samfund'*) on historical grounds. International co-operation was a requisite, but this could not mean surrender of national sovereignty. Protestant countries in particular had come far in development terms, be it economically or otherwise. It was, for instance, only the Protestant countries that had managed to introduce efficient income taxation. Scandinavia and the US were among the most prominent members of this club of practitioners of advanced and progressive social engineering.[25] It is not difficult to discern lines of continuity from this mental – and political – demarcation of Europe in the 1960s. These lines not only stretch back to the 1930s and earlier, they also extend forwards to the debate on Europe around 2000, where

---

[23] Paper given by Roger Johansson, University of Lund, at a workshop at the European University Institute on social and political violence, organised by Bo Stråth and François Demier, 16th and 17th October, 1998.

[24] Misgeld, 1990, p. 137.

[25] Ekström, Myrdal and Pålsson, 1962.

a collective memory and a foundation myth have been moulded around dichotomies like power and poverty, progress and backwardness, history and modernism, and peasant pragmatism and social engineering.

Neutrality and Welfare in One Mythical Web

As we have seen, the concept of neutrality was contested in the 1920s when the Conservatives in particular used it as an argument for a strong army while the Social Democrats argued for international co-operation and disarmament. During World War II, the tension in the neutrality concept was visible. After the Soviet assault on Finland in November, 1939, the foreign minister, Richard Sandler, left the Social Democratic Government in disagreement over the degree of Swedish support for Finland. The new all-party Government (all except the Communists) established their foremost goal as keeping Sweden outside the war, in keeping with the neutrality concept. (With regards to Finland in the 'Phony War', Swedish policy made use of the concept of non-belligerence, which, in international law, allowed for material assistance). During World War II, and in the 1950s during the Cold War, the neutrality concept took on sacred proportions, and historical legitimation was sought in the situation in 1834 when the concept was used for the first time. A collective memory of uninterrupted neutrality since that time was constructed, neglecting obvious deviations from the doctrine on several occasions.[26]

During World War II, the content of the neutrality myth shifted with the direction of the conflict: before 1943 it was more pro-German, while after this time it became more pro-Allied. Throughout the entire war, the Social Democratic Prime Minister, Per Albin Hansson, in the role of the calm father of the people, convincingly explained the continuous adjustment to the power situation around Sweden with ritual reference to the neutrality concept.

After the war, the success of the neutrality policy provoked a need to find some interpretations and *ex post* rationalisations that went beyond pure luck. This was particularly the case given that there was a more or less openly expressed bad conscience for not having done enough for the neighbouring occupied countries during the conflict.

---

[26]   Cf Stråth, 1993, pp. 179-206.

This feeling of guilt was an active force in the search for historical continuity. In particular, the transportation by train along the Swedish west coast of German soldiers on leave from occupied Norway was a painful thorn in the collective conscience. When the Cold War set in, neutrality became both the formula for explaining what had been, and an action orientation for the future. The bronze, eagle-like profile of King Karl XIV Johan, who had first used the neutrality concept in 1834, and the father-like persona of the prime minister ('Per Albin'), mediated and brought together Swedish greatness and historical continuity. This was an image with which the Social Democratic Government liked to identify itself after the war. Per Albin, as the guarantor of neutrality, gave the government the initiative in the field of security policy thanks to the support for his policies during the war years. In 1949, Liberals and Conservatives mounted a brief campaign for Swedish membership of NATO and closer links to Western powers, but they were dismissed by the Social Democrats as 'adventurers'. Thus it was that neutrality, guaranteed by the Social Democrats, totally dominated Sweden's security policy throughout the 1950s. The historical derivation of neutrality was neither questioned nor problematised, and the Social Democratic government acquired priority in the interpretation of the concept. If the government argued that something was incompatible with the neutrality policy, that issue was, as a rule, removed from the political agenda and the action was justified by the collective memory of historical continuity. This memory completely ignored the situation in the 1920s when it was the Conservatives who had stood for Swedish neutrality.[27] The historical legitimisation of the neutrality concept in the 1950s and 60s presented a vision of undisturbed continuity since the 1830s, and obscured the fact that up to World War II, neutrality was much more of an option than a norm or constant element of the Swedish self-image. It was World War II that represented the watershed in this respect.

The theoretical legitimisation of the pragmatic politics during the war years, together with the dictates of the Cold War, gave the neutrality doctrine much more form and content than the politics during World War II. In the 1950s, 'neutrality' was used to develop an identity associated with a 'third way', in which Sweden was not only seen as a neutral state between the two superpowers, but also as a supporter of liberation movements in the Third World. The self-image

---

[27]   *Ibid.*, pp. 196-200.

that emerged was one of conciliators and intercessors in processes of disarmament. The Swedish angels of peace located themselves in opposition to the colonial powers that were responsible for the economic and political exploitation of less developed countries. In the course of the 1960s, this oppositional image was modified and Sweden increasingly set itself in opposition to the images of an imperialistic USA and the rich man's club of the EC. This 'third way' identity found its expression far away from Sweden, where national security interests were not so directly involved in the East-West conflict. In giving support to struggles for independence in the Third World, Sweden was able to develop and promote a form of independence at the verbal level. Indeed, the role of critical mediator and world conscience provided much more nourishment to the Swedish self-image of a nation with a particular international position than did the threatening Cold War scenario in the immediate surroundings. The neutrality fixation associated with Per Albin and Karl Johan began to fade away. The United Nations took over the role of *lieu d'espérances* for Swedish security which the League of Nations had played in the 1920s, but this time derived from, and not in demarcation to, the neutrality concept.

The language of neutrality was linked to the language of welfare, and the two combined in a consistent self-image. Sweden had already been used as a xenostereotype in the 1930s in order to argue for the New Deal in the US. Similarly, after the Second World War, the image of the progressive organisation of Swedish society emerged in political debates in countries like Britain and Germany.[28] In the 1960s, foreign interest in the welfare arrangements of a country that had remained outside the war came to focus particularly on the organisation of the labour market, which was perceived as peaceful ('consensual') and was regarded as promoting high productivity and economic performance. The Swedish xenostereotype which was constructed gradually came to be incorporated in an autostereotype of a model for the rest of the world. In the emerging self-image, welfare merged with neutrality and Third World morality. The position on the power-poverty axis in the collective memory shifted once more towards power, but this time power in a moral rather than military sense.

---

[28] *Ibid.*, p. 206.

This feeling of power was generated by the attention given to Sweden in other countries. In the mutually reinforcing xeno – and autostereotypes, incompatible entities were combined in contradictory but consistent ways. Sweden was exotic, particularly with respect to sex, and mysterious (the films of Ingmar Bergman were an influential factor in establishing this mystery), but at the same time it was a rational and efficient industrial nation that demonstrated economic high-performance.[29] The world exhibition in Stockholm in 1930, a symbol of modernity, was an icon in this latter view. The image as a whole contained a history that hardly mentioned Goths, Vikings and military aggression, but emphasised instead poverty and suffering which had, for once and for all, been overcome in the 1930s. In the 1960s, this decade of economic depression and mass poverty was constructed as a decisive historical divide. From this point, the movement back from the poverty fixation towards power in a new sense, could begin. At the same time, the memory of poverty remained as the past where it had all started.

The merging of neutrality, Third World rhetoric and welfare politics in the 1960s had to confront not only the conflict between West and East in the Cold War, but also the emerging European integration project (which, *per se*, must be seen in the Cold War framework, of course). There was considerable concern in Sweden over this movement towards European power, because it disturbed Sweden's sense of having found an equilibrium point in the Cold War. Moreover, the integration project was regarded as particularly capitalistic and Conservative, and was therefore seen as a threat to the Social Democrat's welfare building. All the same, the demarcation with respect to Europe was motivated both in welfare terms, as the book by Myrdal *et al* mentioned above demonstrates, and with reference to neutrality. The old mental demarcation established in the 1930s between progressiveness in the North and reaction in the South

---

[29] For a discussion of this kind of xeno- and autostereotyping, in which German stereotypes of a sexually free Sweden can be seen as projections of German taboos, and where this construction of an exotic Other was incorporated into Swedish self-understanding, see Schröder, 1996. Cf. Beindorf, 1996. These kind of stereotypes often contain incompatible elements of rational and irrational types. See, for instance, the mythologisation of a German national character based on both rationality and 'irrational' exotic mystery, although here philosophy and romanticism rather than sex, as in Sweden, expressed the exotic element.

was reactivated through the Social Democrats' language of welfare and neutrality.

The preconditions of the Social Democratic welfare state changed dramatically in the 1970s, although the depth of this structural transformation was scarcely appreciated at the time. In the 1970s and 80s, following the decolonisation process and the Vietnam War, Third World rhetoric became so universal that it could hardly continue to contribute to the sense of being a selected people. In the 1980s, the Cold War came to an end and thus ceased to provide the cement of cohesion. All this was accompanied by considerable mental disorientation and the erosion of established interpretative frameworks and collective memories. In this growing void, a neo-liberal/neo-conservative counter-image was constructed, an image in which the 1930s were no longer seen to mark the decisive divide. Instead, it was the 19th century that emerged as the new divide in this view. This was the period when entrepreneurship, political innovation, inventive genius and the leadership of captains of industry had established a capitalist Sweden and lifted the country out of poverty.[30] Poverty therefore remained as a reference point in the collective memory, but the watershed period, when poverty was pushed back as a result of political reforms, was located in an earlier period, while the reform content was no longer Social Democratic. The state was replaced by the market as the key concept in the political debate, and it was the market rather than the welfare state which was provided with domestic historical legitimacy.

In this new language, which invoked a different collective memory, Europe emerged as an opportunity, with the result that the old division between Sweden and Europe had to be broken down. In the euphoria around 1990, Carl Bilt, the leader of the Conservative Party, suggested a referendum on membership of the EC/EU. Not that there was any real need to ask the people (other than indirectly, through Parliament), since opinion polls revealed massive support for the project among the public, and the political establishment was equally enthusiastic. Although technically unnecessary, the referendum was perceived in neo-liberal circles as a ritual manifestation of the popular will to mark the end of more than 50 years of Social Democratic power.

---

[30] Stråth, 1998.

However, the euphoria around 1990 soon turned into anxiety over the uncertain future, and many began to look for security in the Sweden that was. 'Back to the *folkhemmet*' became a mobilising motto, and the referendum over membership of the EC/EU became a manifestation of diverse popular wills. The European question resulted in a fierce battle over the self-image of the Swedish model, including not only the country's demarcation with respect to Europe, but also the collective memory that provided the legitimation for the model. In this battle two contrary views on the relationship Sweden-Europe emerged. For the Conservatives and the Liberals the battle-cry was "Europeanise Sweden" and make the country 'normal' after 50 years of Social Democratic rule. For the Social Democrats the missionary motto was "Swedenise Europe", *i.e.* translate the Swedish welfare model into a European model. At this battle, provoked by the interest in using the European issue for parliamentary power, the concord about a Swedish entrance into the EC/EU split up and the political elites were challenged from basis protests. It was a struggle about how, if at all, the model and its collective memory could or should be integrated into future-oriented action, and, of course, the place of Europe in this mediation between past and future. It was also a struggle over the old demarcation line between Sweden and Europe and over the collective memory that this line had nurtured. A superficial perspective on this situation might describe this struggle in terms of polarisation, with a high degree of conviction on either side of the dividing line. Indeed, the referendum showed two almost equally strong voting blocks. However, a closer examination not only reveals polarisation and growing social tension, but also considerable uncertainty and disorientation in the rewriting of the collective memory.

The lack of consensus over the collective memory and the collective oblivion on the threshold of the 21st century has provoked questions about how neutral Sweden really was; that is, how pro-German it was during World War II and how pro-American during the Cold War. Truth commissions of historians are working with the question of 'how it really was', with the aim of definitively shaping the collective memory. The collective oblivion that will in all likelihood also ensue from this undertaking, will encompass the historical conditions under which a concept like neutrality emerged and under which Sweden's division from Europe was built. The truth, in the Swedish case, just as everywhere else, is seen from the privileged position of knowing what happened later. We can observe, reflected in our rear-view mirror, not only a specific time or event, but the entire road that has been covered from that event up to our present. More than this, we are free to make a choice of the events to focus upon and those to ignore. This is why history, memory and myth come together in one point, a point that is located, not in the past, but in the present.

The processes of collective memory construction are complex and contradictory, and they are never free of political conflict. They are far from being the easy manipulation of the masses by the elite. In the Swedish case, the political conflict has involved key concepts like neutrality and welfare, Europe, the Third World and international co-operation, and has centred on how to fill these concepts with content. This struggle has occurred in the framework of a trope or plot, which, simultaneously, has also been confirmed through the struggle. The divisions have kneaded together and confirmed the plot of a collective memory (and collective oblivion), where the organising principle has been the axis between power and poverty.

In the 1990s, when the feeling of power produced by welfare and the international respect derived from offering a 'good example' in moral terms ceased to work, a more glorious past was invoked. This shift of memory was compatible with the neo-liberal shift of the 'poverty line' from the 1930s to the 19th century, but went one step further. A spectacular museum exhibition about the period of great power symbolised this shift, as it once again became legitimate not just to talk about this period in Swedish history, but to talk positively about it.[31] There was less attention given to the wars, and more to the organisation of society around an effective state administration. Lutheran State Church harshness was a part of this efficiency, and peasant freedom was mixed with social discipline through authoritarian rule. This was a historical heritage with which the Social Democrats could identify as much as the Conservatives.

This new interest in the period of great power did not, however, exclude poverty and moralistic puritanism from the trope. Nothing illustrates this better than the cover of a book which the Social Democratic Minister of Finance, Kjell-Olof Feldt, published in 1991 after he had resigned from the government in disagreement with an

---

[31] Concerning the museum exhibition, see Bohman, 1997, pp. 134-145.

economic policy dictated by an perceived need to heal the split between the Social Democratic government and the trade unions.[32] The cover shows Feldt, the lonely wanderer, bending under the weight of the budget and finance bill which he carries on his back. He is stubbornly struggling onwards and upwards through the uncleared snow on the third way, leaving behind the two broader and easier paths of unemployment and expansion, both of which lead downwards. It is a picture full of purposefulness and the spirit of self-sacrifice and therefore carries pervasive force in Swedish political culture. The privation and the barrenness of the landscape depicted on the cover is full of Biblical undertones: the choice of the narrow gate rather than the broad path, and the strenuous journey that follows in order to reach the ultimate reward of salvation; Christ's deprivations in the wilderness that confirmed his spiritual strength; the 40 years which the Israelites spent in the desert before finally arriving in the land of Canaan. The Biblical spirit of self-sacrifice and the invocation of Swedish poverty appealed to deep emotions. It could also be found in the report by the government commission on productivity, which was published in the same year Feldt published his book. The report warned expressly against the broad way which had been travelled upon in the politics of the 1970s. This emotional chord was already discernible in the construction of a new society in the 18th and 19th centuries after the collapse of the position of great power. And it was also discernible in the *folkhemmet* construction in the 20th century. Per Albin Hansson had hardly held out the prospect of an affluent society when he, as a Social Democratic leader in the 1930s, transformed and appropriated the Conservative image of a people's home to represent a household where meagre resources were distributed in a more fair and just way. The chord was also discernible when the Social Democratic Minister of Finance during World War II talked about a poverty which was better endured if it was shared by all, and again in the 'petty people' government coalition between the Social Democrats and the Farmers' Party in the 1950s. The references to the tradition of poverty disappeared for a while in the 1960s, when a belief in universal affluence emerged, however, the appeals to poverty returned in the 1990s, both in the neo-liberal rhetoric calling for restraint and moderation, and in the politics of the Social Democratic government, with its obvious attempts to recreate the 'petty people' coalition of the 1950s. This appeal to deep emotions which the

---

[32]   Feldt, 1991. Cf. Stråth, 1998, pp. 307-308.

poverty concept provoked is by no means value-free, on the contrary, it is something intended to legitimate political and economic power. 'Sacrifice now in order to reap the reward later' is a well-known theme, and not just in Sweden. It had, however, in its Swedish version an obvious resonance with ideals based on centuries of historical experiences.

In the Swedish foundation mythology, images of primordiality, civility and sacrality, in permanent transition, have merged and bridged dichotomies like power and poverty, state church hierarchy and free church egalitarianism, collectivism and individualism, monarchical authority and peasant ('popular') independence. The construction of a threatening Other has been an effective instrument in this bridge-building. The collective identity that has emerged out of these processes occurred in particular in demarcation to images of a tsarist Russia ('the sworn enemy')/a Communist Soviet Union and/or a Catholic and Capitalist Europe. The main outcome was pragmatism rather than fundamentalism, although this was a pragmatism that radiated moralism much more than value relativism and nihilism, and puritanism much more than pluralism.

Bibliography

Books and periodicals

Adorno, Theodor W. *Negative Dialektik.* Frankfurt/M.: 1992.

'A miskolci pogrom – ahogyan Rákosiék látták' with the preface of Éva Standeisky, *Társadalmi Szemle,* 45. November 1990.

Agulhon, Maurice. *Marianne into Battle. Republican Imagery and Symbolism in France 1789-1880.* Cambridge: 1981.

Agulhon, Maurice. 'Die Nationale Frage in Frankreich: Geschichte und Anthropologie' in Etienne Francois. *Nation und Emotion.* Göttingen: 1995.

Ahronson, Shlomo. 'Zionism and post-Zionism: The Sociological Context of the Historiographical Debate' in Y. Weitz (ed.). *From Vision to Revision; A Hundred Years of Historiography of Zionism.* Jerusalem: 1997, pp. 257-274.

Alatri, Paolo. 'Lettere inedite di Antonio Scialoia'. Part I. Movimento Operaio. 1956, no. 1-3, pp. 149, 156, 161.

Althusser, Louis. 'Du «Capital» à la philosopie de Marx' in *Lire le Capital* (ouvrage collectif) new edition, Paris: 1996 [1968].

Amalvi, Charles. 'Le 14 juillet, du *Dies Irae* à jour de fête' in Pierre Nora (ed.). *Lieux de mémoire.* Paris: 1984.

Andersen, J. *Stemmer fra højre – om Søren Krarup, nynazisterne og alle de andre.* Copenhagen: Forlaget Systime a/s. 1988.

Andersen, L. J. 'Hr. Søren til Seem'. *Jyllands-Posten,* November 29, 1987.

Anderson, Benedict. *Imagined Communities: Reflections on the Origin and Spread of Nationalism.* London: 1990.

Andreasen, R. 'BZAT af revolutionens ånd'. *Det fri Aktuelt,* 29 May, 1993.

Ankersmit, Frank R. 'Danto on Representation, Identity, and Indiscernibles' in *History and Theory.* Vol 37 no. 4, 1998.

Ankersmit, Frank R. 'Trauma und Leiden. Eine vergessene Quelle des westlichen historischen Bewußtseins' in Jörn Rüsen (ed.). *Westliches Geschichtsdenken: eine interkulturelle Debatte.* Göttingen: 1999, pp. 127-145.

APU, 'Roubaix : L'APU 2. stratégie du capital et stratégie populaire'. *Place*. No 6, Winter 1977, Paris.

APU, 'Roubaix : L'APU. Naissance d'un mouvement populaire de résistance aux expulsions'. *Place*, Autumn 1976, Paris.

APU-CSCV, 'La démarche au quotidien'. pp. 17-38 of *Roubaix Alma-Gare. Lutte Urbaine et Architecture*, Editions de l'Atelier d'Art Urbain, Bruxelles, 1982.

Artzi, Yossi Ben. 'On the Historiography of the War of Independence'. *Cathedra* 65, 1992, pp. 159-167 (Hebrew).

Assmann, Jan. 'Kollektives Gedächtnis und kulturelle Identität'. In Jan Assmann and Tonio Hölscher: *Kultur und Gedächtnis*. Frankfurt/M.: 1988, pp. 9-19.

Assmann, Jan. 'Zur Metaphorik der Erinnerung,' Aleida Assmann and Dietrich Harth (eds). *Mnemosyne. Formen und Funktionen der kulturellen Erinnerung*. Frankfurt/M.: 1991, pp. 13-35.

Atkinson, David. 'The Road to Rome and the Landscapes of Fascism' in Catherine M. Gulliver, Wolfgang Ernst, Friedemann Scriba (eds). *Archaeology, Ideology, Method*. Canadian Academic Centre in Italy: 1993, pp. 39-53.

Attman, Artur. *Ryssland och Europa. En handelshistorisk översikt*. Skrifter utgivna av Ryska Institutet vid Stockholms Högskola. Stockholm: 1946a.

Attman, Artur. *Till det svenska Östersjöväldets problematik. Studier tillägnade Curt Weibull*. Göteborg: 1946b.

Balibar, Etienne. *Spinoza et la politique*. Paris: 1985.

Balsby, E. 'De autonomes bydel'. *Weekendavisen*, 6 January, 1995.

Banfield, Edward C. *The Moral Basis of a Backward Society*, New York: 1958.

Barszczewska-Krupa, Alina. *Historia-Mity-Interpretacje*. Łódź: 1996.

Barthes, Roland. *Mythologies*. London: 1974, pp. 109-10.

Beindorf, Claudia. *Sie tanzte nur einen Sommer*. Arbeitspapier 4 des Gemeinschaftsprojektes. Florence and Berlin: 1996.

Bellanger, Claude (ed.). *Histoire Générale de la Presse Francaise*. Paris: 1972.

Beltzén, Nils and Arne. *Arthur Engberg – publicist och politiker*. Stockholm: 1973.

Bendix, Reinhard. *Kings or People. Power and the mandate to rule*, Berkeley: 1978.

Benjamin, Walter. 'Über den Begriff der Geschichte,' in *Gesammelte Werke*, Bd. I/2, 3. ed. Frankfurt/M. : 1990 [1940].

Berggren, Lars. *Giordano Bruno på Campo dei Fiori. Ett monumentprojekt i Rom 1876-1889*. Lund: 1991.

Berggren, Lars. 'Arte monumentale e topografia politica. Alcuni progetti a Roma alla fine dell' Ottocento' in *Analecta Romana Instituti Danici*. 1994: pp. 135-151.

Berggren, Lars and Lennart Sjöstedt. *L'ombra dei grandi. Monumenti e politica monumentale a Roma 1870-1895*. Rome: 1996.

Berliner Extrablatt. Hg. vom Förderverein Berliner Stadtschloß e. V., Januar und Juli 1998.

Berliner Tageblatt. 1898 ff.

Bertrand, Michèle. *Spinoza et l'imaginaire*. Paris: 1983.

Bishara, Azmi. 'The Arabs and the Holocaust'. *Zemanim* 53, Summer 1995, (Hebrew), p. 5.

Björck, Staffan. *Heidenstam och sekelskiftets Sverige*. Stockholm: 1946.

Bjørgen, Hildegunn. *Nasjonaldagsfeiring som politisk redskap?* Oslo: 1997.

Bjørgo, T. 'Ekstremnasjonalisme i Skandinavia: Retorikken om 'modstandsbevegelsen'. 'landsvikerne' og 'invasjonen av de fremmede'. *Internasjonal Politikk*. Vol 52, no. 1, 1994, pp. 3-34.

Blædel, L. 'Den danske Forening og antisemitismen'. *Weekendavisen*. Oktober 27 – November 2, 1995.

Bloch, Marc. 'Mémoire collective, traditions et coûtumes' in *Revue de synthèse historique*, 1925, vol. 40, pp. 82 ff.

Bloch, Peter. 'Denkmal und Denkmalkult' in *Ethos und Pathos. Die Berliner Bildhauerschule 1786-1914. Beiträge* (Jahresgabe des Deutschen Vereins für Kunstwissenschaft), Berlin: 1990.

Blondel, Charles. *La psychanalyse*. Paris: 1924.

Blondel, Charles. *Revue philosophique*, 1926.

Bodenschatz, Harald. *Berlin – Auf der Suche nach dem verlorenen Zentrum*. Hamburg: 1995.

Bohman, Stefan. *Historia, Muséer och nationalism*. Stockholm: 1997.

Bois, Jean-Pierre. *Les anciens soldats dans la societe francaise au XVIe siècle.* Paris: 1990.

Borup Jensen, T. 'Besættelsestidens digte og sange som udtryk for national oplevelse og bevidsthed' in O. Feldbæk (ed.), 1992. *Dansk Identitetshistorie,* vol. 4, 1992, pp. 9-391.

Borup, N. H. 'Exorcisme og ytringsfrihed'. *Højskolebladet.* vol. 106, no. 21, 1981a.

Borup, N. H. 'Søren Krarup – en ukvalificeret kritiker'. *Højskolebladet.* 1981b.

Bosworth, Richard J. B. *Explaining Auschwitz and Hiroshima: historians and the Second World War 1945-1990.* London: 1993.

Bottazzi, L. 'Hitler in Italia – gli ingressi trionfale dell' urbe'. *Le Vie d'Italia,* XLIV, 5, Maggio, pp. 607-614.

Bramming, T. 'Tidehverv 1926-1992 – at være jorden tro' *Kredse,* vol 58, no. 2, 1992.

Bramming, T. *Tidehvervs historie.* Copehagen: ANIS. 1993.

Braun, Robert. 'The Holocaust and Problems of Historical Representation' in *History & Theory* 33 (May 1994), pp. 172-194.

Braun, Robert. *Holocaust, elbeszélés, történelem.* Budapest: 1995.

Brice, Catherine. *Monumentalité publique et politique à Rome. Le Vittoriano.* Rome: 1998.

Brimnes, N. 'Dansk kolonihistorie mellem historievidenskab og antropologi – et forslag til metode'. *Den Jyske Historiker.* No. 60, 1992, pp. 101-118.

Brinks, Jan Herman. *Die DDR-Geschichtswissenschaft auf dem Weg zur deutschen Einheit. Luther, Friedrich II und Bismarck als Paradigmen politischen Wandels.* Frankfurt/M.: 1992.

Brubaker, Rogers. *Citizenship and Nationhood in France and Germany,* Cambridge: 1994.

Brunner, Otto; Werner Conze and Reinhart Koselleck (eds). *Geschichtliche Grundbegriffe. Historisches Lexikon zur politisch-sozialen Sprache in Deutschland.* 7 Volumes plus register volume. Stuttgart: 1972-92.

Bryderup, I. M. & H. Schjerup Hansen. 'Ingen klassekamp – uden pudekamp' in Turid Skarre Aasebø (ed.). *Ungdomskultur ungdomsoprør og ungdomspolitik.* Aalborg: 1986.

Bryld, C. & A. Warring. *Besættelsestiden som kollektiv erindring: historie- og traditionsforvaltning af krig og besættelse 1945-1997.* Roskilde: 1998.

Bryld, T. & J. Reddersen (eds). *Lokummet brænder.* Viborg: 1987.

Butler, Judith. *Bodies that matter: on the discursive Limits of Sex.* New York: 1990.

Butler, Samuel. 'Philosophie des Unbewußten'. Leipzig: 1869 in *Unconscious Memory.* London: 1924 [1880].

Byriel, L. 'For Lidt Revolution'. *Politiken.* 30 May, 1993.

Byrnes, Timothy A. 'The Catholic Church and Poland's Return to Europe.' *East European Quarterly.* Vol. XXX, no. 4, January 1997, pp. 433-448.

Camille, Michael. *The Gothic Idol.* Cambridge: 1989.

Cassirer, Ernst. *Symbolische Formen*, vol. 3. Darmstadt: 1994 [1923-1929].

Cathy Caruth. *Unclaimed Experience. Trauma, Narrative and History.* Baltimore and London: 1996.

Cederna, Antonio *Mussolini urbanista. Lo sventramento di Roma negli anni del consenso*, Bari, Laterza: 1980.

Chabod, Federico. *Storia della politica estera italiana dal 1870 al 1896*, Bari: 1951.

Charle, Christoph. *Les Professeurs de la faculté des lettres de Paris, Dictionnaire biographique 1909-1939* Vol. 2, Paris: 1986.

Combs, James. E. and Dan Nimmo. *Mediated Political Realities.* London, New York: 2nd ed., 1990.

Confino, Alon. *The Nation as a Local Metaphor.* London: 1997.

Connerton, Paul. *How Societies Remember.* Cambridge: 1989.

Coser, Lewis A. (ed.). *Maurice Halbwachs: On Collective Memory.* Chicago: 1992.

Courtois, Stéphane, Nicolas Werth, Jean-Louis Panné, Andrzej Paczkowaki, Karel Bartosek, Jean-Louis Margolin, *Le Livre Noir du Communisme. Crimes, terreur, répression.* Paris: 1977.

Croce, Benedetto. Storia del Regno di Napoli, Bari: 1925.

Croce, Benedetto. *Il carattere della filosophia moderna.* Bari: 1963 [1941].

Crone, N. 'Identitetskrise'. *Berlingere.* 8 January, 1995.

Cuoco, Vincenzo. *Saggio storico sulla rivoluzione napoletana del 1799.* Manduria-Bari-Rome: 1998 [Milan 1800].

Davenport, F. Garvin. *The Myth of Southern History; Historical Consciousness in Twentieth-Century Southern Literature.* Nashville: 1967.

Davis, Norman. *God's Playground. A History of Poland,* vol. I and II. Oxford: 1981.

De Autonome. *En bog om og af de Autonome.* Copenhagen: 1994.

De Felice, Renzo. *Italia Giacobina.* Napoli: 1965.

De Felice, Renzo. *Mussolini il Duce.* Torino: 1974.

De Felice, Renzo. *Mussolini il rivoluzionario, 1883-1920.* Torino: 5th ed., 1976a.

De Felice, Renzo. *Mussolini il fascista.* Torino: 5th ed. 1976b.

De Felice, Renzo. *Fascism: An Informal Introduction to its Theory and Practice.* New Brunswick: 1976c.

De Felice, Renzo. *Mussolini il Duce:* vol. 2. Torino: 1981.

De Felice, Renzo. *Mussolini: L'alleato.* Torino: vol. I: 1-2-II. 1990-1997.

De Felice, Renzo and Goglia, Luigi. *Mussolini: Il mito.* Bari: 1983.

De Sanctis, Francesco. 'La Quistione Napoletana', *Diritto,* 25 october 1855 (II, n. 251), reprinted in Idem. *Scritti vari inediti o rari.* Edited by Benedetto Croce. Napoli: 1898, pp. 193-199.

De Sanctis, Francesco. *La Giovinezza; memorie postume seguite da testimonianze biografiche di amici e discepoli.* Gennaro Savarese (ed.), Turin: 1961 [1888].

Del Boca, Angelo. L'Imperoin Mario Isnenghi (ed.). *I luoghi della memoria. Simboli e miti del Italia moderna.* Roma, Bari: 1996, pp. 415-437.

Der Tagesspiegel, 1994 ff.

Derrida, Jaques. *La dissémination.* Paris: 1972.

Derrida, Jaques. *L'écriture et la différence.* Paris: 1979.

Deutsches Historisches Museum in Berlin. *Mythen der Nationen-ein Europäisches Panorama.* Berlin: 1998.

Di Ciommo, Enrica. *La nazione possibile: Mezzogiorno e questione nazionale nel 1848.* Milan: 1993.

Dickie, John. '*A Word at War: the Italian Army and Brigandage 1860-1870*'. History Workshop Journal, 1992, 33: pp. 1-24.

Die Tageszeitung, 1992 ff.

Diner, Dan. *Kreisläufe. Nationalsozialismus und Gedächtnis*. Berlin: 1995.

Dubiel, Helmut. 'Niemand ist frei von der Geschichte. Die national-sozialistische Herrschaft' in *Der Debatten des Deutschen Bundestages*. Munich: 1999.

Dubois, Claude Gilbert. *La conception de l'histoire au XVIe siècle (1560-1610)*. Paris: 1977.

Egebak, N. 'Teoriens uundgåelige konsekvens'. *Information*. January 23, 1993.

Eisenberg, E. 'Modpolernes mekanik'. *Jyllands-posten*. 2 October, 1994.

Eisenstadt, Shmuel Noah and Bernhard Giesen. 'The Construction of Collective Identity' in *European Journal of Sociology* XXXVI, 1995, pp. 72-102.

Eisenstadt, Shmuel. *Fundamentalism, Sectarianism, and Revolution*. Cambridge: 1999.

Ekström, Tord; Gunnar Myrdal and Roland Pålsson. *Vi och Västeuropa. Uppfordring till eftertanke och debatt*. Stockholm: 1962.

Ellenius, Allan. *Den offentliga konsten och ideologierna*. Kungliga Vetenskapssamhällets i Uppsala handlingar. Stockholm: 1971.

Ellereit, Rudolf /Horst Wellner (ed.). *Kampf um den Palast*. Berlin: 1996.

Ettore Pais, Roma. *Dall' antico al nuovo impero*. Milan: 1939.

Fedorowicz, J. K. (ed.). *A Republic of Nobles: Studies in Polish History to 1864*. Cambridge: 1982.

Feldt, Kjell-Olof. *Alla dessa dagar... I regeringen 1982-1990*. Stockholm: 1991.

Feuer, Lewis Samuel. *Spinoza and the Rise of Liberalism*. Boston: 1958.

Fischler, Raphael. 'Strategy and History in Professional Practice. Planning as World Making'. In Helen Ligget, David C. Perry (eds). *Spatial Practices*. London, New Dehli: 1995, pp. 13-58, esp. 23ff.

Fiszman, Samuel (ed.). *The Polish Renaissance in its European Context*. Bloomington: 1988.

Flamane, A. S. 'De autonome'. *Information*, 3 January, 1994.

Fog Olwig, K. 'Et "Gyldent minde"? Tropiske troper i dansk identitet' in J. Liep & K. Fog Olwig (eds). *Komplekse liv, kulturel mangfoldighed i Danmark.* Copenhagen: 1994.

Foreign affairs. Neue Botschaftsbauten und das Auswärtige Amt in Berlin. Berlin, Basel, Boston: 1997.

Foucault, Michel. *L'archéologie du savoir.* Paris: 1969.

Foucault, Michel. *Surveiller et punir : naissance de la prison.* Paris: 1975.

Foucault, Michel. *Histoire de la sexualité.* vol. 1. *La volonté de savoir.* Paris: 1976.

Franchetti, Leopoldo and Sidney Sonnino. *Inchiesta in Sicilia.* Edited by Enea Cavalieri. Florence: 1974 [originally *La Sicilia nel 1876.* First published in 1877].

Frei, Norbert. *Vergangenheitspolitik.* Munich: 1996, 2.

Freidin G. and Bonnel V. Televorot. 'The Role of Television Coverage in Russia's August 1991 Coup'.Nancy Condee (ed.). *Soviet Hieroglyphics: Visual Culture in Late Twentieth Cetury Russia.* Bloomington: 1995.

Frye, Northrop. 'Introduction' in *ibid. The Great Code. The Bible and Literature.* London, Melbourne: 1982.

Furet, François and Ernst Nolte. *Fascisme et Communisme.* Paris: 1998.

Gadamar, Hans Georg. *Truth and Method.* London 1975.

Galasso, Giuseppe. 'La capitale inevitabile' in P. Piovani (ed.). *Un Secolo da Porta Pia,* Napoli: 1970, pp. 5-24.

Gammelgaard, A. *Mennesker i malstrøm. Tyske flygtninge i Danmark 1945-1949.* Copenhagen: 1981.

Garin, Eugenio. *Filosofia e politica in Bertrando Spaventa.* Napoli: 1983.

Geertz, Clifford. *The Interpretation of Cultures.* New York: 1973.

Gerber, Gerold. 'Doing Christianity and Europe: An Inquiry into Memory, Boundary and Truth Practices' in Bo Stråth (ed.). *Europe and the Other and Europe as the Other.* Brussels: 1999.

Germania, 1900 ff.

Gerner, Kristian. 'Två hundra års europeisk felutveckling – karaktäriserat av nationalismen, rasismen och territorialstaten – går mot sitt slut' in *Nord-Revy.* Nr 3, 1990.

Giesen, Bernhard and Kay Junge, 'Vom Patriotismus zum Nationalismus. Zur Evolution der "Deutschen Kulturnation"' in Bernhard Giesen (ed.).

Nationale und kulturelle Identität. Studien zur Entwicklung des kollektiven Bewußtseins in der Neuzeit, Frankfurt: 1991, pp. 255-303.

Giesen, Bernhard. *Intellectuals and the German Nation: Collective Memory in an Axial Age.* Cambridge: 1998.

Giesen, Bernhard. 'Lost Paradise, Failed Revolution, Remembered Victims' in Neil J. Smelter and Jeffrey C. Alexander (eds). *Cultural Trauma.* Berkeley, London: 2000.

Giesen, Bernhard. *Triumph and Trauma.* Berkeley, London: 2000.

Gilroy, Paul. *The Black Atlantic: Modernity and Double Consciousness.* Cambridge: 1993.

Gjesing, K. B. 'De uværdige sønner – om Danskeren og Den Danske Forening'. *Højskolebladet,* vol. 115, issue 46, 1990.

Gladstone, William. *Two Letters to the Earl of Aberdeen, on the state prosecutions of the Neapolitan government.* London: 1851 (11th edition). First Italian edition, translated and with an introduction by Giuseppe Massari. *Lettere al Lord Aberdeen.* Turin: 1851.

Glasgow Herald, 1961 ff.

Gobetti, Piero. *La Rivoluzione Liberale: saggio sulla lotta politica in Italia.* Turin: 1964.

Goffman, Erving. *Asylums.* London: 1968.

Goldhagen, Daniel Jonah. *Hitler' s Willing Executioners: Ordinary Germans and the Holocaust.* New York: 1996.

Gorbals History Research Group. *Third Time Lucky?: the history and hopes of the Gorbals,* Clydesdale Press, *n.d.* [ca. 1990].

Gramsci, Antonio. *Quaderni del carcere.* Critical edition of Istituto Gramsci edited by Valentino Gerratana. Turin: 1975.

Haberlik, Christina and Gerwin Zohlen. *Baumeister des Neuen Berlin.* Berlin: 1997.

Hageneier, B. Søren Krarup. Mod Strømmen? Et portræt. Hovedland: 1989.

Halbwachs, Maurice. *La topographie légendaires des Evangiles en Terre Sainte.* Paris: 1971 [1941].

Halbwachs, Maurice. *La mémoire collective.* Paris: 1987 [1925].

Halbwachs, Maurice. *Das kollektive Gedächtnis.* Frankfurt/M.: 1991 [1925].

Halbwachs, Maurice. *Les cadres sociaux de la mémoire.* Paris: 1994 [1925].

Halicz, Emanuel. *Polish National Liberation Struggles and the Genesis of the Modern Nation: Collected Papers.* Odense, Denmark: 1982.

Hall, Stuart. 'Introduction: Who needs "Identity"?' in Stuart Hall and Paul du Gay (eds). *Questions of Cultural Identity.* London: 1996.

Hariman, Robert (ed.). *Popular Trials.* London – Tuscaloosa: 1990.

Hasselbalch, O. *Opinionskampen 1933-45.* The homepage of the Danish Association: 1995.

Hasselbalch, O. *Viljen til modstand.* Tidehvervs: 1990.

Häussermann, Hartmut. 'Lebendige Stadt, belebte Stadt oder inszenierte Urbanität'. in *Foyer* lll, 1995, pp. 12-14.

Haynes, Deborah J. *The Vocation of the Artist.* Cambridge: 1997.

Hegel, Georg Wilhelm Friedrich. *Werke in zwanzig Bänden.* (Theorie-Werkausgabe) Bd. 20: *Vorlesungen über die Geschichte der Philosophie III.* Frankfurt/M.: 193, ed. 1971 [1833, 1844].

Heinz, Rudolf. 'Maurice Halbwachs' Gedächtnissbegriff,' *Zs. für philos. Forschung* 23 (1969): pp. 73-85.

Henningsen, Bernd. *Die schwedische Konstruktion einer nordischen Identität durch Olof Rudbeck.* Arbeitspapier 9 des Gemeinschafts-projektes. Florence and Berlin: 1997.

Herf, Jeffrey. *Divided Memory. The Nazi Past in the Two Germanys.* Cambridge: 1997.

Hertl, Günter: *Birne contra Historie.* Berlin: *n.d.*

Hildebrand, K. G. 'Till Karl XII-uppfattningens historia' in *Historisk Tidskrift.* Stockholm: 1955.

Hillebrecht, Frauke. *Skandinavien – Die Heimat der Goten?* Arbeits-papier 7 des Gemeinschaftsprojektes. Florence and Berlin: 1997.

Hobsbawm, Eric J. *Primitive Rebels: Studies in Archaic Forms of Social Movement in the 19th and 20th Centuries.* New York: 1965 [1959].

Hobsbawm, Eric J. and Terence Ranger (eds). *The Invention of Tradition.* Cambridge, Cambridge University Press, 1983.

Hobsbawm, Eric J. *Nations and Nationalism since 1780: programme, myth, reality,* Cambridge: 1990.

Hroch, Miroslav. 'Specific Features of the Nation-Forming Process in the circumstances of the "Small nation"' in Øystein Sørensen (ed.). *Nationalism in Small European Nations*. Oslo: 1996.

Huntington, Samuel. *The Clash of Civilizations and the Remaking of World Order*. New York: 1996.

Iggers, Georg, 'Historiography and the Challenge of Postmodernism' in Bo Stråth and Nina Witoszek, *The Postmodern Challenge: Perspectives East and West*. Amsterdam: 1999, pp. 281-301.

Information, 21 February 1989. 'Søren Krarup: Khomeinis dødsdom er en krigserklæring mod Vesten'.

Internationaler Städtebaulicher Ideenwettbewerb Spreeinsel. 2. Phase. Ausgelobt von der Bundesrepublik Deutschland und dem Land Berlin, vertreten durch das Bundesministerium für Raumordnung, Bauwesen und Städtebau, die Bundesbaudirektion, die Senatsverwaltung für Stadtentwicklung und Umweltschutz. Durchführung: Arbeitsgemeinschaft Wettbewerb Spreeinsel. Berlin, Bonn, Januar 1994 (The Spreeinsel International Competition for Urban Design Ideas).

Jameson, Frederic. *The Political Unconscious. Narrative as a Socially Symbolic Act*. Ithaca, NY: 1981.

Janion, Maria, 'Polski korowod' in *Mity i stereotypy w dziejach Polski*. Warsaw: 1991.

Janion, Maria. *Płacz generała. Eseje o wojnie*. Warszawa: *Sic*! 1998.

Jann, Werner. 'Regieren im Netzwerk der Regionen – das Beispiel Ostseeregion' in Carl Böhret and G. Wewer (eds). *Zwischen Globalisierung und Regionalisierung*. Opladen: 1993.

Jensen, C. (ed.). *BZ Europa – Ungdomsbevægelser i 80' erne*. Copenhagen: 1982.

Jensen, H. G. 'Den retfærdige sags umulighed'. *Information*. March 2, 1993.

Kasthol, C. 'Når gaden bestemmer'. *Politiken*. 10 October, 1994.

Klemperer, Victor. *Ich will Zeugnis ablegen bis zum letzten: Tagebücher*. Berlin: 1995.

Klemperer, Victor. *So Sitze ich denn Zwischen allen Stühlen. Tagebücher 1945-1959*. Edited by Walter Nowojski assisted by Christian Löser. 2 vols, Berlin: 1999.

Klinge, Matti. *Runebergs två fosterland*. Söderströms: 1983.

Knapp, Steven. 'Collective Memory and the Actual Past' in *Representations* 26 (Spring 1989), pp. 123-149.

Kochanowski, Jan: *Poems by Jan Kochanowski*. Trans. Dorothea Prall Radim *et al.* Berkeley: 1928.

Komiteen mod Flygningeloven. *Hvad med Danmark?*. Tidehverv: 1987.

Korte, Karl-Rudolf. *Geschichte der deutschen Einheit*, Vol. 1, *Deutschlandpolitik in Helmut Kohls Kanzlerschaft*. Stuttgart: 1998.

Koselleck, Reinhart. 'Historia Magistra Vitae: Über die Auflösung des Topos im Horizont neuzeitlich bewegter Geschichte' in *Vergangene Zukunft: Zur Semantik geschichtlicher Zeiten*. Frankfurt/M. : 1989.

Krarup, S. *Det moderne gennembrud. 1789-1984*. Copenhagen: 1984.

Krarup, S. *En måned i efteråret. Rapport fra en borgerkrig*. Tidehvervs: 1987.

Krarup, S. *Fundamentalisme på dansk*. Copenhagen: 1988.

Krarup, S. 'Fundamentalister i krig'. *Jyllands-Posten*. March 4, 1989.

Krarup, S. 'Nazismen om hjørnet' *Kroniken i Politiken*. February 5, 1989.

Krarup, S. *Bidrag til en folkelig frimodighed*. Tidehvervs: 1990.

Krarup, S. *I virkeligheden. Af dagens strid*. Kontrast/Tidehvervs: 1986/1990.

Krarup, S. *Dansk Kultur*. Copenhagen: 1994.

Krarup, S. *Tres års Danmarkshistorie. I min livstid*. 1998.

Kreth, R. and M. Mogensen. *Flugten til Sverige. Aktionen mod de danske jøder, oktober 1943*. Copenhagen: 1995.

Kreuzzeitung, 1895 ff.

Kridl, M. and J. Wittlin. *The Democratic Heritage of Poland. For Your Freedom and Ours: An Anthology*. London: 1944.

Krogh, K. O. 'Hvad ville Søren Krarup gøre uden Khomeini?'. *Information*. March 2, 1989.

Król, Marcin. *Podroż romantyczna*. Paris: 1986.

Król, Marcin. *Mity i stereotypy w dziejach Polski*. Warszawa: 1991.

Kvist, J. 'Danmarks dissident'. *Aktuelt*. December 19, 1992.

La Croix, 1905 ff.

La Petite République, 1897 ff.

La Repubblica, 1998 ff.

Laqueur, Walter. *Fascism: past, present, future*, New York: 1996.

Laux, Henri. *Imagination et Religion chez Spinoza: La* potentia *dans l'histoire*. Paris: 1993.

Le Figaro, 1900 ff.

Le Goff, Jaques. *Histoire et mémoire*. Paris: 1985.

Le Temps, 1896 ff.

Leggewie, Claus. *Vom Schneider zu Schwerte: das ungewöhnliche Leben eines Mannes, der aus der Geschichte lernen wollte*. Munich: 1998.

Lehmann, Hartmut. 'Friedrich von Bodelschwingh und das Sedanfest'. *Historische Zeitschrift*. No. 202, 1966.

Leith, James A. *The Idea of Art as Propaganda in France 1750-1799. A Study in the History of Ideas*. Toronto: 1965.

Lepetit, Bernard and Denise Pumain (eds). *Temporalités Urbaines*. Paris: 1993.

Lepetit, Bernard. 'Une hermeneutique urbaine est-elle possible?' in Bernard Lepetit and Denise Pumain (eds). *Temporalités Urbaines*. Paris: 1993, pp. 287-299.

Lepetit, Bernard (ed.). *Les Formes de l'expérience*. Paris: 1995.

Lepetit, Bernard. 'Le présent de l'histoire' in Bernard Lepetit (ed.). *Les Formes de l'expérience*. Paris: 1995, pp. 273-297.

Lequin, Yves and Jean Métral, 'Auf der Suche nach einem kollektiven Gedächtnis. Die Rentner der Metallindustrie von Givor,' in Lutz Niethammer (ed.). *Lebenserfahrung und kollektives Gedächtnis. Die Praxis der Oral History*. Frankfurt/M. : 1980, pp. 249-271.

Lévi-Strauss, Claude. *Myth and Meaning*. London: 1978.

Lindroth, Sten. *Reformation och humanism. Ny ill. svensk litteraturhistoria 1*. Stockholm: 1955.

Lindstrøm, C. 'De autonome og "systemet"'. *Det fri aktuelt*. 2 September, 1994.

Lübbe, Hermann. *Zwischen Trend und Tradition*, Zürich: 1981.

Lyotard, J. F. *La condition postmoderne – rapport sur le savoir*. Paris: 1979.

Maczak, Antoni and Henryk Samsonowicz (eds). *East-Central Europe in Transition: From the Fourteeneth to the Seventeenth Century*. Cambridge, New York: 1985.

Maier, Charles. 'A Surfeit of Memory' in *History and Memory* 5, 1993, pp. 136-51.

Mannheim, K. ' The Problem of Generations' in *Essays on the Sociology of Knowledge*. London: 1952 [1928], pp. 276-322.

Massey, Doreen. *Space, Place and Gender*. Cambridge: 1994.

Massey, Doreen. 'Places and Their Pasts'. *History Workshop Journal*, Issue 39, Spring 1995, pp. 182-192.

Massey, Doreen and Pat Jess (eds). *A Place in the World? Places, Cultures and Globalisation*, Oxford: 1995.

Mastriani, Francesco. *I Vermi: le classi pericolose in Napoli*. Napoli: 1994 [1863].

Matheron, Alexandre. *Individu et communauté chez Spinoza*. Paris: 1969.

Matheron, Alexandre. *Le Christ et le salut des ignorants chez Spinoza*. Paris: 1971.

Matheron, Alexandre. 'Spinoza et le pouvoir' in *Anthropologie et politique au XVIIe siècle (Etudes sur Spinoza)*. Paris: 1986.

Mathiasen, A. P. & N. Thorsen. 'I skyggen af det kantede kors'. *Politiken*, September 25, 1994.

McArthur, A & H. Kingsley Long. *No Mean City*, Corgi Books, 1957.

Michel, Karl Markus. 'Liebknechts Balkon. Oder die Vergangenheit als Denkmal dargestellt am Beispiel Berlins'. in *Kursbuch* 112 (1993), pp. 153-173.

Micheovo, Mattheo di. *Maciej, z Miechowa. Historia delle due Sarmati* Trans. signore Annibal Maggi. In Vinegia: 1581.

Mickiewicz, Adam. *Forefathers*. London: 1968.

Mickiewicz, Adam. *Konrad Wallenrod and, Grazyna*. Trans. by Irene Suboczewski. Lanham, Md. : 1989.

Milosz, Czeslaw. *A History of Polish Literature*. London: 1969.

Misgeld, Klaus. 'Socialism och religion. En debatt inom den Socialistiska internationalen på 1950-talet – utan relevans för Sverige?' in *Signum* (Sweden) Nr. 1 1983a.

Misgeld, Klaus. 'Socialism och religion II. Internationalen diskuterar "religion och socialism"' in *Signum* (Sweden) Nr 2 1983b.

Misgeld, Klaus. 'Den svenska socialdemokratin och Europe från slutet av 1920-talet till början av 1970-talet. Attityder och synsätt i centrala uttalanden och dokument' in Bo Huldt och Klaus Misgeld (eds).

Socialdemokratin och svensk utrikespolitik: från Branting till Palme. Stockholm: 1990.

Mitscherlich, Alexander. *Die Unfähigkeit zu trauern. Grundlagen kollektiven Verhaltens*, Munich: 1994.

Moe, Nelson. '"Altro che Italia!" Il Sud dei Piemontesi (1860-61)'. *Meridiana*: 1992, 15: pp. 53-89.

Molik, Witold, 'Polen "Noch ist Polen nicht verloren"' in *Mythen der Nationen: ein Europäisches Panorama*, herausgegeben von Monika Flacke. Berlin: Deutsches Historisches Museum, 1998: 295-320.

Møllenbach Larsen, T. 'Tidehvervs Start. En undersøgelse af debatten i Tidehverv intil 1934'. *Arken.* No. 14. 1982.

Moreau, Pierre-François. *Spinoza*. Paris: 1975.

Moreau, Pierre-François. *Spinoza: L'expérience et l'éternité*. Paris: 1994.

Morris, Benny. *The Birth of the Palestinian Refugee Problem, 1947-49.* Cambridge: 1988.

Mosse, George. *The Nationalization of the Masses*, New York: 1975.

Mosse, George. *Nationalization and the Masses: Political Symbolism and Mass Movements in Germany from the Napoleonic Wars Through the Third Reich*, Cornell: 1991.

Mussolini, Benito. *Opera Omnia di Benito Mussolini*. Edoardo e Duilio Susmel (ed.)., vol. XV, Florence.

Namer, Gérard. *Mémoire et société*. Paris: 1987.

Namer, Gérard. *Maurice Halbwachs, Les cadres sociaux de la mémoire*. Paris: 1994.

Namer, Gérard (ed.). *Halbwachs, mémoire collective*. Paris: 1997.

Namier, Lewis. *1848: The Revolution of the Intellectuals.* London: 1946.

Neil McWilliam, 'Monuments, Martyrdom, and the Politics of Religion in the French Third Republic' in *The Art Bulletin.* 1995:2, pp. 186-206.

New York Times, 1926 ff.

Nielsen, F. C. 'Professoren er altid kampklar'. *Jyllands-Posten.* April 23, 1995.

Nielsen, J. 'Med jerntanterne i landsretten'. *B70.* No. 1992, pp. 610-611.

Niethammer, Lutz. 'Fragen – Antworten – Fragen. Methodische Erfahrungen und Erwägungen zur Oral History' in Lutz Niethammer and Alexander von Plato (eds). *'Wir kriegen jetzt andere Zeiten'. Auf der*

Suche nach der Erfahrung des Volkes in nachfaschistischen Ländern. Berlin/Bonn: 1995, pp. 392-445.

Niethammer, Lutz in collaboration with Axel Dossmann. *Kollektive Identität. Heimliche Quellen einer unheimlichen Konjunktur,* 2 vols. Reinbek: 1999.

Nietzsche, Friedrich. *Sämtliche Werke. Kritische Studienausgabe.* Berlin: 1988 [1852-1889].

Nipperdey, Thomas. 'Nationalidee und Nationaldenkmal in Deutschland im 19. Jahrhundert' in *Historische Zeitschrift,* Vol. 206, München: 1968, pp. 529-585.

Nissen Styrk, M. 'For Søren Krarup er ikke demokraties men nationalisme og militarisme hovedsagen'. *Information.* 18 December, 1981.

Nora, Pierre. *Les lieux de mémoire.* Paris: 1984-1986.

Nora, Pierre. 'Between Memory and History: *Les lieux de mémoire*'. Transl. Marc Roudebush, *Representations* 26, Spring 1989, pp. 13-25.

Nora, Pierre (ed.). *Realms of Memory: Rethinking the French Past.* New York: 1996.

Nordin, Jonas. 'I broderlig samdräkt? Förhållandet Sverige-Finland under 1700-talet och Anthony D Smiths *ethnie*-begrepp' in *Scandia. Tidskrift för historisk forskning.* Lund, Sweden: 1998.

Norris, Christopher. *Spinoza and the Origins of Modern Critical Theory.* Oxford: 1991.

Olesen, S. 'Vredens dag'. *Jyllands-Posten.* 28/9 1986.

Olser, Krystyna M. (ed.). *For Your Freedom and Ours: The Polish Progressive Spirit from the 14th Century to the Present,* 2nd ed. New York: 1981.

Olwig Fog, K. 'Et "Gyldent minde"? Tropiske troper i dansk identitet' in J. Liep & K. Fog Olwig (eds). *Komplekse liv. Kulturel mangfoldighed i Danmark.* Copenhagen: 1994.

Oredsson, Sverker. 'Karl XII och det svenska stormaktsväldets fall i historieskrivning och tradition' in Sverker Oredsson (ed.). *Tsar Peter och kung Karl. Två härskare och deras folk.* Stockholm: 1999.

Østergård, U. 'Hvad er det danske ved Danmark?'. *Den Jyske Historiker.* No. 29-30, 1984.

Østergård, U. 'Denationalizing National History – The Comparative Study of Nation States'. *Culture and History.* No. 9-10, 1991, pp. 9-41.

Østergård, U. 'Peasants and Danes: The Danish National Identity and Political Culture'. *Comparative Studies in Society and History*, vol. 34, number 1, 1992, pp. 3-27.

Østergård, U. 'From National Catastrophe to National Compromise 1864-1993, *Scandinavian Journal of Development Alternatives*. Vol. 12, no. 4, 1993, pp. 51-70.

Paggi, Leonardo (ed.). *Le Memorie della Repubblica*. Florence: 1999.

Papazu, M. 'Karaktermord på Krarup'. *Information*. February 8, 1994.

Pape, A. 'Fra Handelsbanken til Ungdomshuset'. *Information*. 12 August, 1984.

Pappe, Ilan. 'Critique and Agenda: The Post-Zionist Scholars in Israel'. *History and Memory*, Vol. 7/1, Spring/Summer 1995, pp. 66-90.

Pappe, Ilan. 'Fifty Years Through the Eyes of "New Historians" in Israel'. *MERIP* (Middle East Research and Information Project), No. 207, Vol. 28/2, Summer 1998, pp. 14-16.

Pasek, Jan Chryzostom. *The Memoirs of Jan Chryzostom z Goslawic Pasek*, trans., with an introduction and commentaries by Maria A. J. Święcicka. New York: 1978.

Pavone, Claudio. *Una guerra civile: Saggio storico sulla moralita nella Resistenza*. Torino: 1991.

Pavone, Claudio. *Alle origine della Repubblica: Scritti su fascismo, antifascismo e continuita dello stato*. Torino: 1995.

Pedersen, Thomas. 'Kapitulationen of afviklingen af den tyske besættelse af Danmark'. *Den Jyske historiker*. No. 71, 1995.

Pekacz, Jolanta T. 'Antemurale of Europe; From the History of National Megalomania in Poland. '*History of European Ideas*. Vol. 20, no. 1-3, 1995, pp. 419-423.

Petersen, H. U. 'Danmark og Hitlerflygtningene fra Czekoslovakiet 1938-45' in B. Blüdnikow (ed.). *Fremmede i Danmark. 400 års fremmedpolitik*. Odense: 1987, pp. 211-248.

Petersen, H. U. 'The Historical Perspective in Denmark: The Treatment of Refugees in the 1930' s' in *Rescue – 43. Xenophobia and Exile*. Copenhagen: 1993, pp. 27-38.

Petersen, P. (ed.). *Fugle større end vinden... en bog om og omkring begivenhederne i Ryesgade 58 og BZ-bevægelsen*. Copenhagen: 1986.

Peukert, Detlev J. K. *Max Webers Diagnose der Moderne*. Göttingen: 1989.

Pichierri, Angelo. 'The (Re-)Emergence of Urban Economies? The Play and the Playwright' in Bo Stråth (ed.). *After Full Employment. European Discourses on Work and Flexibility*. Forthcoming.

Plessner, Helmuth. *Die verspätete Nation: über die politische Verfügbarkeit bürgerlichen Geistes*. Frankfurt/M. : 1992.

Poulsen, H. 'Dansk modstand og tysk politik'. *Den jyske Historiker*. No.71, 1995.

Putnam, Robert D. *Making Democracy Work: Civic Traditions in Modern Italy*. Princeton: 1993.

Qvortrup, Lars. 'Stedfortrædene eksorcisme'. *Information*. January 25, 1994.

Renan, Ernest. *Vie de Jésus*. Paris: 1863.

Renan, Ernest, *Qu'est-ce qu'une nation ?* London: 1992 [1887].

Rescue – 43. Xénophobia and Exile. Copenhagen: 1993.

Ribbe, Wolfgang. *Gescichte Berlins*. Munich: 1990.

Ricci, Corrado, A. M. Colini & V. Mariani. *Via dell' Impero*. Rome: 1933.

Ricoeur, Paul. *Lectures on Ideology and Utopia*. Columbia, New York: 1984.

Ritter, Joachim (ed.). *Historisches Wörterbuch der Philosophie*. Bd. 3; col. 417. Basel: 1974.

Rohleder, N. 'Profession: Autonom'. *Information*. 5 January, 1995.

Rosén, Jerker. *Svensk Historia. I*. Stockholm: 1961.

Rousso, Henry. *Le syndrome de Vichy de 1944 à nos jours*. Paris: 1987.

Rousso, Henry & Eric Conan. *Vichy, un passé qui ne passe pas*. Paris: 1994.

Rubin, Miri. *The Making of the Host Desecration Accusation: Persuasive Narratives, Persistent Doubts*. manuscript, 1993.

Rutherford, Jonathan. 'Identity. A place called home' in Jonathan Rutherford (ed.). *Identity. Community, culture, difference*. London: 1990.

Ryan, Marie-Laure. 'Truth without Scare Quotes: Post-Sokalian Genre Theory'. *New Literary History*. Vol. 20, no. 4, Autumn 1998.

Rydal, O. 'Det folkelige Tidehverv'. *Århus Stift*. Vol 26, 1988, pp. 64-70.

Said, Edward W. 'Bases for Coexistence'. *Al-Ahram Weekly.* 15 November 1997.

Sampson, S. 'The Threat to Danishness. Danish Culture as seen by Den Danske Forening. Taking the Xenophobic Right Seriously' in *Multiculturalism in the Nordic Societies.* Tema nord: 1995.

Schellack, Fritz. *Nationalfeiertage in Deutschland 1870-1945.* (Doctoral thesis), Frankfurt/M. : 1990.

Schieder, Theodor. *Das Deutsche Kaiserreich als Nationalstaat.* Göttingen: 1961.

Schmale, Wolfgang. *Scheitert Europa an seinem Mythendefizit?* Herausforderungen Historisch-politische Analyse Bd 3. Bochum: 1997.

Schnyder, André. 'Der Dichter als Monument. Ein Kapitel aus der Geschichte der Rezeption Walthers von der Vogelweide' in *Archiv für Kulturgeschichte,* 1989: 2, Köln & Wien: 1989, pp. 395 ff.

Schröder, Stephan Michael. *Mehr Spaß mit Schwedinnen? Funktionen eines deutschen Heterostereotyps.* Arbeitspapier 3 des Gemeinschaftsprojektes. Florence and Berlin: 1996.

Schultheiss Europäischer Geschichtskalender, 1895, Berlin: 1896.

Scriba, Friedeman. *Augustus im Schwarzhemd? Die Mostra Augustea della Romanità in Rom 1937-38,* Frankfurt/M. : 1995.

Sebastiani, Silvia. 'Race as a Construction of the Other. Americans and Africans in the 18th Century Edition of the Encyclopaedia Britannica' in Bo Stråth (ed.). *Europe and the Other and Europe as the Other.* Brussels: 1999.

Senatsverwaltung für Bau- und Wohnungswesen Berlin (ed.). Parlaments- und Regierungsviertel Berlin. Ergebnisse einer vorbereitenden Untersuchung. Berlin: Mai 1993 (Städtebau und Architektur, Bericht 17, 1993).

Senatsverwaltung für Verkehr und Betriebe (ed.). *Unabhängige Kommission zur Umbenennung von Straßen. Abschlußbericht vom 17. 3. 1994.* Berlin: 1994.

Settembrini, Luigi. *Lettere dall' ergastolo.* Edited and with the introduction by Mario Themelly, Milan: 1962, p. 81.

Shils, Edward. *Tradition,* Chicago: 1981.

Silverston, Roger in James W. Carey (ed.). *Media, Myths, and Narratives. Television and the Press.* London: 1988.

Sjöberg, T. ' International Refugee Assistance During the Interwar Period and World War II' in *Rescue – 43. Xenophobia and Exile*. Copenhagen: 1993, pp. 39-52.

Sørensen, N. A. 'En traditions etablering og forfald. Befrielsen fejret 1946-1985'. *Den Jyske Historiker*. No. 71, 1995.

Sørensen, Niels Arne. 'Commemorating War: some Anglo-Danish comparisons' in Uffe Østergaard and Peter Bang (eds). *European Identity and Identity Politics*, Roma: 1999.

Sørensen, Øystein (ed.). *Nordic Paths to National Identity*. Oslo: 1993/95.

Sørensen, Øystein and Bo Stråth (eds). *The Cultural Construction of Norden*. Oslo: 1997.

Sørensen, Øystein and Bo Stråth. 'Introduction: The Cultural Construction of *Norden*' in Öystein Sørensen and Bo Stråth (eds). *The Cultural Construction of Norden*. Oslo: 1997.

Sovetskaia Rossia, 1998 ff.

Spalinska, Magdalena. 'Naga, niewinna Polska'. *Zycie*. 27 May 1998, p. 8.

Spinoza, Benedict. *The Chief Works of Benedict de Spinoza, translated from the Latin, with an introduction by R. H. M. Elwes*. Vol. 1-2. London: 1883.

Stadtforum, 1991 ff.

Sternhell, Zeev. *Neither Right nor Left: Fascist Ideology in France*. Princeton: 1996.

Storsveen, Odd Arvid. *Henrik Wergelands norske historie. Et bidrag til nasjonalhistoriens mythos*. Oslo: 1997.

Stråth, Bo. 'Die bürgerliche Gesellschaft Schwedens im 19. Jahrhundert. Soziale Struktur und politischer Wandel' in Jürgen Kocka (ed.). *Bürgertum im 19. Jahrhundert. Deutschland im europäischen Vergleich*. Vol 1. Munich: 1988.

Stråth, Bo. *Folkhemmet mot Europa*. Stockholm: 1993.

Stråth, Bo. *The Organisation of Labour markets. Modernity, Culture and Governance in Germany, Sweden, Britain and Japan*. London: 1996.

Stråth, Bo. *Mellan två fonder*. Stockholm: 1998.

Stråth, Bo. 'Introduction: Europe and the Other and Europe as the Other' in Bo Stråth (ed.). *Europe and the Other and Europe as the Other*. Brussels: 1999.

Sulzer, Johann Gottlieb *Allgemeine Theorie der Schönen Künste*, I-IV, Frankfurt & Leipzig: 1798.

Svensson, P. & L. Togeby. *Højrebølge?* Århus: 1991.

Szakolszai, Arpad. *Max Weber and Michel Foucault: Parallel life-works.* London: 1998.

Szymanska-Barginon, Katarzyna & Magdalena Spalinska. 'Naga prawda o Polsce i Europie'. *Zycie.* 23/24 May 1998, p. 5.

Taylor, William. *Cavalier and Yankee; The Old South and American National Character.* New York: 1957.

Tazbir, Janusz. *A State without Stakes Polish Religious Toleration in the Sixteenth and Seventeenth Centuries.* New York: 1973.

Tazbir, Janusz. *Poland as the Rampart of Christian Europe: Myths and Historical Reality.* Trans. Chester A. Kisiel. Warsaw: 1988.

Thompson, E. P. *The Making of the English Working Class.* London: 1980 [1963].

Thompson, E. P. 'The Politics of Theory' in R. Samuel (ed.). *People' s History and Socialist Theory.* London: 1981, p. 407.

Thorsen, Arve T. *Nasjonaldagsfeiringene i Paris og Berlin 1895-1905. To nasjonaldagsfeiringer – ett komparativt nasjonalismebarometer.* Publications from the Norwegian Research Council, the KULT-series. No. 86, Oslo: 1997.

Thorsen, N. 'Idealisterne'. *Politiken.* 16 October, 1994.

Tibor, Lukács. *A magyar népbírósági jog és a népbíróságok (1945-1950).* Budapest: 1979.

Topolski, Jerzy (with Raffaello Righini). *Narrare la storia. Nuovi principi di metodologia storica.* Milan: 1997.

Tosel, André. *Spinoza ou le crépuscule de la servitude. Essai sur le traité théologico-politique.* Paris: 1994.

Trinchera di Ostumi, Francesco. *La Quistione Napolitana.* Italy: 1855.

Tuan, Yi-Fu. *Space and Place. The Perspective of Experience.* Minneapolis: 1977.

Turner, Victor. *The Anthropology of Experience.* Urbana: 1986.

Turner, Victor. *The Ritual Process.* New York: 1995.

Tyvaert, Michel. *Recherches sur les histoires générales de la France au XVIIe siècle,* Thèse de doctorat présentée à l'Université Paris I. No date.

Unabhängige Kommission zur Umbenennung von Straßen. Abschluß-bericht vom 17.3. 1994. Hg. von der Senatsverwaltung für Verkehr und Betriebe. Berlin: 1994.

Unverfehrt, Gerd. 'Arminius als nationale Leitfigur. Anmerkungen zur Entstehung und Wandel eines Reichsymbols' in *Kunstverwaltung, Bau – und Denkmal-Politik im Kaiserreich*. Berlin: 1981, pp. 315-340.

Valeur, E. 'Bag om et dramatisk fjende-billede'. *Information*. 2 June 1993.

van Gennep, Arnold. *Le folklore de la Flandre et du Hainaut français*. Brionne: 1981, and *Coutumes et croyances populaires en France*. Paris: 1980.

Vico, Giambattista. *La scienza nuova*. Milan: 1977 [1725].

Viganoni, Giovanni. *Mussolini e i Cesari*. Milan: 1937.

Villari, Pasquale. *Le lettere meridionali ed altri scritti sulla questione sociale in Italia*. Florence: 1878.

Villemoes, L. 'Den autonome virus'. *Weekendavisen*. 28 May-3 June. 1993.

Villemoes, L. 'De anonymes kampbrigade'. *Weekendavisen*. 11 June-17 June 1993.

Villemoes, L. 'Historien om den røde bande'. *Weekendavisen*. 4-10 June, 1993.

Voglis, Polymeris. *Becoming a Subject: Political Prisoners in Greece in the Civil War, 1945-1950*. PhD thesis, European University Institute, Florence: 1999.

Voltaire. *La philosophie de l'histoire*. Paris, Genève: 1996 [1765].

Von Proschwitz, Gunnar (ed.). *Voltaire, Carl XII:s historia. Med tolkning, inledning och kommentar*. Stockholm: 1997.

Vörös, Éva. 'Kunmadaras. Újabb adatok a pogrom történetéhez'. *Múlt és Jövő* 5,Vol. 4, 1994.

Vorwärts, 1895 ff.

Walicki, Andrzej. *Philosophy and Romantic Nationalism: the Case of Poland*. Oxford, New York: 1982.

Walicki, Andrzej. 'National Messianism and the Historical Controversies in the Polish Thought of 1831-1848' in *Culture and Nationalism in*

Nineteenth-Century Eastern Europe. Edited by Roland Sussex and J. C. Eade. Columbus, Ohio: 1983, pp. 128-142.

Walicki, Andrzej. *Russia, Poland, and Universal Regeneration: Studies on Russian and Polish Thought of the Romantic Epoch.* Notre Dame: 1991.

Wandycz, Piotr Stefan. *The Lands of Partitioned Poland 1795-1918.* Seattle: 1974.

Warring, A. *Tyskerpiger – under besættelse og retsopgør.* Copenhagen: 1994.

Watts, Stephen. 'New Miracle in the Gorbals'. *New Yorker Magazine,* 1959, reprinted in *Evening Times.* 11 Jan, 1960, p. 5.

Weinrich, Harald. 'Typen der Gedächtnismetaphorik'. *Archiv für Begriffsgeschichte.* 1964: pp. 23-26.

White, Hayden. *Metahistory. The historical imagination in the nineteenth-century.* Baltimore: 1974.

White, Hayden. 'Response to Arthur Marwick'. *Journal of Contemporary History,* Vol. 30/2, April 1995, pp. 233-246.

Young, James E. *The Texture of Memory.* New Haven/London: 1993.

Zac, Sylvain. 'Durée et Histoire' in *Philosophie, Théologie, Politique dans l' œuvre de Spinoza.* Paris: 1979.

Zac, Sylvain. *Spinoza en Allemagne. Mendelssohn, Lessing et Jacobi.* Paris: 1989.

Zenobi, Giuseppe. *Il triumviro Aurelio Saliceti.* Teramo: 1959.

Zølner, M. *Re-imagining the Nation.* EUI-Working paper series, Florence: 1999.

Zukin, Sharon. 'Postmodern Urban Landscapes: Mapping Culture and Power'. In S. Lash, J. Friedman, eds, *Modernity & Identity.* Cambridge/Mass. : 1992, pp. 221-247.

Zukin, Sharon. *The Cultures of Cities.* Cambridge/Mass. : 1995.

Archives

Abbreviations and files used:

AMR: the Archives de la Mairie de Roubaix, ('Trois autres quartiers changent de visage, *Périodique d'information municipale*, August 1974).

ANE: the archives of *Nord Eclair*, Roubaix, (*Nord Eclair*, 'Roubaix: Nos lecteurs posent des questions aux candidats'. Friday 11 March 1977, p. 9.).

AIR: archives of the Association Inter-Quartiers de Roubaix. (*Bulletin d'adhésion*, CSCV, handwritten; CSCV, APU, letter re. la réunion du Groupe de Travail, 8. 6. 77).

BFL: Budapest Főváros Levéltára (Budapest City Archives) (V 56032/1, V 56032/2, V 56032/1, V 56032/2).

ML: Mitchell Library (*The Gorbals View*, 1967 ff. [subsequently retitled *The View*]).

RG: National Archives, Washington D. C., State Department Records (Record Group 59, Decimal Files 124. 01).

Websites

www.berlin.de/deutsch/politik/hauptstadt/standorte_parlament/B1S3D/index.html

www.upenn.edu/ARG/archive/R&R2.html

About the Contributors

Péter Apor is a Doctoral Researcher in the Department of History and Civilisation at the European University Institute, Florence. He has previously worked for the Open Society Archives, Budapest and has taught modern history at the University of Miskolc. His broad research interests cover the historical and anthropological analysis of Communism in Central and Eastern Europe.

Lars Berggren is a Lecturer and Associate Professor in the Department of Art History and Musicology at the University of Lund. He has published extensively on public monuments in 19th century Europe, including *L'Ombra dei Grandi. Monumenti e politica monumentale a Roma (1870-95)* (co-author L. Sjöstedt), 1996. He is currently working on a project entitled 'Public Monuments and Memorials in the Construction of National and Regional Identities in Sweden 1750-1950.'

Beate Binder is a Research Assistant at the Institute for European Ethnology at the Humboldt-University, Berlin. Her current research project is entitled, 'Stagings of Power: Making the Berlin "Government Quarter" a Representational Space' and concerns the present transformation of Berlin into the new German capital.

Ewa Domańska is an Assistant Professor of Theory and History of Historiography at Adam Mickiewicz University, Poznan, Poland. She has published, *Encounters: Philosophy of History After Postmodernism*, 1998 and *Microhistories: Encounters In-Between Worlds*, 1999, (in Polish).

Steen Bo Frandsen is Vice-Director of the Danish Institute of Science and Art in Rome. He is currently researching the role of Italian cities during the 19th century. His publications include articles and books on regional history in Denmark and Danish-German relations in the 19th and 20th centuries.

Bernhard Giesen is Professor of Sociology at the University of Konstanz. He has held visiting positions at various institutions including the European University Institute, Florence, and the Center for Advanced Study in the Behavioral Sciences at Stanford University. He has published extensively on social theory and on the issue of collective identity. His latest publication in English is

Intellectuals and the Nation. Collective Identity in a German Axial Age (1998).

Thomas Hippler is a Doctoral Researcher in the Department of History and Civilisation at the European University Institute, Florence. His thesis is entitled, 'The History of Military Service in 19th Century France and Germany'. He has studied history, philosophy and music in Berlin and Paris, and his general research interests include contemporary French philosophy.

Wolfgang Kaschuba is Professor of European Ethnology at the Humboldt-University in Berlin. His main research interests lie in the fields of culture and everyday history, European national and ethnic discourses, history of ethnological science and anthropological theory. He has recently published *Einfuhrung in die Europaische Ethnologie*, 1999.

James Kaye is currently a researcher at the European University Institute in Florence. His research addresses questions of comparison, belonging and alienation within a "Germanic" language and symbol world of the late 19th and 20th centuries. He has also worked as a curator of exhibitions and events in Austria and Italy with a specific interest in the juxtaposition of art and science.

Michael James Miller is a Doctoral Researcher in the Department of History and Civilisation at the European University Institute, Florence. His thesis addresses urban planning and protest movements in postwar Britain and France. His interests include theories of place and identity, urban history and geography.

Lutz Niethammer is Professor of Modern and Contemporary History at the Friedrich Schiller University, Jena, and Jean Monnet Fellow at the European University Institute, Florence, 1998-9, where he is working on the history of the future in 20th century Europe. His most recent publication will appear in 1999, and is entitled, *Kollektive Identität. Heimliche Quellen einer unheimlichen Konjunktur.*

Ilan Pappe is the head of the International Relations Unit at the University of Haifa University and the Academic Head of the Institute for Peace Research in Givat Haviva, Israel. His most recent publications include, *The Making of the Arab-Israeli Conflict, 1947-1951* (1992) and *The Israel/Palestine Question* (1999).

Marta Petrusewicz is Professor of Modern European History at the City University of New York. She has numerous publications, including *Latifundium: Moral Economy and Material Life in a*

European Periphery (1996), and is currently completing a manuscript entitled, *'The Natural Order of Things': Programs and Visions of Harmonious Development in 19th Century (Ireland, Poland and the Two Sicilies).*

Ron Robin lectures on History and Communication Studies at the University of Haifa, Israel. His most recent books include. *The Barbed Wire College: Re-educating German POWs in the United States During World War II* (1995), and, *A Military-Academic Complex: War and the Behavioral Sciences from Korea to Camelot* (forthcoming).

Bo Stråth is Professor of Contemporary History in the Department of History and Civilisation/Robert Schuman Centre at the European University Institute, Florence. He has published widely on political and economic processes, and his research focuses on modernisation and democratisation processes in Western Europe in a comparative context, with particular reference to labour market organisation.

Arve Thorsen is Research Fellow at the 19th International Congress of History, Department of History, University of Oslo. He is currently working on a doctoral thesis dealing with the interrelations between religion, confession and national ideology in France and Germany in a comparative perspective.

Hayden White is Professor of Comparative Literature at Stanford University and former University Professor at the University of California. He has recently published, *Figural Realism: Studies in the Mimesis Effect* (1999).

Mette Zølner is Assistant Professor in French Studies in the Department of Intercultural Communication and Management at Copenhagen Business School. Her doctorate from the European University Institute, Florence, was a comparative study of national identities and memories in contemporary France and Denmark. She is currently working on a research project entitled, 'Identity Constructions and Transformation Among French Business Elites'.

Andrei Zorin is Associate Professor of Russian Literature at the Russian State University for Humanities, Moscow. In 1999 he has been Visiting Professor of Slavic Languages and Literature at Harvard University. He has published extensively on Russian literary and cultural history of the late 18th and early 19th centuries as well as on the culture of post-Soviet Russia.

"Multiple Europes"

Multiple Europes is a series that aims to describe and analyse, in a historical perspective, the variety of ways in which social community and images of cohesion have been constructed in Europe. Particular emphasis is given to the idea of "nation", which, without doubt, has been one of the most persistent community categories of the last two hundred years. Various myths, memories, and historical heritages, often contradictory, always shifting, have been mobilised in the processes of community construction, and, taken together, these emphasise the multiplicity of Europe.

It is not only the processes of construction that are multiple - so too are the images of Europe that are produced as a result. Historically, images of Europe has been both utopian and dystopian. The experience of war has given rise to pacifist dreams, while atomism and disintegration have produced a longing for holism and wholeness. Indeed, the tension between war and peace, atomism and holism, is one of the most obvious elements in the construction of community in Europe. The continent's self-images have oscillated between pride and shame, between, for example, Europe as civilisation and Europe as degeneracy, and these self-images have emerged through various demarcations between Us and the Other. A crucial aspect of such demarcations is the views they project of minorities and immigrants, either as refugees from political regimes and war or as economic migrants.

Another crucial question addressed in the *Multiple Europes* series is how, since the French Revolution, with its rousing call for *liberté, égalité, fraternité*, images of social justice have been used in the construction of community, and how, in political processes, efforts have been made to minimise the evident tension between concepts like freedom and equality.

In this series, the analysis focuses on the levels of both the political, economic and intellectual elites, and the everyday, and considers these levels not only as reflected constructions, but also as unreflected practice. It is in this space between construction and practice that Europe, in its multiple forms, emerges.

Series Director: Professor **Bo Stråth**, Contemporary History Chair, History Department, Robert Schuman Centre, European University Institute (Italy)